a Man's place

masculinity in transition

joe l. dubbert

A SPECTRUM BOOK

Prentice-Hall, Inc., Englewood Cliffs, New Jersey 07632

Library of Congress Cataloging in Publication Data

Dubbert, Joe L
  A man's place.

  (A Spectrum Book)
  Bibliography: p.
  Includes index.
  1. Men—United States.   2. Sex role.   3. Masculinity
(Psychology)   I. Title.
HQ1090.D82   301.41′1′0973   79-246
ISBN 0-13-552059-2
ISBN 0-13-552042-8 pbk.

Editorial/production supervision
and interior design by Eric Newman
Cover design by Len Leoni, Jr.
Manufacturing buyer: Cathie Lenard

A SPECTRUM BOOK

10 9 8 7 6 5 4 3 2 1

Printed in the United States of America

PRENTICE-HALL INTERNATIONAL, INC., *London*
PRENTICE-HALL OF AUSTRALIA PTY. LIMITED, *Sydney*
PRENTICE-HALL OF CANADA, LTD., *Toronto*
PRENTICE-HALL OF INDIA PRIVATE LIMITED, *New Delhi*
PRENTICE-HALL OF JAPAN, INC., *Tokyo*
PRENTICE-HALL OF SOUTHEAST ASIA PTE. LTD., *Singapore*
WHITEHALL BOOKS LIMITED, *Wellington, New Zealand*

for Kimberly and Marshon

CONTENTS

PREFACE

My interest in writing a book about masculinity emerged from my understanding and perceptions of the women's liberation movement. For that I owe a great debt to many women—and some men—who introduced me to what has been the plight of women throughout American history and the part we men have played in shaping it. For an author to state that it all started with Betty Friedan's *The Feminine Mystique* may sound like a cliché, but in my case at least it underscores a fundamental truth: What we think we know about ourselves as men and women often involves a considerable amount of fanciful projection and myth often defying logic and rationality. Like many American men who grew up in middle-class homes, I, too, attended school, wanted to be popular, went out for sports, worked to achieve success, got married, and experienced parenthood—all under the influence of an array of social and psychological pressures never fully understood at any of these times. Teaching American social and intellectual history over the past decade, I have become aware that American men have to struggle with a mystique about being male, just as women have to contend with certain assumptions about what it means to be female, and that it has not always been easy for men to articulate, much less resolve, many of the problems spawned by the mystique. That is what this book is about.

The formality of notes does not begin to indicate the gratitude I have to the many individuals whose scholarship on sex roles and interpretations of American history I have used in writing this book. Gene Wise of the University of Maryland set me to thinking about historical methodology, and David Noble of the University of Minnesota influenced me with his interpretations of the American frontier experience. Myron Brenton and Warren Farrell provided some important directions with their books on the contemporary male paradigm. I am deeply grateful to Joe Pleck at the Center for the Family, Amherst, Massachusetts, who read the entire manuscript and offered valuable criticisms and suggestions. Muskingum College supported my work by granting a sabbatical leave in 1974–75 to pursue my research; the Mack Foundation of Homer City, Pennsylvania, helped with several modest grants.

Thanks are due many others, among them several of my students from over the years at Muskingum, including Mary Beth Hirsch and Tim Halverson. Most of all, I owe a special thanks to Jane Edwards, who helped me clarify several methodological perspectives and assisted the work throughout with a careful attention to style and accuracy of detail. Eric Newman of Prentice-Hall gave superb editorial direction and was a delight to work with. I also want to express my thanks to William P. Lester, also of Prentice-Hall, for giving freely of his time and his talents and for his invaluable assistance in helping to finish the project. Among my faculty colleagues, I wish to thank David Skeen of the Psychology Department for some useful advice, and Ronald Mulder of the History Department for just being around. Marge Hawkenberry graciously gave of her time to type portions of the rough draft, as did Rosalyn Zatezalo and Carol Stanton. Galen Wilson typed the final draft.

Without the help of Mariana Dubbert, there simply could not have been a book. She helped make time available and, most of all, her skillful proofreading and good judgment about content matters were highly significant contributions.

Grateful acknowledgment is hereby made to the following for granting permission to reprint material:

The quotation from Margaret Mead on page 1 is from *Male and Female* (William Morrow and Company, Inc., 1949), p. 318, and is reprinted with the permission of William Morrow and Company, Inc., and that of Victor Gollancz Ltd, London (1950).

The quotation from William James on page 13 is from *The Moral Equivalent of War* (New York: Harper & Row, Publishers, 1971), p. 36, edited and with an introduction by John K. Roth.

The quotation from Lewis Mumford on page 163 is from *Technics and Civilization* (New York: Harcourt Brace Jovanovich, Inc., 1934), p. 307.

... maleness in America is not absolutely defined; it has
to be kept and rearned every day. ...

Margaret Mead

1

INTRODUCTION:
THE CASE
FOR STUDYING
MEN AND MASCULINITY

"The American Republic stands before the world as the supreme expression of masculine force," proclaimed the Illinois Association Opposed to Women's Suffrage in 1910. According to every empirical test, American men had affirmed their commitment to progress by subduing nature, then successfully capitalizing on nature's resources. The free, competitive economic system had advanced the human race in all aspects further and faster than ever in recorded history. The growth of commerce, transportation, and agriculture was impressive. "All these are purely masculine enterprises. They require exclusively masculine brains as well as brawn." Of course the womenfolk were around too. In fact, "They have an influence over the men of their own nation such as the women of no other country possess." In 1910, few men seemed to doubt this in spite of the fact that one-fourth of the states denied women the right of property ownership and one-third of them disallowed claims on women's earnings. Thirty-six states even denied women equal guardianship of their children. How can such an anomaly be explained? To read again from the Illinois antisuffrage publication is instructive. "They [the women] owe this influence in a large degree to the fact that they are spared the hard material labor to which men in the pursuit of their natural career devote themselves and are thus given leisure and opportunity for the culture of those tender spiritual graces for the possession of which men set them upon a pedestal . . . and grant them whatever favors . . . they as a sex desire."[1]

In 1910, organized women were asking for the vote, but many men were disturbed by suffragism specifically and by feminism more generally, both of which came together in the popular press under the heading "the woman question." The issues it included as perceived by many men not only turned their attention to women and their associated provocative activities, but it had an equally profound effect of forcing men to think about themselves: who they were, what they were doing with their lives, and how they were to get along in the future. Since progress was seen as a masculine achievment, giving in to women was seen by some men as reducing the virile force of the republic to the standard of the "weaker sex."[2] And as one widely regarded male authority had said, "We men are (rightly) very jealous of our virility."[3]

Compared with what we know about the identity problems of women, we know relatively little about the American male's struggle with his identity. Perhaps Ralph Luce was right when he commented that popular assumptions about masculinity might be so much a part of our natural coloring that they simply don't need to be discussed. Whatever the reason, social historians have not paid much attention to the American male image, except for the few, like Irvin Wyllie and John Cawelti, who have dealt with the self-made-man themes and the idea of success.[4] However, in the past decade, with the emergence of the women's liberation movement, attention has finally shifted toward an analysis of the male role. The premise on which this perspective has been based assumes that "for every woman rethinking *her* role . . . there's probably a man somewhere rethinking *his*."[5] Just as women have been trapped by a historical identity and role definition known to some as the feminine mystique, men too have been trapped by a masculine mystique. There is an assumed framework of doctrines emphasizing male power, superiority, and domination in the sexual, social, political, and intellectual life of the United States. What some of these studies on male behavior have pointed out is that many contemporary males suffer from a distorted view of themselves in terms of what they think society has always expected of them as American men. Myron Brenton notes that when middle-class males talk candidly about themselves, they often manifest a feeling of being harried and trapped by events and circumstances. Nostalgia for the good old days, full of idealizing about the past and the place of men in it, is fairly common. Yet, according to Brenton, if history were studied seriously by those men seeking a confirmation of what the American male once was, they would be in for a shock.[6] Since the middle of the nineteenth century, the masculine power structure has been assaulted by the women's rights movement, the problems of an intensely competitive individualistic economic system, and the emergence of a technological, urban civilization. The now-common assumption of male domination in America is certainly weakened, considering how the power, control, and sexual aggression of America's men were so roundly criticized by so many women and simultaneously were being rendered obsolete by technology and automation.

Karl Bednarik concludes that modern males are suffering from a whole series of basic problems affecting their masculine life. Most of all, men think opportunity is exhausted, and know that only a few ever get to be company executives. Such a realization plunges some men into depression and despair and, according to Bednarik, tends to make others violent because they see their futures so limited. In self-defense and in justifying their behavior, some men have become classic chauvinists, a condition in which every situation they face at work, at home, or at the gym is interpreted in terms of supremacy, control, and domination.[7] Michael Korda studies this phenomenon and suggests that such men cannot be very happy because they suffer from self-doubt, paranoia, and frustration. "The truth is," writes Korda, "that men are not very happy with the world they have created. . . ."[8]

Thayer Greene observes that once upon a time it was easier for boys to proclaim their manhood than is presently the case with an increasingly feminine influence. In the "initiation process" of the tribe or group, adolescent males were expected to reveal courage and bravery in performing some feat in such an exemplary fashion that the young boy could be considered a man. In another diagnosis of male attitudes, H. R. Hayes focuses on the male concept of women as witches commenting that males have adopted a long series of defensive measures to protect themselves against feminine evil. In the extreme, there is a psychological urge for rape of and physical violence toward women, perhaps as retaliation against female encroachment into male territory.[9]

Marc Fasteau describes the male stereotype as "an ideal image of masculinity shared, with minor variation, by nearly every male in America." Part of the stereotype is "obsessive competitiveness," a "principle mode by which men relate to each other." How men perform in their workplace is the principle validation of their masculinity and has been a basis of defining a division of labor and distinguishing sex roles. Although Fasteau offers no historical evidence to suggest just how the male stereotype was created, he senses (and rightly so, it seems) that it has affected just about everything men do. For example, he argues that men often have a difficult time relating to children because of the inflexible nature of their masculine personalities. Because of men's perception of their personality, assuming superior, reasoned male logic, a child's emotional needs seem frustrating and annoying. Fasteau recognizes the widely held assumption that sports build character (more precisely, sound masculine character). Even as spectators, men vicariously identify with performing athletes in such a way as to strengthen their masculine identities through intelligent observation and by plotting counter-strategy. It is not surprising that many fathers push sons toward Little League as an early step on the way toward true manhood's legendary hall of fame.[10]

"Unconscious conspirators, parents and society" weave the masculine mystique into "the psyche of every developing boy." Dr. Harvey Kaye argues that the dream of being superman is embedded in the recesses of men's minds and that it significantly affects the way men behave. The mystique that men try to cultivate is at such variance with reality that many succumb to ulcers and heart attacks in trying to fulfull its complex configurations. Kaye believes the male will continue to dangle in inert suspension as long as men remain unliberated from the masculine mystique.[11]

Like the writers mentioned above, Warren Farrell has come to the conclusion that the extraordinary effort men have made to appear successful and up to par in all things at all times, in spite of their limitations and weaknesses, has been confining and humiliating. Male liberation, which can be said to have been born with the works of these writers, is a process of breaking down stereotyped sex roles, and in so doing finally discovering who men really are as human beings. Farrell stresses but does not overestimate the problem of overcoming the emotional frigidity of men in their exaggerated sense of individualism and their commitment to dominate women. He offers a compendium of advice about male consciousness-raising, with the objective of helping men get in touch with their true selves, creating a condition whereby they can see through those aspects of their personal-identity inventories that have altered men's perception of reality to conform to a predefined male image.[12] It may mean admitting that one detests sports and would be happier playing the piano or making bread on a free day, or it may mean just wanting to be with children. Such a process of self-discovery does not necessarily guarantee a repudiation of all the behavior traits connected with the old image of manliness. Yet it may result in a new sense of genuine sports appreciation in which the emphasis is on recreation and exercise rather than on performing up to the standards set by other men or even professionals.

In most books about masculinity and in many recent articles on the male role in a changing society, there is constant reference to the masculine stereotype in America and the image of manliness it has projected. But what is this peculiar stereotype and image? What do we really know about it from a historical point of view? Few of these studies go very far toward explaining the *formation* of the male image in American history. None have sufficiently studied the essential ingredients of manly character and related them to the broader social context. How has the ideal masculine image influenced the way American men have regarded women and children? How has the concept of manliness survived in times of war and depression? And why have so many men become so defensive and confused about their masculine image? The time has come for historians to seriously study these questions. Whatever chances male liberation may have will depend in large part on the ability of American males to understand more clearly where they are in relation to where they have been and where the liberationists may want to lead them.

Historians have had little to say about the male image in America, partly because of the nature of such terms as *status*, *image*, and *identity*. Status, for example, in an individual context involves the assessment of one's self in terms of what that individual thinks others think of him. Having an identity is a process of fulfilling and living by a particular sense of what a person thinks he should be and what others may also think he should be. Image involves portrayal and projection of a person as he would like others to see him. The image may or may not coincide with reality, for many reasons, but it can be inferred that such a portrayal is important to the individual because recognition results from it. Quite obviously, in seeking to write historically about character formation, image, and identity as they combine to help influence sex roles, historians must confront the serious problems of method and evidence. Specific information regarding such personal matters is difficult to locate except as it turns up in some autobiographies, diaries, and personal correspondence, mostly from men of middle- and upper-middle-class backgrounds. This volume, therefore, basically concerns the historical imagination and activity of these men. Historians interested in further male-sex-role/identity research would do well to study and compare, for example, immigrant groups, black males, and men from different occupational backgrounds, or homosexuals, which this more general survey of the American masculine image does not do.

Seldom do individuals describe just how they regard their personal status, image, or identity. Readers of autobiographies usually have to judge for themselves those aspects of life based on an interpretation of a subject's behavior in responding to other people and events throughout his or her life. Even if some autobiographies plainly revealed such insights of a personal nature, how many such autobiographies would be sufficient to substantiate an interpretation regarding masculine status or attitudes about women? An abundance of evidence that could be considered irrefutable proof of a specific masculine identity simply does not exist. After all, one characteristic of American men is that they simply do not reveal their feelings; to do so would imply where they are vulnerable and thus would compromise their masculinity. Yet there have been discussions in a variety of sources about the male role and self-concept, particularly in relation to women. Many of these sources have been investigated by historians studying American women, studies that have traced the feminist movement and attempted to explain the feminine character and influence of women on American civilization. Furthermore, women organized at various levels for a variety of purposes, and they left records and impressions of their activities and feelings about their role as women. But there never has been a "masculine movement" or even "masculinism" to correspond with the feminist movement and feminism in American historiography. Without an organization and a movement to define and promote the interests of males as such, as women have done for women, the existing impressions about American men are the more general ones taken from studies of American character that discuss men shaping history through business, politics, and associated activities.

In the post–World War II era, sociologists and social psychologists have published a variety of studies on the male role. Joseph Pleck has broadly classified these studies of the male role into traditional and modern versions. In the traditional male role, described in works by William Whyte and Mirra Komarovsky, the forms of achievement used to validate masculinity are physical. The modern male role, however, requires a greater interpersonal involvement and keener intellectual skills to positively validate masculinity. In the traditional male role, emotionality and intellectualism are eschewed; impulsive behavior and vigorous physical action are emphasized as validating criteria. In the modern situation in which men find themselves, male dominance is less pervasive and the trend is toward greater interdependence with other men and with women.[13] Times have changed. The old frame of reference of the frontier and a high degree of individualism, which men used to validate their masculinity in the past, simply does not exist any more. The problem, then, for American men, is to adjust to these new realities that affect men's sex-role identity. The question for historians is whether they can provide men with a focus on the continuities and conflicts of their masculine past to help them better understand the present goals of men's and women's liberation. Sociobiologists, of course, would argue the case of an innate male imperative, as opposed to a sex-role identity, shaped by social and cultural forces. This does not, however, satisfactorily account for the many choices and decisions men have made organizing their environment and structuring their social interactions, to say nothing of the disagreements between men (and with women) pertaining to such choices. Men choose one kind of work over another kind, choose to mate or not, choose to play games or not, and so on. Men create myths and pass them on; they paint, write, sing, and argue, not just for the sake of survival but to implement ideas of progress, which are a vital part of their intellectual and psychological being.

It has been more than two decades since William Langer addressed the American Historical Association on the value of integrating other disciplines, especially psychology, into the study of history to foster a deeper understanding of the past.[14] Langer's recommendation has been expanded by Robert Waelder, who has presented a case for applying psychoanalysis to history. While determining what actually happened, historians must go further to interpret human action or inaction in terms of external situations and influuences, and according to the "human nature or the characteristics of the people involved." Waelder stresses the value of focusing on the so-called "private facts" as much as the "historically relevant facts." He notes that psychological reasoning has been applied in the past by historians to evaluate sources on the assumption that there may be conscious motives to alter the appearances of a given action.[15]

Gene Wise has pointed out in his provocative analysis of American historical scholarship that historians have too often tended to concentrate their studies on the *expressed content of thought*. The rules of evidence in attempting to write objective history cause them to ignore the underlying function of an individual's verbalized thoughts. Missing is the process of idea formation and how ideas are used and assume strategic value as they become significant in justifying or validating certain behavior patterns. Wise echoes Thomas Kuhn's argument that attention should be given to form and process rather than to results as major scientific paradigms rise and fall. What is particularly rewarding for Kuhn (and potentially rewarding for many others following his example) is the cognitive insights to be gained when traditional theories of reality fail to function properly and thereby pass into a stage of crisis as a new paradigm forms. History, for Kuhn, then, is much more than a repository of chronological anecdotes. History is most exciting and rewarding when studied as imagination, where individuals work out or adopt a view of the world with reference to their experience in it. For Wise, experience is the key, because in searching out the cognitive one deals with experience and explanations of experience. One must consider not only objective reality and truth but also how mental images were formed based on what was happening in the world.[16]

But what does this have to do with masculinity in American history? Forming an identity is a process of the imagination that takes place on all levels of mental functioning as individuals throughout time (American males in this case) encounter experience. In practice, as Erik Erikson describes it, identity formation takes place as individuals constantly judge themselves in ways and on terms by which others would seem to be judging them. In other words, identity formation is a process of reflection and comparison as individuals (again, men in our case) seek to live up to a prescribed model and role considered to be manly or typically masculine. Long before Erikson uttered his observations on identity, Elisabeth Woodbridge anticipated, in 1914, the same thesis quite forcefully: "For if a man, at certain periods and in certain moods, strongly desires to meet the standards set for him by women, he also desires, almost all the time, and in almost every mood, to meet standards set for him by men."[17] Just how these standards were perceived and how the male sex role came to be established is a central problem in the male-identity-formation process examined in this book.

What I will attempt to establish is that middle-class American males had to contend with a paradigmatic revolution in self-perception during the nineteenth and twentieth centuries. In 1800, a vast, unsettled continent stretched before American men. It was possible for men to move (with or without families) from point to point in space. They blazed trails, cleared land, built crude buildings, and likely as not moved again to repeat the process. The era produced a host of legendary heroes, such as Daniel Boone, Kit Carson, and Davy Crockett, who were prototypes for James Fenimore Cooper's Leatherstocking tales. These legendary figures were adventurous, courageous, strong-willed, autonomous males who survived mostly on the strength of their natural animal instincts. Not only in their day but long afterward they were regarded as the most manly of men who existed in frontier space without attachment to community or institutions. For them and for Americans who followed their paths into the wilderness, nature signaled the possibility for total human fulfillment. In moral terms these men were seen, as the historian George Bancroft saw Boone, as agents guaranteeing the salvation of the young nation by leading Americans away from corruption. Their heroics coincided with and were an integral part of the major interpretation of history as progress, a history moving relentlessly onward toward its ultimate manifest destiny.

In spite of the many criticisms leveled against Frederick Jackson Turner's thesis that the frontier gave rise to American democracy, the frontier *as space* did exist and was a very real factor in the construction of a paradigm of democratic progress to which masculine ability was highly relevant. Quite obviously, not all American males could move into the open space of the frontier, but studies dealing with American ideals and expectations (for example, the much-sought-after American Dream) reveal that the frontier as fact and fantasy was prominent in the American imagination. Americans from all classes, races, and origins have sensed an urge to identify with the frontier. One of the most striking examples of the masculine mystique is the continuing popularity of cinema and television westerns in which powerful and forceful men (like Matt Dillon of "Gunsmoke" and Ben Cartright of "Bonanza" during the 1960s) gave evidence time and again of their manliness. The Davy Crockett fad in the 1950s, the television episodes of Daniel Boone, and movies like *High Noon, Gunfight at OK Corral,* and *The Wild Bunch* remind Americans of a heroic past in which men were men and proved it.[18]

The identity of these heroes was directly dependent on their relationship with space. Boone, it will be remembered, knew it was time to move on when he could spot the smoke of another campfire in his valley—a highly symbolic attitude for anyone searching for a deeper meaning of the American experience. The anthropologist Edward Hall suggests that all animals, including humans, need space between themselves and others in order to function. Culture is the hidden dimension of human space, he argues, and it is the culture that molds the experience in space and shapes behavior. The theory of proximics, as Hall calls it, varies in degree among different cultures, but for Americans more space seems necessary in order to live and work comfortably. Bednarik's study also considers the male identity in a spatial context. Because of the phallic nature of the male, the primordial drive has always been to expand and dominate situations and territory.[19] Males made deals where possible or acted otherwise to advance their positions. When successful, their status and reputation were substantially augmented. Once they were successful, laws were made to secure gains and metaphysical sanctions postulated to underwrite actions. White male culture displaced the Indians by force and gave no regard to the rights of minorities or women. As long as this process went true to form, as it could and generally did during the early years of the republic, stress was absent.

Nevertheless, as the frontier line receded across the continent and while urbanization advanced, the frontier became important as a myth and symbol, which Henry Nash Smith documents in *Virgin Land*. Beginning with Cooper, in fact, Smith notes that the chief problem was to introduce Leatherstocking to civilization: to women, game laws, settlements, fences, and politics. The power and appeal of the myth exaggerated frontier virtues and life-style all the while it was disappearing. The perception of open and uninhabited space formed a unique American perception in which men could envision their existence as that of action-oriented adventurers and manipulators.[20] By 1890, however, the frontier was officially closed, according to the Census Bureau. If the perception of progress was linked to the availability of virgin land and if the moral destiny of America depended on expanding onto new frontiers, as Turner said it did, then what was to happen when the frontier no longer existed? Here was a crisis for American males as the *space* paradigm was threatened. They now had to accept living in *place*, in a community, in a social environment, interacting with other men doing the same, and facing the very real possibility that they might become fathers with children to support. Judging from the popular and scholarly literature around 1900, from works of fiction, biographies, and autobiographies, there is an explicit concern about the masculinity and virility of the race. It was not through a cartoonist's flight of imagination that Theodore Roosevelt maintained his cowboy image right into the White House. Many men, as will be shown in following pages, identified with a masculine image that was part of the space paradigm but had little to do with the realities of modern life, such as what to do about corporate competition and the "new woman." Or, how were men to ensure the maintenance of strong character so widely proclaimed in the pastoral days? The old paradigm of masculine dominance, supremacy, and control of events already seemed questionable by 1900. By mid-twentieth century the image had broken down. Not only had the sense of open space long since passed, the trends of modernization, further democratization through federal legislation, women's liberation, and the specialized, technical, bureaucratic nature of work presented a very real "closing in" on another and more serious kind of space.

Notes

[1]*Men and Women*, Bulletin No. 3 (Chicago: Illinois Association Opposed to Women's Suffrage, 1910).

[2]Ibid.

[3]Grant Allen, "Plain Words On the Woman Question," *Popular Science Monthly XXXVI (December, 1889)*, 174.

[4]Ralph Luce, "From Hero to Robot: Masculinity in America—Stereotype and Reality," *Psychoanalytic Review*, LIV (1967), 53–74; John Cawelti, *Apostles of the Self-Made Man* (Chicago: University of Chicago Press, 1968); Irvin Wyllie, *The Self-Made Man in America* (New Brunswick: Rutgers University Press, 1954); see also Lawrence Chenoweth, *The American Dream of Success* (North Scituate, Mass.: Duxbury Press, 1974).

[5]Barbara Katz, "Women's Lib Auxiliaries," *National Observer* (December 29, 1973), 8.

[6]Myron Brenton, *The American Male* (Greenwich, Conn.: Fawcett Publications, 1966).

[7]Karl Bednarik, *The Male in Crisis* (New York: Alfred A. Knopf, Inc., 1970).

[8]Michael Korda, *Male Chauvinism* (New York: Random House, Inc., 1972), p. 160.

[9]Thayer Greene, *Modern Man in Search of Manhood* (New York: Association Press, 1967); H. R. Hayes, *The Dangerous Sex* (New York: G. P. Putnam's Sons, 1964).

[10]Marc Fasteau, *The Male Machine* (New York: McGraw-Hill, 1974), pp. 2, 11.

[11]Harvey E. Kaye, *Male Survival* (New York: Grosset and Dunlap, 1974), p. 3.

[12]Warren Farrell, *The Liberated Man* (New York: Random House, Inc., 1975).

[13]Joseph H. Pleck, "The Male Sex Role: Definitions, Problems and Sources of Change," *Journal of Social Issues*, XXXII (Summer, 1976), 155–64; Mirra Komarovsky, *Blue Collar*

Marriage (New York: Random House, Inc., 1962); William Whyte, *Street Corner Society* (Chicago: University of Chicago Press, 1955).

[14]William Langer, "The Next Assignment," *The American Historical Review*, LIII (January, 1958), 283–304.

[15]Robert Waelder, "Psychoanalysis and History: Application of Psychoanalysis to Historiography," *The Psychoanalytic Interpretation of History* (New York: Basic Books, 1971), p. 6.

[16]Gene Wise, *American Historical Explanations* (Homewood, Ill.: The Dorsey Press, 1973), pp. 45–50; Thomas Kuhn, *The Structure of Scientific Revolutions* (Chicago: University of Chicago Press, 1962), pp. 1–9.

[17]Erik Erikson, *Identity: Youth and Crisis* (New York: W. W. Norton & Co., 1968), pp. 22–23; Elisabeth Woodbridge, "The Unknown Quantity in the Woman Problem," *The Atlantic Monthly* (April, 1914), 514.

[18]Frederick Jackson Turner, "The Significance of the Frontier in American History," *The Frontier in American History*, (New York: Holt, Rinehart and Winston, 1920), pp. 1–38; Will Wright, *Six Guns and Society* (Berkeley: University of California Press, 1975); see also Orrin Klapp, *Heroes, Villains and Fools* (Englewood Cliffs, N.J.: Prentice-Hall, Inc., 1962).

[19]Edward T. Hall, *The Hidden Dimension* (Garden City, N.Y.: Doubleday and Co., 1966), pp. 138–40; Karl Bednarik, *The Male in Crisis* (New York: Alfred A. Knopf, Inc., 1970), pp. 14–15.

[20]Henry Nash Smith, *Virgin Land: The American West as Symbol and Myth* (New York: Alfred A. Knopf, Inc., 1950).

In rough terms we may say that a man who energizes below his normal maximum fails by just so much to profit by his chance at life; and that a nation filled with such men is inferior to a nation run at higher pressure.

William James, 1906

Sexual intercourse is not necessary to preserve health and manly vigor. The natural sexual impulse can be kept under control by avoiding associations, conversations and thoughts of lewd character.

U.S. Health Service Poster Series #22, 1922

SHAPING THE IDEAL DURING THE MASCULINE CENTURY

Social historians owe a great debt to Philippe Ariès, who describes and analyzes the emergence of the modern family since the Middle Ages with specific reference to the discovery of childhood. Following the detail of Ariès's study, one is struck with the integrated nature of the medieval community. During the Middle Ages, children were regarded as small adults who participated with big adults in the household and community in virtually all aspects of work and play. They slept, ate, and conversed in the same room in the big house that customarily included many adults and children, more than just a mother, father, brothers, and sisters. The community was characteristically a very sociable one from which the children seldom wandered and from which they hardly ever moved as adults. This collective life, as Ariès describes it, "carried along in a single torrent all ages and classes, leaving nobody any time for solitude and privacy."[1]

How different modern man was to become! If any one contrast impresses us as particularly significant about the basic changes that have taken place since 1500, it is that modernization was a profoundly segregating experience. As modern man began to trade and travel, his tastes and preferences were substantially revised, and with those revisions came the slow but steady emergence of the modern family. As the modern family evolved through the seventeenth and eighteenth centuries, it tended to be isolated from the larger community, "to hold society at a distance," according to Ariès, "to push back beyond a steadily extending zone of private life."[2] As the quest for privacy and personal intimacy increased, sociability and a sense of community participation decreased. Houses were constructed with separate rooms so that children and adults could be separated and their unique functions distinctly defined. Once an affair of the group family and the apprenticeship system, education became increasingly a matter of the school. Pressed to a logical conclusion, the evolution of the modern family has encouraged and sustained autonomy while interdependence and sociability have diminished.

THE AMERICANIZATION OF MASCULINITY

Nowhere was the transformation to the modern family more noticeable than in America, where the prospects of isolation and privacy were virtually guaranteed because of the reality of living in frontier space. Here individualism became synonymous with Americanism. Progress was defined as the breaking down of traditional barriers to self-development and fulfillment as individual men sought to capitalize on the main chance and become successful producers in a state of nature abundant with possibilities. Even the Puritans were deeply involved in the segregating experience of modernization. The seventeenth-century family consisted of an adult couple,—a husband and wife—and their own children with the addition, in some cases, of grandparents and perhaps a servant. By 1700, "Yankeeization" seriously challenged the Puritan community as it became impossible to regulate the 'out-livers," those who struck out on their own for personal gain. Such individuals did not desire to be restricted by regulations that they thought served community interests more than their own. Since space was available, why not move beyond the hills or up the river, beyond the jurisdiction of settlement company and crown? In the new world, it became exceedingly difficult to maintain for very long any consistent pattern of law and order or even community loyalty.[3] It is little wonder, then, that John Adams could claim that the origins of America's revolution could be found in the very first settlements of the 1600s, in which authority was overtly undermined by self-seeking men. In the larger perspective of time, it was to mean that any authority would be difficult to establish and maintain in a nation with a weak central government and in which expansion into unsettled land was a constant attraction. It became a familiar pattern for American men as they addressed themselves to business and personal advancement to resist any restraint or restriction on their actions. Perhaps that is the ultimate meaning of the term "frontier spirit." Nothing was too big, too dangerous, too far, or too powerful in human or physical dimensions to thwart dedicated American males from achieving their objectives. As Richard Bartlett writes, "One of the most valid ways to build an understanding of the new country society is to begin with the conscious realization of its masculinity. . . ."[4] The government policies of laissez-faire prepared the way for what was to become an extremely materialistic society and culture in the nineteenth century, which in retrospect can be seen as "the masculine century." Although the accomplishments of some women cannot be denied, it was, however, almost exclusively the men who were expected to cash in on an abundance of opportunities to maximize their gains and minimize their losses. Gone was the emphasis on faith as a means to salvation, and replacing it was an emphasis on work. A man's status could be determined by what he could acquire and control in a lifetime. It could be material goods, land, or even people. Such a frame of reference stressed individualism and personal accomplishment, and did not invite a consideration of the needs of others. To have done so would have signaled sentimentality, a symptom of weakness that manly men avoided.

Yet one of the often-repeated slogans in America was that behind every successful man was a good woman. There was much truth to this, because clearing the land, building a business, or just surviving required an extraordinary amount of effort from men *and* women. The processes of American civilization even served to enhance the woman's position when compared with that of her European counterpart. It is one of the genuine anomalies of nineteenth-century America that while women assumed a more prominent role in the family, they were excluded from politics, business, and most professions. Thus a careful distinction needs to be made at the outset. Women were important in America because they exercised considerable *influence*, especially in the role of wife and mother. But men held legal, social, political, and economic *power* as providers and protectors in a nation that believed in an ideal of progress that was essentially masculine by definition.

Alexis de Tocqueville pointed out in 1835 that there were distinctly different notions about marriage, and, hence, about women's roles, in trading nations and religious communities. In trading nations, or those communities in which commerce abounded, women were necessary for the security and maintenance of an orderly household, and in religious communities women were pledged to uphold purity and to preserve morals. America was unique because it was both a religious community with a traditional faith in a covenant of grace and a trading nation with a strong faith in a covenant of works. The roles of women, highly important to the development of American civilization, were to keep order in the home, have babies to perpetuate the race, and maintain moral order.[5] Taken together it meant that the cult of true womanhood was to consist of purity, piety, submissiveness, and domesticity. "Put them all together and they spelled mother, daughter, sister, wife—woman."[6]

In 1840, Sarah Lewis emphasized that women had a divine mission to shape destiny through their influence (although she conceded that men held the reigns of power). From the male point of view, Winslow Hubbard urged that the elevated position of women be recognized by men, but, he added that it should not mean the suppression of men, a reservation that was to prove exceedingly troublesome.[7] Many other writers of the time echoed the importance of elevating women to the pedestal because, as one writer stated, "God has endowed her." Another writer stated that although the home was the woman's province, her influence was not limited to there. "Society is her empire, which she governs almost at will. . . ." Most of all, the woman was considered to be "naturally religious" for "hers is a pious mind." Religion was exactly what gave women the dignity that best suited their dependence.[8] Working in the church was a perfectly acceptable "outside" activity for women because, unlike any other outside activity, church work reinforced the divine duties of the home. Tocqueville was impressed, as he observed American women in the 1830s, by how firmly established these notions were and how readily young women surrendered their independence to accept their sacred duties.[9]

Men, on the other hand, were involved in the worldly pursuit of things—manipulating objects and making deals. They had power. Since their attention was constantly focused on worldly things and getting ahead, they were always threatened by corruption. No true woman should ever venture into such a tempting environment. And no man should ever induce a woman to treat lightly her piety. The chance that such would happen hounded the lives of many American men and women, for it was just assumed that the male would sin and sin again and was helpless to do anything about it. Ironically, however, it became a mark of masculine honor that these same corrupt males were expected to uphold the character and dignity of a woman in order that she discharge her sacred duties.[10]

MOTHERHOOD AND MASCULINITY

What is apparent, then, is that in no other area of domestic life did women excel in exerting their high moral influence quite as much as they did in performing their role as mothers. In turn, a strong argument can be made that few problems were as perplexing to adolescent males as the one that involved them in working out a masculine identity in a home context dominated by a mother's stern moral influence. By defining the ideal role and function of womanhood as domestic and moralistic, men did not have to compete against women in the masculine world of politics and markets. In a sense, men could think of women as safely contained and out of the way of men on the make. On the other hand, women's dedication to home duties resulted in such a formidable set of behavioral structures and ideals that it came to be known as "momism" in the twentieth century. By then, momism was condemned as emasculating by writers like Philip Wylie, and as "misplaced paternalism" by Erik Erikson.[11] Among women writers, it was defended by traditionalists who believed in ranking home duties ahead of career, and criticized by other women as a restricting feature of the feminine mystique.

The basis of momism evolved out of a complex set of theological views and social circumstances. By the Jacksonian era, noted for its glorification of the common man, many books and articles on family life were dedicated to the proposition that motherhood was a divine mission, the highest of earthly callings. A mother's importance was underscored by the modern concept that children were no longer viewed as miniature adults, but as children who needed a special kind of attention. For mothers following the assumption of infant damnation, a devoted mother had to save her child by emphasizing to her offspring the danger of sin and the requirements necessary for salvation. If mothers were influenced by Locke and Rousseau to see their children as neutral and innocent, waiting to be impressed, mothers had to be sure that nothing would corrupt their children. Whatever their view of child nurture, mothers determined the "moral culture" of the society, according to the *Christian Family Magazine*. In the home, the true mother "seizes the first tender years of childhood, and improves them as the golden seedtime of life to her child."[12] *Mrs. Whittelsey's Magazine for Mothers* proclaimed that "God has made you a mother, and entrusted you with the parental authority in order that you may habituate that child as its first great law, to filial obedience," a discipline, the magazine added, that had to be enforced, not reasoned.[13] Throughout the nineteenth century, mothers took over roles previously occupied by fathers and grandfathers as those men abdicated their place in the family, in education, and in the cultural life. William Eliot viewed men as incapable of child care because of their temperament. Only mothers possessed the "exceptional love" required for children. Even sisters were reminded of their distinctive influence on their brothers. A growing boy formed an early estimate of the female sex based on a sister's character. Another writer reminded sisters that boys were often awkward and harsh, and that reforming a brother was no easy task. Patience was necessary, but it would all pay off in developing a "noble, and pure minded man, who will respect and honor woman [*sic*] for his sisters' sake."[14] Clearly, as fathers left the home for the industrial shop, the business office, and the fields, women were taking over at home.

Most of those who wrote about mothers and child-rearing during the nineteenth century agreed that girls were easier to manage than boys. The latter were inclined to be more worldly, more venturesome, and more vulnerable to temptation than girls. Opinions varied as to why this difference existed. Were little boys inherently "bad," or was it a process of socialization that made them so vexatious? Little girls were made of "sugar and spice and everything nice" and little boys were made from "frogs and snails and puppy dog tails," according to the old nursery rhyme, ingredients symbolic of a more earthy interest. Because such items were more stimulating to the imagination of little boys, it was harder for mothers to convert them to an appreciation of things spiritual. Therefore, mothers were told to "break the will" of these boys to make them conform, or run the risk of having them become immoral monsters as adult men. Boys who grew up in a happy home governed by a strong mother would be set for life, safe from temptation, and sure of success. In the home and even at school, the goal was to raise a moral child. Everything else hinged on how perfectly his character could be shaped. Business success depended on it; so did his worth as a citizen. The schoolbooks of the nineteenth century extolled love of country and love of God, stressed obedience to parents, and praised the accumulation of property as a guarantee of progress and perfection.[15]

Taking this concept to the extreme, Frances Hodgson Burnett created Little Lord Fauntleroy in the 1870s in a book depicting the perfect boychild. The little man in Burnett's book had soft, golden, curled hair that fell in beautiful ringlets on his shoulders. His manners were impeccable and his mature, innocent behavior impressed everyone. Remarks of praise filtered back to his proud, successful mother, the ultimate reward for her devotion to maternal duty. So inspired were some mothers that Little Lord Fauntleroy attire, consisting of a fur-trimmed velvet waistcoat worn over a starched white shirt with ruffled sleeves, became quite fashionable.*[16]

PARENTAL AUTHORITY
AND IDENTITY CONFLICT

Whether or not the little fellow inside this costume lived up to the standards of the fictional model is quite another question, one that plunges close to the heart of the identity conflict experienced by many boys in the nineteenth century who grew up under strong maternal influence. Grover Cleveland, born in 1837, was raised in a home that was a model of civilized morality. High standards of conduct and moral living based on a puritan ancestry were expected. Cleveland's father, a minister, wielded a strong influence over his son by encouraging hard work and self-discipline. Yet Allen Nevin's research has found young Cleveland to have been a roistering young fellow who knew the inside of many saloons. Although he was brought up in an atmosphere of culture and refinement, Cleveland wanted to be a "man's man." He avoided polite society as much as possible because it seemed effeminate. He preferred the smoke-filled room, card-playing, and hunting, and generally avoided women altogether. Yet, it was well known that he fathered at least one illegitimate child.[17]

The same conflict over parental authority and male identity troubled young Floyd Dell. Dell, who was born in 1887, wrote in his autobiography that "for me there always would be, in almost every region of beauty and

*For some exquisite photographs of Little Lord Fauntleroy costumes, see *This Fabulous Century, 1870–1900* (New York: Time-Life Books, 1970), p. 194.

knowledge the sweet ghostly presence of my mother. . . . " She tried to instill in her young son an appreciation of poetry and music, all the while keeping her growing boy in curls. "Mothers do things like that to their pet little boys," Dell wrote, "but little boys do not have to stand for it." His mother pushed him in school to advance her career image of him (to be a lawyer and then a Republican president), only to have him come under the influence of female teachers who extended the powerful motherly influence. But there were ironies in the mother-and-son relationship that at first seemed only curiosities but represented some fault lines in the general patterns of nineteenth-century family relationships. Why, for instance, did Mother Dell, who stressed moral integrity, not want her son to play with black children? And later in life, why did she not tell him of the mysteries of love and sex? In time, why did his mother resent Floyd's wife? Although a number of contributing causes may have been pivotal in answering these questions, Dell's autobiography strongly implies that his mother's domination early in life cut him off from sources of information and masculine models, especially from his father, all of which might have been highly advantageous to him in later life.[18] One can sense that many young men struggled with Dell's problem of how to gain some moral freedom from the suffocation of a mother's protective love. Lincoln Steffens, who was ten years younger than Dell, concluded in his autobiography that one of the great wrongs suffered by boys of that age was that they were smothered by mother love. Steffens's point was that nineteenth-century boys received the affection and devotion from their mothers so early and so totally that they never learned to genuinely love in return, a serious liability when it came to courtship and marriage.[19]

WHERE IS FATHER?

Although the ideology of motherhood and praise of mothers in general was a frequent topic in nineteenth-century journals and magazines, one searches mostly in vain, however, for a concept of fatherhood, or even of an opinion of what a good father might be. In the fictional literature about families and children written by women, it is especially notable that fathers are missing. In some of the novels and stories fathers were either foolish adventurers, psychologically inept, or else they were dead. Donald Meyer has suggested that during the period around the Civil War, female authors may have been trying to present an image of independent and responsible women who did not need men, symbolizing the rejection of males on behalf of American women.*[20]

Alternatively, it was generally conceded that fathers were preoccupied with their male roles and activities, too engaged in the competitive struggle to pay much attention to children and family life. Yet men were expected "to be ahead of the wife," set an example of "manly virtue" to the children and practice reverence in the home. The conservative Heman Humphrey, president of Amherst, recommended that fathers be more dictatorial in creating the proper moral atmosphere in the home. Timothy Dwight urged American fathers to restore their dominance in the home, even if it meant slowing down the rapid pace of their business pursuits to spend more time with their children. Reverend Winslow Hubbard also worried about the imbalance between men and women in the home. But all these men shared the dominant view that if progress were to continue, sex-role differences had to be maintained. From every available source, it is clearly evident that girls and boys were raised by mothers who were faithful to the standards of motherhood. Fathers were generally absent from the home. Men lived a masculine existence "out there," which, from decade to decade, seemed more isolated from the feminized home life of "in here." This alienation from home was to be one of the most diabolical features of modern family life.[21]

On the surface, Victorian family life may have seemed healthy and contented while industry and agriculture expanded and productivity increased. In the 1830s, Tocqueville was confident that the decline in the status and prestige of American fathers was a positive development, leading to a new democratic spirit. Where European fathers had been trapped by an authoritarian past, American fathers had no past to trap them, just space and opportunity in which all males theoretically could participate equally. That there might be conflicts within the process of child-rearing that Americans subscribed to was not seriously considered. What most mothers especially wanted was the perfect child from the perfect home.[22]

In reality, the Victorian family situation and rigid sex-role patterns contained some highly ambiguous features that were bound to affect the ways American children were to perceive their future and their sex-role functions. As agent and teacher of the civilized morality in America, the

---

*The reader can find examples of this mentality in *Wide Wide World* by Susan Warner, *Little Women* by Louisa May Alcott, and *Rebecca of Sunnybrook Farm* by Kate Wiggins.

mother had the role of preaching about the evils of the external world. She set the standards of decent Christian conduct in the home for her children. It meant, however, that the American mother could succeed with only half her children. How was it possible for a mother to offer appropriate guidance to a son when she had not experienced the kind of existence American society and culture assumed that men would eventually seek? If a mother saw the external world as essentially evil and corrupt, it meant that she would have to protect herself from her contaminated husband and her son from his father in order to truly succeed at her task. Such an atmosphere made it difficult for a male child to know the truth about the life ahead of him. Since the modern family was becoming increasingly segmented by fathers' "going off to work," what or who was to provide a viable model and direction with which sons might seek to identify in order to fulfill their destiny as men? And finally, might not sons conclude that girls were far better off than boys and more valuable to society, because some day the girls would be mothers, with the highest of all missions to perform? In the words of the *Public Ledger and Daily Transcript* of July 20, 1848, "one pretty girl was equal to ten thousand men and a mother was, next to God, all powerful."[23]

IDEALIZATION OF WOMANHOOD

A study of pre–Civil War literature strongly implies the concept that men were born of the flesh and were heirs to constant temptations. It was up to the fearless, patient, persistent American woman to marry the man and "save" him. Worshiping a woman as a moral savior, however, could and did lead to some serious problems in the marriage, since some men felt they dared not express themselves sexually to a goddess. A short story in an 1855 *Harpers* catches the somber mood of the Victorian morality that held people apart. "I did do reverence to her," stated a young beau about his girl. "I was a boy before her. She was my whole life, my idol, in every sense of the word. I did not know or care that there was a God above us both—I worshiped but her." But the young couple scarcely knew each other; they certainly did not know of love and sex. Within six months the dream of love was over. "We occupied separate rooms, seldom met in the house or in society, never sat together, never folded each other in our arms . . . never pressed our lips to each others cheeks or lips . . . It was all over . . . I sat long nights alone in my library when she thought I was reading [while] I was struggling with the agony of my life." But true to the ideal of womanhood that he held, the young man added that "still I trusted her, still I believed her mine, still she was magnificently beautiful."[24] There can be little doubt that this worship of women by men was intense and that, at the same time, alienation and ostracism were common as people separated into masculine and feminine spheres of existence.

Autobiographies, letters, and diaries from the nineteenth century support an additional contention that many boys were estranged from their fathers, not only because sons did not see their fathers often enough to get to know them, but also because they sensed a latent tension between a mother and father. Out on the range, where one is told that "seldom was heard a discouraging word," many women were discouraged with the existence to which men subjected them. Hamlin Garland's frequent moves with his parents were not greeted with much enthusiasm by his mother, who usually suffered in silence while breaking up a household and moving on. William Allen White's mother was bored with frontier drudgery and longed for something more engaging. For other women, on the move to help make America great, there were always thoughts of the comfortable homes left behind and doubt about the wisdom of the move. "The wagon train is divided," Lucy Ide confided in her diary. "Some want to turn back; others favor going on. A decision is reached at noon; the train is to move on."[25] Another pioneer woman put it into verse:

> *My husband, I pity he is wasting his life*
> *To obtain a scant living for his children and wife.*
> *The Sabbath which once was a day of sweet rest*
> *Is now spent toiling for bread in the West.*
> *After five years hard toiling with hopes that were in vain*
> *I have such despair on this desolate plain.*[26]

Belittling the wanderlust existence of a husband and father was bound to affect adolescent attitudes, indicating that the mother wanted to raise her son in such a way that he would reject a reckless, wasteful life like that of his father.[27]

Boys from upper-class families who seldom ventured anywhere experienced a similar confusion about their fathers and towards life. Charles Francis Adams, who was born in 1835, yearned to "know" his father but never succeeded, confessing in his autobiography, "I have suffered from it all through life." Adams complained that rigidities of pre–Civil War America, in which everyone was pumped full of Puritanism, left him incapable of enjoying leisure with his father. Not until young Charles went to college did he have occasion to compare his diary with his father's, discovering what sort of man his father had been.[28] Growing up in the 1860s, John R. Commons recalled that his "father just left the children to mother," a stern, moralistic disciplinarian who mocked her husband's dealings and his friends. Mrs. Commons, in fact, had to support the family as her husband's struggle to achieve success in business failed. Her fight to maintain Calvinistic orthodoxy led her to support the temperance movement and oppose the study of evolution. She set high standards for her son, wanting him to be better than his father, to become a minister; she had the boy learn Greek and Latin in preparation. She fretted over his choice of playmates, fearing "bad associates," no doubt like those who she thought plagued his father. The final touch was to keep John in curls to give him that angelic look, which made him bitterly protest, but he proudly remembered not crying when whipped, retaining at least a shred of boyhood respectability. All the while his father remained silent, quite apart from these family proceedings.[29]

AN AMERICAN FAMILY

One of the most illuminating case studies that reflects the tangled problems of nineteenth-century male adolescent behavior and the parental sex role identity conflict is that of the Henry James family. Henry James, Sr., born in 1811, recalled the high moral standards and expectations set for him by his parents, expecially the "not-to-dos" of their stern Presbyterian home. But the boy hardly knew his father, who, like many men of that time, was preoccupied with an expanding business, leaving home life to Henry's mother. By the age of ten, Henry was stopping regularly on his way to and from school at a shoemaker's shop for a nip of brandy or gin. As Leon Edel suggests, it may have helped establish his manliness among playmates, but the habit also served as a defiant gesture against a God who created such dull Sundays and against his father, who to him was virtually a god. The wrath of God caught up with him, however, when a playtime accident at the age of thirteen cost him a leg. The ordeal showed him that his mother had greater self-control in coping with the tragedy than his father. Through his painful convalescence, Henry James also had a long time to contemplate the enmity that surely existed between a boy and the god of his parents. How could any boy, whose natural instincts of spirit and body were so limited by the moral governance of parents, ever be a creative and productive man? Henry James made the most of life by going to college and acquiring a forceful, aggressive eloquence that he put to use as a philosopher-teacher.[30]

Henry James, Sr., had four sons, one of them Henry, Jr., born in 1843. As a child in Victorian America, the younger James remembered his mother as "our protecting spirit, our household genius," a mother who set the rules, preached restraint, and encouraged achievement. But Henry James, Jr., was bewildered by his mother's frequent concessions and reversals bordering on contradictions, and he wondered about the different standards observed by his mother and father. Mrs. James kept the family organized and disciplined, but Henry Sr., who was robust and virile, seemed "softer," willing to indulge the juvenile ambitions of his children, allowing them a peek at the Christmas gifts—but warning them not to tell their mother. While the son acknowledged the authoritarian position of his mother, even though she seemed contradictory and confusing, the relationship between mother and father proved especially confusing. Why had his father always seemed to defer to his mother? Why did the senior James not teach his sons more about masculine life? While an identity with his mother seemed easier to recall, why was the memory of the relationship with his father so vague? Did Henry James really respect his father, or had he been so "effeminized" by his wife that father–son affection and admiration had been impossible? Few nineteenth-century American writers were to pay as much attention to these problems of parental role functioning as Henry James, who observed in later years that "we wholesomely breathed inconsistency and ate and drank contradictions." Young Henry's memory of his boyhood pictured his mother as enveloping the entire family, even his father, who disappeared in her "enclosing lap." "She *was* he, *was* each of us," he wrote many years after her death. Perhaps it was because Henry James, Sr., was crippled that he depended so heavily on his wife. Given the social and moral conditions of Victorian life, however, one suspects that Henry James, Sr., was no atypical in his reliance of his wife. In fact, when she died, "he passed away, or went out with entire simplicity, promptness and ease, for the definite reason that his support had failed."[31] That Henry Sr. was such a passive, dependent figure prompted mild contempt from the son in an age when most men were aggressive, domineering doers. It is, of course, hazardous to speculate on the degree to which Henry's later personal life may have been affected by his parents' relationship. The culture and social thought of the time had placed women at the center of the family, even over men, and the question remains as to what was the effect on nineteenth-century children, especially boys.

In glimpsing at life histories like these, which relate childhood attitudes about parents and behavior, it is instructive to note Erik Erikson's thesis that when mothers dominate the home, boys have a tendency to grow up with a sense of inadequacy. Being constantly held accountable by mothers and sisters may have encouraged self-doubt in a boy and a feeling that he really was a repulsive creature. In the long run, pathological consequences may have become manifest in a condition of hysterical denial or self-restriction in which individuals were kept from living up to their inner feelings and powers of imagination. In examining Erikson's suggestions further, we find that some men may have overcompensated with a tireless drive, regardless of the psychological and physical results. Applying this to American men during the masculine century, with its extraordinary emphasis on morality, work, success, and accomplishments, to become a "self-made man," one senses that many men may have been harried and desperate to achieve an estimation of themselves set for them by their stern, moralistic parents. John R. Commons, for example, eventually suffered a nervous breakdown trying to fulfill the ideals prescribed for him by his mother and nineteenth-century Victorian America. Finally, however, he was "born again" when he entered the University of Wisconsin in 1904. He became an admirer of Robert LaFollette, a man who had both willpower and success. Another illustrative example is that of Charles Francis Adams, who searched in vain for a strong male figure on the Harvard faculty, but found none with whom he could identify. It was not until the Civil War that his search for the manly ideal was completed.[32] Other men may have thrown themselves into business with such a zeal that there could be no question about their worth and caliber as men exemplifying the ideals of American progress. What Adams, Commons, James, and others like them searched for was a realistic masculine figure, some reliable masculine source or model with whom they might identify and gain that valuable counsel through precept and example. While many young men may have been confused by parental influences shaping their masculine identity, there did exist an ideal of manhood just as there was an ideal of true womanhood.

A MASCULINE AVATAR

One source for the ideal can be found in the hundreds of guidebooks published to counsel young men on the proper approach to a vigorous, productive manhood.[33] Many of the same sources are useful in gaining perspectives on the ideal of true manliness as it was viewed in America before and after the Civil War. In no way do these sources document what may have constituted the private behavior of individuals. The autobiographies like those mentioned above provide much more information and insight, even though these sources are the historian's poor equivalent to the psychoverbal probings that are available today. The guidebook literature is one of the very best available sketches of Victorian ideals, establishing a frame of reference that reflected Victorian morals and standards, giving men some indication of how to go about fulfilling them. This literature was produced and read mostly by native-born middle- and upper-middle-class males. It can be contended, however, that, after all, this was the dominant class in the masculine century, the group that set standards it hoped others would value and emulate.

Guidebook literature on morals and etiquette had existed before, but around 1830 the number of such books increased and their tone became more serious, especially in discussing sexual purity. The decline of federalism and with it the decorum, standards, and ideals of the founding fathers may help account for this. With the rise of the common man and the emphasis on individualism, there was concern that social order might disintegrate. As more immigrants came to America, there may have been fear that the dominant class might be too weak to match the energies and proliferation of the newcomers. There was considerable interest in perfectionism by a number of groups and societies, all of which emphasized right living according to the true ideals of manhood and womanhood. And finally, too, the importance of the ever-increasing sexual distinctions between male and female made it necessary to delineate over and over again the proper social spheres of each. But most of all, the guidebooks seem to have been written for young men who these authors apparently felt needed direction that was not being supplied—especially by fathers. Whatever the case, the tone and substance of these little volumes, often repetitious and polemic, reveal much about the culture and what some thought was involved in being a man.[34]

SPIRITUALITY AND SUCCESS

Above everything else, the guidebooks stressed that manliness assumed material and/or professional success. But success almost always depended on good character. Although it is true that all societies, to some degree, recognize standards of character and praise success, manly success in America came to be closely associated with highly competitive occupational and business achievement. Because much of American business and industry was in a rapid growth stage, attention was naturally drawn to those who did well, and they served as models to many other men hoping to succeed. The success ideal was extended to others, as well as to the military man and politician, but generally because these men reflected the views of business.[35] In 1864 T. L. Nichols noted that when Americans spoke of a man's *worth* it was a measure of him *personally*.[36] Therefore, "nowhere is money sought so eagerly," reflecting a familiar cultural premise that God rewarded the righteous man. The Reverend John Todd, a prominent spokesman on successful manliness, published a sermon on character that represented the widely held view on the relationship of character and success. Citing the Revolutionary War, Todd claimed that the unique personal character of such men as Adams, Otis, and Ames, was the key to the success of the revolution against England. And before them there was the sterling example of the eighteenth-century theologian Jonathan Edwards, whose strong, manly character shaped his generation. According to George W. Burnap, manliness derived from strong internal character, which made the individual ready to face life's combat like a soldier in war.[37]

The truth was, wrote Timothy Dwight, that man's most substantial part was his spirit; the body was only a form "organized and built up from inert material particles. . . . It is this spiritual body which is the true man." This internal force had no power of vision of its own, explained Dwight, yet it was cognizant of everything in the outer and lower world of matter. A man's spirit could perceive truth and direct the body to function obediently toward the truth. Thus, according to Dwight, a man's spiritual body was the core element of his character, upon which perceptions and impressions were founded.[38] George Peck described "true manhood" as "little less than angelic—it is the grandest exhibition of divine power and wisdom—the culminating point of the world's greatness." The power within every man to shape his environment was a common theme that many guidebook authors followed with discussions of how best to be strong of mind and body.[39]

PHYSICAL HEALTH AND MANLINESS

Good health was essential if young men were to become dynamic and forceful. Physical exercise, preferably field work, or at least some form of physical exertion, was assumed to be basic in the formation of good character. Farm boys were usually considered to possess a distinct advantage over their urban contemporaries in building masculine physiques and in the all-important and related task of molding good character.[40] In fact, a basic indication of masculinity that was stressed in virtually all the guidebooks and generally throughout nineteenth-century society was *action*. The truly masculine male was active, energetic, always on the go. It followed, then, that the truly feminine woman was inactive, passive, and withdrawn, all of which contributed greatly to sex-role stereotyping. Dwight assured his male readers that inaction was not the rest that reinvigorated the exhausted energies of either the mind or body. The best rest was always more activity, only of a different kind. Unless this activity was maintained, the current of thought could flow undirected and unchecked, dangerously out of control, threatening the power of the mind. While not disavowing leisure activity completely, the guidebooks took a firm stand against idleness, which was assumed to be an enemy of manhood because it invited unwholesome activity, such as gambling and billiards. Such pastimes wasted valuable energy that could be used to advance more productive ends.[41]

A youth's failure to attend to the physical aspects of manhood might result in weakness of body and possibly even in feminine delicacy. Following this kind of advice, Theodore Roosevelt went west after his Harvard days to improve his health and become a man by riding and hunting. The fact that he wore spectacles, however, caused some to doubt his manliness. Such a physical weakness was taken as a sign of a defective character. This sort of stereotyping often prompted many smaller, homely, or "insignificant men" to physically assert themselves and overcome their disadvantaged bodies. According to G. Stanley Hall, physically large men were more frequently found among natural, self-made pioneers, chiefs, bosses, and captains of industry. However, noted Hall, big men were not necessarily healthier than average middle-sized men. Nevertheless, the point stuck in the minds of nineteenth-century men that a physical life in the open air was far more enhancing to masculinity than a constricted life and a vocation in a city.[42]

Guidebooks often depicted life as a "great battle," not only against external forces but against internal temptations of the flesh as well. Since every successful man needed to be armed with "patience, fortitude, energy and intense thought," he could never afford to indulge in alcohol or tobacco, which would weaken the perceptive powers of his manhood upon which he relied to capitalize on opportunity.[43] Many private and public institutions adopted behavior codes, based on the theory that they were saving the young man's character and ensuring his success as a man if they restricted his personal indulgences. As Ruth Elson has remarked, the nineteenth century emphasized the moral child rather than the educated or even the contented one, with virtually all behavior ultimately serving as an evaluation of personal character.[44]

THE MAN OF ACTION

Since manliness was the province of the action-oriented individual, it followed that intellectual or aesthetic pursuits were not part of being manly. In his discussion of anti-intellectualism in America, Richard Hofstadter contrasts what Americans felt was the decadent artificiality of European education and civilization with the vigor and originality of nature's school in America. There was no question as to which was superior according to Hofstadter's analysis: While European men theorized and planned, American men acted on the basis of their primitive instincts and imagination to advance a new world order based on individual abilities and accomplishments. Reverend Todd concluded that one of the chief evils to which many young men fell victim was crowding their minds with superfluous information. This diverted energy from more important things. It was charged that intellectual stimulation led to reflection and contemplation, ending with doubt or hesitation; such was not the stuff of a vigorous, active manhood. Because of his intellectualism, Thomas Jefferson, for example, was considered not half the man Andrew Jackson was when it came to brave deeds and manly accomplishments. Part of Jefferson's problem was his aristocratic nature and his intellectual curiosity, which no doubt contributed to making him a deist, Todd intoned. Those who wrote about the ideal of true manhood agreed that the speculative person was impractical, usually inefficient, and seldom active. Cultivated men were said to be effeminate and too sentimental to get along in the real man's world.[45] In George Bancroft's words, Andrew Jackson was a "nursling of the wilds" and grew to manhood "little versed in books, unconnected by science with the tradition of the past. . . . "[46] And as Michael Rogin has suggested, Jackson experienced personal regeneration and subsequent popularity through his violence and celebrated independence. He was controlled more by the raging conflicts of civilization than by restraint, understanding, or compromise. He could not indulge mutuality, viewing life only in terms of domination or submission. Such a "masculine" interpretation of his existence influenced all of his actions, whether with friends or adversaries, be they the Indians or the British. He embodied the half-alligator-half-man legend of the invincible, savage American backwoodsman.[47]

Throughout American history, men of force like Jackson have drawn higher praise and more attention than men known for intellectual or aesthetic contributions. In fact, the strong man who got things done was the one usually chosen for leadership roles because in him was seen the greater possibility of accomplishing some kind of action. To intellectuals, this kind of preference, which was clearly indicated in the guidebook literature, posed the serious problem of how one might reconcile the desire to be simultaneously a man of heroic action and noble thought.

This conflict between thought and action as a masculinity-validating criterion deeply troubled Ralph Waldo Emerson. Born in 1803, the son of a minister, he grew up in a strict home and followed his father into the church. But Emerson left the ministry, in part because he could not be the kind of man he really wanted to be and be a minister at the same time. Throughout his life, Emerson relentlessly pursued the meaning of the ideal heroic style and virtuous masculinity. Growing up in an era of intense economic and social fervor, Emerson was witness to a nation of energetic men, symbolized by the dynamic Andrew Jackson, who came from boyhood poverty, served in the military, performed heroically, bought land, and finally was swept into the White House amidst the tumult and shouting of the common man. The philosophical Emerson was suspicious of Jackson, however, reasoning that a man who did things on the spur of the moment was untrustworthy and therefore, from Emerson's perspective, unmanly.[48] But, in contrast, what realistic claims to heroic manhood could Emerson, a man of letters and learning, possibly make? The cant of the time registered a strong suspicion of new ideas, the possession of which never lead to ownership of stocks and bonds.

On a trip to Europe, Emerson wrote to a friend that he was searching for a teacher, a master, or "the man." The Emersonian key to powerful and effective manhood was self-confidence and self-reliance. "Whoso would be a man must be a nonconformist." Probably as much to convince himself as anyone else, Emerson adopted the view that the man of ideas who confidently pursued the truth, wherever it might lead, was as manly as the man of action who carried a gun and wielded an axe.[49] Emerson, however, seems not to have succeeded in convincing himself about the role of contemplators, conceding that poets were thought to be weak, which explained why they "talk themselves hoarse over the mischief of books and the effeminacy of bookmakers." The man of action was practical, engaging in perceivable means-and-ends relationships that required investments of energy, money, and a will to succeed. Those unwilling or unable to make those investments were considered unmanly. Realizing the truth of all this, Emerson admitted that men were usually ashamed of their intellect; those with scholarly attributes usually played them down. "The poet counsels his own son as if he were a merchant," indicating a desirability for practical accomplishments.[50]

The best education, then, was self-education, "natural wisdom," based on experience. William Eliot wrote that there was no profession better calculated to enlarge the mind and elevate the character than the pursuit of commerce. By the end of the century, the concern about the over-civilized man was quite common, and the criticism that the mind was being developed at the expense of the body was frequently heard.[51] One author contended that a formal education might help some young men advance their careers by helping them save time. But it was quite possible to "overread" with the unfortunate consequence of weakening a sense of purpose and dissipating energy. J. M. Buckley added that it is better to know less and to have more spirit than to know more and be tame, spiritless, and unproductive. Natural or self-education—or self-culture, as it was often called—depended on a viable imagination. Imagination was described by George Peck as the "power which modifies the images once received, creates new ones of them and gives them contents which do not originally belong to them." Such was the key to true greatness for men and the country. In other words, writers of these books and essays published about men and their accomplishments were fond of pointing out how men should rely on native instincts, not book learning, to direct their careers.[52]

COURAGE AND MASCULINITY

In a century known for its pioneering and belief in Darwinism, it is not surprising to find many of the guidebooks written in a "life is war" frame of reference. To be prepared for the active life, a bona fide man had to have a powerful will and courage sufficient to execute it. Courage was recognized as the manliest of all attributes. Courage meant persistence, or the determination to have one's own way, coupled with contempt for safety and ease. But one could never be certain of having courage until it was tested. The most severe test of manly courage occurred on the battlefield, but relatively few men were ever so tested before the Civil War. There were, however, countless other occasions, according to Thomas Hughes, in which an individual's courage could be put on the line, "for we are born into a state of war; with falsehood and disease, and wrong and misery in a thousand forms lying all around us, and the voice within calling on us to take our stand as men in the eternal battle against these."[53] One became manly as the conflict with evil was pursued courageously and relentlessly to the finish. Conversely, it was a sign of weakness and cowardice not to fight. After reading some of the proclamations about manliness and courage, one can more easily understand the violence and high homocide rate in many nineteenth-century American communities. No right-thinking man, true to himself and seeking recognition from his peers, could walk away from a fight. In a Darwinistic tone, Sylvanus Stall proclaimed enthusiastically that every man liked a good fight, and the stronger the opponent the better the individual was for the battle.[54]

A boy who lacked courage and avoided a fight was considered a sissy—a term commonly used by the end of the nineteenth century, one signaling an alarming problem to parents, especially fathers, who feared for their sons' reputations. Although the word *homosexual* was not often used in the public media, frequent references were made to the effeminate or sissy type of male to such an extent that an assumption developed associating him with the homosexual. Such an assumption explains the fear many parents had about sons who they thought were not developing "normally" by participating in "man's activities." Common factors in describing a sissy were the element of dependence and an inability to "take" what a given situation required. The sissy was just the opposite of the ideal masculine man praised in the moralistic nineteenth-century literature. Rafford Pyke described the sissy as "a somewhat effeminate young person" who, because of his appearance, inspired "a vague yet insurmountable feeling of *malaise.*" Usually, the sissy had a voice lacking in timbre, resonance, and carrying power. The face and form of the sissy lacked the sharp features of the ideal manly figure. His neck was long and his Adam's apple prominent. The sissy usually was polite and overly anxious to please. He liked to be with the ladies (but for the wrong reasons) and in a way, according to Pyke's description, the ladies liked him. In some ways he provided an important function for young women because of his willingness to "fetch and carry" for those whom he wanted to impress. Such an individual was a harmless type whose life was usually devoted to performing some sort of social or public service, a sharp contrast with the productive man of accomplishments and achievements.[55] Only after a man had "proved" himself through some masculine accomplishment (frequently it was of a military nature like Jackson's) could he be considered an authentic public servant.

There were other types of sissies not as physically recognizable, but who had "sissy souls." These unmanly men giggled when they laughed and whined when they were hurt. They were "chicken-hearted, cold and fearful." What they did with themselves was always inconsequential. Usually they preferred to copy others. When with men, the air of manliness they tried to project was scorned and provoked laughter. However much these individuals may have liked to impress, they simply had no daring or adventurous qualities. Women hated such men, Pyke stated, because they were flabby and feeble and affected women and other men "with a sort of moral nausea."[56]

The moral virtues men liked most in men, according to Pyke, included, above all, a sense of honor. Manly honor demanded fair play and the vigorous pursuit of every ideal. Justice was the basis of honor, which Pyke called "the most masculine of virtues, because it was the only one in which no woman ever had a share." It was this vision of "God's gift to man alone," that placed Pyke among those who saw sex differences as biologically determined. Reasonableness was another virtue that appealed to men when found in other men, for it was vital to success. Courage, generosity, and dignity were other virtues all truly masculine types should possess. And finally, Pyke carefully explained, another quality all true men had to have was gentleness. This was not to be confused with effeminacy, which all men disliked. Gentleness was acceptable as a masculine trait as long as the individual was strong. If he lacked physical and moral strength but was gentle, then he was usually considered effeminate. Yet the touch of gentleness gave all the other masculine qualities an accent, and the man a fineness of character. Gentleness was the key to the intuition, sensitivity, and imagination that helped show the way to great achievement.[57]

LITERATURE FOR BOYS

While the masculine style was being described and defined in guidebooks and advice manuals for boys and young men, there was a corresponding emphasis in boys' fiction and biography on masculine accomplishment and heroism. Many boys were thrilled by the adventure stories of Rudyard Kipling and by tales of Napoleon or other leaders from the past who demonstrated masculinity by being brave, courageous, and true to the concepts of masculine honor. Before the Civil War, there were the popular stories by Jacob Abbott, whose little Rollo, only nine years old, was a symbolic hero of the age. This character was disciplined and flawless; his confidence was full and reassuring. There was the constant anticipation of a great test at every turn in the Abbott stories, and with each step in the testing process the little fellow was made to feel more like a man.[58]

Daniel Boone was probably the most widely celebrated adventure hero. Timothy Flint's biography of the Kentuckian, one of the most illuminating discussions of the ideal male character, and one widely read, highlighted the strength and power of Boone. He was decisive and courageous, never failing to do the manly thing. One biographer contended that Boone left North Carolina because he was incensed at the effeminacy of the slave owners there. The epitome of the nonintellectual, Boone was raised in the woods, where nature trained and governed his instincts. In 1868, Flint prefaced another of his Boone biographies with the remark that the frontiersman possessed the best virtues of true manhood: fearlessness, strength, energy, and sagacity. And "we suspect he rather eschewed books, parchment deeds and clerkly contrivances as forms of evil; and held the dead letter of little consequence."[59]

That succeeding generations of Americans have seen in Boone a representative ideal man can be documented by claims such as the one in a 1912 Philadelphia newspaper that "God never made a grander man than Daniel Boone and in every public school in the land the story of his life should be made a regular part of the children's study."[60] Whether authors consciously deviated from evidence they possessed about their heroes is impossible to determine, but the very effort to create an ideal image promoted sanitized, larger-than-life male heroes, evidence of a concentrated effort to define moral masculinity. Boone was five-foot-eight and weighed 175 pounds. Kit Carson, another "big man," considered by Daniel Beard and others to be worthy of emulation, was five-foot-six and weighed only 135 pounds. Carson drank, swore, and was indifferent to religion, although stories about him stressed the opposite. Buffalo Bill also had a fondness for liquor, although he too was always portrayed as an ideal moral figure, a man of action who possessed no bad habits.[61]

HORATIO ALGER

Guidebooks dwelling on self-help and advancement themes argued the indispensable virtues of thrift, industriousness, and perseverance. Taken all together, these virtues were held to be vital if a man was to be independent and autonomous. Claims of masculinity could hardly be taken seriously if a man relied on others in any way, a suggestion of physical and mental weakness. On these points, the famous Horatio Alger books are good illustrations, as the author frequently associated themes of courage, self-reliance, and manliness. Through his more than one hundred novels for juveniles, Alger preached that engaging in the evils of alcohol, smoking, and loose living was a sure way of destroying manliness and preventing success. Even if boys were on life's wrong road, there was always hope for them, a theme that helps explain why the Alger legend epitomized the American-dream ideal. There was always the possibility of moral salvation followed by almost certain economic success and power. Virtually nothing was impossible for the boy who had pluck and drive, if he could save and invest shrewdly.

Alger's personal life hardly typified the exemplary qualities he put into his fictional heroes. His life fluctuated dramatically from periods of relative happiness and contentment to periods of intense loneliness and despair, when he ceased to be creative at all. Alger suffered the misfortune of being a child of exceptionally zealous parents, especially his overpowering father, a minister of the gospel, who prescribed the course his son's life should take. From Alger's birth in 1832 until their deaths, his parents constantly reminded him of the sinfulness of the world, assuring him that it would only be through the efforts of God's virtuous ones (like the Algers) that the unvirtuous slithering lot of humanity would be saved. Such stern parental governance made Horatio the object of ridicule and teasing when he showed up for school in Sunday clothes. "Holy Horatio," his classmates called him. To add to young Horatio's problems, he was a small, timid, sickly youth, virtually nontalkative.[62]

When Horatio Alger went to Gates Academy, a prep school in Marlborough, Massachusetts, however, the dam of repression broke, and it was not long before his parents learned that their son was expressing his youthful manliness through mischievous deeds, and even fighting. Later, at Harvard, he reverted to withdrawal and fits of loneliness, perhaps to avoid facing the proposition, put to him by a friend, that religion was a "barrier to mental growth." In October 1849, Alger rebounded from his doldrums when he met Patience Stires, one of the few people he was to truly love. His father refused, however, to consent to their marriage, sternly reminding Horatio about his "duty to God and conscience." Again Horatio Alger resorted to an introverted existence, torn between being a minister, which would have pleased his father, and being a writer. "I want to live to be great," he wrote after finally escaping to Europe. "Suppose it is in vain," he wondered, yet, "all great men are vain. What have they got that I need to be like them?" Apparently it was experience— experience in all of life's facets. With that resolution behind him, Alger took the plunge into riotous living and adventure in Paris. Perhaps not unexpectedly, considering Alger's sheltered background, women took advantage of him in a couple of bewildering affairs that caused no end of anguish and frustration but did not make Horatio Alger the great man he yearned to be.[63]

While many American men his age achieved heroic acclaim from serving in the Civil War, Alger never made it into the fighting. Instead, attracted to the plight of urban youth deserted by their parents and society, he found himself writing stories for young boys. By this point he had virtually renounced women and, as his biographer notes, Alger began living an existence that was "homosexual in nature if not in fact." There are no doubt many interpretations that could be drawn from his experiences; however, one is compelled to contemplate the tragic elements in Alger's life as he struggled to be a great man, finally achieving recognition as an author of boy's books, perhaps because he knew he could not write for adults. After another affair turned out badly, he fell into an unstable mental condition, from which he never fully recovered—still convinced that he was going to write the great book. Symbolically, he had all the boys' books he had written removed from his room, as if to prepare himself for the task ahead. But he died before he started, a lonely and frustrated man who had nevertheless gained a great reputation for postulating the ideal of success and fame.[64]

By the end of the nineteenth century, the moral messages and pontifications of the guidebooks were found in numerous boys' magazines, such as *Tip Top Weekly*, *St. Nicholas*, *Pluck and Luck*, *Brave and Bold*, and *Work and Win*. In short, action-packed stories featuring such heroes as Fred Fearnot, the reader was often swept into a crisis situation that called for courageous action or a moral resolution, all of which was to help induce fresh incentives to be good.

FRANK MERRIWELL AND BURT STANDISH

Among the most popular of the young heroes was Frank Merriwell, a strong, healthy, moral, athletic, and good-looking young man who never shirked his duty or complained. "His handsome proportions, his graceful figure, his fine kingly head and that look of clean manliness · . . . stamped him as a fellow of lofty thoughts and ambitions." The creator of this image, Burt Standish, known as Gilbert Patten to his audience, wrote about twenty thousand words a week and reached over twenty-five million readers, according to one estimate.[65]

Born in 1866, Burt Standish was raised according to the stern Christian discipline of his mother and father. Young Standish resisted the parental pressures to lead a moral and contrite life. He smuggled into his possession every soft-covered, cheap, yellow-backed book he could find and read them assiduously, forming a vivid childhood imagination and the basis of a rich fantasy world. His mother and father reprimanded him for fighting and quarreling with playmates, which only alienated the parents from their son. No self-respecting young boy could avoid fighting and maintain any respect from his peers. A pacifistic ethic was one of the initial indications of a sissy—something his parents did not understand about the younger generation of the 1870s. In time, Burt began reading the Beadle dime novels and thrilled at the heroic situations that the men of those novels often confronted. Even though his reading time interfered with his schoolwork, there was little doubt that Burt Standish felt it was worth it. The novels gave him a sense of purpose and the respectable manly model every boy needed. Boys of those days, he observed, who were called "good" by society were often little more than lackadaisical prigs without courage or inclination to take chances. Standish made it to respectability when he smoked a two-cent cheroot, a "bully experience" as he called it, proving he was no softie.[66]

But many young men of that age were perplexed by two conflicting tendencies. The "bad boy" image of Huck Finn and Tom Sawyer urged youth toward rebellion against parental restraints in favor of mischief. Young Standish felt a unique masculine identity with the gang by smoking and drinking, common initiation rites for thousands of young men. Drinking and smoking became a testimony of a young man's individuality and evidence that he had not conformed to social norms and customs set by women. Yet when, as Gilbert Patten, he wrote the famous Merriwell stories, his hero conformed to the ideals of righteous manhood found in the guidebooks. Frank Merriwell loved his mother and his country and was devoted to his school, first to Fardale Academy and then to Yale. He abhorred the bully, the social misfit, and bad sportsmanship. And Frank Merriwell never lost an athletic contest. He won at boxing, was an extraordinary football player, and excelled at baseball with a pitch that curved in two directions. He was outstanding at hockey, golf, bicycling, and track. He stood for honesty and decency among men by helping to outwit thugs and Texas rustlers. For twenty years, Frank Merriwell stories thrilled young readers with an exciting image of virile manhood never defeated or compromised. Although the hero was too perfect to have been real, and even though there was little of Merriwell's perfection in his creator, Patten stated that "I know I would have chosen to be like Frank had fate made it possible, and I believed all respectable, clean-minded boys felt the same." Many a young man sought to emulate Frank Merriwell so completely that they nearly ruined their arms trying to borrow Frank's special "double shoot curve." Privately, however, Standish confessed disgust that his famous character was so priggish, and that he was stupid for letting the other fellow strike the first blow. This feeling, which may suggest a latent contempt for the ideal image, was growing among many young men by 1900, a time when their masculine identity was becoming more and more confusing to them.[67]

SEX AND MANHOOD

When the authors of the guidebooks and advice manuals got around to the subject of marriage and sex, vagueness and inconsistency prevailed. In other words, as long as the focus was on juveniles, their physical development, and the attributes of success, courage, and masculine honor, the genre was at its best in dispensing shibboleths about manliness. Sooner or later, however, the Frank Merriwells and Fred Fearnots of the real world faced the prospect of female relationships, courtship, prospects of marriage, and, most confusing of all, sex. A key reference point in mate selection was mother, not surprising in view of the role mothers had in the lives of their sons and families. O. S. Fowler urged every boy to "behold thy mother! Make love to her, and her your first sweetheart. . . . Nestle yourself right into her heart, and hers into yours."[68] That such an enthusiastic celebration of mother love might lead to some conflicts in a basic male–female relationship with other women did not seem to occur to those offering such advice. This classic state of confusion is reflected in the writing of Indiana Senator Albert Beveridge in 1906. "Be a man; that's the sum of it all—be a man," he wrote. "Be all that we Americans mean by those three words." Eight pages later, however, the reader finds Beveridge urging that young men yield to their mothers' moralities in life. In fact, "be mother's own boy."[69] T. S. Arthur had so argued fifty years earlier, while Daniel Wise warned young men to be always on guard against skeptical women, especially in times of radicalism and ultraism. Such women had a latent tendency to become unfeminine moral monsters, capable of "unmanning" a man. Henry Beecher contended that no man could have good luck if he had a bad wife. Beecher warned young men that they especially be on guard against extravagance, one of the chief evils in women, and one that would surely work against the prospects of a man becoming successful. Specific advice on mate choice, according to a study by Michael Gordon and Charles Bernstein, not unexpectedly emphasizes finding a woman willing to accept her domestic role. Men were urged to serve their women well, that is, make them happy in order that they would perform their duties cheerfully. The three basic criteria of mate choice included religious conviction, good physical health, and moral character. Apparently it was assumed that if one paid close attention to these points, marital happiness and adjustment would follow. Guidebooks rarely if ever mentioned rationality, spontaneity, or a respect for others' emotions in marriage.[70]

Nineteenth-century marital happiness, then, depended heavily on the religion of both male and female. Through the methods of promoting good character, which guidebooks profusely outlined, the theory was that a perfection of the physical aspects of marriage would automatically follow. By emphasizing "male continence," withdrawal before ejaculation, John Humphrey Noyes carried the theory to the extreme in his commune at Oneida, New York, where complex marriage was practiced.* Another philosophy popular before the Civil War was Swedenborgianism, which dated back to eighteenth-century Europe. According to this philosophy, which grew in popularity in the late 1840s, followers of Emanuel Swedenborg, like their Swedish master, believed that the perfect society was created through a holy marriage that placed the conjugal love at the highest level of transcendental contemplation, a point somewhere beyond earthly or physical reality, that bound two souls together in perfect harmony. The object was an exalted vision of progress arrived at through

---

*Regarding sexuality and the masculine role, the views of John Humphrey Noyes are quite different from those discussed here. Those views offer some distinct alternatives.

heavenly refinement of sexuality, one in which men and women had their physical lives completely under control.[71] Few, if any, conventional guidebook authors treated sexuality in terms bearing even the faintest mark of reality. Considering the Victorian age through autobiographies and personal memoirs, the best assessment of the attitudes toward sex is that it was a thoroughly bewildering problem. Ideas about moral purity, notions of romantic love, the natural physical desires, medical advice and suggested therapy seriously confounded sexual relationships.[72]

ABSTINENCE AND HEALTH

The rise of the common man in the early to mid-nineteenth century and the emerging transformation of America into an industrial society spurred growing anxiety about sexual morality and promiscuity, fostering a sexual-purity crusade. For many of the same reasons that middle- and upper-class Americans were agitated about the effects of alcohol and related social evils, they sensed a special threat to social order if greater freedom were permitted with regard to sex and personal morals in a society as diverse and undisciplined as nineteenth-century America. The translations of purists, such as Samuel Tissot and Benjamin Rush, that appeared around 1810, had warned about the grave dangers of excessive sexual indulgence. By 1830 the concern about sexual control was augmented by the concurrent "discovery" of adolescence and new theories about child nurture. Phrenologists, for example, became popular with their "scientific method" of analyzing human behavior by studying cranial shape. They claimed they could tell who was likely to be pure and who would be lusty. Sylvester Graham, a principle figure of the purity crusade, championed temperance, eventually incorporatiog it in all things to ensure proper health. Thus, along with many other reformers and reform organizations to promote it, the interest in sexual purity and control became a basic concern to Victorian Americans.*[73]

Benjamin Rush labeled excessive sex as an illness, contending that if men were to let themselves go, other afflictions, such as vertigo, dyspepsia (a disturbed digestion), loss of memory, pulmonary consumption,

*A representative text, *Search Lights on Health: Light on Dark Corners: A Complete Sexual Science and a Guide to Purity and Physical Manhood* (Napier, Ill.: Nichols & Co., 1895) by B. G. Jeffries and A. M. Nichols, reportedly sold more than one million copies.

hyphchondriasis (depression), impotence, epilepsy, and even death might follow. According to Rush, a mere "fondness for obscene conversation and books" could bring on these maladies, or even "a wanton dalliance with women" could trigger erotic aspirations in the male constitution. Intercourse wasn't even necessary.[74] In 1833 Sylvester Graham lectured that all the organs of the body were closely related through the nerves, and that the whole system was, in effect, closed. If energies were spent in one way, through intellectual activity, for example, one could not expect to have as mcuh physical energy. In other words, there was only so much the body could be expected to do with its allotted energy. "All extraordinary and undue excitements . . . whether caused by mental, moral or physical stimuli, increase the excitablility and unhealthy activity of the nerves of organic life; and tend to induce diseased irritability and sensibility in them, which is more or less diffused over the whole domain. . . ." Even daydreams were dangerous pastimes because this "adultry of the mind" was one of the chief sources of "effeminacy and disordered functions" in men. Fortunately, God gave man powers of intellect and moral integrity to avoid such excesses. For married men, Graham argued, sex should be only infrequent—so as not to undermine masculine strength for other pursuits. He reasoned that as a husband and wife "became accustomed to each other's body, and their parts no longer excite an impure imagination," except for those "natural and instinctive excitements . . . intercourse is very seldom." Graham refused to be specific about the frequency of connubial indulgences allowable without doing harm to the system. Some men, he reasoned, who were vigorous and possessed a lot of energy could indulge in sex more frequently, but even they could very easily transgress the "constitutional laws" of good health and well-being and be overtaken by lustful desire, which could undermine their manhood. Good-looking females were the most dangerous because they inspired the lewd thoughts and sexual excitement that often resulted in a waste of masculine energy.[75]

The idea that sex could actually result in a "wasting infirmity" for men was believed true from the time of Benjamin Rush through the popular writings of John Cowan, reprinted well into the twentieth century. G. J. Barker-Benfield had labeled the problem one of the spermatic economy, based on the assumption that males produced only so much sperm within their systems and that they would have to exercise care as to how it was "spent," just as one should carefully spend money. Cowan theorized that a young man's undischarged semen was absorbed back into the bloodstream, thereby producing masculine traits and energy. The voice deepened, the figure changed, hair grew, manly strength developed, and the mind became active. Any careless spending of the precious energy-saving semen would arrest the development of these masculine traits and precipitate a near-certain decline of physical and mental energy.[76]

Medical doctors like Rush, Cowan, and P. H. Chevasse simply deferred to the "laws of nature" to support their arguments, contending that no man seeking the status of true manhood and manly success would ever ignore such laws. In 1919, Winfield S. Hall was still offering these same ideas. The key word for him was *virility*, the physical manifestation of everything that was associated with the ideal of manliness.[77]

As all men found out sooner or later, and most likely sooner, sexual temptation sneaked its way into their lives. What to do about it and how to respond with a workable "cure" preoccupied nineteenth-century sexual purists. One suggested preventative was a proper diet, consisting mostly of unseasoned vegetables, a form of control favored by Rush and later by Graham and his diet-reform movement of the 1830s and '40s. Benjamin Rush cited the example of a man who had nearly extinguished sexual desire by living on a bread-and-water diet! Seasonings, spices, and alcoholic beverages of all kinds were cited as stimulants to be avoided to stave off sexual arousal. Being properly employed, avoiding leisure moments, and especially not dallying with women were all listed as ways to forestall the dangers of sexual arousal, which undermined manhood. City living was highly suspect as a contributing cause of a sexual imagination. Vice and diversions of all sorts constantly threatened to attract men and pollute them with evil thoughts, making them lose control of themselves. William Alcott, one of the most widely read lay authorites during the 1840s and '50s, described a man of only thirty-five years who, because of his urban environment, had succumbed to "all the infirmities of three score and ten [meaning that he had aged as much as a man of 70]." The cause: "solitary and social licentiousness." And worst of all, Alcott lamented, "thousands of youth on whom high expectations have been placed are already on the highway that will probably lead down to disease and premature death."[78]

Such dire predictions of calamity brought with them a host of treatments for those afflicted. Dio Lewis advanced a program of physical exercise designed to divert energy from the sexual organs and distribute it to other parts of the body. Another method was the water cure, whereby the body was literally filled with water to cleanse it of impurities, sometimes with painful and dangerous side effects. Electric shock was also used to forestall corruption of the body and guarantee a moral, masculine existence. In fact, the sexual purists who diagnosed such maladies made such extraordinary predictions and recommended such extreme cures became so pervasive by the 1870s that they had virtually taken over the advice manuals on marriage and manhood.[79]

Marriage was the only legitimate outlet for those ridden with sexual desire, but, as noted, a man could never be sure how often he could spend his sexual energies without risking his manliness. There were those who advised restraint and temperance in all things, expecially in sex, while some others, John Cowan among them, believed sex should be only for procreative purposes.

Many believed a man should marry and have sexual experience only when the body was fully matured and capable of handling the strain. Cowan observed that such maturity was attained at about age twenty-eight or thirty. Serious, debilitating consequences could be expected if a man married too soon or otherwise had excessive sexual intercourse. "A life other than strict continence arrests the growth of his body, weakens his entire system, his muscles become pale and flabby, nerves weak, brain forever oppressed and clogged, and he is no more capable, in his work in life's vineyard to make a name for himself among the earth's great ones, than the veriest barn fool." Husbands and wives must thoroughly understand the seriousness of maintaining a healthy marriage. This would be greatly augmented if men and women anticipating marriage were certain that their respected traits of character were equal in all ways. Cowan warned men to above all avoid the "hysterical woman," because her sensuous behavior was a direct threat to manliness. All men should "leap out of bed as soon as they awake in the morning," he advised, to avoid the possibility of sexual intercourse. P. H. Chevasse, another physician who argued for continence, claimed that when men brought their instincts under control, they not only proved their native nobility but their "hero power" as well.[80] Another recommendation argued that "a single bed is always preferred both for married and unmarried people. Where two persons sleep in the same bed, the one who [has] the stronger physical power is likely to absorb the vital forces of the weaker one."[81] Cowan dismissed birth-control theories and devices because of the dangerous delusion implied that frequent intercourse was possible and acceptable without procreation. Withdrawal before ejaculation, practiced by some traditionalist groups, was dangerous, he charged, because it did not allow the reabsorption of semen into the blood stream, and once the system was thrown out of balance, the overall slippage of health was sure to result. The rhythm method was not reliable, he went on, because the arousal of the female caused the release of the eggs earlier in the menstrual cycle, often resulting in pregnancy.[82]

"SELF-ABUSE" AND "SELF-RELIEF"

Masturbation, the so-called "secret sin," described as "self-pollution," was one of the biggest concerns for sexual purists and masculinity idealists. The very fact that it was "secret" and private, and that young men allegedly practiced it more than older men, made it especially alarming. The worst consequence of masturbation was not only that it wasted valuable masculine energy and reduced the productivity of men, but that it was a major cause of insanity, epilepsy, and a host of other physical and emotional ailments, according to Joseph Howe.[83]

Frederick Hollick, who spoke frequently on the subject during the 1840s, produced a study that revealed that half of the reported insanity cases among merchants, students, printers, and shoemakers started with masturbation. Among carpenters, blacksmiths, and those who had an active form of employment, only thirteen percent of the insanity cases came from masturbation. The conclusion was clear: Youths should be kept busy at active jobs away from "the monotonous inactivity of a counting-house desk," away from an office, and they should avoid the "merely intellectual profession[s]."[84]

As for the causes of "sex pollution," the reasons varied. Improper diet was thought to provoke a masturbatory impulse—especially certain stimulating foods and beverages, such as pickles, coffee, and alcohol. Overeating and not chewing food properly were listed as other reasons. Lewd conversation and obscene pictures were said to be a primary cause; this emphasizes the significance of Anthony Comstock's attack on the smut peddlers in the 1870s. Joseph Howe blamed nurses and servants for not watching young children more closely. Howe favored a statute that would deter, if not stop, "depraved nurses from transfering their lewdness" to the children under their charge. He also listed certain gymnastic exercises, and even the climbing poles, as stimulation inducing masturbation. Sleeping in a soft bed with too many bedcovers in a room not properly ventilated added to the likelihood that a boy would be troubled by the self-polluting urge. Whatever the reason, masturbation was thought to be a serious disease, and even if a victim did not show any physical effects, there would be a scar on the soul. To be a man meant resising masturbation by following the many recommended cures: sleeping on a hard bed with the window open, taking cold baths, walking before breakfast, and, above all, avoiding erotic thoughts. To resist such desires was a mark of bravery in normal men for "it is . . . the impure life which either effeminates [i.e., weakens] or else compels a naturally brave man to do things which he knows are abhorrent to his sense of manhood."[85]

Doctors and moralists also had to deal with the problem of nocturnal emissions. Generally it was felt that these occurrences were less harmful to masculine development, although a high frequency of these "wet dreams" could weaken the body. Sylvanus Stall explained them as nature's self-relief of an excess build-up of fluid in the male organs and commented that such emissions did not necessarily mean a loss of manly power. But George Beard maintained that spermatorrhea could result in sleeplessness, headaches, and depression. Such emissions "are the effects as well as the cause of disease, and should be so considered."[86] Frank Harris took the problem of nocturnal arousal and emission seriously enough to tie a cord around his penis before retiring so that when it swelled he would be awakened in pain. Later, Harris, tortured by the thought of his sinfulness (as well as by his rope), fantasized that maybe Christianity was just a pack of lies after all, and that none of the warnings and repressions of the age were really necessary.[87]

GUILT AND CONFUSION

The impact of Victorian sexual restraints and moral imperatives on men in their quest of true manhood surely must have been troublesome, although few men wrote down their actual feelings. One who did was Upton Sinclair, who constantly wrestled with sexual cravings during his adolescence. In his autobiography he recalled the confusion, restlessness, and misery regarding women he met on the street, often fantasizing about sexual relations with them. Occasionally, when women were openly flirtatious and suggested intimacy Sinclair was flooded with temptation, "but then would come another storm—of shame and fear." Having grown up in a society that placed women on a pedestal (shunning sex at the same time) left young men, like Sinclair, floundering for self-understanding and guidance. "My chastity was preserved at the cost of much emotional effort. . . . " The fear of sex, the mere suggestion of it, had overwhelmed him even when he studied Renaissance art and confronted that "mass of nakedness" in his art books. At sixty-five, Sinclair confessed that he still had difficulty facing the sexual facts and understanding himself in his youth.[88]

Believing that sexual permissiveness was bad, many people were left miserable by the denial and repression of sex. The journalist Oswald Garrison Villard echoed a similar frustration and annoyance at a moral code that either succeeded in driving young people apart or induced a feeling of guilt, leading some young men to seek the secret companionship of "outcast women." Raised in a home in which his mother's influence was supreme ("one could hardly refuse that mother anything"), he grew up believing that sexual sin was the worst of all offenses. His mother was open-minded enough to recognize changing mores, but because she was so sure of the correctness of her position, she often strained the feelings of those who least wished to offend.[89] Meanwhile, young William Borah's parents discouraged his interest in stage plays and refused to condone his reading for variety. He was counseled that the only way to manliness and greatness was to pursue work and live by the old codes. By the time he married in 1895, Borah had become so accustomed to concentrating on his political career that he paid hardly any attention to his wife.[90]

The experiences of Villard, Sinclair, Borah, and others suggest that even as American society was changing during the nineteenth century, the ideals of true manhood, which were based in part on the expectations of sexual purity, were reiterated with such vehemence and steadfastness that they created serious obstacles to realism and maturity. The evidence bears out the contention that these obstacles and issues invaded every element of sensuality—especially marital relationships. The tragic result was that many young men were taught by parents. usually mothers, and by guidebooks about the evils of sensuality rather than about its proper place in their lives. Nevertheless, the mere pretention of upholding the ideal gave the age a certain reassurance that moral and material progress was being made in America amid the morally dangerous trends of immigration, urbanization, and industrialization.

CURES AND CONFLICTS

What must have been especially vexing to many nineteenth-century men was that much of the advice was quite contradictory. Regarding spermatorrhea, for example, one extreme cure recommended inserting a wooden plug into the rectum to create a pressure that was thought to prevent emission. On the other hand, some doctors actually prescribed illicit sex for unmarried men to reduce spermatorrhea. Then there was the very real confusion that resulted from the emphasis placed on a man's physical development, the advice being that exercise and activity, prescribed to the point of exhaustion in some instances, was essential to promote muscle growth and development. In fact, one of the concerns of the physical-culture movement (discussed in Chapter 6 of this book) was that muscles would wither if not exercised. But should the same argument not be applied to the male sex organs? Some doctors, recognizing this seeming inconsistency, discounted the moralists and accepted "the principle that a muscular organ is invigorated by moderate exercise."[91] On another subject, John Kellogg contended that constipation was a source of sexual excitement that led to those dreaded consequences described above, while Frederick Hollick maintained that, in fact, constipation was a cause of sexual weakness and thereby inhibited virility. Although in retrospect it might seem that impotence would have been ideal in an age that emphasized sexual purity, there was much discussion about impotence and how to remedy it. Hollick, who was a very popular lecturer, even recommended the use of marijuana as one means of stimulating men. Other Victorians prescribed everything from opium to electric shock to excite sexual desire. The same confusion can be found surrounding the advice on alcohol. Some thought it highly stimulating to sexual functioning; others thought just the opposite, that it undermined a man's health and sexual vitality.[92] Finally, one wonders about the mood and mind of a society that preached sexual control and restraint in the interests of order and stability but worried about being overtaken by lower racial stocks who allegedly multiplied much faster than they.

Whatever the conflicts and the resulting confusion about male sexuality, morality, and identity may have been, it should not be concluded that the men, or women either, of the Victorian era were an unhappy and unstable lot. In fact, one can speculate whether subsequent generations were not just as confused or misled, perhaps even more so in their own way, about the intertwined relationships of men and work, men and women, men and men, men and their environment, and the whole spectrum of sexual activity. After all, nineteenth-century men were productive and creative in their dedication to a vision of progress that, as suggested here, bacame the American masculine mystique.

How men behaved, what they thought of the opposite sex, and how they saw themselves performing in masculinity-validating experiences must be seen in the larger context of trying to fulfill that elusive American dream of fame and good fortune, which the mystique demanded. Since the ideal of progress assumed a strong, forceful manhood to achieve its ideals, no danger, no threat of failure, whatever it might be, whether a lack of courage, an overindulgence in sexual passion, or artificiality of any kind, could be tolerated. The task before every young man was "to make himself the most perfect specimen of a man, in all the elements that enter essentially into right character, and while doing it, to help others as powerfully as possible to do the same thing." The paradigm of progress, with its strong orientation toward active individualism and success, put good character on the top line of the social contract of the time. The purpose was "not solely to make money, but to make manhood, while making money, not to win fame, but to make a character worthy of fame. . . ."[93] The making of such a character, the likes of which a Daniel Boone had surely possessed, seemed attainable to young men in the middle years of the century. But as implied here, serious problems lay ahead. Men and women were divided over sexuality and men divided further against one another as they operated their affairs and pressed deals as forceful and, they hoped, successful men. It would not be hard to make the case that Boone's heroic appeal to succeeding generations of men was that he was able to avoid effeminizing civilization and all that went with it. When Kentucky filled with people, Boone, according to legend, left because his personal sense of manhood could only be worked out in a spatial context, beyond the line of civilization that counseled refinement, restraint, and sociability. But escape to frontier space was not a realistic option for men of the twentieth century. Nevertheless, the power and force of the mystique tantalized them as if it were.

Notes

[1] Philippe Ariès, *Centuries of Childhood*, trans. Robert Baldick (New York: Alfred A. Knopf, Inc., 1962), p. 411.

[2] Ibid, p. 398.

[3] John Demos, *A Little Commonwealth* (New York: Oxford University Press, 1970), pp. 180–90; Richard Bushman, *From Puritan to Yankee* (New York: W. W. Norton & Co., 1967).

[4] Richard Bartlett, *The New Country: A Social History of the American Frontier 1776–1890* (New York: Oxford, 1974), p. 343. Copyright © 1974 by Oxford University Press, Inc. Reprinted by permission.

[5]Alexis de Tocqueville, *Democracy in America*, II (New York: Random House, 1945), p. 212.

[6]Barbara Welter, "The Cult of True Womanhood," *American Quarterly*, (Summer, 1966), 152.

[7]Sarah Lewis, *Woman's Mission* (Boston: Crosby & Co., 1840), p. 13; Winslow Hubbard, *Woman As She Should Be* (Boston: T. H. Carter, 1838), p. 11.

[8]Eileen Kraditor, *Up From the Pedestal* (Chicago: Quadrangle Books, 1968), p. 47.

[9]Barbara Welter, "The Cult of True Womanhood," *American Quarterly* (Summer, 1966), 153; Alexis de Tocqueville, *Democracy in America*, II (New York: Random House, 1945), p. 212.

[10]Thomas Branagan, *The Excellency of the Female Character Vindicated*, quoted in Barbara Welter, "The Cult of True Womanhood," *American Quarterly* (Summer, 1966), 155.

[11]Philip Wylie, *Generation of Vipers* (New York: Rinehart, Pocket Books, Inc., 1955), pp. 184–205; Erik Erikson, *Childhood and Society* (New York: W. W. Norton & Co., Inc., 1963), p. 292.

[12]*Christian Family Magazine* (January, 1842), 107.

[13]*Mrs. Whittlesey's Magazine for Mothers* (New York: Henry Whittlesey, 1850–51), 171.

[14]William Eliot, *Lectures to Women* (Boston: Crosby Nichols, 1880), pp. 80–85; L. B. Adams, "Farmer's Boys," *Agricultural Report* (Spring, 1866), 311–12.

[15]Robert Sunley, "Early Nineteenth Century American Literature on Child Rearing," in Margaret Mead and Martha Wolfenstein, eds., *Childhood in Contemporary Cultures* (Chicago: University of Chicago Press, 1955), p. 152; *Mothers Magazine*, II, No. 8, 113–15; *Mrs. Whittlesey's Magazine for Mothers*, I (1850–51), 210–11; Ruth Elson, *Guardians of Tradition* (Lincoln; University of Nebraska Press, 1964), pp. 8–11, 337–39; Eric Dingwall, *The American Woman* (New York: Rinehart & Co., Inc., 1956), p. 58.

[16]*This Fabulous Century, 1870–1900* (New York; Time-Life Books, 1970), p. 194.

[17]Allen Nevins, *Grover Cleveland* (New York; Dodd, Mead & Co., 1962), pp. 5–6, 13, 23, 57, 71; George Parker, *Recollections of Grover Cleveland* (New York: Century Co., 1911).

[18]Floyd Dell, *Homecoming* (Port Washington: Kennikat Press, 1933), pp. 5–6, 22–26.

[19]Lincoln Steffens, *Autobiography* (New York: Harcourt Brace Jovanovich, Inc., 1931), p. 77; see also Doris Kearns, *Lyndon Johnson and the American Dream* (New York: Harper and Row, 1976).

[20]Donald Meyer, *The Positive Thinkers* (Garden City, N.Y.: Doubleday & Co., Inc., 1965).

[21]Heman Humphrey, *Domestic Education* (Amherst: Adams, 1840); Timothy Dwight, *The Father's Book* (Springfield: G. & C. Merriam, 1834); "Father's Influence," *Mrs. Whittlesey's Magazine for Mothers*, I (1850–51), 255–57; Winslow Hubbard, *Woman as She Should Be* (Boston: T. H. Carter, 1838); Lyman Cobb, *Evil Tendencies of Corporal Punishment* (New York: M. H. Newman and Co., 1847); "Decay of Family Affections," *Nation* (April 15, 1869), 291–92.

[22]Alexis de Tocqueville, *Democracy in America* (New York: Random House, 1945), pp. 202–08; Bernard Wishy, *The Child and The Republic* (Philadelphia: University of Pennsylvania Press, 1968), pp. 26–28.

[23]*Public Ledger and Daily Transcript* (Philadelphia), July 20, 1848, p. 2.

[24]"First and Last Love," *Harpers* (October, 1855), 655; Margaret Fuller, "The Great Lawsuit: Man vs. Woman, Woman vs. Man," *The Dial*, IV (1843), 1–47; see also William

Wasserstrom, *Heiress of all the Ages*: *Sex and Sentiment in the Genteel Tradition* (Minneapolis: University of Minnesota Press, 1959).

[25]Lucy Ide as quoted in *This Fabulous Century*, 1870–1900 (New York: Time-Life Books, 1970), p. 78; William Allen White, *Autobiography* (New York: Macmillan, 1946), pp. 34–35.

[26]*This Fabulous Century, 1870–1900* New York: Time-Life Books, 1970), p. 94.

[27]Erik Erikson, *Idenity: Youth and Crisis* (New York: W. W. Norton & Co., 1968), p. 63.

[28]Charles Francis Adams, *Autobiography* (Boston: Houghton Mifflin, 1916) pp. 4–35.

[29]John R. Commons, *Myself* (New York: Macmillan, 1934), pp. 9, 11, 15–16.

[30]Leon Edel, *Henry James: The Untried Years, 1843–1870* (New York: Lippincott, 1935), pp. 21–23, 49–53; Copyright © 1953 by Leon Edel. Reprinted by permission of J. B. Lippincott Company. F. O. Matthiessen, *The James Family* (New York: Alfred A. Knopf, Inc., 1948), pp. 23–38.

[31]Leon Edel, *Henry James: The Untried Years, 1843–1870* (New York: Lippincott, 1953), pp. 49–53. Copyright © 1953 by Leon Edel. Reprinted by permission of J. B. Lippincott Company.

[32]Erik Erikson, *Identity: Youth and Crisis* (New York: W. W. Norton & Co., 1968) pp. 117, 120; John R. Commons, *Myself* (New York: Macmillan, 1934), p. 95; Charles F. Adams, *Autobiography* (Boston: Houghton Mifflin, 1916), p. 35.

[33]Irvin Wyllie, *Self-Made Man in America* (New York: Macmillan Co., 1954); John Cawelti, *Apostles of the Self-Made Man* (Chicago: University of Chicago Press, 1965).

[34]Ronald Walters, *Primers for Prudery* (Englewood Cliffs, N.J.: Prentice-Hall, Inc., 1974), pp. 10–12; G. J. Barker-Benfield, *The Horrors of the Half-Known Life* (New York: Harper and Row, Publishers, Inc., 1976).

[35]Robin M. Williams, *American Society*: *A Sociological Interpretation*, 2nd ed. rev. (New York: Alfred A. Knopf, Inc., 1960).

[36]T. L. Nichols, *Forty Years of American Life*, 2 vols. (London: J. Maxwell & Co., 1864).

[37]John Todd, "An Address to Young Men" (Amherst: n.p., 1833), pp. 5–11; see also G. J. Barker-Benfield, *The Horrors of the Half-Known Life* (New York: Harper & Row, Publishers, Inc., 1976), pp. 135–74; George W. Burnap, *Lectures to Young Men (Baltimore: John Murphy, 1848)*.

[38]Timothy Dwight, *Advice to Young Men* (n.p.), pp. 22–23.

[39]George Peck, *The Formation of a Manly Character* (New York: Carlton & Phillips, 1853), p. 3; see also Henry Ward Beecher, *Twelve Lectures to Young Men* (New York: Appleton and Co., 1890); Frank Ferguson, *The Young Man* (Boston: n.p., 1848); William Alcott, *The Young Man's Guide* (Boston: T. R. Marvin, 1846); William Arnot, *The Race for Riches* (Philadelphia: Lippincott, Grambo and Co., 1853); Freeman Hunt, *Worth and Wealth* (New York: Stringer and Townsend, 1856); Charles Seymore, *Self-Made Men* (New York: Harper and Brothers, 1859); William Guest, *The Young Man Setting Out in Life* (New York: American Tract Society, 1868).

[40]Horace Mann, *A Few Thoughts for a Young Man* (Boston: Lee and Shepard, 1870), p. 13.

[41]Timothy Dwight, *Advice to Young Men* (n.p.), p. 72; William Eliot, *Lectures to Young Men* (Boston: American Unitarian Association, 1882), pp. 45, 115, 117; Horace Mann, *A Few Thoughts for a Young Man* (Boston: Lee and Shepard, 1870), p. 66.

[42]George Peck, *The Formation of Manly Character* (New York: Carlton and Phillips, 1853), pp. 11–12; Theodore Roosevelt, *Autobiography* (New York: Charles Scribner's Sons, 1913), p. 37; G. Stanley Hall, *Adolescence* (New York: D. Appleton and Co., 1904), pp. 38–39.

[43]Timothy Dwight, *Advice to Young Men*, (n.p.) pp. 72–73; Horace Mann, *A Few Thoughts for Young Men* (Boston: Lee and Shephard, 1870) p. 60; Timothy Arthur, *Advice to Young Men* (Boston: Phillips Sampson & Co., 1855), pp. 142–45; William Eliot, *Lectures to Young Men* (Boston: American Unitarian Association, 1882), pp. 94 ff; Phineus Barnum, *Art of Money Getting* (Philadelphia: International Pub., n.d.).

[44]Ruth Elson, *Guardians of Tradition* (Lincoln: University of Nebraska Press, 1964), pp. 1–2, 8–11, 337–39.

[45]Richard Hofstadter, *Anti-Intellectualism in American Life* (New York: Alfred A. Knopf, Inc., 1962), pp. 148, 158–59, 186; John Todd, "An Address" (n.p.), p. 11; George Peck, *Formation of a Manly Character* (New York: Carlton and Phillips, 1853), p. 116; J. W. Kasey, *Young Man's Guide to Greatness* (published by the author, 1858), p. 265 and passim.

[46]Quoted in John W. Ward, *Andrew Jackson: Symbol for an Age* (New York: Oxford University Press, 1962), p. 73.

[47]Michael Rogin, *Fathers and Children* (New York: Alfred A. Knopf, Inc. 1975), pp. 13, 48; John W. Ward, *Symbol for an Age* (New York: Oxford University Press, 1962).

[48]Ralph W. Emerson, *Complete Works*, Vol. XI (Boston: Houghton Mifflin Co., 1883), p. 521.

[49]Ralph W. Emerson, *Essays* (New York: John B. Allen, 1885), p. 47; Ralph W. Emerson, *Complete Works*, Vol. X (Boston : Houghton Mifflin Co., 1883), pp. 268–73.

[50]Ralph W. Emerson, *Complete Works*, Vol. X (Boston: Houghton Mifflin Co., 1833), p. 264; Ralph W. Emerson, *Representative Men* (Boston: Houghton Mifflin Co, 1903), p. 2; "Emerson Reconsidered," *New Republic* (January 1 and 8, 1972), 27–29.

[51]William Eliot, *Lectures to Young Men* (Boston: American Unitarian Association, 1882), p. 48; William Mathews, *Getting On in the World* (Chicago: Griggs and Co., 1883), pp. 52–53; Joseph Conwell, *Manhood's Morning* (Vineland, N.J.: Homini's Book Co., 1896), pp. 160–64 and passim.

[52]J. M. Buckley, *Oats or Wild Oats: Common Sense for Young Men* (New York: Harper, 1885), p. 2; George Peck, *The Formation of a Manly Character* (New York: Carlton & Phillips, 1853), p. 55; James S. Kirtley, with introduction by Henry Hopkins, *The Young Man and Himself* (Napierville, Ill.: Nichols and Co., 1902), p. 304.

[53]Thomas Hughes, *True Manliness: From the Writings of Thomas Hughes Selected by E. E. Brown* (Boston: D. Lothrop and Co., 1880), p. 20; Horace Porter, "The Philosophy of Courage," *Century Magazine* (June, 1888), 253; Henry Van Dyke, *Sermons to Young Men* (New York: Scribners, 1893), pp. 53–55.

[54]Sylvanus Stall, *What A Young Man Should Know* (Chicago: Winston, 1897), p. 158; James F. Scott, *The Sexual Instinct (New York: E. B. Treat, 1902), pp. 130*–31; T. S. Arthur, *Advice to Young Men* (Boston: Phillips Sampson & Co., 1855), p. 127; see also William McAdoo, *Crowded Years* (Boston: Houghton Mifflin Co., 1931) p. 35.

[55]Rafford Pyke, "What Men Like in Men," *Cosmopolitan* (August, 1902), 405–06; Eric Dingwall, *The American Women* (New York: Rinehart and Co., Inc., 1956), p. 137.

[56]Rafford Pyke, "What Men Like in Men," *Cosmopolitan* (August, 1902), 405

[57]Ibid., pp. 405–06.

[58]Bernard Wishy, *The Child and The Republic* (Philadelphia: University of Pennsylvania Press, 1968), pp. 58–61.

[59]Timothy Flint, *Life and Adventures of Daniel Boone* (Cincinnati: U. P. James, 1868), preface, and pp. 226–27; Timothy Flint, *The First White Man of the West* (Cincinnati: E. Morgan and Co., 1850), preface; Timothy Flint, *Biographical Memoir of Daniel Boone* (Cin-

cinnati: N. G. Guilford & Co., 1833); Stewart White, *Daniel Boone: Wilderness Scout* (Garden City, New York: Doubleday, 1928), p. 4.

[60]Quoted in Dixon Wecter, *The Hero in America* (New York: Charles Scribner's Sons, 1941), p. 188.

[61]Kent Stekmesser, "The Frontier Hero in History and Legend," *Wisconsin Magazine of History* (Spring, 1963), 168–69.

[62]Dixon Wecter, *The Hero in America* (New York: Charles Scribner's Sons, 1941), pp. 312–14; Ralph D. Gardner, *Horatio Alger* (Mendota, Ill.: Wayside Press, 1964), pp. 60–62.

[63]Ralph D. Gardner, *Horatio Alger* (Mendota, Ill.: Wayside Press, 1964), passim; John Tebbel, *From Rags to Riches* (New York: Macmillan Publishing Co., Inc., 1963), pp. 23–32, 49–50.

[64]John Tebbel, *From Rags to Riches* (New York: Macmillan Publishing Co., Inc., 1963), pp. 69, 133–34.

[65]*This Fabulous Century, 1900–1910* (New York: Time-Life Books, Inc.), 107–09; Gilbert Patten, ed., *Burt L. Standish: Frank Merriwell's Father* (Norman, Okla.: University of Oklahoma Press, 1964), pp. 13–16, 26–27, 32–37); Robert H. Boyle, *Sport: Mirror of American Life* (Boston: Little, Brown, 1963), pp. 241–71.

[66]Gilbert Patten, ed., *Burt L. Standish: Frank Merriwell's Father* (Norman, Okla.: University of Oklahoma Press, 1964), pp. 13–16, 26–27, 32–33.

[67]Ibid., pp. 37–41.

[68]Orson S. Fowler, *Perfect Men, Women and Children in Happy Families* (New York: Fowler and Wells, 1878), p. 170.

[69]Albert Beveridge, *The Young Man and the World* (New York: Appleton and Co., 1906), pp. 53, 61.

[70]T. S. Arthur, *Advice to Young Men* (Boston: Phillips Sampson & Co., 1955), pp. 99–100; Daniel Wise, *Young Man's Counsellor* (New York: n.p., 1854), p. 245; Henry W. Beecher, *Twelve Lectures to Young Men* (New York: Appleton and Co., 1890), p. 31: James R. Miller, *Young Men: Faults and Ideals* (Boston: Thomas Crowell, 1893), p. 13; Michael Gordon and Charles Bernstein, "Mate Choice and Domestic Life in the Nineteenth Century Marriage Manual," *Journal of Marriage and the Family*, XXXII (November, 1970), 665–74.

[71]Maren L. Carden, *Oneida: Utopian Community to Modern Corporation* (Baltimore: Johns Hopkins Press, 1969), pp. 49–52; Whitney R. Cross, *The Burned-Over District* (New York: Harper and Row, 1950), pp. 341–47.

[72]John S. Haller, Jr., and Robin Haller, *The Physician and Sexuality in Victorian America* (Urbana: University of Illinois Press, 1974), pp. 91–137.

[73]Ronald Walters, *Primers for Prudery: Sexual Advice for Victorian America* (Englewood Cliffs, N.J.: Prentice-Hall Inc., 1974); David Pivar, *Purity Crusade: Sexual Morality and Social Control, 1868–1900* (Westport, Conn.: Greenwood Press, Inc., 1973); Richard Shryock, "Sylvester Graham and the Health Reform Movement, 1830–1870," *Mississippi Valley Historical Review*, XVIII (September, 1931), 172–83; Charles E. Rosenberg, "Sexuality, Class and Role in 19th-Century America," *American Quarterly* XXV (May, 1973), 131–53.

[74]Ronald Walters, *Primers For Prudery* (Englewood Cliffs, N.J.: Prentice-Hall, Inc., 1974), p. 33; James F. Scott, *The Sexual Instinct* (New York: E. B. Treat and Co., 1902), p. 35.

[75]Sylvester Graham, *A Lecture to Young Men* (Providence: Weeden and Cory, 1834), pp. 17, 33.

[76]John Cowan, *The Science of a New Life* (New York: John Cowan, 1870), pp. 90–91.

[77]P. H. Chavasse, *Man's Strength and Woman's Beauty* (San Francisco: Jones Bros., 1880), pp. 392–404; Winfield S. Hall, *From Youth to Manhood* (New York: Association Press, 1919), pp. 45–47.

[78]Ronald Walters, *Primers for Prudery* (Englewood Cliffs, N.J.: Prentice-Hall, Inc., 1974), pp. 35, 60–62, Ill.

[79] Ibid., pp. 121, 163–66; John S. Haller, Jr., and Robin Haller, *The Physician and Sexuality in Victorian America* (Urbana: University of Illinois Press, 1974), pp. 15, 207.

[80]John Cowan, *The Science of a New Life* (New York: John Cowan, 1870), pp. 32, 41, 51; P. H. Chavasse, *Man's Strength and Woman's Beauty* (San Francisco: Jones Bros., 1880), pp. 404–5.

[81]Sylvanus Stall, *What a Young Man Ought to Know* (Philadelphia: Vir Publishing Co., 1897), p. 104.

[82]John Cowan, *Science of a New Life* (New York: John Cowan, 1970), p. 111.

[83]Joseph Howe, *Excessive Venery, Masturbation and Continence* (New York: E. B. Treat, 1887), pp. 92–108.

[84]Frederick Hollick, *The Male Generative Organs in Health and Disease from Infancy to Old Age* (New York: American News Co., 1877), pp. 289–91, 330–31; Ronald Walters, *Primers for Prudery* (Englewood Cliffs, N.J.: Prentice-Hall, Inc., 1974), p. 58.

[85]Joseph Howe, *Excessive Venery, Masturbation and Continence* (New York: E. B. Treat and Co., 1887), pp. 62–68.

[86]Sylvanus Stall, *What a Young Man Ought to Know* (Philadelphia: Vir Publishing Co., 1901), p. 152; George Beard, *Sexual Neurasthenia* (New York: E. B. Treat and Co., 1905).

[87]George Beard, *Sexual Neurasthenia* (New York: E. B. Treat and Co., 1905), pp. 118–21; Frank Harris, *My Life and Loves* (Paris: n.p.), p. 46; John S. Haller, Jr., and Robin Haller, *The Physician and Sexuality in Victorian America* (Urbana: University of Illinois Press, 1974), p. 215.

[88]Upton Sinclair, *Autobiography* (New York: Harcourt Brace Jovanovich, Inc., 1962), pp. 46–47.

[89]Oswald Garrison Villard, *Fighting Years: Memoirs of a Liberal Editor* (New York: Harcourt Brace Jovanovich, Inc., 1939), pp. 21, 45, 65.

[90]Claudius Johnson, *Borah of Idaho* (New York: Longmans, Green and Co., 1936), pp. 3, 36, 67.

[91]John S. Haller, Jr., and Robin Haller, *The Physician and Sexuality in Victorian America* (Urbana: University of Illinois Press, 1974), pp. 219–21.

[92]John H. Kellogg, *Plain Facts About Sexual Life* (Battle Creek, Mich.: Office of the Health Reformer, 1877), p. 114; Frederick Hollick, *The Male Generative Organs in Health and Disease from Infancy to Old Age* (New York: American News Co., 1877), pp. 303–05; Ronald Walters, *Primers for Prudery* (Englewood Cliffs, N.J.: Prentice-Hall, Inc., 1974), pp. 63, 118–20.

[93]James J. Kirtley, with introduction by Henry Hopkins, *The Young Man and Himself* (Napierville, Ill.: Nichols and Co., 1902), p. 17.

. . . besides the material results of the Civil War, we are all, North and South, incalculably richer for its memories.

Theodore Roosevelt

3

THE CIVIL WAR: MANLINESS THROUGH COMBAT

The imperatives for shaping a manly character described in guidebook literature were put to their sternest test during the Civil War. Having the courage and bravery to stand and fight for one's convictions and having moral honor and the physical stamina to see the battle through were the crucial attributes any manly American male was supposed to possess. The same kind of masculine tenacity and dedication that drove the pioneer and the Indian fighter prevailed during the Civil War, only to degrees more extreme in terms of objectives and results. Throughout history, war had been seen as a test of endurance and courage, or, as some might put it today, the ultimate evidence of "guts."

No less a figure than William James, a pacifist, tended to agree that nothing stirred humanity quite like a war, for the victor as well as the vanquished. Like many war apologists, James understood the horrors of war as a cheap price to pay for the unattractive alternative of a world made up of "clerks and teachers, of co-education and [philosophy], of 'consumers leagues' and 'associated charities,' of industrialism unlimited, and feminism unabashed. No scorn, no hardness, no valor any more!" And although James hated war, he believed the only way to preserve peace was to "make new energies and hardihoods continue the manliness to which the military mind so faithfully clings." Writing in 1910, James observed that the martial arts must be "the enduring cement; intrepidity, contempt of softness, surrender of private interest, obedience to command, must still remain the rock upon which states are built." To that end, James advised the conscription of all youths into a military organization, in which the virtues of hardihood could be equally instilled.[1]

A GENERATION REDEEMED

Probably few young men going into military service in 1861 in America were as eloquent about the virtues of war as was James. Yet that war was to be every bit the test of fidelity, cohesiveness, tenacity, physical vigor, conscience, and heroism that James described, and it left an extraordinary legacy. To young Charles Francis Adams, going into the army was to be born again. His search for manliness was finally fulfilled after having missed everything resembling manly companionship all his life. The war, he wrote, "gave me just that robust, virile stimulus to be derived only from a close contact with nature and a roughing it among men and in the open air which I especially needed." Raised in a home rigid in moral discipline but lax on physical experience, young Adams worried about being weak. "So far as my physique is concerned, I from my army experience got nothing but good." Adams, who went on to a brilliant career as a historian, businessman, and lawyer, remembered the Civil War as the greatest event in his life. In his autobiography, Adams did not confine the war's significance to himself personally. Antietam and Gettysburg were names common to a whole generation, and for those who had been there those names recalled a vivid testing. There was carnage, attack, repulse, and breathless suspense, but through it all the men of those days found their manhood in bravery and courage sufficient for ultimate victory.[2]

The war affected virtually all classes and segments of society, and the records, diaries, letters, and tales of the conflict bear witness to the personal significance Adams attached to the crisis. Few groups, however, wrote as vividly about the personal meaning of the war as did the young, educated men of America's learned class. In the decade preceding the Civil War, American intellectuals virtually withdrew from everyday existence into a life of contemplation. Like Emerson, they wrote about self-culture and transcendental idealism, a few of them becoming abolitionists. The Civil War had a significant impact on these men because it gave them an opportunity to transform their idealism into social action.[3] In a society suspicious of men known for their talk and seldom for their deeds, the prospect of military service, in which a man's manly qualities were put to the severest test possible, offered an exciting prospect for masculine fulfillment. Few men were as sensitive to this participation of the young scholar as Ralph Waldo Emerson. Thinking, no doubt, of his own scholarly patrician environment, and concerned about the validity of his own masculine identity, Emerson warned the young men of ideas against becoming "effeminate gownsmen." Never should the young man of letters take his calling so lightly that he reclined in a life of comfort. The intellectual must be powerful too, armed with moral strength and courage in the same sense that other men were equipped with firearms on the battlefield. Nothing could be more manly, according to Emerson, than actually going into combat to fight for high principles. The Civil War gave thousands of boys the right to claim their true manhood because war always tested the true strengths of the nation's young men. Speaking in 1863, Emerson called upon every young man to complete and enrich his manhood through military service. It was no time for the "helpless angel to be slapped in the face" by disregarding "the Styx of human experience, and made invulnerable. . . ."[4] This premonition apparently overtook many young genteel Bostonians, who, according to Thomas Wentworth Higginson, turned to manly, practical things after the war. As for Higginson himself, the war experience blunted his enthusiasm for a literary life. For the nation as a whole, Francis Parkman, as well as Emerson, thought the Civil War would significantly improve the standards of manhood from their prewar mediocrity.[5]

When word arrived of the death of a beloved son or friend, it often prompted a eulogy that, as George Fredrickson has noted, provoked an assessment of the whole generation of young men fighting for the noble cause. By implication, one is led to think that serious reservations may have existed about America's young men before the war. Perhaps the young scholar could only talk, lacking the manly courage to act decisively on his convictions. Perhaps the whole generation had gone soft and lacked the determined convictions of its forefathers. But war's harsh testing proved America's young men belonged with the youth of all great civilizations in service and sacrifice. Upon the death of Robert Gould Shaw, Henry Ward Beecher expressed his pleasant surprise at the voracity in the cultivated class. "Our young men seemed ignoble; the faith of the old heroic times had died . . . but the trumpet of this war sounded the call and O! how joyful has been the sight of such unexpected nobleness in our young men! . . . Youth, beauty, birth, wealth, position" were all fully substantiated.[6]

The Civil War, then, was to have a profound impact not only on the young poet and scholar, but also on many of the young men of prominent families who were raised in the genteel tradition. As children of Americans with social standing, they often had been reared by strict parents who practiced the Protestant work ethic. Their parents' success was considered proof enough that the old values still had relevance and were worthy of being pursued, particularly at a time when social disintegration seemed to threaten the very existence of America. Upper-class young men often attended private schools and academies in which they read the best literature and studied classical languages. They were carefully instructed on how best to express themselves in order to exhibit a strong image of substance and good character. But what was often missing in the lives of these young men was a sense of action and motion, something the vast majority of young men in America during the middle years of the nineteenth century experienced daily.

THE RED BADGE

Oliver Wendell Holmes was raised to believe in the genteel style, in which social grace and tradition were paid high respect. But was not there more to life? young Holmes wondered. To descend from soldiers or to be a soldier ready to give one's life rather than suffer defeat and disgrace was undoubtedly more manly than being a gentleman. Like many boys of his social class and background, Holmes had known a relatively sheltered and strict childhood as his parents sought to help him assume his place in polite society. But he yearned for adventure and distinction, which the Civil War finally gave him. Holmes went into the war with a very practical sense of social service, concerned more about being a hero than fighting on the side of justice in a holy crusade. While humanitarianism and ideology may have had a great appeal to the learned man of that era, the heroic ideal, explained in military terms, was far more relevant to those young men who participated in the Civil War. To put it another way, the Civil War was Holmes' real college and testing ground. It presented him the opportunity to "share the passion and action of his time at the peril of being judged not to have lived." Wounded at Ball's Bluff in October 1861, Holmes came home to recuperate and recount his heroic moments to a "semicircle of young Desdemonas" who admired this fine display of manhood. Holmes returned to the fighting and suffered two more wounds, one in the neck and the other in the heel, both requiring convalescence, and both affirming the experience of war as necessary to manhood, as comprehended by Oliver Wendell Holmes, Jr., at the age of twenty-three.[7]

Although the deeds of warfare may have inspired some to claim a new personal worth for themselves, the Civil War baffled and bewildered other men. Henry James was one of those "temperamentally unsuited for soldiering."[8] He had no taste for violence and the painful testing some men seemed so anxious to encounter. In fact, he had no fondness for peacetime competition with his brothers, or even that of business enterprise. As noted, however, young Henry already felt the pressure to be like other young males and experienced fear and anxiety when he realized that perhaps he could not match their qualifications to be "one of the boys." To begin with, Henry James, Sr., was not like the other strong-willed aggressive fathers his son knew. The loss of his leg obviously restricted his physical movement, but the elder James was also patently sentimental, a trait no "real man" should possess. Dear old homebody Papa James reveled in put-downs from his wife, apparently for the sake of his own amusement. Furthermore, there was the very real problem of Henry Sr.'s occupation, which his sons had difficulty explaining to the satisfaction of their school fellows. Describing their father as a philosopher, seeker of truth, or a lover of mankind failed to convince young playmates that the elder James was much of a man, and perhaps no one suffered more than Henry Jr. His father's dual nature of a family man who was manly and in his own way robust, yet feminine, weak, and yielding, posed a serious ambiguity about his masculine identity.[9]

Then came the pressure on young men to enlist in the army. Henry Sr. was of no help to his sons, confessing that "affectionate old papas like me are scudding all over the country to apprehend their patriotic offspring and restore them to the harmless embraces of their mamas."[10] Meanwhile, as their brothers Wilky and Robertson went to war, sensitive young men like Henry and William James could read the lines of Dr. Holmes:

> *Listen young heroes! Your country is calling*
> *Time strikes the hour for the brave and the free!*
> *Now, while the foremost are fighting and falling,*
> *Fill up the ranks that have opened for you.*[11]

But neither William nor Henry helped fill the ranks. An accident suffered just prior to the war apparently kept Henry out of the service. It was described as a "horrid if obscure hurt," about which little is said by James himself, but an injury that became a central factor in a personal test of his masculinity. Critics were to charge later that he had become impotent, and they implied that his injury had been used as an excuse to avoid military service. That Henry James never married was taken as evidence supporting the emasculation theory. But James's biographer contends that it was probably a back injury, maybe a slipped disc, which caused occasional pain. Whatever the injury may have been, it did not prevent him from riding horseback, lifting weights, and walking long distances. But missing the Civil War while his two brothers had such romantic opportunities during their careers troubled Henry James. How could a man who claimed throughout his life to write about experience be authentic when he missed (or dodged) the experience that set apart a whole generation?[12]

IN PRAISE OF BATTLE

The journals and diaries written by rank-and-file soldiers at the beginning of the Civil War reveal that many young men who filled the ranks voluntarily did so enthusiastically. Generally, these accounts continue in a vein that strongly implies that the military experience had a profound effect upon the shaping of a more manly character. One can find remarks to the effect that "1863 was the most memorable year of my life" and admonitions that "every man would do well to begin his adult life by spending three years in the army."[13] James Garfield tells of being "strongly and powerfully drawn to the men of the Forty-Second. It was a splendid army, not so much in numbers but in character borne out by the test of battle."[14] The war offered men of diverse means and backgrounds a chance to vouch for their bravery. After a fierce hand-to-hand combat in which he was engaged, D. M. Kelsey wrote, "I guess they won't call us kid-gloved soldiers anymore."[15] But another soldier candidly confessed that the manly boastfulness often vanished when the cannons began to roar. "Between the physical fear of going forward, and the moral fear of turning back, there is a predicament of exceptional awkwardness, from which a hidden hole in the ground would be a wonderfully welcome outlet."[16] Another soldier at the front wrote of the importance of hearing from the "true women of our land, whom we respect and honor, and for whose welfare we fight." In the hospitals, camps, and trails of the war zone the cry of "God bless the women" was frequently heard. The same account also noted that "I have seen men who never flinched in battle, or faltered when one comrade after another fell by their side, weep like children because the mail brought no messages from home."[17]

COMPARING COURAGE

Soldiers from the East and West in the Union Army frequently disputed who were the best. Western Yanks often considered the Easterners soft, effeminate, liquor-soaked, money-mad dandies who knew how to have a good time, but not fight. General McClellan's less-than-vigorous execution of the Eastern campaign during the winter of 1861–62 invited snide remarks about the Easterners and a feeling that the hardy Midwestern farmboys, toughened by hard physical work, had to take charge of the war in the Western campaign. "The final assault on Petersburg was rendered a failure by the the gross cowardice of the Potomac Army," wrote an Illinois soldier. Eastern Yanks, however, were not to be outdone in boasting about their own military accomplishments. They viewed the Western campaign as little more than raids by an unruly mob that had no discipline and low morals. And even Grant himself, from Illinois, was quoted as saying in 1864 after taking command in the East that he had never seen such fighting before, and "that our Western army never had any *such men* to fight as we have."[18]

Foreigners who served were closely scrutinized as to their attitudes and personal habits. Did they have the mettle and fortitude of native men? Because courage was the most tangible mark of a man, bravery in battle could ease doubts about a recent immigrant's manhood or patriotism; he could then usually count on winning the respect of his comrades. In fact, the military experience helped weld together many diverse national strains and instructed many young men of foreign backgrounds in the ways of Yankee manhood.[19]

When Billy Yank perceived the enemy across the way, he often thought of them as cowardly men who would not stand and fight: "[T]hey know we can whip them with mitens [*sic*] on," wrote one Northern soldier. Another felt they would fight hard but would never stand their ground if a bayonet were coming at them. Still another soldier observed that the Rebs were at their best only when they could get behind trees. Other accounts contradicted these generalizations about cowardice but added that the Rebs could fight well only if emboldened by whiskey. Some Yanks, however, praised the manliness of their Southern foes, some even to the point of doubting the ability of the North to defeat such strong-willed men whose purpose and resolve drew admiration.[20] Conversely, many Southern men thought that the men in blue were too soft to fight, too docile and passive, too citified and sissified. The Rebs, however, saw themselves as the true men of nature, descendants of a hardy, virile frontier tradition, "conscientious brawlers," to use Wilbur Cash's term.

THE SOUTHERN MALE AND THE MILITARY

In many respects, the Rebs had known a harder life than their adversaries. They had lived a more isolated and autonomous existence. Southern life was based on an exaggerated sense of personal honor and pride. There was always that image of plantation life that tantalized middle-class farmers with the dream that one day, if everything went right, they too would own a mansion and bask in the success of that life. But more realistically, in the foreseeable future, white Southern males viewed as a primary task the defense of Southern women against the black male, who lurked in the slave quarters fantasizing about his freedom and, possibly, revenge and rape. What an outrageous prospect, to think of a profane black penis penetrating a white woman, the goddess whom Southern men worshipped and protected! For again, as Wilbur Cash suggests, "it is obvious that the assault on the South would be felt as, in some true sense, an assault on her also, and that the South would inevitably translate its whole battle into terms of her defense." Given the nineteenth century's idealization of woman as mother and perpetuator of the race, the extent to which Southern men would go to defend her against the black savages— for the sake of white male pride if nothing else—is a crucial factor in understanding Southern male attitudes about race and sex.[21]

For a long time, the South had trained some of its young men in the specifics of warfare. Almost every state had a military academy, some quite well established. Parents were often sold on the wisdom of choosing a military-school education for their sons because of the perfect discipline taught in the academies. An official in Virginia, arguing for military education, contended that "habits of unrestrained indulgence have frequently laid the foundation of ruin of youths, who, if submitted to proper discipline and restraint at this trying season of life . . . would otherwise have become useful and distinguished members of society."[22] Military education paid close attention to the physical growth of men, helping build sound, strong bodies that would help in induring life's hardships. Whatever these graduates did, they would retain the "modest and manly bearing of the soldier instead of the impudent leer and blustering swagger of the rowdy."[23] It is easier to understand the South's optimism on the eve of war even though outmanned four to one by the North, if one understands the deep feeling of confidence in the preparation of the South's young men for war. The spirit was contagious to those not brought up through the academies. "No man who had the least regard for his character would keep out of the army," according to one observer.[24]

When the war came, however, the sources of Southern masculinity that had lionized Southern men proved to be a liability. Enlisted men did not accept military regulations and discipline gracefully, because it had not been their custom to recognize any authority beyond their own will. Although many Southern men rushed to enlist, their enthusiasm waned when confronted with army regulation and routine. According to an Alabama enlisted man, "a soldier is worse than any Negro on the Chatohooche river [sic]. He had no privileges whatever. He had worse taskmasters than any Negro. He is not treated with any respect whatever. His officers may insult him and he has no right to open his mouth and dare not do it."[25] Southern enlisted men tended to resent marching in orderly ranks, and many deserted the army when disenchantment overwhelmed them. Independence, individualism, and resentment of social-class privileges, all qualities any true man possessed, accelerated the South's undoing. Above all else, the improved man was what the South needed in order to defeat the North, said General Wise. But just what constituted "an improved man" begged many questions about values and Southern masculinity that were beyond answering at the time of the Civil War, not only in the South, but in the North as well. It was still a world in which heroes performed deeds to maintain individualistic codes of honor.[26]

WARTIME MORALS

Since engagement under fire was not a full-time situation, there were often long hours for recreation and bull sessions, providing many a young man with fascinating new challenges to enhance his sense of manhood. Sports and games, especially baseball, became a popular pastime for Civil

War soldiers. Prize-fights and wrestling bouts were often engaged in to find out who the toughest man of the company really was. (The most notable was the "Great Prize Fight" of 1863 between Mike McCool and Joe Coburn, just ten days after the Chancellorsville battle.) Many soldiers read "dime novels" about Revolutionary War heroes and heroic frontiersmen. Dixon Wecter credits the surge of paperback-book publications with having a significant effect on Northern wartime psychology. At least initially, the dime novels reflected the tenets of manly character similar to those of the guidebooks. Male heroes were portrayed as rugged individualists, self-reliant to the core, unflinchingly brave and courageous. Seldom did these dime-novel heroes sip a drink of whiskey and only occasionally did they play a hand of cards, usually only to expose the flawed character of an opponent. Nor were they profane, which brought praise from many people, including President Lincoln. Blood was a different matter. To kill, maim, or destroy the enemy, even if in a manner bordering on sadism, was quite tolerable, perhaps expected, when considered in the context of a truly manly character having to verify itself by opposing evil.[27]

There was a marked contrast, however, between the ideal of true manliness described in nineteenth-century guidebooks and war novels that the soldiers might have read about, and the soldiers' actual behavior during their own military life. Wartime offered new experiences away from home and mother and away from moralizing sermons preaching uprightness achieved through repression and self-denial. The men who learned to fight hard and live hard were the men who had saved the Union, not the high-minded moralizers and philosophers. The war helped alter the accepted masculine image somewhat into one of roughness and toughness, even ruthlessness, which was frequently manifest in crude and vulgar behavior. A city-bred Easterner wrote home that camp life was a "hard school" and that scores of men were ruined in morals by succumbing to lewd and crass conduct. A year later, the same soldier reported, "The more vulgar a man is, the better he is appreciated and as for morals . . . [the army] is a graveyard for them." Without the presence of women, and perhaps because it was a unique freedom, swearing became routine. Orders were issued against swearing, backed up with the threat of fines, but the habit continued. "Hell" and "damn" became common expletives. "Jesus Christ," "kiss my arse," "go stick it up——" were frequently heard imploring violent action and were a credit to the earthy manliness of the proclaimer.[28]

Virtually all the guidebooks had strongly counseled against gambling, but during the war the practice became widespread, bringing one Yank to remark that according to his observation, nine out of ten men played cards for money. Some did so even in the thick of battle, survivors hurrying back to scoop up their playing cards and resume their game. Drinking often accompanied card-playing and, like gambling, was more frequent in 1865 than it had been in 1861. Even the most pious of troops, such as New York's Forty-Eighth, under the command of a minister named James M. Perry, could not refuse the temptation to go on a glorious drunk. The Civil War also presented many men with their first opportunity for real sexual adventure. Most big cities noticed a sizeable increase in the number of prostitutes and bawdy houses. Washington, D.C., was reported to have 450 houses of ill repute with some 7,500 prostitutes. More than 182,000 reported cases of venereal disease were a sad commentary on the search for sexual manhood.[29]

After the war, many Northern soldiers returned home to cheering throngs of people who praised the deeds they had read about in the newspapers. As if to vouch for their part in the triumph, many Yanks brought home souvenirs, emblematic of the ultimate event that was to document their manly adventure.

Even for those who were less chauvinistic, it would have been virtually impossible to escape being emotionally touched by the Civil War and the fervor it stirred, which went far beyond the ranks of the military. A large body of literature grew out of the events of the 1860s, much of it praising heroic and manly behavior. Examining reviews of some of the short stories and novels of the 1860s, one historian noted a prurient hunger to sensationalize the test of war on young men and women. There is the common image of a lady pleading with her noble young gentleman with "raven curls clustering about a marble brow" not to go to war. But then she learns of the war's moral dimension, hears of evils committed by the other side, reconsiders her position, and sends her soldier-hero dashing into combat. He enters the fray, giving a noble account of his manliness in battle, and then turns up missing, presumably dead. But the life of the hero is gifted and he returns, perhaps limping, to her open arms, a legend in his own time.[30]

NEW ATTITUDES

Such scenes, whereever they appeared, whether in fact or fiction, lay at the heart of this earnest query from Emerson: "Is an armed man the only hero?" For the Civil War had an impact far beyond the battles to preserve the Union and end slavery. The strength, power, and will to succeed on the battlefield drove hom to an entire generation of men that, whether in the institution of the army or as individuals, men could attain goals and achieve success far beyond what they had ever imagined. No doubt the technological and managerial techniques learned during the war helped, but there was more to it. After the Civil War, men were more preemptory and cocky, not as docile and passive as they had been before. In the years after 1865, American culture, buttressed by social Darwinsim, gave the highest praise to individualism. Society honored those who let nothing get in their way, just as the North had praised Sherman's march to the sea. It meant that in the years after 1865, many people, not the least of whom were a man's family, especially his wife, were to pay a price. The bread-winning role of the American male was not just one of survival; it had become a criterion for defining the extent of a man's honor and character. Back of it all, wrote Henry Adams some years later, was a dear lesson learned in the Civil War: "Action was the highest stimulation—the instinct to fight." Such men were the new heroes, the new forces of nature—building, shaping, controlling everything in their wake.[31]

If action was the "highest stimulant," reflection and introspection were now more than ever damning characteristics, which might explain why political and social reform made such little headway during the last third of the nineteenth century. A social conscience, to be touched emotionally by the condition of humanity, was now taken as a genuine sign of effeminacy. Such men were "namby-pamby, goody-goody gentlemen." Senator Ingals of Kansas denounced them as "the third sex." Senators Conkling and Blaine viewed such men as foolish, impractical, farcical, and although insignificant, nevertheless a bother to the real, manly men of America who got things done. In the 1870s, this sense of militant masculinity was manifest in a critical and unreceptive attitude towards the humanists, the college graduates, and young men who had been trained to use their minds to evaluate the functioning of institutions. The Civil War had helped prove what Andrew Jackson had symbolized earlier (and society now seemed willing to take quite literally)—that it was the practical man of action who was the most manly, a concept that has survived into very recent American history. Implicit in the attack upon educated reformers was the view that politics was, after all, a man's affair and must remain so. The trouble with men such as George Curtis, editor of *Harper's*, was that he had been softened by female sentimentality. It followed that if women were ever encouraged to get into politics, they would become more masculine and, according to Horace Bushnell, their basic temperament would be altered for the worse.[32]

The Civil War not only served to stimulate the American male to greater individualistic activity, but it also lured some women out of the home and into public service, sexual trends that were bound to conflict sharply in later years. Even if a woman did little more than roll bandages or volunteer to serve in a hospital, it was an important step in getting women out into the world. Conservatives, who may have thought it was a dangerous precedent, could hardly protest, given the national emergency.

Some mothers thought it degrading to see their daughters go to work, but the trend established during the war continued as many young women pursued careers in nursing or in education, a situation men would later refer to as "the woman problem."[33]

THE SOUTHERN MALE
AFTER THE WAR

In the South, the legacy of the war was unique, if only because the South had lost. During the war many Southern women were found capable of doing jobs men had always done, proving that women were not as dependent as men had always thought. In fact, the war opened new positions, such as teaching, to the women of the South, jobs they took, and in many cases kept, over the objections of fathers, brothers, and husbands who felt disgraced that their women had to work to support themselves. Moreover, it was Southern women, as well as men, who struggled to bring order out of the chaos of defeat. Some men, according to several accounts, were so depressed and forlorn that they loafed in saloons for some time after the war and sought comfort from their mothers.[34]

Some men felt an understandable psychological letdown once the guns fell silent and the intense action of war ceased. But the perception of the manly ideal remained. Women and homes still had to be protected, the land farmed, and order re-established to promote the good life, because, if anything, the war made the South more Southern. It is not surprising that many Southern men sought affiliation with organizations that restored a sense of purpose and commitment to the South and to their own lives. At the heart of those organizations was the promise of the restoration of masculine power and control. The Ku Klux Klan became one of the most famous examples of the type of organization that appealed to defeated Southern males. Started by some returning soldiers who lived near Pulaski, Tennessee, the Klan appealed to conscientious Southern men, individuals who believed in law and order. This meant punishing or intimidating disloyal Negroes and Southern whites who sympathized with radical reconstruction, which was the ultimate invasion of Southern space. Klan members were required to demonstrate manly character and courage.[35] According to the Klan ritual, as an alien approached the Klavern for his naturalization (initiation into the Klan), he was commanded by the Kladd to "Follow me and be a man." In the ceremony the Klokard prays:

> *God give us Men! The invisible Empire*
> *demand strong*
> *Minds, great hearts, true faith and ready*
> *hands.*
> *. . .*
> *Men who possess opinions and a will*
> *Men who have HONOR; men who will NOT*
> *Lie*
> *. . .*
> *God give us men!*
> *Men who serve not for selfish booty,*
> *But real men, courageous, who flinch not at*
> *duty*
> *Men of dependable character; men of sterling*
> *worth;*
> *Then wrongs will be redressed, and right will*
> *rule the earth;*
> *God give us men!*[36]

The purpose of the KKK, which surged to prominence after 1865, was ostensibly to intimidate Negroes, but its more subtle mission was to reclaim the South for Southern gentlemen. After emerging from a searing conflict, in which Southern manhood had been defeated in spite of all it had going for it, Reconstruction added insult to injury. The Klan attracted men who had never quite succeeded as well as they thought they should have. It gave such men a platform upon which to stand and proclaim that their manhood was still viable, and that they were as willing as ever to defend their beloved traditions as all other great men had done. In the South, for young men home from the war, the Klan served a noble cause and provided a psychological remedy at the same time. In large measure, the same psychological attraction existed after 1920, when the Klan was revived. Men who had been in a war, the outcome of which was a shock, found their sense of manhood rehabilitated when given the opportunity to extend the noble fight for the Christian ideals professed by the Klan. The Klan in the 1920s, like that of the post–Civil War era, idealized he old virtues of strong character, sanctity of home and womanhood, the power of manhood, and patriotism, at a time when both political parties seemed indifferent to those ideals, and at a time when the economy, upon which men relied to support their claims of industrious vigor, was falling apart. Viewed in this context, the Klan was the ultimate legacy of an idealism about manhood and war.[37]

"WAR MEMORIALS"

The generation of men whose fate it was to fight in the Civil War was memorialized in countless ways. But the most significant of those many memorials was probably the one stamped on the imagination of the young men born after 1865. Sons and grandsons were frequently told by veterans such as Oliver Wendell Holmes, who observed in an 1884 Memorial Day address that "the generation that carried on the war had been set apart by its experience." Holmes once related that when "you meet an old comrade after many years of absense he recalls the moment when you were nearly surrounded by the enemy, and again there comes up to you that swift and cunning thinking on which once hung life or freedom— shall I stand the best chance if I try the pistol or the sabre on that man who means to stop me?" And where did such strength originate? Holmes attributed it to the Puritans, whose legacy, as he saw it, lived on through the heroic deeds of the Civil War soldiers. "For the Puritan still lives in New England, thank God! and will live there so long as New England lives and keeps her renown. New England is not dead yet. She still is mother of a race of conquerors—stern men, little given to the expression of their feelings, sometimes careless of the graces, but fertile, tenacious, and knowing only duty."[38]

Popular and scholarly magazines, such as *Century*, gave considerable space to Civil War reminiscences praising the manliness and individualism of the soldiers, which added to the impression that they had indeed been special men of moral character and physical vigor. Long after the last battle, testimonials flourished that extolled the tenacity of the youthful hearts that had been touched with fire and the young men who had scaled the "snowy heights of honor." The Civil War had enshrined the men of bold and forthright action.

Politicians who wanted to get elected found it necessary to identify themselves with the Civil War in some manner. The reasoning was that philosophers did not make good leaders because they lacked that crucial ability to act, being basically timid and vacillating. From the time of Washington's presidency, in fact, there was an underlying assumption that military men were better men to run the country. Men of ideas and culture were seen as impractical, even wasteful of time and energy, in a nation that was rapidly making a fetish of practical, manly action.[39]

What these Civil War accounts did to the generation of young men in their twenties and thirties during the 1870s and '80s was to instill a feeling that all the great challenges to the republic had been confronted and conquered. There was nothing left for these young men to do but cherish the fruits of victory given them by their older relatives and friends. But living vicariously was not living realistically. It prompted self-doubt and a sense of guilt that the youth of the 1880s was living off his parents' glory. Walter Hines Page said that any young man at a famous boys' school he knew of suffered a distinct disadvantage if he did not have a military background.[40] The nobility of the war contributed to young men's feelings that their's was a purposeless generation. Social Darwinism preached *laissez-faire* and assumed a deterministic course of progress. The Civil War, however, had provided a situation in which there could be action and commitment to a cause. Victory on the battlefields for the North had become a measure of personal victory and worth. Even those who survived defeat could claim at least a personal victory over a crisis condition in which they had given their best. In the dullness of the 1880s, what was left to be done? What cause could be their's to endow the new generation with a treasury of memories and a sense of purpose? Or was it the fate of young men of that time to live dull and uninspiring existences?

In some of the postwar memorials and popular accounts of battles and events, there was a note of skepticism that succeeding generations would never measure up to the boys of '61. Young men of the late 1880s, it was charged, did not appreciate the true meaning of partiotism because a genuine partriot had to contribute to the permanent benefit of the principles of government he lived under. In other words, true patriots, the war veterans specifically, made personal sacrifices to strengthen their nation. "Surely," the Civil War veteran H. R. Howbert wrote, "voters must be impressed with the great obligation they had to those men who had lived by the awful thunder of the cannon." Howbert implied that, perhaps, young men of modern times were not as capable of proving themselves as responsible and as dutiful to the nation's honor and tradition as his generation was during the Civil War. Strongly believing that modern times had softened youth's will and commitment, in words that were to have a significant psychological impact on many young men of the time, Howbert observed that the lesson of history was to "make more history or die." The heroism of the past had preserved freedom, but those heroic acts had to be lionized as models by all Americans if they desired to maintain that freedom.[41]

Undoubtedly, the Civil War strengthened the attitude that military service was the most meaningful way to vouch for one's patriotism and manliness. Many schools and even some churches developed units that drilled and marched in parades and even engaged in mock battles. The Grand Army of the Republic—a society of men who fought for the North—passed a resolution urging military instruction and training in the public schools. The rationale was that these organizations were an excellent means to develop the physical culture whereby boys would learn to discipline their bodies and be courageous. Former President Benjamin Harrison emphatically agreed, noting that military drills would help reduce the sluggishness of young men. At least one churchman, B. O. Flowers, was highly critical of fostering the "war spirit" among young people. Flowers was scandalized by one account in *Corner Stone Magazine* that spoke of twenty-seven church–military organizations, the largest being the Baptist Cadets. To any lover of peace, such a preoccupation with military routine and custom was sickening.[42] The practice, however, was consistent with logic of the times: Being a strong, religious, and brave young man prepared to fight was a benchmark of American nationalism as much as it was a testimony of one's masculinity.

Biographers of Civil War veterans did their part to portray their subjects as fit models for all masculine young men to imitate. In the case of Ulysses S. Grant, however, it was hard to create such a model. Albert Richardson, who took on the task, conceded that Grant was not particularly bright in school, nor was he particularly imaginative or a good athlete. He was awkward at dodge ball, but the high point for Richardson was that Grant did not cry when he was hit with the ball. He did, however, always prefer the company of men, and from an early age young Grant, according to this account, admired military heroes and traditions. Not particularly an exemplary cadet at West Point, Grant nevertheless possessed within him the foundation of a strong, manly character, so that when the test of war came, Grant assumed leadership naturally. His rugged, unpolished demeanor cast him in the Boone tradition.[43]

A good example of the manliness theme is found in *Admiral Farragut*, written by Alfred Mahan, who was himself in search of a strong and manly identity. Mahan had gone to West Point, but a failure in math led to his transfer to Columbia College. There, he lived with his half-brother, Reverend Milo Mahan, who was to exert a strong religious influence on the young Alfred. Still seeking a military career, Mahan finally went to the naval academy. His reserved manner failed to impress the midshipmen, one of whom attributed it to his "effeminately beautiful face which was enough to prejudice his classmates against him." However, Mahan rigidly disciplined himself to overcome his apparent manly deficiencies. He was attracted to Admiral David Farragut partly because of his firm, resolute, confident nature. He was fearless, strong, an expert in physical exercises, and religious, a combination of traits that Mahan was to incorporate into his own life.[44]

Autobiographies of men and women born in the years after 1865 frequently alluded to the Civil War and the part their parents and relatives played in it. Joseph Bristow of Kansas, for example, heard much about the war, its heroes, and, significantly, Republican patriotism.[45] Just five years old at the end of the Civil War, Hamlin Garland vividly remembered the war's end and his father's repeated stories of marching with Sherman. Those must have been "passionate and poetic years," he recalled, as he was frequently reminded of the manly nobility of Grant, Sherman, Lincoln, and others who had answered destiny's call.* No doubt the war had much to do with his father's restless pioneering, as he would bring virgin soil under the plow only to leave it for a new homesteading adventure farther west. Young Garland was duly impressed with this spirit of adventure and the demonstrated courage of warriors: "Aside from the natural distortion of a boy's imagination I am quite sure that the pioneers of 1860

---

*Grant was noble and a hero to people in the North, of course, during the period immediately after the Civil War. In later years, however, he probably was not considered as noble a man considering his political career and the corruption surrounding it.

still retained something broad and fine in their action, something a boy might honorably imitate."[46] Like Garland, the Indiana poet James Whitcomb Riley admired the heroics of past pioneers, especially the '49ers, and was sure they must have possessed extraordinary powers. Veterans' organizations, memorial celebrations, and Civil War statuary gave rise to a feeling that his parents' and their parents' generations really had been significant and heroic. Hearing the war tales, the new generation undoubtedly thought that their fathers would be forever unmatched in vigor and will. The children of these brave and courageous men were to grow up with a strong sense of "lost adventure, of having been born too late."[47]

STEPHEN CRANE

No one who wrote about the Civil War joined the realism of combat with the idealism of courage and sacrifice quite the way Stephen Crane did in *The Red Badge of Courage*. Crane's personal life was a deep struggle with many of the moral precepts preached to him during the 1880s. His parents were strict New Jersey Methodists, his father a minister. Crane wrote: "[U]pon my mother's side everybody as soon as he could walk became a Methodist clergyman." Crane grew up to detest his parents' dogmas. After his father's death, Crane's mother tried to take full command of her son and break his devilish will, as good mothers were supposed to do. But Crane was a hopeless case, or so it must have seemed to his mother. He drank, swore, smoked, and seemed to relish rowdiness, behavior hardly typical of a boy with a righteous moral character. Stephen's mother sent him to a military school to have him taught discipline. After attending Lafayette College and Syracuse University, he headed for New York and a life of reporting and general wandering.[48]

Crane's restlessness typified one aspect of the 1890s: an unquenchable desire for action. Crane sought in history an era in which he could find out about war and heroic men. The Civil War fascinated him, and one should note that his best work, *The Red Badge of Courage*, a novel about the Civil War, appeared shortly before America entered another war (the Spanish-American War). The philosophy implicit in *The Red Badge of Courage* is that war was the ultimate catharsis in life that tests true manhood. Henry Fleming, the raw recruit, is subjected to battle and finds himself driven by contending inner forces, leading him to self-doubt: "How do you know you won't run when the time comes?" Later, alone in his tent, "he saw visions of a thousand-tongued fear that would babble at his back and cause him to flee, while others were going coolly about their country's business." The next day, he panics in his baptism of fire and runs, but shame overwhelms him and he returns to his regiment and renews his commitment to fight for the noble cause of his country and the cause of his own soul. Throwing himself into the next great battle, he demonstrates courage and self-assurance. "He felt a quiet manhood, nonassertive but a sturdy and strong blood. . . . He was a man." Crane had thrust Fleming into the total experience of war because only through such a totally consuming experience could one become disciplined and develop the character necessary for manhood.[49]

A MAN'S PROFESSION

Crane's quest for action and experience to authenticate his manhood took him to wars in Turkey, Cuba, and Greece as a reporter. During the Spanish-American War, Crane recklessly rushed along the front line, following the Rough Riders, exposing himself to enemy fire to get his story. One suspects that Crane was testing his courage, so that it could never be said that he was found wanting when his moment of testing had arrived. The Spanish-American War offered that kind of opportunity to many young men brought up to believe in social Darwinism, the virtues of war, and the adventures of Kipling during the last quarter of the nineteenth century.

Crane was one of several young correspondents in Cuba, all of whom found in newspaper reporting a vocation that took them to the scene of the action. Richard Harding Davis, admired as much for his extraordinary masculinity as he was for his reporting, summed it up by saying that "the good reporter, like the good soldier, must look upon war as the supreme adventure in the great drama called life."[50] But it was no easy decision for Davis to remain a reporter and pass up the real experience of soldiering. He was offered a commission to serve in the army, but he reluctantly turned it down because he felt he would have more freedom for adventure as a reporter. It was a "question of character," he said. The discomfort he felt in turning down a chance to serve in the army, however, was partially compensated when he later threw himself into a skirmish by snatching an available carbine and charging a Spanish position, a feat that, of course, drew praise from Colonel Roosevelt. Davis had fulfilled his definition of a soldier of fortune: "a man who in any walk of life makes his own fortune, who when he sees it coming leaps to meet it, and turns it to his advantage."[51]

Reporting the war for *Harper's Magazine,* Frederic Remington exalted in it. For whatever the hazards of war were to him personally, it was great to fulfill a lifelong urge to see men do the greatest thing that they could be called to do. In Major General Adna R. Chaffee, Remington found a composite of the manly warrior type who brought to the present age strengths that were present only when the race was young and strong. Regrettably, Remington said, men like Chaffee were hard to find in the present age, adding that his contemporaries were too complicated.[52]

Henry Watterson wrote that one found in Cuba the best representatives of American manhood. The men were rugged, determined, and individualistic, having a variety of opinions, occupations, and faiths. The common bond holding them together was their manly spirit of adventure. They were big-game hunters and cowboys, and, according to Watterson, every field officer and captain had at one time or another owned a ranch. The majority of all the soldiers came from the uncomplicated western part of the country. Ninety percent had been native born; most of them had been athletes. In the war, these young men tested their manhood and, to judge from Watterson's book, the nation would have nothing to fear, considering the accomplishments and sacrifices of the young men in Cuba. One of those who paid the supreme sacrifice was twenty-six-year-old Hamilton Fish. "He was of powerful build," Watterson reported, an athlete in school. But the most striking thing to the reporter was his "magnetized animal spirit" and his "love of danger." When death came to young Fish, he met it with the simplicity of a hero; "he died without complaint."[53]

THEODORE ROOSEVELT

Joseph Foraker confided that of the young men of his generation born after the Civil War, there was a keen "moral resolution" to get into the war with Spain.[54] Leading them all was Theodore Roosevelt, who, more than any other person, public or private, symbolized militant, aggressive manhood. Born in 1858 into the New York gentry, Roosevelt worked religiously to build up his frail body. He went West to ranch and hunt, to live and proclaim the virtues of the strenuous life. He was enthralled by Cooper's Leatherstocking tales. Hurry Harry, Ishmael Bush, and

Deerslayer were like personal friends to him. "I have bunked and eaten with them. They were mighty men and they did the work of their day and opened the way for ours."[55] This attitude never left Roosevelt, not even when he sat in the White House. He was always the cowboy with a cowboy's view of the world, a perspective fundamentally important if one is to understand Roosevelt and the perception of Roosevelt and his manliness by the generation of the 1890s.

The Spanish-American War, in which Roosevelt's Rough Riders gained wide acclaim, was said to be not much of a war, but the best one to be found at the time. Even to Remington, for all the war did for him personally, it was a disappointment, because he "wanted the roar of battle, which same I never did find."[56] But to the men of that era, the war, whatever it turned out to be, seemed highly necessary. It was not just to remove the menace of Spain from the American sphere of influence in order to benefit trade and commerce. Nor was it fought to bring Anglo-Saxon progress and other benefits to the heathen. That these motives figured into the whole complex set of impulses cannot be discounted, but in the context of the 1890s, as civilization was rendering the frontier traditions obsolete, as urbanism loomed ahead, and as society was being tamed by the "new woman," it was an ideal moment for young men to assert their virility and be memorialized. It is this philosophy that lay behind Roosevelt's remark of 1895 that, after hearing the peace sentiment in America, he became convinced that what the country needed was a good war.

In 1905, Roosevelt gave a speech at the dedication of the Sherman monument in Washington, D.C. What he said on that occasion recapitulates the basic sentiment of what it seems his generation had come to believe about the past, in terms of what it should teach men of the present:

> We of the present, if we are true to the past, must show by our lives that we have learned aright the lessons taught by the men who did the mighty deeds of the past; we must have in us the spirit which made the men of the Civil War what they were . . . the spirit which gave the average soldier the grim tenacity and resourcefulness that made the armies of Grant and Sherman as formidable fighting machines as this world has ever seen. We need their ruggedness of body, their keen and vigorous minds, and, above all their dominant quality of forceful character. Their lives teach us in our own lives to strive after, not the thing which is merely pleasant, but the thing which it is our duty to do. The life of duty, not the life of mere ease or mere

pleasure, that is the kind of life which makes the great man as it makes the great nation.[57]

Notes

[1]William James, *The Moral Equivalent of War and Other Essays*, ed. John K. Roth (New York: Harper & Row, Publishers, Inc., 1971), pp. 6–7, 12.

[2]Charles F. Adams, *Autobiography* (Boston: Houghton Mifflin, 1916), p. 129.

[3]George Fredrickson, *The Inner Civil War* (New York: Harper & Row, Publishers, Inc., 1965), pp. 175–76 and passim.

[4]Ralph W. Emerson, *Complete Works*, Vol. X (Boston: Houghton Mifflin, 1883), pp. 251–52.

[5]Bliss Perry, *Life and Letters of Henry Lee Higginson* (Boston; The Atlantic Monthly Press, 1921), pp. 233, 536; George Fredrickson, *The Inner Civil War* (New York: Harper & Row, Publishers, Inc., 1965), pp. 173–74.

[6]George Frederickson, *The Inner Civil War* (New York: Harper & Row, Publishers, Inc., 1965), p. 15.

[7]Max Lerner, ed., *Mind and Faith of Justice Holmes* (Boston; Little, Brown, 1943), pp. xxiv–xxv, 17–18.

[8]Leon Edel, *Henry James, The Untried Years* (New York: Lippincott, 1953), p. 170.

[9]Ibid., pp. 49–53.

[10]Ibid., p. 171.

[11]Ibid.; Oliver W. Holmes, "The Sweet Little Man, dedicated to the Stay-at-Home Rangers" (n.p.).

[12]Leon Edel, *Henry James, The Untried Years* (New York; Lippincott, 1953), pp. 171, 173–79, 183.

[13]Albert O. Marshall, *Army Life From a Soldier's Journal* (Joliet, Ill.: n.p., 1882), pp. 16–17; Joseph Foraker, *Notes of a Busy Life* (Cincinnati: Stewart and Kidd, 1916), p. 26; Charles Coffin, *The Boys of '61 or Four Years of Fighting* (Boston: Estes and Lauriat, 1896).

[14]Frederick D. Williams, *The Wild Life of the Army: Civil War Letters of James Garfield* (East Lansing: Michigan State University Press, 1964), pp. 73, 251.

[15]D. M. Kelsey, *Deeds of Daring by Both Blue and Gray* (Philadelphia: Scommell & Co., 1888), p. 94.

[16]G. F. R. Henderson, ed. Jay Luvaas, *The Civil War: A Soldier's View* (Chicago: University of Chicago Press, 1958), pp. 132–33.

[17]Lydia Post, *Soldiers' Letters* (New York: Bunch and Huntington, 1965), pp. 202–3.

[18]Bell Wiley, *The Life of Billy Yank* (Indianapolis: The Bobbs-Merrill Co., Inc., 1951), pp. 321–23.

[19]Ibid., pp. 312–13.

[20]Ibid., pp. 349–53.

[21]Wilbur Cash, *The Mind of the South* (New York: Alfred A. Knopf, Inc., 1941), pp. 116–20; Edward Sears, *Monthly Religious Magazine*, XXV (June, 1861), 376–84.

[22]Quoted in John H. Franklin, *The Militant South* (Boston: Beacon Press, 1956), p. 138.

[23]Ibid., p. 139.

[24]T. L. Nichols, *Forty Years of American Life*, I (London: J. Maxwell & Co., 1864), p. 377.

[25]Quoted in Edmund C. Burnett (ed.), "Letters of Three Lightfoot Brothers, 1861–64," *Journal of Southern History*, XXV (May, 1959), 180.

[26]Grady McWinney, "Who Whipped Whom? Confederate Defeat Re-examined," *Civil War History*, XI (March, 1895), 5–26; David Donald, "The Confederate as a Fighting Man," *Journal of Southern History*, XXV (May, 1959), 178–93.

[27]Dixon Wecter, *The Hero in America* (New York: Charles Scribner's Sons, 1941), pp. 342–44.

[28]Bell Wiley, *Billy Yank* (Indianapolis: The Bobbs-Merrill Co., Inc., 1951), pp. 247–49.

[29]Ibid., pp. 247–62.

[30]Ibid., p. 79; George W. Smith and Charles Judah (eds.), *Life in the North During the Cvil War* (Albuquerque: University of New Mexico Press, 1966), p. 302.

[31]Henry Adams, *Education of Henry Adams* (New York: Houghton Mifflin Co., 1918), p. 265; William Wasserstrom, *Heiress of All the Ages* (Minneapolis: University of Minnesota Press, 1959), pp. 30–31; Charles Ferguson, *The Male Attitude* (Boston: Little, Brown, 1966), pp. 196–207.

[32]Alfred L. Conkling, *Life and Letters of Roscoe Conkling* (New York: C. L. Webster and Co., 1889), pp. 538–49; Richard Hofstadter, *Anti-Intellectualism in American Life* (New York: Alfred A. Knopf, Inc., 1962), pp. 185–90.

[33]Amy L. Reed, "Female Delicacy in the Sixties," *Century* (October, 1915), 885–64; H. F., "Letter from the Homestead," *Country Gentleman* (July 21, 1864), 40–42.

[34]Thomas C. De Leon, *Belles, Beaux and Brains of the Sixties* (New York: G. W. Dillingham, 1909), pp. 369–71; Stephen Powers, *Afoot and Alone: A Walk From Sea to Sea by the Southern Route* (Hartford, Conn.: Columbian Book Co., 1872), p. 43.

[35]John C. Lester and Daniel L. Wilson, *Ku Klux Klan*, (New York: Neale Publishing Co., 1905), pp. 52, 65, 75, 102; William G. Brown, *The Lower South in American History* (New York: Macmillan Co., 1903), pp. 196–201.

[36]*Kloran* (Atlanta: W. J. Simmons, 1916), pp. 31–32.

[37]Walter C. Cook, "Secret Political Societies in the South During the Period of Reconstruction," (address given at Western Reserve University, n.d.), pp. 23, 27–28.

[38]Max Lerner (ed.), *Mind and Faith of Justice Holmes* (Boston: Little, Brown, 1943), pp. 11–13.

[39]Richard Hofstadter, *Anti-Intellectualism in American Life* (New York: Alfred A. Knopf, Inc., 1962), pp. 147–48.

[40]Arthur Calhoun, *Social History of the American Family From Colonial Times to the Present*, Vol. III (New York: Noble, 1917), p. 25.

[41]H. R. Howbert, *Reminiscences of the War* (Springfield, Ohio: Globe Printing and Publishing, 1888), pp. 362–72.

[42]B. O. Flower, "Fostering the Savage in the Young," *Arena*, X (August, 1894), 422–32; Benjamin Harrison, "Military Instruction in Schools and Colleges," *Century* (January, 1894), 468–69.

[43]Albert Richardson, *A Personal History of Ulysses S. Grant* (Hartford, Conn.: Winter and Hatch, 1885), p. 59.

[44]Alfred Mahan, *Admiral Farragut* (New York: Appleton and Co., 1892), pp. 57, 312–25.

[45] A. Bower Sageser, *Joseph L. Bristow* (Lawrence: University of Kansas Press, 1968), pp. 1–2; Larzar Ziff, *The American 1890's* (New York: The Viking Press, 1966), p. 78.

[46] Hamlin Garland, *A Son of the Middle Border* (New York: Macmillan, 1927), pp. 5, 7–8, 11, 63, 139, 313; see also Everett Wheeler, *Sixty Years of American Life* (New York: Dutton and Co., 1917); B. A. Botkin, *A Civil War Treasury of Tales, Legend and Folklore* (New York: Random House, 1960).

[47] Larzar Ziff, *The American 1890's* (New York: The Viking Press, 1966), pp. 149, 306.

[48] Richard W. Stallman, *Stephen Crane* (New York: George Braziller, 1968), pp. 4, 14–19.

[49] Stephen Crane, *The Red Badge of Courage* (New York: New American Library, 1952), pp. 27, 134; Richard W. Stallman, *Stephen Crane* (New York: George Braziller, 1968), pp. 170–71.

[50] Quoted in Charles B. Davis, ed., *Adventures and Letters of Richard Harding Davis* (New York: C. Scribner's, 1917), pp. 240–41.

[51] Quoted in Fairfax Downey, *Richard Harding Davis and His Day* (New York: Scribner's, 1933), p. 130; see also Richard Harding Davis, *Soldiers of Fortune* (New York: C. Scribner's, 1897).

[52] Frederic Remington, "With the Fifth Corps," *Harper's* (November, 1898), 962–75; Charles Brown, *The Correspondent's War* (New York: Charles Scribner's Sons, 1967).

[53] Henry Watterson, *History of the Spanish-American War* (Chicago: Smith Publishing, 1898), p. 216.

[54] Joseph Foraker, *Notes of a Busy Life* (Cincinnati: Stewart & Kidd Co., 1916), p. 26.

[55] Quoted in James Morgan, *T. R.: The Boy and the Man* (New York: Grosset and Dunlap, 1919), p. 53.

[56] Frederic Remington, "With the Fifth Corps," *Harper's* (November, 1898), p. 970.

[57] Quoted in Abbe Felix Klien, *In the Land of the Strenuous Life* (Chicago: McClurg, 1905), pp. 328–29.

What else is a woman but a foe to friendship, an inevitable penance, a necessary evil, a natural temptation, a coveted calamity, a domestic peril, a pleasant harm, the nature of evil painted over with the colours of good; wherefore it is a sin to desert her but a torment to keep her.

a thirteenth-century Franciscan

4

CURRENTS OF CONFUSION: MEN AND WOMEN, 1880–1900

When Thomas Jefferson negotiated the Louisiana Purchase, he was extending the space in which the American ideal of progress was to become manifest. In that ideal was assumed the uninterrupted course of human moral and material development. As we have seen, American women largely assumed responsibility for the moral standards of the nation's development by keeping children isolated from corruption and implanting in their sons the basics of good character. Man, as pioneer, moved into frontier space "to fight with nature," according to Frederick Jackson Turner. "He came from a civilization based on individual competition, and he brought the conception with him to the wilderness where a wealth of resources, and innumerable opportunities gave it a new scope."[1] By the 1890s, a different situation confronted the sons of the nineteenth-century pioneers. The frontier was settled; the natural environment that had produced a Boone, and a rugged, virile manhood in his wake, was being rapidly transformed into an urban nation. The competitive system had favored some individuals over others. Corruption was common. Business and government had become complicated.

ECONOMICS AND MANHOOD

Some men had authenticated their masculinity by becoming extraordinarily successful, building businesses and huge industrial combinations, often at the expense of other men and whole social classes, all of which could be justified by the logic of social Darwinism. Such men epitomized David Riesman's inner-directed men, men who drew inspiration and guidance from parents, a familiar idealized image, or from some frontier hero and followed through to exert their own character in the conquering of a frontier conjured in their imagination.[2]

One of the most successful men, J. P. Morgan, liked "yachts, solitaire, beautiful women, power." He was a man who in every respect fulfilled the ideal of nineteenth-century manliness with his forcefulness and concentration. He was blunt, dictatorial, driving himself and those around him with a harsh vigor. He was not inclined to intellectualism and disliked weakness in other men. Because of his commanding physique, piercing eyes, and frequent outbursts of temper, a meeting with Morgan was once likened to meeting an express train at full throttle.[3] But unfortunately, for every Morgan who succeeded so magnificently there were many tragic failures, men who may have had lots of pluck but not much luck. The economy was dying in the 1890s, with some 6,000 reported business failures and bank closings. What could be said about the masculinity of those individuals who had failed? Were they victims of an economic cycle, or of a flaw in their manly character? The impression one gets from reading the Dun and Bradstreet reports on business failures, beginning with the year 1890, is that personal factors, incompetence, inexperience, extravagance, and neglect explained the majority of business failures. And since the factors explaining business failures were personal, what then was happening to American men? For the male of the 1890s, faith in progress and America's masculine power and ability to see it through was shaken.

Women were posing problems too. There was evidence that many were restless with their assigned domestic roles. This was the case of the "new woman," who joined clubs, became interested in causes, wanted an education, and, in some cases, even a career. The trend was going to continue, according to one account published in 1890, and it was stated that women might even prove to be better workers than men. There were charges that American women were becoming more masculine and threatened to Europeanize American society with their newly discovered "outside" interests. A British visitor, James Burn, was astonished at the assertiveness of American women during the Civil War. Many women flaunted a strong sense of personal independence and were selfish and extravagant. Burn predicted the degeneration of moral standards if American men did not react against the offending women.[4]

By 1900, a century of manly striving toward material success and a century of female influence were producing a mounting social tension that would affect the very essence of what it was to be masculine or feminine in America. On the one hand, men had learned how to do little else than make money. Women, on the other hand, had long been acknowledged as moral guardians, possessing a conscience enriched by their sentiment and emotion. Upper-middle-class men had used their wives as status symbols; they were "the peg on which he hangs out his fortune," according to one account. Men lavished their good fortunes on their wives, as did Cornelius Vanderbilt, who put a $250,000 pearl necklace around his wife's neck, perhaps because he did not know what else to do with his money. For many women, their husbands' wealth meant more leisure time, less drudgery in the home, and opportunities to entertain and discuss matters of the day. Never before in American history had women had as many aspirations or the potential for realizing them as they did by 1900. But if they succeeded, it would surely challenge traditional sex-role norms. This, in fact, was happening, but men were so absorbed in their pursuit of power and wealth that they cared little for their wives' new interests. All they wanted was for women to remain content in their own sphere, which, from most indications, they were not going to do. Some women, sensing change in the air, urged their husbands on to greater success to enhance their social means. But the more men worked, it seemed, the greater their estrangement from wife, family, and society. By the early twentieth century, one could read that the American male was a bore and even a failure because he was so limited in interests and knowledge. Who was to blame? Some blamed the money madness of the culture itself. Others blamed women for driving their men onward to advance their feminine status. Whatever the case, it was clearly evident to many men that the masculine hold on society was in jeopardy.

WOMEN AND THE
MASCULINE SOCIETY

In 1867, Elizabeth Willard, in a remarkable, insightful analysis of nineteenth-century sex roles, surveyed the male creature going through the motions of competitive production and consumption and concluded that the masculine world was not operating in the best interests of human progress. "The masculine law is the law of division and antagonism, the law of discord, combat and destruction." Women had been misled by men into thinking that the artificial divisions men had created were good. One of the most obvious examples Willard saw of women's being duped was in the South, where women had followed men right down the path into the slaughter of the Civil War.[5]

Even some men, obviously not the conventional masculine types, shuddered at the viciousness of masculine competition. The old forms of aggressive "rude masculinity" of will and force "must yield in a redeemed world to the influence of humanity." The author of this thesis in the *Baptist Quarterly* asserted that ugly masculine government and temper must be redeemed. And he looked to women as the source of the redemption.[6]

By the 1880s, it was apparent that many women had grown restless and bored with the exclusive role assigned them of keeping order at home and raising children. Magazine articles challenged the male domination and control over women, and the treatment of them as objects much like the terrain and trees men were plowing under. Women possessed a basic human compassion, and it was time the masculine world be so informed. Mary F. Armstrong argued that "while the process of evolution has pushed us so far forward that there is no longer in our dealings with men, any serious question as to superior abilities, there still remains between our moral standards and theirs the same gap that had existed ever since the purity of women was tacitly recognized as essential to civilization." The moral superiority of women must be allowed to triumph or men would corrupt everything—including women—and chaos would result. Men could read in magazines such as *Cosmopolitan* that, based on "thousands of letters" and "thousands of confessions," women thought men were actually weak.[7] Thus, one very disturbing theme to men of that time was the assertion of many women that the male world was essentially a failure and needed saving by women. Not even the exalted fraternalism of men during the 1880s and '90s spared males from the charge that they were ravaging beasts. Most often, the brotherhood ideal was a device for political or industrial benefit. The admiration men had for one another was usually based on commerce, having little to do with human growth and development.[8]

Because of their pure and pious influence, women had enlisted in a number of reform movements dating far back into the nineteenth century. Dress reform and abolitionism were well known to women before the Civil War. After 1865, feminism broadened its base considerably to constitute what Eleanor Flexner has termed "a veritable domestic revolution." Seen from the male perspective, men were being swept toward a woman's world in which life was going to be ordered according to the feminine touch. But what could men expect? Female influence over matters of mores and morals had long been acknowledged by men and women alike. Whatever reforms loomed ahead, they were a logical outgrowth of women's influence and their domestic role, combined with hhs social inertia of men.[9] One of the most comprehensive reform organizations, originally the Home Protection Drive, was the Women's Christian Temperance Union, which had been growing since the 1840s. The W.C.T.U. organized various departments to accommodate the diversity of interests the women of America were manifesting. But at the heart of the organization was the campaign against alcohol, in effect, attacking what to some was one of the prominent badges of virile masculinity in nineteenth-century America.[10]

MEN, WOMEN, ALCOHOL, AND SOCIAL REFORM

A sip of the spirit allegedly bolstered the courage of many a hard-driving man, while for some men drinking was an act of social rebellion and a denunciation of feminine manners and morals, as suggested by Stephen Crane in the novel *George's Mother*. George Kelcy's mother was the embodiment of the moral universe trying to restrain her son from drunken rowdiness. "She was convinced that she was the perfect mother rearing the perfect son." But George disregarded her pronouncements on the evils of drink and the behavior of men in saloons. "As he drank more beer, Kelcy felt his breast expand with manly feeling," wrote Crane. Kelcy could never be comfortable in his mother's moral universe, which jeopardized his freedom to assert the masculine identity he defined as proper for a man. Through all indications, this pattern of rebellion through the use of alcohol and tobacco was fairly common by late in the nineteenth century.[11]

The novelist and adventurer Jack London, one of the era's most celebrated champions of the Nietzchean–superman ideal, confessed he did not like liquor and preferred to avoid it, but he proclaimed nevertheless "my manhood must compel me to appear to like wine. . . . I shall so appear. But no more than is unavoidable." But London found alcohol hard to resist and spent a fortune in drinking bouts with chesty men who "put their seal on their comradeship by drinking." It was not uncommon for London to get into drunken brawls, which, to him, was a confirmation of authentic manliness, the road all *real* men took who were full-blooded and virile.[12]

To be sure, not all men so openly declared an association of beer with manliness, and nineteenth-century morality still assumed a strong stand against Demon Rum. Men of "good character," men who sought manly leadership and success, were admonished again and again to abstain from the evil of alcoholic beverages. But there was a tacit recognition, especially among many middle- and lower-middle-class men, that the hard-driving man drank his share of liquor and smoked or chewed tobacco.

While the W.C.T.U. gained a reputation of attacking the bars and saloons in which men drank beer and celebrated their masculine rites, other women's organizations across the country fostered a variety of new activities that seemed clearly dangerous to thousands of American men. Painting, art, literature, and social and cultural activities were becoming the preoccupation for many newly sophisticated women. Men involved in the work-a-day world obviously fell behind in knowledge and understanding of the fine arts (although not all women's clubs studied the fine arts). One motivation behind these fast-growing women's organizations was a sense of mission, that women had to save the world before men destroyed it with their alleged unbridled selfishness in the pursuit of material gains. The interest in social reform was a common denominator that brought many women of different ethnic and class backgrounds together. Women like Margaret Robins of Boston's elite, and Mary Anderson, a Swedish immigrant, discussed world peace, health and sanitation issues, recreation for children, and a host of other current topics, all designed to reshape masculine America.[13]

One of the most important of the new pursuits of women that was to have a profound impact on American men was education for women. In 1853, colleges in America began admitting women in increasing numbers.

The first was Oberlin (Ohio) College, the first coeducational college in the United States. But it was not until the 1880s that female education really became a "problem" for some men. By that time, the restlessness of women was more noticeable. It was argued by women that they wanted what was best, not only for themselves, but for their country. The mission of the educated woman, according to Mary F. Armstrong, in a stinging rebuke to men, was to provide a means whereby her superior abilities could be recognized and trained. The only way women could be sure of maintaining their position in society was to be more independent. To deny the new woman her independence would allow the baser instincts of men to corrupt women in the future, "which is a consummation most devoutly not to be desired." Such a claim alarmed many men because it implied the superiority of women. "We realize, often in bitterness of heart, that our moral life, the life of our aspirations, is upon a plane which, as yet, the average man has not reached." Modern women could not afford to backtrack down the trail and lend their stumbling and fumbling men friends assistance, because it would jeopardize progress too much. Yet, there was some hope for man, as "we stand ready to welcome him whenever he can bridge the chasm and make our standards his."[14] In the old order of established sex roles, women had no place to apply their talents, express their views, or participate in what men called "the game of life." Suzanne Wilcox advanced the idea that day-care centers ought to be established to care for children and free mothers for a greater sense of fulfillment. And once men understood the versatility of women and their competence, there would be a more realistic appreciation of them.[15]

WOMEN AND THE VOTE

More than anything else, the vote symbolized the ultimate invasion of the male domain by women in their drive to save the Republic. Suffrage had been discussed since 1848, but by the 1890s it became a focal point of reform for many women. Hundreds of resolutions and bills were introduced in state legislative bodies across America and were accompanied by some vigorous campaign support by women. Even when the suffrage issue appeared to have reached an impasse between 1890 and 1910, the discussion and rhetoric about women's suffrage was intense, bordering on desperation for some women. "Let me get the reins in my hands," wrote one woman, "and I will make men temperate; I will make them pure; I will cut corruption out of their politics."[16]

Men had often reacted against such claims in very specific language, contending that male dominance and control of politics must be preserved. The women's rights movement inspired complaints that feminism would confuse the meaning of masculinity. In the 1850s and '60s, *Putnam's Monthly* tacitly supported womens' rights but maintained that men had rights too, and that their rights superseded those of women. For example, men had legal responsibility for women and children, and because this fact derived from a natural phenomenon, it was unalterable. Women were created to serve men, the magazine emphasized, but added that feminine sentiment was putting logical consistency (defined as masculine virtue) on the defensive. In 1869, a *Putnam's Monthly* article expressed the fear that women were getting so interested in worldly affairs, discussing the policies of the German leader Otto von Bismarck, for example, that they were becoming impure. A plea that American women return to the humble station of their grandmothers was made on the basis that they had better understand their own high and true nature or they would risk corrupting it.[17]

Horace Bushnell went so far as to argue that women would be physiologically damaged if they got the vote. Women would grow larger, develop heavier brains, and lose their unique feminine mannerisms and features. Worst of all, women would endanger their purity and morality if they entered the political arena.[18] This argument, used by men against women's suffrage, was one of the most revealing because it served to illustrate the psychological and moral distance that had come between men and women. In analyzing the "real case" against the suffrage, a male author acknowledged that, regarding the present age, many men "are heartily ashamed of its brutality," but then added, "what is written is written"; men had been decreed the possessors of force, the main actors in accomplishing American progress. Government, to function properly, depended on male force, "and this is embodied in the male sex." Women were outside this process, in fact above it, and should never be plunged into the sordidness of male existence by obtaining the vote. It was not so much that women should be denied suffrage but that they should be *exempt* from it because of their lofty position and female role. "There is a very real distinction between being placed among the beasts, and being placed among the 'ministering angels.' "[19]

What is important to note, as is the case in the above quoted article, is the very clear distinction of sex-role functions and definitions, which many men, and women too, agreed on in their opposition to women's suffrage. It was because women stood so high that their political interests were deplored. The practice of politics was in no way ennobling for women, nor was it useful in educating them about good citizenship because it emphasized "chicanery, cunning, the arts of party management, the market price of manhood, skill in offering rewards for service."[20] None of this the true woman could indulge in without paying the price of her superior womanly virtue. The implication that the male world was sordid and corrupt and that a man's activities were shameful was evident when the case against women's voting was stated this way. Many women agreed that they had a superior influence to exercise and dared not subject themselves to situations likely to compromise their virtue. That such a conclusion did not beg some very distinct conflicts for men and women about their sex identity and self-definition is hard to imagine. How could the masculine ideal of progress be maintained if the active life of force and power upon which politics rested was so sordid?

Some men were willing to concede that the male domain was selfish and sordid, but they resented and, in fact, resisted attempts of women to reform them. Pretenses of feminine reform were annoying because they countered traditional masculinity-validating behavior such as forcefulness, assertiveness, practicality, and the desire to uphold male honor. The "woman question" was not so much a question as a fear voiced by men that they would lose control over society, and that control had been central to the male understanding of what progress had entailed. To some, the moral "titaness," as Henry Beer called her, was a kind of female robber baron, muscling into the existing order with a casual disregard as to what she might upset or break down. An article in *Harper's New Monthly Magazine* warned male readers about the growing number of women's journals that openly asserted the deficiency of men. Most of all, the article warned men not to underestimate this growing journalistic fashion featuring femine cultural and intellectual musings.[21] An unidentified (but no doubt male) author complained that the new woman wanted constant pampering, like a hedonist, and that she often called men selfish because they did not accommodate her every whim. Women were more interested in Ibsen and Shakespeare and the psychological fiction of the day than they were in understanding their husbands. The American cult of true womanhood was being destroyed because of women's growing interest in society and culture. The "new woman" was ridiculed as a status-seeker, threatening to bring Europe's worldliness to America. All the while, it was charged that American husbands were slaving at their jobs, driven to distraction and exhaustion by the Anglo-Saxon society woman. As the mania for notoriety increased among women, they could be expected to enter the male world in increasing numbers, which would threaten the very existence of society.[22]

A WOMAN'S PLACE

According to Hugo Munsterberg, a scholar and world traveler, American women were taking over the culture, and male predominance was being destroyed. Munsterberg warned that if the United States were womanized, the nation would be irreparably weakened and progress arrested. The prospects were not good that American males would correct the dangerous trend, because men were unable to develop cultural interests of their own to compete with women's. An English visitor to the United States, P. A. Vaile, observed what he called serious psychic strains affecting American males. Women were avoiding their responsibilities of raising children and providing good homes for their husbands. The effect women did have, Vaile noted, was to effeminize the men and their sons.[23] Other foreign commentators noted that the American male was dispirited, passionless, overworked, and that men and women were seeking to escape from one another. Paul Bourget, a Frenchman, wondered, "How does it come to pass that the men of this country—so energetic, so strong-willed, so domineering—have permitted their wives to shake off masculine authority more completely than in any other part of the world?"[24]

Grant Allen, a free-thinking English biologist and an advocate of the new morality in England, generally sympathized with the feminist movement. He believed that a woman's life ought to be made as easy as possible, but he argued that some women had gone too far in asking for total emancipation, which he, and many others, predicted would have terrible consequences. For Allen, the fundamental concern to which all other questions were subordinate was to define the American community in terms of its basic goals to create and sustain a strong race. To this end, women must remain wives and mothers, and all the education they acquired should be directed toward that end. Education of women for any other purpose would serve only to make women masculine in all but virility and "we men are (rightly) very jealous of our virility." Just as no man would want to denounce his masculinity, no woman would dare to "unsex" herself to the point of not wanting a family. So, on with women's education as far as Grant Allen was concerned, as long as it was within the man's framework, subordinate to his existence, and serving his needs. Allen added in a subsequent article that American men would probably prevail against the trend in edcuation to "unsex women," and that they would select wives according to principles of traditional masculine preferences. In their proper (conventional) place women would positively contribute to the emotional resonance of society by generally patronizing the arts, music, and culture. Women were good at relating to people; men, however, would continue to relate to the world of things.[25]

Theodore Roosevelt and Grover Cleveland agreed with Allen that a woman's place was in the home. Both men, who had had exceptionally strong fathers, perceived progress as preordained, men and women having distinct roles to play in its natural evolution. It was the duty of every woman to understand her calling, to be a helpmate just like Eve in the Garden. "I would have them happy and contented in following the Divinely appointed path of true womanhood," wrote Cleveland, hinting that he would have no objection to easing domestic drudgery if this were what the "new woman" desired. The true loving wife, however, should attend to her husband's every need and especially to dissuade him from pessimistic viewpoints undermining his self-confidence. Cleveland was hostile to the National Federation of Women's Clubs, which he saw as subversive. It only encouraged women to transcend the home and acquire an interest in possessions to the point of making men feel guilty when they could not provide them. Some hostile club women seemed intent on punishing their men for years of neglect. These women did not understand "the saving womanly traits that distinguished us above other nations." Cleveland warned them that the "strength and beauty of our domestic life are put in peril" by the activities of these women.[26]

Grover Cleveland's views and feelings represent the attitudes that many middle-class white American males had about the new activities of women. Perhaps men recognized that if women through committed social action changed their role or redefined feminity in any way it would invade male territory, force men to evaluate their masculine image and role, and perhaps even alter the allocation of social, economic, and political power. The same general challenge faced white society when the black civil-rights movement became a threat and, like men of ths 1880s who saw it as "the woman problem," whites of later years issued diatribes describing "the Negro problem." As in the case of blacks, who were described as "unfit" for a wider participation in American society, women were also "scientifically" scrutinized by an impressive roster of male scientists and were found to be deficient in physical and mental capacities. One scientific "fact," for example, expounded upon by many male researchers was that the female's smaller brain should be taken as proof that men had superior intellectual powers.

THE DIFFERENCE BETWEEN THE SEXES

Where women did excel was in their power of perception, according to one view. They were acknowledged to be more affectionate, devoted, and modest. They were clearly more self-sacrificing than men, and they had a stronger aesthetic sense. Men and women fell into conflict when man brought his coarser, selfish, masculine nature from the competitive world into the home, where it offended a woman's delicate sensibilities. The proof that this situation was quite natural came from Darwin. The male of the species had always struggled for dominance and had succeeded, thereby proving his natural superiority. To understand evolution better, one had only to recall Darwin's other point of natural selection: Males admired women who were instinctively feminine, and, conversely, women were attracted only to distinctly masculine types. Such was the "law of inheritance" as limited by sex.[27]

G. T. W. Patrick of the University of Iowa agreed that women had smaller brains and that they were not as ambidextrous as men. Because their perception of detail was less accurate, they were neither reliable critics nor good judges of reality. Having more nerve tissue than men, women were more excitable and emotional, a point of "scientific fact" that many men were to exploit rather widely. As for psychological differences, however, Patrick saw women as conservative in nature because of their physiological reproductive function, while men were liberal and forward-looking because of their role as producers. The sociologist Lester Frank Ward agreed that women were cautious and more conservative than men because of their biological helplessness. That helplessness, however, contributed to their quicker instinct in sensing danger. Ward perceived women as the "balance wheel of society, keeping it in a fixed condition of growth." Women contained within them a composite of the race as it had evolved to its present stage of development. According to Patrick, women had been the best at preserving the "underlying qualities," such as good manners and good taste in matters of etiquette. Men contributed the qualities of courage, endurance, and muscular strength, which made them more adaptable than women to a changing environment.[28] Another sociologist, W. I. Thomas, saw woman as the core of society, the "fixed point," while man existed in space, often violent and spasmodic as he struggled to overcome his environment. Both, of course, were assumed to be complementary.[29]

Ward advocated female equality because men and women were needed to balance nature between active and passive elements and furnish each other with inspiration. But Ward, too, drew sharp distinctions between sex-role functions. Men were powerful and forceful by nature with active, aggressive characteristics. To succeed, males had to act on their inherent shrewdness and diplomacy. In an apparent effort to placate the often shrill protest of women reformers, Ward explained that women's reforming zeal could be more correctly understood as quite conservative. Hers was the kind of reform not really directed at the masculine world, but one to protect herself and her offspring. What made feminine reform appear so dangerous was that women tended to abolish bad institutions rather than change them. In other words, they were revolutionists and, after all, Ward explained, revolution was really complete conservatism carried out for self-preservation. While men sustained and continued the race, women could be expected to protect it from evil influences. Where men acted courageously to promote masculine interests, women could be expected to act prudently to protect feminine "selfhood." Although the two traits may be viewed as antithetical, they were essential to the delicate balance of nature, Ward assured his readers.[30]

W. K. Brooks, in still another effort to account for sex differences, suggested that men possessed a greater variability because they had cells called *gemmules*. This variability, he vaguely contended, passed through the ovum, described as a "material medium," which was where the law of heredity manifested itself. The ovum, then, was the conserving element in racial transmission, while the male element was the progressive, or variable, factor in evolution. The female, by the very nature of her sexuality, was supposedly anabolic, the storehouse of instincts, habits, intuition, and proper conduct, whereas the male was catabolic, building upon these instincts and extending them into new fields.[31]

One of the most common arguments men used against the new woman was that education of women would threaten stability and progress. Again, "proof" of this came from the male scientific community. It was assumed that woman's chief purpose was to bear children and that the reproductive system would not function properly if the female body was rigorously taxed or if the brain became too active. Therefore, a responsible woman was expected to conserve her energy for her chief function of life. Edward Clarke, who explored this mind–body connection, distressingly concluded that American women were not being very faithful to their purpose of motherhood and domesticity, and he went so far as to predict that American men would have to import wives after another generation if they were going to perpetuate the race.[32]

G. Stanley Hall collected, studied, and related many of these theories in an exhaustive two-volume work. Hall, who earned his doctorate at Harvard and taught at several prestigious American colleges, was greatly interested in childhood development. If there is any overall theme in his work, it is that every child recapitulated the life history of the race. Hall, the first president of the American Psychological Association, perpetuated the opinion that it was harder to describe the typical male than the typical female, subscribing to the thesis that males were more variable than females. Hall was disturbed by the trend toward further education of women because, like so many other men, he believed it was a sign of regression. The purely intellectual woman was a deformity, according to Hall. Bookishness was a bad sign in women, suggesting artificiality, pedantry, and "the lugging of dead knowledge." Hall contended that women should be taught nothing that did not have practical application to enable them to retain their common sense.[33]

Edward Thorndike believed the effort to educate women was fruitless because not more than two percent of the truly gifted in society were women. The few women who were so distinguished were not worth the effort of educating them and so the conclusion of this man was clear: "[M]ediocre grades of ability and achievement should be reckoned with by our education system."[34]

But what about knowledge of the Bible, about which it can be surmised women probably knew more than most men? During the nineteenth century, women played a very active role in church organizations and Sunday-school work. Pursuits of a religious nature, however, did not disturb the female balance, according to Hall, because religion was an affair of the heart and out of the range of intellectualism. Yet Hall conceded that many young girls desired a more intellectual education rather than the prescribed household-arts training. Hall was disturbed by a survey that revealed that eighteen out of one hundred college girls confessed they would rather be men than women. Studies also demonstrated that more and more young girls did not have female models for their lives but were attracted to the great men of history.[35]

Clearly, the American ideal of true womanhood was disintegrating, and Hall urged that the dangerous trend be stopped. To guarantee sex-role divisions and standards, Hall urged that boys and girls be separated in the classroom. This segregation would be good for both sexes. Boys would benefit in Hall's estimation, because they were suffering from too many female teachers, who exacted forms of discipline that humiliated the boys' manly ideals. There was something wrong with a boy in his early teens if he could be called a "perfect gentleman." The gentlemanly ideal was appropriate only later in life, after the brute and animal element had had time to be absorbed into manhood in a normal and healthy way. It followed that girls needed to be segregated from boys to guard against the girls' developing masculine interests and risk being rejected by men. When the sexes were together in the classroom, the impulse for each to be at their best grew lax because "each [sex] comes to feel itself seen through, so that there is less motive to indulge in the ideal conduct. . . ." Thus, familiar camaraderie produced disenchantment and diluted the "mystic attraction of the other sex."[36]

Hall admitted that some of his reflections remained only hypothetical, but, nevertheless, he believed that sexually integrated schools were at least one cause for a declining marriage rate. As for school administration and instruction, Hall believed that the secondary schools were overly feminized, much to the detriment of male teachers. "It is hard, too, for the male principals of schools with only female teachers not to suffer some deterioration in the moral tone of their virility and to lose in the power to cope successfully with men." Men were forced to make too many compromises in discipline and pedagogy to go into teaching, and therefore the ideal male types did not choose careers in teaching, depriving schoolboys of a model of manly excellence. If each generation were to repeat the essential life history of the race, then sex-role functions and patterns would have to remain stable in order to ensure masculine competitiveness and feminine domesticity, upon which the concept of American progress depended.[37]

Personal contention and strife during the late nineteenth century arose when females moved from their fixed place into male space. Lawrence Irwell, for example, had no objections to women's being educated or even voting, but if girls were coeducated with boys in their preparation for a man's work, irreparable harm might come to the women, for they "are not adapted to compete with men." Women would lose certain crucial immunities if they tried to enter the world of men, it was argued. Although Irwell lacked conclusive proof of any connection, he observed that insanity among women was increasing in the United States. The only justifiable reason for a woman to be educated was purely for the sake of learning itself. Education that would lead to a rivalry with males invited disaster.[38]

From his perspective in 1906, the sociologist W. I. Thomas said that anthropological studies revealed the human mind to have been fixed in the earliest times when the species was fighting, contriving, and evolving from one stage to another. Into the present situation of human evolution, Thomas contended, all of these early conflicts had been extended. Scientific and business pursuits were analogous to the "hunting, flight, pursuit and courtship and capture of early racial life." Modern morality through education demanded more pleasant and more serviceable analogies to society than the traits of primitive man. But there was risk involved, for if the modern woman ventured too far into higher education, seeking the pleasant, serviceable analogies that she thought were most likely to complement her feminine tastes, she would deceive herself and the masculine figures around her by distorting reality. Man should not and could not be considered anything but what he was basically intended to be from the beginning of the species.[39]

THE GROWING CONFLICT

The discord between the sexes stretched far beyond the implications of temperance and suffrage and involved more than just club women's "getting out." At stake was the whole spectrum of personal relationships between men and women that revolved around human sensitivity, emotions, and various perceptions of love. Few novelists dealt with these issues as suggestively as Henry James, who observed the American scene from Europe. James's view was that men derived their strength from the women they married, but women had become so influential that they endangered the welfare and freedom of their husbands. Women had been directed to assume moral leadership, but they were now dominating the lives of their husbands through womanly expectations and restraints. This vicious circle, found in much of James's writing, was labeled "the vampire theme" by Leon Edel, his biographer. Fathers demanded and got complete attention from a wife and mother, but at the same time women had the influence to command their husbands like quasi-slaves. From this pattern, one can deduce that, in James's work, love was really a renunciation of self. In the nineteenth century, for the American male, love was a denial of masculine power and instinct, a condition of stultifying dependence, in conflict with the masculine mystique. Marriage, then, was a form of death. In James's short story "Longstaff's Marriage," for example, Longstaff suffers great personal agony because of his love for Diana, but upon her rejection of him he rapidly recovers and it is Diana who suffers miserably and eventually dies of a broken spirit. In *The Secret Fount*, *The Ambassadors*, and *Roderick Hudson*, the relationships between people, especially between wives and husbands, endure great strain and tension. Youthful energy, compassion, and creativity were often tragically destroyed by the new feminine vultures, a view shared by Henry's brother William.[40] "There is a strange thinness and femininity hovering over all America," wrote William James to his brother Henry in 1893. Upon his return to the United States, William James was astonished that America was "so different from the stoutness and masculinity of land and air and everything in Switzerland and England." It made James strangely sad to reckon with the American social order, in which men were losing out to women. How different Europe was, where men had fought stubbornly to maintain their place, a lesson American men would do well to copy.[41] "The whole generation is womanized," exclaimed Basil Ransom, the hero of *The Bostonians*. "The masculine tone is passing out of the world; it's a feminine, a nervous, hysterical, chattering, canting age, and age of hollow phrases and false delicacy and exaggerated solicitudes and coddled sensibilities," which was leading straight to flat and flabby mediocrity. "The masculine character, the ability to dare and endure, to know and yet not fear reality, to look the world in the face and like it for what it is . . . that is what I meant to preserve, or rather, as I may say, recover. . . ."[42]

James, William Dean Howells, and many other writers suggested that personal relationships between men and women were strained, and that love, especially, was misunderstood or not understood at all by men. While many men professed their love to women, it was a narrow sense of love, often expressed only materially. If women needed protection and support, then loving a woman had its own purchase price. Furthermore, men wanted to be loved in return, which really meant that men wanted to be admired for their manly accomplishments and heroic feats. The social record indicates that once men felt they had gained such recognition, they often neglected their wives and took the love relationship for granted. Women, on the other hand, could not complain about being taken for granted and neglected without raising the ire of their husbands and society at large. They could, and, most often, did suffer in silence. Explanations and accountability for this tension varied. One woman advised caution, explaining that men were subject to laws and forces of competition that women did not understand. It was natural, she reasoned, for a woman to register jealousy and contempt at the male devotion to worldly pursuits, but she advised obedience to womanly virtues as a woman's contribution to her husband's life.[43]

Marriage was criticized by another woman for having been founded on a concept of distorted love, resulting from sex-role functions that served neither men nor women very well. Through the courtship period, men affectionately praised the angelic quality of their chosen mate. Once married, however, male behavior usually oscillated between masculine aggression and domestic docility, but in either extreme, the husband was basically ungrateful for wifely duty. Soon women found themselves left alone by men indifferent to them and unsympathetic to their wishes.[44] In a most insightful and well-balanced essay, Junius H. Browne explained why feelings between the sexes were strained. American men had historically idealized women, adorning them with fruits symbolic of material conquests. This was one way masculinity advertised itself. Yet Browne and other observers agreed that most men did not really desire the companionship of women. Companionship implied "the highest, broadest, truest love," but in America, men and women seemed to have no appreciation of mutuality, in or out of wedlock, because of the exaggerated sense of sex-role polarities. It would be ages, Browne predicted, before the sexes understood each other well enough to contribute to one another the essential requisites to build a basic companionable relationship.[45]

In the 1890s, it was claimed, women were socializers, but the male's peculiar sense of destiny left him with a "wandering, capricious disposition." What had been the goal of male existence for a century—to live in space beyond confinement and restraint—still prevailed. "There was something mentally enervating in feminine companionship." Men preferred to be alone, with other men, or, best of all, "out in the open air, as it were, roughing it among the rough as a mental tonic."[46] As Browne and many others noted, American men seemed bewildered by the home and the women in it.

LEISURE TIME AND THE WOMAN

A woman's life and work seemed to be changing rapidly, more rapidly than a man's. By 1900, the Sears catalogue was advertising no end of gadgets and appliances designed to ease the burden of home chores and leave women with time for club meetings devoted to topics that men might not have understood or would have preferred women not discuss. Another sign of the times was that by 1905 the Sears catalogue gave twice as much space to musical instruments as it did to stoves, reflecting this trend of a more diverse cultural interest. Thousands of women took part in the bicycling craze that swept the nation in the 1890s. This popular pastime was perhaps a factor that encouraged women to dress more for their personal comfort and convenience than to uphold the dress standards observed by their mothers. Certainly not all men objected to the changes and experiences affecting women. There were men, however, who expressed concern that women's new widely publicized pursuits would detract from the more important male responsibility of achieving progress.

Along with her many other interests, the woman of the 1890s had more time to read. Many of the new magazines and periodicals featured hundreds of short stories about young women, their many moods, and romances. These gushy stories portrayed beautiful young women on the verge of "falling" or in a state of "falling in love" with a charming man of polish and significance. Dana Gibson, who illustrated many of these stories, portrayed in pen and ink what came to be known as the "ideal American girl" of the time, the Gibson girl. While her physical features and apparel became American standards, it was her sullen, mysterious qualities that seemed to enchant her male following. The women in these stories usually came from solid, middle- and upper-class backgrounds and were raised to expect adult life to be happy and secure. The same conditions did not always auger well for their real-life readers. One woman complained that too many young girls had been raised in a materialistic culture in which each had been "petted and indulged at home." The problem was that a girl assumed that such a life would continue into marriage, only to find that her husband soon became bogged down in business and expected his wife to be a "helpmate unto him." But, according to the same report, many women resented the time and interest men devoted to their business world, and they were no longer content to practice the womanly virtues of patience, consideration, and submissiveness.[47]

THE AMERICAN MALE AND HIS HOME

By 1900, the very institution of marriage itself was founded on terms that were bound to cause problems. The place accorded by society to women as moral guardians forced men to subdue male aggressiveness and put on "false" behavior in their own homes. Men suffocated in their own homes, and many inwardly rebelled against it, walking on egg shells to avoid wounding the feelings of their wives. It was not surprising that many men found it necessary to work late and take frequent business trips to escape their own household. Many American men came to regard home as a place to eat and sleep but preferred to get away from it at the earliest moment. It is indicative of the state of relations between men and women during the 1890s that the idea of a "den" became fashionable in the modern home. It was an exclusive male retreat, a room, one woman writer commented, women would not like.[48] Many men found more ease and comfort at the country club, saloon, or the lodge. By 1900, the numbers of such places had increased enormously, with all the attendant rituals and ceremonies that further separated men from women, as if the latter were an invasion force to be staved off. Men could be safe behind the walls of such clubs as the prestigious Union League Club of New York, which advertised "no women, no dogs, no Democrats, no reporters."[49] How unique the American man was when compared with his British counterpart. According to one comparison, the Briton left his home later each morning and returned earlier in the evening. "An Englishman is continually going home; an American is continuously going to business."[50]

What accounted for this domestic estrangement can be traced to men's having deferred to women, for a century, on matters of culture and morals. "Men cannot deny this inferiority, for to this day they make woman's standards of conduct a higher one than their own, from an instinctive conviction that only under a woman's lead can civilization advance in this direction."[51] Women wanted a society that was tasteful and polite, but there was implied a degree of sociability that men were not intellectually and emotionally prepared to adopt. Men were autonomous individuals running businesses and farms, and proving their manhood doing it. New York meant business; Washington politics were symbolic of the masculine state of mind.[52] Even if men were to be civilized, it was conceded that women were so clearly morally superior that most men would still probably prefer to avoid them. Most men, in fact, according to Junius Browne, never dreamed of camaraderie with women, since it was not perceived within the framework of their masculine identity or disposition as rugged individualists to indulge in the interests of the new woman. Those few men who were comfortable in the presence of women were often derided by other men as effeminate, weak, or "Miss Nancyish." Hence, those men who were more or less companionable were afraid of being embarrassed, not so much by women but by other men. It was one of those irrefutable credos of true manliness never to appear as anything but robust and virile to other men:

> Man is, it must be acknowledged, still semi-barbarous, as is shown by some of his tastes and not a few of his pleasures. Woman, who is civilized, and, in the main, enlightened, feels this savagery in him without comprehending it, and marvels at its existence. It constantly wounds and shocks her; but the feeling she reserves, having learned that self-repression is the price she must pay for the maintenance of peace.[53]

It is not surprising that genuine communication between men and women was strained and that many commentators alluded to a frustrated state of male–female companionship. According to Browne, men, in their relations with women,

> are conventional, artful, anxious to create an impression: women in dealing with men, sacrifice everything in their effort to be agreeable; hide nature, and pervert truth with this intent. There is no chance for companionship between them. It cannot breathe in so artificial an atmosphere. Men alter their language to suit women. You get no more idea of their sentiments or actions from what they say to women than you do of real women from what [they say] to men.[54]

Hence, the mystique at work. It was important to always give the appearance of success and progress to prove one's masculinity, even if it meant distorting reality. But Browne complained that men too were being deceived, especially by the vanity of the new woman. The way she dressed and presented herself in public made it appear that she was trying to be something other than her true self. Hair dyes, makeup, pads, and corsets were available to help make women attractive. Women could send away for lotions and potions, such as Dr. Worden's Female Pills and the "world famous La Dore's Bust Food," to enhance feminine appeal. How could such interest in altering one's appearance be the basis for an honest relationship with a sincere (and unsuspecting) man?[55]

IRRECONCILABLE DIFFERENCES

W. I. Thomas tried to put the new, glittering female into perspective, by noting that, having arrived at a state of dependence in human evolution, women had to fix themselves up to win the courtly favors of young men. Since males were so autonomous, independent, and selective, women had assumed an almost aggressive attitude toward courtship to be sure of getting a mate. Other male writers interpreted the new appearance as part of a conspiracy for "conquest, power, supremacy." Women wanted men at their pretty feet. "They like to torture [men], as naughty children torture flies." Too often, men submitted to these artificial contrivances. "Indeed, man in this country has deferred to her so long that woman is beginning to think she has the force that compels deference and not the weakness that woos it." It was a crisis situation. Women were beginning to imitate the masculine animal, whom, in fact, they despised, stated one writer. Meanwhile, for men, "doubt is in the air. There is an upheaval of old traditions and conventionalities. . . . With no firm ground to stand upon, the self-confidence of the past has vanished. Disbelief in everything involves disbelief in one's self."[56] The words point directly to the crisis of the male paradigm, which had been conceived in strength and power to achieve progress but now faced deception and potential defeat.

Everywhere white middle-class men looked, it seemed as if the ideal of masculine power and virtue—as perceived in a Boone, the Civil War hero, pioneer, or wheeler-dealer—were threatened by a new historical process of urbanization, civilization, and feminization. The new woman was not the only thing affecting the masculine state of mind. Banks and railroads were going bankrupt, and farmers saw their farms taken over by land companies. Unemployment and restlessness were abroad in the land. Through it all, men struggled to maintain their heroic self-respect. In many cases, this may have meant deceiving associates, wives, and families about the real state of their business. No man, not in America at least, could admit defeat or talk openly about his problems. Men had been socialized to be rational and tough and conditioned to get to the top and win, all a part of the validation of masculinity. One medical doctor, Cyrus Edson, urged wives not to nag their husbands (a habit that he regarded as a very serious threat to masculine health), and to say nothing to disturb their peace of mind. Coming home from a struggle at business, men needed to rest and be left alone. Edson warned that, in time, more and more men would revolt against their wives' accusations, and that some husbands would even become violent. It was better for men that they be allowed to suffer in silence. As a result of this silence, few women ever understood their husbands' problems and occasional intemperance. The strain of commercial relations was so enormous, said *Nineteenth Century*, that more than any other nation, America has departed from "conditions suitable to the normal healthy male."[57] With women becoming more restless, demanding and indulging in more leisure activities, males had to support them by working even harder. A century of hustle had already resulted in a condition of overworked men and nervous, unsatisfied women. Some believed sterility had increased in America to such a degree that the dominance of the Anglo-Saxon race was in doubt. Such a prospect was especially frightening, considering the higher birth rate of ethnic minorities and especially the rising yellow race.

During the 1880s, G. M. Beard gained wide acclaim for his study of neurasthenia—nervous exhaustion—and its debilitating effects. Beard concluded that no former generation or nationality had ever suffered such a wide variety of irritation and nervousness as he found in America, all of which he attributed to the pressures of modern civilization. One of the specific elements of modern civilization, listed by Beard, contributing to the pressure of life was the mental activity of women. Their pursuit of a wider range of social and cultural activity was creating confusion in the social order by undermining traditional lines of masculine authority and influence. Spiritual and moral sanctions for the old order seemed less clear, and the emphasis on materialistic matters was also cited as a cause of nervous exhaustion. Beard stated that men had caught up with women in mental depression and morbid fear, and he even suggested that nocturnal emissions—so-called "wet dreams"—were the effect, as well as the cause, of depression and disease. His recommendation, like that of many other physicians of the time, was to separate the sexes, to have them sleep apart until such time as good health and attitudes were restored.[58]

All of this turn-of-the-century theorizing was no doubt a major factor stimulating the home-in-peril theme of countless books and magazine articles. One representative work, by Frank Hagar, argued for the continuation of masculine dominance and supremacy as necessary to preserve the family. Blending theology, historical examples, and sociological theory, Hagar argued that progress was rooted in paternal power, which was central to the Christian family. He warned that the greatest danger to the family was sexual equality. It encouraged conflict and strain, discouraging some men from honoring their obligation to extend progress and perpetuate the race. Hagar was not alone in his concern about masculine sterility, usually attributed to the "nervousness of the age," which in turn was caused by the extraordinary American drive to succeed.[59] Hagar claimed that the most fatal mistake was the trend toward the higher education of women. The intellectural life had the regressive effect of producing indifference in girls or even sex aversion. An education encouraged young girls to assume that they had equal power and opportunity. The effect of coeducation, then, was a blurring of sex identity, all of which seriously strained modern marriage. "Perhaps," Hagar wrote, "the mistake in the higher education of women had not been that it is high, but higher than that of men." To remedy the strains current in America at the turn of the century, Hagar urged a return to traditional values in order to ensure a Christian culture. Preservation of the family was how a Christian culture was ensured. In a confused age, Hagar saw the family as the best answer to individualism, since he believed the family structure was inherently democratic.[60] All the evidence, however, suggested that men were not ready to surrender their autonomy, for it was an integral part of their criteria of masculinity to be and remain individuals. Attempts to change them into anything different were met with contempt.

Arthur Calhoun's 1917 study of the American family is an indispensable source for understanding male and female attitudes of the nineteenth century. Calhoun's research led him to a conclusion similar to that of Hagar: that the structures of an orderly society were dependent on the family and male dominance. But women had succumbed to what Calhoun called the "butterfly spirit," which had led them to reckless expenditures and, in increasing numbers, to divorce. Calhoun, like many others, thought American men were working exceptionally hard to support the parasitic women of the late nineteenth century. And of those women who had taken jobs, Calhoun was critical because of the inherent implication to the male that he was weak, inefficient, or not productive enough at his work to support her. Furthermore, the revolt of women had undermined the husband's sense of accountability for his wife's conduct and family responsibility.[61] In short, the family was becoming a burden to men, whose egos had always been inflated by an exaggerated sense of selfhood and independent action. Calhoun's documented study shared the general male view that the "rise of women" was not going to produce a new spirit of humanity in which men and women would circumvent old sex-identity standards to discover sharing and love in the family.[62] The feminine revolt was creating tension and confusion and challenging the masculine paradigm. From the vantage point 1925, F. P. Milard concluded that it was the rare man who would admit that the wife he had subdued and conquered was ever any help to him. The men in a society that so highly praised *individual* action could hardly be expected to openly seek their wives' support or grant them credit when it might be due.[63]

THE NEW WOMAN
AND INCREASING DIVORCE

Robert Grant, a jurist and popular novelist, roundly condemned the new, mobile woman, the woman anxious to be freer from home duties, because she was vulnerable to the disease of social ambition. In Grant's novel *Unleavened Bread*, the aggressive Selma White destroys a succession of well-meaning men who are unlucky enough to cross her path. Women like White, according to Grant, displayed a smug sense of self-importance in their efforts to enrich the home and enliven culture, but, in fact, they confused personal ambition with social objectives. Grant predicted, in the long run, the coming of a family composed of just a mother and children. Husbands and fathers would be driven away because of their inability to cope with modern women.[64]

In the years between 1880 and 1916 the rate of divorce increased from one per twenty-one marriages to one divorce per every nine marriages. The rate rose most sharply during the 1880s, when the divorce accelerated from one per twenty-one to one per twelve marriages. Numerous reasons were cited to explain the alarming trend. *The Nation*, which opposed any liberalizing of divorce codes, blamed the increase on a decline in a faith in immortality and saw it as an atonement for earthly sins. The habits and practices encouraged by the new morality were singled out as dangerous to the future of marriage, as was the improved transportation system, which took people to places where they hadn't been before and filled them with "other desires." Inherent in such arguments was the belief that social mobility was directly proportionate to social order and moral standards.[65]

The growing number of divorces would later prompt some Progressives to argue for a revitalization of American ideals and values. Theodore Roosevelt, among others, was fearful of Anglo-Saxon race suicide if more marriages did not survive, Edward Bok, editor of *Ladies' Home Journal*, believed that if young men got married they would be more likely to get and hold a respectable job because any "true" woman would demand it. She would protect her husband from wasting his manly energies on loose women, gambling, drinking, and other vices that could ultimately destroy a man—a philosophy of marital functionalism dating far back in the American experience,[66]

Basic to the increase in divorce, however, beyond the sociological implications, was the nature of marital relations, and, more specifically, the problem of changing sex roles. The author of an 1868 *Nation* article alluded to women's becoming more self-assertive as one reason why more American males preferred the single life. No man could be expected to tie himself to a wife unless he could be sure of having supreme authority in his marriage. As women became more masculine—meaning that they were more active and less submissive and domestic—fewer men would be inclined to marry them. In other words, marriage had to take place strictly within the framework of existing sex-role definitions. These dictated that if males were not supreme, a marriage could not be expected to survive.[67]

One suspects that another reason middle-class men generally opposed women's assertiveness was that male lives seemed so dull by comparison. The routines of business life and the office were tedious and boring, and the effects surely must have been felt by many men who heard about wives and women who were experiencing a greater variety of activity in their lives. Moreover, the rigors of work were so confusing and exhausting that men were unprepared physically or emotionally to keep up with the new interests of women. To women, business work seemed static. To Rafford Pyke, who reported on what American women liked and did not like about American men, the conclusions were not flattering. American men seemed "too coarse to appeal to the finer needs of a woman's nature." The old rugged manly qualities seemed to be of little importance to women seeking husbands. As women became more sophisticated, they also became more discriminating, less willing to accept men whose attitudes would conflict with women's new interests. What the new woman seemed to want in her man was good looks, refinement, and some knowledge of polite society. If this was the stuff upon which a lasting marriage depended, the possibility of a happy marriage was doubtful, women wanted a "new man" whose image was different from that of his ancestors. But most men still idealized the old image. There was a conflict between the old and the new image of man in Pyke's analysis, because he also asserted that a man should never let a woman be wholly sure of him, and that to please a woman, a man should have sexual experience and be aggressive.[68] The question was, how could the male be socially refined, tamed, and domesticated and yet still be aggressive and dominant?

The image of an ideal woman that men had was of a beautiful creature whom they could possess but who would not possess or control them. They instinctively disliked "superior women." But apparently, this desired woman was a memory from a time when males were dominant in marriage and family matters.[69]

BRINGING MEN AND WOMEN TOGETHER

How much masculine and feminine ideals troubled late-nineteenth-century Americans can be seen in the number of articles and books written specifically about coming to terms with marriage. One of the most popular authors on marriage was Mona Caird, who sharply contrasted the degree of freedom men enjoyed with the freedom of women. It was a misconception to think of America as a society of individualism, she argued, because this was only half true. Only males had achieved independence, whereas women could have no interests separate from those at home. "If a woman obeys her husband, for that she is exalted to heaven." A wife could not be a companion to her husband because in so doing she would compromise her womanhood by moving into the male world. Caird saw women as virtual prostitutes within the marriage bond and called upon the state to help mothers find work and become self-supporting. She urged the passage of more-liberal divorce laws to free women from their assigned role of *having* to provide sexual release for their husbands. Several other new moralists, as William O'Neill called them, were highly critical of the rigid cultural and social distinctions and sex roles.[70] Grant Allen called upon men to treat women more like comrades in love and sex. It was part of a bargain he proposed to women in which they would remain committed to their traditional duties but would be "rewarded" by a new spirit of love. This implied a new sensitivity on the part of males, and Allen believed that men had to understand female sexuality if marriage was to survive. Moreover, this philosophy would perpetuate the race when the conditions and psychology of love were altered to complement feminine desires and interests.[71]

An English author, widely read in the United States, Edward Carpenter, castigated the American male for his lack of social maturity and sexual knowledge, both of which greatly affected marriage and the ultimate happiness of husband and wife. While making significant technical and mechanical progress, which aggressive and assertive males seldom restrained from proclaiming, the truth was, according to Carpenter, that their "human and affectional side seems at times an utter failure." As a consequence, marriage was seldom understood, usually clouded over by an illusion of glamor. Once the bloom faded, couples often found themselves frustrated and annoyed with each other, resulting in boredom and "even nausea." All too often, male egoism and desire for satisfaction were the main causes of such a deplorable condition. Carpenter urged a broader, freer, more healthy marriage that would allow women and men much more freedom than the stagnant, selfish marriage relationship in which couples conformed to distinct sex-role definitions. A marriage that allowed for more freedom and mutuality would be happier for both men and women. Carpenter did not specify the exact nature of his new freedom, but it is clear that he saw the marriage vows and pledges made in the heat of romantic love as not irrevocable. An understanding of the dynamic social interactions of people would lead one to new experiences that might even involve extramarital affairs and would certainly not lead to ostracism for any person obtaining a divorce.[72]

When Frederick Howe finished writing his autobiography, his wife skimmed it and remarked that he had never mentioned his marriage. "Oh yes," answered her husband. "I forgot that. I'll put it in." Lincoln Steffens thought that this anecdote accurately summarized the attitude about marriage held by many men of his generation. Love, as the basis for marriage, was seldom understood, although most men thought they understood sex, as it was physical. But sex and love were never the same thing, although Steffens believed they should have been. It would have to be women and "such effeminate men as poets" who would write a science of love, if there ever were to be one, because the American male seemed completely confused about love, sex, and marriage. Upton Sinclair recalled that when he was young it was generally taken for granted that marriage had to be ill-sorted and that couples quarrelled with each other. Steffens and Sinclair were deeply confused about sex and love in their respective boyhoods and both had difficulty coping with it in their adult masculine lives.[73]

PROSTITUTION

Throughout the nineteenth century, there were always ways for men who were frustrated with marriage, or who felt stifled by Victorian mores, to find sexual release and excitement. Before 1865, Southern gentlemen had the slave quarters, and Northern men, depending on class and location, had the prostitute or mistress. Brothels existed in many American cities, North and South. There were, of course, harsh warnings to men of all ages about consorting with prostitutes, especially about "social (venereal) diseases." Sexual-purity crusaders warned that the prostitute was a killer of manhood because of her ability to drain manly energy, weaken masculine nerves, destroy sound reasoning, and corrupt other sensory faculties. One author depicted prostitution and the diseases prostitutes carried as a "foul blot upon humanity," a "loathsome ulcer," and a "malignant leprosy" that shows its hideous deformities among the fairest results of modern culture. Henry Ward Beecher exclaimed that "NONE THAT GO UNTO HER RETURN AGAIN."[74] Despite such vivid language and stern warnings, prostitution flourished in nineteenth-century America. A detailed study of prostitution was published in 1832 by a New York clergyman and in 1858 a history of prostitution by William Sanger was published. Additional studies titled *Sunshine and Shadow in New York* and *New York by Sunlight and Gaslight* indicate the pervasiveness of sex for hire. Chicago's prostitution experienced a tremendous growth between 1865 and 1900. A "gentleman's guide" was even available in some cities to help men locate the better houses and advertise the services of individual prostitutes.[75] According to vice-commission reports published in Chicago in 1911, the city had 192 houses of prostitution with 2,343 rooms, 1,012 "inmates" (as they were called in the report), and 189 madams. The commission noted there were 272 additional flats with 960 rooms containing 419 "inmates" who also served the sexual needs of men.[76] What was true of Chicago appears to be generally true of most large cities of that time. In New York, the *Social Hygiene Bulletin* of January 1916 reported there were 15,000 prostitutes doing business on any given day in New York City, serving 150,000 patrons daily, many of them regular customers.[77]

Society's reaction to prostitution ranged from passive curiosity to alarm, with frequent calls for suppression. The causes of prostitution, according to conservatives, usually centered on the unhealthy environment of the large city and the temptations that lurked there, preying upon innocent, moral manhood. Throughout history, cities had been associated with sensuous pleasures and reckless living. Some critics claimed that the erotic literature and picture-show bills, which circulated freely in the city, were responsible for prostitution. The arousal caused by this "perverted" literature led to the desire to release the pressures of sexuality. Therefore, the argument ran, to preserve the nation's pure manhood, the erotic stimuli should be suppressed. Prostitution, as an easy avenue toward infidelity and adultery, would then vanish. Such a reaction, which treated any form of extramarital sexual activity in a moralistic framework, only obstructed a more profound understanding of male behavior, in terms of men's attitudes about themselves and toward the society in which they lived. Yet much of the discussion about prostitution was carried out on the religious and theological level, with venereal disease seen as the wages of sin.[78]

Literature on prostitution has usually dealt with the motives of the young women, and from the literature has emerged the generalization that prostitution thrived on the economic needs of young urban women, the majority of whom were immigrants. A far more enlightening analysis might be the motives and expectations of the men who visited prostitutes. Such an examination, even if based only on sketchy evidence, helps identify at least some aspects of the nineteenth-century sexual muddle. The Civil War, no doubt, played a part in forcing some of these changes in American social morality. In 1883 Lester Frank Ward observed that, because of the rigidity and restraint of Victorian society, some form of extramarital sex was essential. Country men, in town to sell their livestock, were among the most frequent customers. Girls like Chicago's notorious Everleigh sisters, whose services were well known, could help men experience elements of sexuality that they might not have enjoyed elsewhere. The prostitute, then, could be seen by many men as more appealing because she was wonderfully uninhibited and knowledgeable about sex.[79] Some years later, Havelock Ellis wrote, "It is well recognized that men sometimes go to prostitutes to gratify the excitement aroused after having fondled their betrothed." Ellis's observation suggests the strange situation in nineteenth-century social relationships in which women dressed and carried on to attract men, to arouse male interest in them as potential lovers; no doubt many men fantasized that the tempting women were more than equal to the occasion. Once they married them, however, the moral rectitude of "true" womanhood replaced the alluring nature of physical womanhood. A wife who accepted the advances of an amorous husband often did so as a dutiful and submissive wife, even though she may have found sex distasteful, or frightening because of pregnancy. That husbands may have eventually looked to other sources of sexual gratification is not surprising. It is hazardous, at best, to guess at the impact of the related expectations, tensions, and fears of men and women trying to live up to the concepts of masculine and feminine ideals. Even Sylvester Graham, the well-known purity crusader of the 1830s, acknowledged that intercourse was probably more exciting outside of marriage. Thus prostitution existed for these married men, not so much as a counterculture, as the Hallers have noted in their recent history of medical advice in Victorian America, but as an integral part of the Gilded Age—as a sort of psychic drainage system.[80]

And what of the unmarried man? There was frequent speculation during the nineteenth century as to why an increasing number of young men did not marry. As noted in the novels of Henry James and others, marriage implied a surrender of oneself to a relationship dominated by the woman. Marriage was seen by many men as a commitment that was defined mostly according to the whims of the new woman. Some young men remained single rather than confront "the titaness," a woman these men knew would gauge them at every station in life, as husbands, fathers, businessmen, and community leaders. Fearing that they might be inadequate in any or all of these tests, many young men opted for the single life, and for release they turned to vice and extravagance, according to a publication by the Equitable Life Assurance Society in 1913.[81] The prostitute offered an ideal relationship in that she demanded none of the social perquisites other women clamored for. In fact, she did not even demand sexual satisfaction. In a very real sense it was a "free relationship," one in which a man could pay a price to exercise his sexuality while remaining totally free from further commitment or testing.[82] Perhaps, along with the prostitute, some men decided that it was more sensible to "surrender virtue" rather than preserve it against the backdrop of an age that was experiencing many other changes, including a trend toward the new morality.

Prostitution was an understandable phenomenon, then, because sexual gratification had become separate from marriage. The most radical position on the subject was advanced by a German woman, Grete Meisel-Hesse, who called for a recognition of the male's "psycho-physical needs" in the modern age. According to her research and study, males felt a need to discharge their sexual desires in a manner in which there would be no serious social or spiritual consequences. "The intensity of their masculine need becomes manifest when we consider how difficult it is for the individual . . . to attain under existing conditions to any satisfying erotic intercourse outside the limits of marriage." Yet women seemed to refuse the reality of this essential masculine need, which Hesse argued could be satisfied only by prostitution. Instead, men were preached to or reformed by overzealous women who were too anxious to possess them and control their desires, resulting in a masculinity crisis often affecting the individual male's performance on the job and in other social relationships.[83]

THE DOUBLE STANDARD

What this survey of prostitution, marital tension, and psychic frustration reveals is that by 1900 men and women were living and working with a vast and complicated double standard. Men had been socialized to believe that women were pure and pious like their mothers surely had been, and that society depended upon women to enforce moral and social standards. But adult men according to their very masculine nature, were expected to sin, apparently failing their mothers' highest expectations of them. The wives men married presented an opportunity for male reform, but the man's perception of masculinity, of the aggressive, strong-willed, forceful individual, presented quite a barrier to male reform. A wife could accept her noble mission to uplift her man but often had to compromise her hopes and look on disapprovingly as her husband went the way of all manly men, toward masculine fulfillment in a materialistic, competitive society that was often corrupt. Men could argue that if women got into business and politics they would surely be corrupted. The argument tacitly admited that the male world was corrupt.

Adultery was just the extreme fulfillment of the double standard. Men could seek out the whore, prostitute, "fallen woman," or mistress for sexual satisfaction. He might see no impropriety on his part because the woman had already fallen, and the man was merely doing what was expected of him. In fact, some might have argued that extramarital sex made a man better adjusted by relieving sexual desire and helping him recognize the moral purity of his wife. This double standard was witnessed in the first American settlements, where the sin of an adulteress was more severely reproached than that of her male accomplice. A man's extramarital sex did not risk introducing "someone else's" offspring into the family. The male was not risking disorder in his life, but it was assumed that a child was the responsibility of the mother, and failure to honor that responsibility led to condemnation.[84] This double standard, based on concepts of what were proper feminine and masculine behavior and expectations, was to be one of the most troubling of all problems affecting male–female relations in nineteenth- and twentieth-century America.

By 1900, the American male confronted a paradoxical situation. American men had the power in their hands but a few men had become so powerful that they could effectively control and manipulate the nation's social and political structures. The male influence seemed to dominate. The future seemed secure. But one consequence of the dynamic American social order at the end of the nineteenth century was that more and more women were beginning to claim a share of the recognition and an opportunity for fulfillment equal to that of men. And many men were confused as to what to do about the emerging new woman. There were those men who contributed funds to start women's colleges, such as Vassar and Bryn Mawr. Many parents wanted their daughters to attend a four-year college. Some men encouraged their wives to assume an active role in the husband's business or profession. For example, a survey revealed that thirty-one of the 200-or-so female lawyers in the United States were attracted to the profession by marrying lawyers.[85]

As could be expected, many men were appalled by the women's rights movement. Anna Howard Shaw, trained in the ministry and medicine, was afraid to tell her family of an invitation to preach her first sermon, sensing that it might cast a personal disgrace on her. Rheta Child Dorr's husband tolerated her writing novels, which was, after all, a passive, *feminine* activity, but he resented her ambition to be a journalist, writing about public controversies, which was, in the nineteenth-century-male view of things, an aggressive, *masculine* activity. Even Frederick Howe, himself an active reformer, had difficulty adjusting to his wife's feminism. If women became serious about reform, what would be the limits of their revisions of the social and political order? What if, for instance, women tried to force an appreciation of the fine arts and sentimental literature on their men? Would it not contribute to the effeminization of men? Since the work week was getting shorter, men had more idle time on their hands, which, one writer predicted, would very likely change men from their traditional active aggressiveness to passive receptivity.[86]

If men conceded to the positions taken by the feminist movement, they risked domination over aspects of their lives that had always been considered as masculinity-validating. The frontier and the rugged, romanticized life style associated with it were already passing. Meanwhile, powerful impersonal economic forces were taking their toll on the individual American male. A convocation speaker at the University of Chicago in 1907 spoke to the men there about "the crushing out of opportunities for young men through the growth of capitalistic combinations." Young men might easily be disturbed by the "disappearance of traditional landmarks."[87]

STRAINS OF THE TIMES

Many of the tensions and problems men faced from the disappearance of the traditional landmarks of masculine achievement and behavior were reflected in some of the novels of the time. Jack London, who was born in 1876, had no respect at all for the soft, sentimental life. He detested what he called "false culture" and romantic philosophy. In *Son of the Wolf*, the wealthy club man and the society dandy were ridiculed as lazy, inactive shirkers who could talk big but cried over a toothache. London attended the University of California but left for the rugged Klondike when gold was discovered there. Although he found no gold, the strenuous and demanding experience contributed to London's philosophy. London felt that basic to man's survival was his unrestrained natural will, as found in animals, which helps explain the author's attraction to the animal world and his fascination with their survival instincts. His most famous novel, *Call of the Wild*, is about Buck, a dog stolen from California and taken to Alaska, where he is trained as a sled dog. Buck adapts to the ruggedness of the North, eventually becomes leader of the sled team, avenges his owner's death by killing his murderers, and then takes up life in the wild, surviving on instinct. London's human heroes were masculine individualists like Jacob Welse, a robber baron (capitalist–industrialist) who made his fortune in the Arctic in *A Daughter of the Snows*, and the ruthless sea-captain Wolf Larsen, who practiced a Nietzchean philosophy in *The Sea Wolf*. But accompanying the action, proclamations of racial superiority, and struggle for domination in London's work there is also considerable ambiguity and contradiction that reflects, in part, the turbulence of changing times and the confusion of London's defining his own masculinity. London seemed unable to resolve just what type of man he really admired: Was it the clod-man of everyday existence who went along with his life and accomplished something, however unspectacular, or was it the God-man who was moral, civilized, and who attracted attention because of his stature? There was sympathy for the underdog and hatred for excessive wealth, which led London to social protest in the 1890s and to Marxian socialism, but there was also an emphatic commitment to social-Darwinian individualism. The women in London's novels tended to be quite feminine, yet athletic and even emotionally superior to men. While London himself wanted to prove his virility by fathering a child, marriage and family troubled him. Although he valued purely natural instincts, there was always the excessive drinking that stimulated his "manly behavior." By the time of his death—which was probably a suicide—in 1916, the forty-year-old London was a physical and mental wreck.

In *A Man's Woman*, *The Pit*, and *McTeague*, Frank Norris emphasized the brutish, primitive, masculine qualities in his male characters. One critic has acclaimed Norris as the "founder of the red-blooded school in America," and with good reason. In a speech to the Hamilton Club of Chicago, Norris said he "hated the timid man, the lazy man . . . the over-civilized man, who has lost the great fighting masterful virtues . . . whose soul is incapable of feeling the mighty lift that thrills stern men with empires on their brains."[88] One finds in the novels by Norris the atavistic theme that every man has the potential of recovering the same rugged spirit of his predatory ancestors. Since nothing had thwarted manly assertion and action in primitive men, so it could be with modern men if they could get in touch with the old instincts. Norris's McTeague offers an extraordinary example of how the primitive impulse took over one man. With Trina in the dentist's chair, helpless before him, McTeague grows obstinate "with all the strength of a crude and primitive man." And on another occasion, when Trina is anaesthetized and helpless in the dental parlor, "the animal in the man stirred and awoke." It is a crisis that McTeague struggles to combat, "the old battle, old as the world, wide as the world—the sudden panther leap of the individual, lips drawn, fangs aflash, hideous, monstrous. . . ."[89] Although he fights off the predatory impulse to seize her, he wonders why he cannot love her purely and cleanly. Eventually, McTeague marries Trina, but the marriage turns sour. It is discovered that he has no license to practice dentistry, and thus the slide downward of the male character, typical of the Norris novels, is begun. Trina works, concealing her income from her husband. McTeague begins to drink because of his enforced idleness, and when Trina counsels against his habit, he grows to dislike her. She annoys him because she is too small, so prettily made, so invariably correct and precise. He becomes unable to love her and eventually she dies from a beating he inflicts. McTeague flees to the desert only to die there of thirst.[90]

Examined from the historical and psychological perspectives of the late nineteenth century, *McTeague* offers one example, in fiction, of the tensions surrounding latent male impulses. Although attracted to Trina, McTeague discovers that he cannot coexist with her refinement and sense of civilization. It drives him to self-doubt and then to violence and self-destruction.

Robert Herrick contributed several novels in which his male characters sought to escape overzealous women. Herrick himself grew up in a home dominated by his mother, who came from old Puritan stock. She took special delight in teasing her children about their poor lives and their lack of glory. She embarrassed her family by trying to live beyond its means. At Harvard, Herrick found no particular excitement or cause that could bring him a sense of fulfillment. In his novels, especially *Together*, Herrick introduced a whole gallery of sophisticated, nagging, intellectual women whose husbands were driven to bankruptcy and some into adultery. What seemed basically wrong with the women of Herrick's novels was that they were too finely organized for plain duties. While they did not want to enter the male world, they did not want to be mothers and have family responsibilities either. The pursuit of fashion and decorous living by these women destroyed the strengths and good character of the men they married. Herrick sympathized with these men and saw their behavior as a consequence of the pressures and strains forced on them by their women.[91]

During a time in which historians have emphasized the results of economic competition as the major problem of national life, these novelists and commentators were grappling with crises deep within the American consciousness. Summing up the situation, Rafford Pyke saw the average male as curiously deficient in self-analysis. While confident in his ability to successfully work out his business affairs in the external world, internally the American male was dazed and helpless. The average man's inability to seriously examine himself was both a source of strength and weakness. It was a strength from the point of view that he tended to approach his existence with few misgivings, hesitation, or doubt. Once a man took a stand, he was firm because his soul gave him a "strenuous assurance that everything which bars his way is wrong and hence is to be dealt with rigorously." This was the practical masculine view of reality. The analytical faculty, according to Pyke, was a "dangerous possession unless it [could] be allied with steady nerves, strong common sense, and a healthy strain of animality." Yet, Pyke realized that some self-analysis was necessary if the male sex were to keep from being "a sort of Dummheit [dummy] which is sometimes ludicrous and sometimes irritating."[92]

There was plenty to contemplate—the end of the frontier, dwindling opportunities, the rise of women, and a whole panoply of complexities involving a change of sex roles. A resolution of the tensions men were feeling about their masculine identities was part of ths motivation that turned many men toward progressivism.

Notes

[1] Frederick Jackson Turner, *The Frontier in American History* (New York: Holt, Rinehart and Winston, 1962), p. 271.

[2] David Riesman, "The Saving Remnant," in John W. Chase, ed., *Years of the Modern* (New York: Longmans, Green, 1949), pp. 114-22.

[3] John Sprout, "Organizing and Rationalizing American Capitalism," in Howard Quint and Milton Cantor, eds., *Men, Women and Issues in American History*, Vol. II (Homewood, III.: Dorsey Press, 1975), p. 18; Irvin Wyllie, *Self-made Man* (New York: Macmillan, 1954), pp. 32–33.

[4] John Habberton, *Our Country's Future* (Chicago: International Publishing Co., 1890), pp. 489–502; Emma Hewitt, "The 'New Woman' in her Relation to the 'New Man,' " *Westminster Review* (March, 1897), 335–37; James Burn, *Three Years Among the Working Classes in the United States During the War* (London: Smith, Elder and Co., 1865), p. 94.

[5] Elizabeth Willard, *Sexology as the Philosophy of Life* (Chicago: J. R. Walsh, 1867), pp. 373, 385; see also Philip Slater, *Pursuit of Loneliness* (Boston: Beacon Press, 1970); Page Smith, *Daughters of the Promised Land* (Boston: Little, Brown and Co., 1970), p. 90.

[6] William Conant, "Sex in Nature and Society," *Baptist Quarterly* (April, 1870), 176–97; Stephen Dana, *Woman's Possibilities and Limitations* (New York: Fleming H. Revel, 1899).

[7] E. Linton, "The Higher Education of Women," *Popular Science Monthly* (December, 1886), 168–80; Mary F. Armstrong, "The Mission of Educated Women," *Popular Science Monthly* (March, 1890), 601–8; Ella Wheeler Wilcox, "Restlessness of the Modern Woman," *Cosmopolitan* (July, 1901), 314–17.

[8] Eric Dingwall, *The American Woman* (New York: Rinehart & Co., 1956), pp. 101–6; Stephen Dana, *Women's Possibilities and Limitations* (New York: Fleming H. Revel, 1899), pp. 95–97. Annie H. Meyer, "Women's Assumption of Sex Superiority," *North American Review* (January, 1904), 103–9; L. H. Harris, "A Man's Relation to the Two Sexes," *Independent* (May 26, 1904), 1190.

[9] Eleanor Flexner, *Century of Struggle* (Cambridge: Belknap Press of Harvard University, 1959), pp. 294–305; Lloyd Morris, *Postscript to Yesterday* (New York: Harper, 1947), p. 53; Edward Hardy, *How To Be Happy Though Married* (New York: Scribner's, 1886), p. 22.

[10] Peter Filene, *Him/Her Self* (New York: Harcourt Brace Jovanovich, Inc., 1974), pp. 80–81.

[11] Stephen Crane, *George's Mother* (New York: Edward Arnold, 1896), pp. 46, 59.

[12] Charmain London, *The Book of Jack London* (New York: Century Co., 1921), pp. 80,

126, 129, and passim; Joan London, *Jack London and His Times* (New York: The Book League of America, 1939), p. 44.

[13]Lois Banner, *Women in Modern America* (New York: Harcourt Brace Jovanovich, Inc., 1974), pp. 71–72.

[14]Mary F. Armstrong, "The Mission of Educated Women," *Popular Science Monthly* (March, 1890), 607.

[15]Suzanne Wilcox, "Unrest of Modern Women," *Independent* (July 8, 1909), 62–66.

[16]Margaret Deland, "The Change in the Feminine Ideal," *Atlantic Monthly*, CV (March, 1910), 298.

[17]"Woman and the Woman's Movement," *Putnam's Monthly*, I (March, 1853), 279–88; "A Word for Men's Rights," *Putnam's Monthly*, VII (February, 1856), 208–13; "Men's Rights," *Putnam's Monthly*, XIII (February, 1869), 212–24.

[18]Horace Bushnell, *Women Suffrage: The Reform Against Nature* (New York: C. Scribner and Co., 1869).

[19]O. B. Frothingham, "The Real Case of the Remonstrance Against Woman Suffrage," *The Arena*, II (July, 1890), 177.

[20]Ibid., p. 178.

[21]Charles Warner, "The Subjection of Man," *Harper's New Monthly Magazine*, LXXX (May, 1890), 972–73; D. M. Murdock, "Concerning Men," *Forum*, IV (September, 1887), 38–48; Henry Beer, *The Mauve Decade* (New York: Alfred A. Knopf, Inc., 1926, 1960), pp. 3–38; Stowe Persons, *The Decline of American Gentility* (New York: Columbia University Press, 1973), p. 97.

[22]"The Anglo Saxon Society Woman," *The Living Age*, CCXXXII (March 1, 1902), 513–22.

[23]Hugo Munsterberg, *Americans* (New York: McClure, Phillips & Co., 1905), pp. 583–88; P. A. Vaile, *America's Peril* (London: Francis Griffiths, 1909), pp. 111, 116, 141.

[24]Paul Bourget, *Outre-Mer Impressions of America* (New York: C. Scribner's Sons, 1895) p. 79; James Bryce, *The American Commonwealth* (New York: Macmillan, 1889).

[25]Grant Allen, "Plain Words on the Woman Question," *The Popular Science Monthly*, XXXVI (December, 1889), 170–81; Allen, "Woman's Intuition," *Forum*, IX (May, 1890), 33–40.

[26]Nicholas Roosevelt, *T.R.: the man as I knew him* (New York: Dodd, Mead, 1967), p. 27; Grover Cleveland, "Women's Mission and Women's Clubs," *Ladies' Home Journal* (May, 1905), 3–4.

[27]George Romanes, "Mental Differences of Men and Women," *Popular Science Monthly* (July, 1887), 383–401; anon., "Biology and Women's Rights," *Popular Science Monthly* (December, 1878), 201.

[28]G. T. W. Patrick, "The Psychology of Women," *Popular Science Monthly* (June, 1895), 209–25; Lester Frank Ward, *Psychic Factors of Civilization* (Boston: Ginn, Co., 1892–1906), p. 177.

[29]W. I. Thomas, "The Adventitious Character of Women," *American Journal of Sociology*, XII (July, 1906), 34–35.

[30]Lester Frank Ward, *The Psychic Factors of Civilization* (Boston: Ginn, Co., 1892–1906), pp. 175–80, 194.

[31]W. K. Brooks, "The Condition of Women from a Zoological Point of View," *Popular Science Monthly* (June, 1879), 154; also Janice L. Trecker, "Sex, Science and Education," *American Quarterly* (October, 1974), 352–66.

[32]Edward Clarke, *Sex in Education* (Boston: Osgood, 1874); James Crichton-Browne, "Sex in Education," *Popular Science Monthly* (September, 1892).

[33]G. Stanley Hall, *Adolescence*, Vol. II (New York: Appleton, 1904), pp. 567, 640.

[34]Edward Thorndike, "Sex in Education," quoted in Leta Stetter Hollingsworth, "Variability as Related to Differences in Achievement," *American Journal of Sociology*, XXI (January, 1914), 510.

[35]G. Stanley Hall, *Adolescence*, Vol. II (New York: Appleton, 1904), pp. 640–41.

[36]Ibid., p. 621.

[37]Ibid., p. 623.

[38]Lawrence Irwell, "The Competition of the Sexes and Its Results," *American Medico-Surgical Bulletin*, X (September 19, 1896), 317, 319; G. T. W. Patrick, "The Psychology of Women," *Popular Science Monthly* (June, 1895), 224; George Romanes, "Mental Differences of Men and Women," *Popular Science Monthly* (July, 1887), 398; T. S. Clouston, "Female Education from a Medical Point of View," *Popular Science Monthly* (December, 1883), 214.

[39]W. I. Thomas, "The Adventitious Character of Women," *American Journal of Sociology*, XII (July, 1906), 44.

[40]Leon Edel, *Henry James, The Untried Years* (New York: Lippincott, 1953), pp. 54–55; William Wasserstrom, *Heiress of All the Ages* (Minneapolis: University of Minnesota Press, 1959), pp. 32–34, 57, 64–65.

[41]Henry James, ed., *The Letters of William James*, Vol. I (Boston: The Atlantic Monthly Press, 1920), pp. 346–47.

[42]Henry James, *The Bostonians* (Baltimore: Penquin Books, Inc., 1966), p. 290.

[43]Rose Cooke et al., "Are Women to Blame?" *North American Review* (May, 1889), 628–29.

[44]Ibid., pp. 630–32.

[45]Junius H. Browne, "Are Women Companionable to Men?" *Cosmopolitan* (February, 1888), 452.

[46]*This Fabulous Century, 1900–1910* (New York: Time-Life Books, 1969), p. 43.

[47]Rose Cooke et al. "Are Women to Blame?" *North American Review* (May, 1889), 627; Ella W. Wilcox, "The Restlessness of Modern Women," *Cosmopolitan* (July, 1901), 314-17,

[48]Octave Thanet, "Men as Friends," *Harper's Bazaar* (October, 1908), 999-1001; Rose Cooke et al., "Are Women to Blame?" *North American Review* (May, 1889), 638; Christine Herrick, "Man the Victim," *Munsey's Magazine* (September, 1902), 889–93.

[49]*This Fabulous Century, 1900–1910* (New York: Time-Life Books, 1969), p. 43; Frank Arnett, "American Country Clubs," *Munsey's Magazine* (July, 1902), 481–89.

[50]Price Collier, "Home Life in England and America," *Forum* (1894), 345; Junius H. Browne, "Are Women Companionable to Men?" *Cosmopolitan* (February, 1888), 352.

[51]Henry T. Finck, "Only a Girl," *Independent* (May 9, 1901), 1062; Frank Crane, "Women," *Independent* (Nov. 3, 1910), 965–67.

[52]Harrison Rhodes, "The Unconquered American Male," *Bookman* (December, 1908), 320–24; Amanda Quasita, "The Unattractiveness of American Men," *Independent* (November 11, 1909), 1065–67.

[53]Junius H. Browne, "Are Women Companionable to Men?" *Cosmopolitan* (February, 1888), 453–54.

[54]Ibid., p. 354; Page Smith, *Daughters of the Promised Land* (Boston: Little, Brown and Co., 1970), pp. 92–93.

[55]*This Fabulous Century, 1900–1910* (New York: Time-Life Books, 1969), p. 173.

[56]W. I. Thomas, "The Adventitious Character of Women," *American Journal of Sociology*, XII (July, 1906), 38; William S. Walsh, "The Conceited Sex," *The North American Review* (September, 1894), 371–72; Caroline Tichnor, "The Steel-Engraving Lady and the Gibson Girl," *Atlantic Monthly* (July, 1901), 105–08; A. W. Warner, "The New Woman and the Old," *Century* (November, 1909), 89–92.

[57]H. B. Watson, "The Deleterious Effect of Americanization Upon Woman," *The Nineteenth Century* (November, 1903), 788; Cyrus Edson, "Concerning Nagging Women," *North American Review* (January, 1895), 29–37; Octave Thanet, "Men as Husbands," *Harper's Bazaar* (December, 1908), 1174–76; L. H. Harris, "The Crab Apple Adam," *Independent* (November 3, 1910), 967–71.

[58]George M. Beard, *Sexual Neurasthenia* (New York: E. B. Treat and Co., 1905); Philip Weiner, "G. M. Beard and Freud on American Nervousness," *Journal of the History of Ideas*, XVII (1956), 269–74; H. B. Watson, "The Deleterious Effect of Americanization Upon Women," *The Nineteenth Century* (November, 1903), 782–92; Frank Hagar, *The American Family* (New York: University Publishing Society, 1905), pp. 144–51.

[59]Frank Hagar, *The American Family*, (New York: University Publishing Society, 1905), pp. 50–55; H. B. Watson,"The Deleterious Effect of Americanization Upon Women," *The Nineteenth Century* (November, 1903), 788.

[60]Frank Hagar, *The American Family* (New York: University Publishing Society, 1905), pp. 139, 155, 169.

[61]Arthur Calhoun, *Social History of the American Family*, Vol. III (New York: Noble, 1917), pp. 120–21.

[62]Ibid., p. 160.

[63]F. P. Milard, *What a Man Goes Through* (Christopher, 1925), pp. 57, 69 ff.

[64]Stow Persons, *The Decline of American Gentility* (New York: Columbia University Press, 1973), pp. 95–98; Robert Grant, *Unleavened Bread* (New York: C. Scribner's Sons, 1900); Robert Grant, *Fourscore: An Autobiography* (Boston: Houghton Mifflin Co., 1934).

[65]"Divorce in South Dakota," *Nation* (January 26, 1893); "The Marriage Scandal," *Nation* (May 18, 1899), 369; D. M. Means, "The Statistics of Divorce," *Nation* (June 18, 1891), 493–94; William O'Neill, *Divorce in the Progressive Era* (New Haven: Yale University Press, 1967).

[66]Edward Bok, "The Young Man in Business," *Cosmopolitan* (1894), 339.

[67]"Why is the Single Life Becoming More General?" *Nation* (March 5, 1868), 190–91; "Why Don't Educated Women Marry?" *Independent* (October 28, 1909), 966–69.

[68]Rafford Pyke, "What Men Like in Men," *Cosmopolitan* (August, 1902), 402–6.

[69]Julien Gordon, "Men's Women," *Lippincott's Monthly Magazine* (February, 1891), 248–51.

[70]Mona Caird, *The Morality of Marriage* (London: G. Redway, 1897), p. 96; William O'Neill, "Divorce in the Progressive Era," *American Quarterly* (Summer, 1965), 203.

[71]Grant Allen, "Plain Words on the Woman Question," *Popular Science Monthly* (December, 1889), 179.

[72]Edward Carperner, *Loves Coming of Age* (New York: M. Kennerly, 1911), pp. 32, 80–81.

[73]Lincoln Steffens, *Autobiography* (New York: Harcourt Brace Jovanovich, Inc., 1931), p. 153; Upton Sinclair, *Autobiography* (New York: Harcourt Brace Jovanovich, Inc., 1962), pp. 45–46.

[74]John S. Haller, Jr., and Robin Haller, *The Physician and Sexuality in Victorian America* (Urbana: University of Illinois Press, 1974), pp. 260–61; Ronald Walters, *Primers for Prudery* (Englewood Cliffs, N.J.: Prentice-Hall, Inc., 1974), pp. 50, 71; Rufus W. Clark, *Lectures on the Formation of Character, Temptations and Mission of Young Men* (Boston: J. P. Jewett, 1853), p. 191.

[75]William W. Sanger, *The History of Prostitution* (New York: Harper and Bros., 1858); Mathew Smith, *Sunshine and Shadow in New York* (Hartford: J. B. Burr and Co., 1869); J. D. McCabe, *New York by Sunlight and Gaslight* (Philadelphia: Douglas Brothers, 1882); David Pivar, *Purity Crusade* (Westport, Conn.: Greenwood Press, Inc., 1973), p. 31.

[76]*The Social Evil in Chicago: A Study of Existing Conditions* (Chicago: Vice Commission of Chicago, 1911), p. 70.

[77]Howard Woolston, *Prostitution in the United States* (Montclair, N.J.: Patterson Smith, 1921), pp. 77–78.

[78]Edwin O. Buxton, "The Social Evil and its Remedy," *American Journal of Politics*, III (1893), 39–50; John Burnham and Robert Riegel, "Changing American Attitudes towards Prostitution," *Journal of the History of Ideas*, XXIX (July–September, 1968), 437–52; David Pivar, *Purity Crusade* (Westport, Conn.: Greenwood Press, Inc., 1973), pp. 132–35.

[79]Lester F. Ward, *Dynamic Sociology* (New York: D. Appleton and Co., 1883), p. 629; Charles Washburn, *Come into My Parlor* (New York: National Library Press, 1936), pp. 103–5.

[80]Havelock Ellis, *Studies in Psychology of Sex* (New York: Random House, 1936), p. 312; John S. Haller, Jr., and Robin Haller *The Physician and Sexuality in Victorian America* (Urbana: University of Illinois Press, 1974), p. 249.

[81]Arthur Calhoun, *Social History of the American Family*, Vol. III (New York: Noble, 1917), pp. 190, 208.

[82]Oswald Schwarz, "The Prostitute and her Customers," in A. M. Kirch, ed., *Men: The Variety and Meaning of their Sexual Experiences* (New York: Dell, 1953), pp. 241–42; Howard Woolston, *Prostitution in the United States* (Montclair, N.J.: Patterson Smith, 1921), pp. 77–80.

[83]Grete Meisel-Hesse, *The Sexual Crisis* (New York: The Critic and Guide Co., 1917), pp. 167–68.

[84]John S. Haller, Jr., and Robin Haller, *The Physician and Sexuality in Victorian America* (Urbana: University of Illinois Press, 1974), p. 238.

[85]Lois Banner, *Women in Modern America* (New York: Harcourt Brace Jovanovich, Inc., 1974), p. 39.

[86]Helen Crew, "The Matter of Idling," *Outlook* (June, 1913), 381.

[87]Albert Shaw, *Outlook for the Average Man* (New York: Macmillan Publishing Co., 1907), p. 12.

[88]Quoted in Ernest Marchland, *Frank Norris: A Study* (New York: Octagon Books, Inc., 1942), pp. 102–3.

[89]Frank Norris, *McTeague* (New York: Boni and Liveright, Inc., 1899), pp. 25, 30.

[90]Ibid.; Donald Pizor, *The Novels of Frank Norris* (Bloomington: Indiana University Press, 1966), p. 21.

[91]Christopher Lasch, *The New Radicalism in America, 1889–1963* (New York: Random House, 1965), pp. 39–46.

[92]Rafford Pyke, "What Men Like in Men," *Cosmopolitan* (August, 1902), 402–3.

There is no place in the world for nations who have become enervated by soft and easy life, or who have lost their fibre of vigorous hardiness and masculinity.

Theodore Roosevelt

Although men are apt to deceive themselves in general matters, they rarely do so in particulars.

Machiavelli

5

THE
BULL MOOSE
MENTALITY

In the year after Theodore Roosevelt's death, Lawrence Abbott wrote, "I am inclined to think that Roosevelt was generally regarded by the public as preeminently a man's man."[1] Even before his legendary charge up San Juan Hill, Roosevelt was well known for his advocacy of the strenuous life, a philosophy that gave title to a book he wrote.[2] No other man of his time combined the essentials of the American masculine ethos quite like Theodore Roosevelt. His was the strenuous life personified. As for his place in American history, another writer summed it up by saying of Roosevelt that "he sought to make the national mind virile, daring, imaginative, aggressive, and eager for distinction in the world."[3] What is notable about Roosevelt is that although he grew up in a genteel Victorian home, he seemed to have overcome any taint of false or artificial acculturation so often associated with wealth and pleasure. Similar to Carlyle and

Kipling, Roosevelt thought the inactive, pleasure-seeking life was contemptible.

GROWING UP RUGGED

Unlike many American boys of his time, Roosevelt had a strong relationship with his father. Young Theodore saw the elder Roosevelt as "big and leonine at the same time that he was tender." No man matched his strength, and although he was a Christian, he did not have a "soft head." "My father was the best man I ever knew," Theodore was to proclaim later.[4] Yet the younger Roosevelt was not without a certain effeminate quality in his youth. He had a high-pitched, squeaky voice, a somewhat sickly physique, and asthma. The asthma, from which he sporadically suffered quite severely, has been interpreted by one Roosevelt scholar as having a significant bearing on the father–son relationship, for it was his father whom Theodore remembered walking the floors with him at night when breathing was difficult. Unlike many nineteenth-century middleclass fathers, the older Roosevelt seldom failed to supply maximum attention to his son—but not as a doting or condescending parent. By the time the boy was ten, Theodore Roosevelt's father was viewing his son's convalescence as very much within his own power. He urged him to get into shape, to push himself into the physical life. Hunting trips, mountain climbing, and the like were such frequent activities that physical perseverance became an all-encompassing value system for the maturing Roosevelt. By contrast, his mother had a fragile personality, a compulsive fear of dirt, and a haunting fear of being abandoned by her husband.[5]

Theodore's schooling was administered mostly by his father and private tutors. Of all the books he read, few influenced him as much as *The Last of the Mohegans*, a story about a vanishing weaker race's being taken over by a fitter civilization. That Roosevelt viewed American civilization in the same framework is documented by his lifelong concern about racial suicide, the fear that Anglo-Saxons would no longer be predominant among America's population, losing out to other racial groups. Roosevelt traveled widely, including a trip to Egypt, during which he hiked and hunted to the point of nearly exhausting his father. In Germany he took up boxing, sporting an occasional bloody nose and black eye, of which he seemed quite proud, no doubt because it demonstrated his aggressive masculinity and proved he was a tough young man who could "take it." He enrolled at Harvard, but academic exercises were not altogether to his liking precisely because they did not incorporate or complement the active, aggressive physical life to which he had become so accustomed. His problem, like that of Emerson, was one of how to have ideals and yet be a man who could act, inspire, and lead. Rigid pedagogy and formalized educational structures seemed bothersome and irrelevant.[6] Thus he wrote in his *Autobiography* that his Harvard education served him in only a most general sense. He got the most help and inspiration from personal contact with those professors to whom he was attracted. He gained a lot from sports, especially boxing, a sport he pursued while in the White House.[7] He abandoned the East in 1884, in part because of his health, and headed for Wyoming, where he invested in a cattle ranch. More important than the ranch, however, was the inspiration of Western life, which brought Roosevelt close to nature and back to the tests of hardiness and endurance faced by America's pioneers. His cathartic experiences as a big-game hunter and cowboy were what inspired his *Hunting Trips of a Ranchman*, *The Wilderness Hunter*, and *The Winning of the West*. Roosevelt filled his pages with both the facts of Western history and the human drama of Western exploration and settlement. It is readily evident that Roosevelt viewed these early Americans as the true standard bearers for Americans to emulate. Their relationship to nature made them strong of body and sound of character, as it indeed did for Roosevelt himself. Hunting was highly valuable to any young man because it got him close to nature and offered a chance to demonstrate manliness and hardiness, cornerstones of the strenuous life. The highest form of success, whether for the outdoorsman or the modern businessman, came to those who never shrank from danger or hardship, those who were intimately acquainted with "toil and effort and strife." Thus any study of Theodore Roosevelt that purports to focus on his intellectual and personal impact on Americans at the turn of the century cannot be complete without appreciating that crucial connection in Roosevelt's mind between the world of cowboys, hunters, and adventurers and the world of politics and power. The two were intimately linked: The tests of manly courage and tenacity encountered in one area made men especially capable in the other.[8]

With the passing of a genuine frontier in the West, Roosevelt's close friend and admirer Owen Wister kept the frontier image alive in novels like *The Virginian*. In this novel, dedicated to Roosevelt in 1902, Wister follows the adventures of the mysterious Virginian whose sensitive inner self is seldom revealed. What is seen is a physical and moral giant, a man of few words and shrewd action who could effectively deal with his fellow men and women. His strength and insight derived not from books or formal learning but from nature's schoolroom. Roosevelt could hardly fail to be impressed at the resoluteness of Wister's character: "Now back East you can be middling and get along. But if you go to try a thing on in this Western country, you've got to do it well."[9] "Fortunately," wrote Roosevelt in his autobiography, "Wister and Remington, with pen and pencil, have made these men live as long as our literature lives." The tales and the heroic actions of the Wister men were not overdrawn, Roosevelt maintained. Many men he worked with out West in the 1880s and soldiered with in Cuba "might have walked out of Wister's stories."[10]

VIGOR AND POLITICS

Roosevelt wrote in *Forum* that one thing that should never be "forgotten by the man desirous of doing good political work is the need of the rougher, manlier virtues, and above all the virtue of personal courage, physical as well as moral."[11] To do good work for the country, Roosevelt maintained that men must be able to hold their own in rough conflict, and be able to bravely suffer punishment and return it in kind. Men living in commercial nations, such as the United States, in which technology had eased the strain of life and increased refinement, ran a risk of growing soft, of losing their "virile fighting qualities." Every man should be taught to stand up for his rights, for the worst enemy of the republic was the coward. Speaking directly to youthful political aspirants, Roosevelt urged them to develop the virtues that the soldier had to have to succeed in battle, a forecast of that remarkable scene in 1912, when Roosevelt, dedicated o moral reform, led the new Progressive Party in singing their battle song, "Onward Christian Soldiers."[12]

Within the concept of progress had always been assumed abundant physical space and a Christian mission to extend the benefits of the virile Anglo-Saxon race to all nations. By 1890 doubt was in the air. Land to explore and settle was virtually gone, and in its place was growing a complicated urban society. To make matters worse, the new woman was perceived to be crowding the masculine domain. Roosevelt's significance lies in his assurance that in America there was still ample opportunity for manly types to control and dominate as they had always done. Roosevelt was confident that any man of adventurous tastes, wanting to maximize opportunities available to him, was beyond measure better off than were his forefathers.[13] In fact, it was possible for more men to travel, have adventure, and be active politically than ever before. Roosevelt argued that, because of modern developments in fields ranging from communication to transportation, it was possible for aggressive men to do more than men before them had ever done. What a tonic Roosevelt's words must have been to a generation of men who felt that life had passed them by, that all the great wars had been fought and causes won. Theodore Roosevelt was able to revitalize men on a personal level as progressivism sought to revitalize institutions on a national level. Everything Roosevelt typified, his courage, human sympathy, and "democratic interest in all sorts of men, when they were real men—attracted the attention of hundreds of young Americans of his own age. They felt, somehow or other, that he was a symbol of what young America could do if it tried."[14] Biographies of Roosevelt written around 1900 called him an "irresistible force." Edward Bok, editor of the *Ladies' Home Journal*, wrote that a talk with Roosevelt left one feeling as if mountains were the easiest things in the world to move. Most accounts agreed that Roosevelt was an ideal model for young boys to follow. It was as if Roosevelt were a surrogate father for a generation raised by too-stern mothers.[15]

A ROLE MODEL

The autobiographies and biographies of some of Roosevelt's contemporaries indicate how Roosevelt influenced them. Elihu Root, Roosevelt's Secretary of State, had suffered several personal rejections during his youth. His father was too busy at the college where he taught to spend as much time with his son as the son would have liked. His mother was a deeply religious woman who exerted a restraining influence in the home. By the time Elihu went off to Hamilton College, he saw himself as a mushy, undistinguished boy.* When he attempted to enlist in the army in 1861, he failed to pass the physical, so he continued his college education. While others fought gloriously for their country, Root was gaining the reputation of an intellectual. Eventually he asked Clara Wales to marry him, but he confessed to his mother that no woman could usurp the place she occupied in his heart. In a manner that was consistent with the pattern of the day, Root did not pay much attention to his wife after their marriage, yet she exercised a considerable influence over him.[16]

---

*The word *mushy* here is not used as the derisive term for someone who is romantic; rather, it refers to a "softness" or lack of boyishness in someone as compared with his peers.

Upon their first meeting, Root was at once overwhelmed by Roosevelt's "virile energy," later noting that everyone he knew was affected individually by Roosevelt. Root confessed an unabashed love for Roosevelt, claiming that the man could renew energies in those he met, just as Roosevelt himself was renewed by the touch of mother nature. What an example he set! The fact that Roosevelt had started out as a frail boy and grew to manly strength should make every American boy his follower. Stripped of all complicating, overcivilizing devices and influences, "[Roosevelt] was a man, not of sentiment or expression, but of feeling and of action."[17]

Roosevelt provided for many young men a model of masculine power and efficiency, which, in many cases, and for a variety of reasons, seemed to be lacking in their lives. The journalist Mark Sullivan attributed the outpouring of epigrams about Theodore Roosevelt to Roosevelt's "capacity for stimulation, the dynamic quality of his personality, the sheer quantity of it." Richard W. Child, a promising young novelist of the time, was quoted as saying that Roosevelt's "personality so crowds the room that the walls are worn thin and threaten to burst outward." Harold Ickes wrote that when Roosevelt died in 1919 something went out of him (Ickes) that he was never able to replace.[18]

Albert J. Beveridge, who represented Indiana in the Senate, was one of Theodore Roosevelt's strongest supporters and eventually presented the keynote address to the Progressive Party Convention in 1912. Born in 1862 and raised in a home dominated by a strong mother, Beveridge was another one of those Americans searching for a new father-leader to restore manliness and masculine purpose to America. Beveridge contributed a fascinating volume on how young men should face the world in the twentieth century. Books as a source of guidance were useless (except, of course, Beveridge's book) because books were artificial, but through nature one could discover what the life of a man should be. A man's life was rugged, challenging, and full of hard knocks. One could learn to cope with life by getting to know successful men and having manly companions. Beveridge advised his readers to visit men's clubs, hear men discuss manly ideas, and read Emerson's essays on self-culture. Most of all, the twentieth-century man needed to do real things and pursue real accomplishments. "Work, work, work," he advised, ". . . keep up your nerve, never despair, and success is certain, distinction probable, and greatness possible, according to your natural abilities."[19]

James R. McGovern has documented the persistence of this "virility impulse" in yet another anxious male of the time, the essayist and novelist David Graham Phillips. A good friend of Beveridge's when they attended DePauw University, Phillips had a strong-willed, dominating mother, much like Floyd Dell's. She was, in fact, a fanatic on the temperance question and conducted her household according to a rigid set of moral precepts. An older sister, Carolyn, also exerted a major influence on Phillips's life, to such an extent that she lived with him from 1902 to 1911, separating from her husband to do so. In other words, as McGovern interprets the facts of David Graham Phillips's life, he "never achieved mature maleness" and remained an "oral, passive personality type."[20] Phillips blamed women's devotion to culture and leisure for the restless condition of many early-twentieth-century men. Culture, he believed, was not human, "not in any way related to the human race," because those who were cultured lived a life apart, a stage life. Women had brought culture to modern civilization, and with it came impracticality and the waste of power and potential of men who had to supply the means for the women to acquire their culture. "Man is dominated by woman to an extent which she perhaps appreciates better than he," Phillips wrote.[21]

McGovern noted in his study that Phillips was disturbed about his passive disposition and therefore avoided "luxurious surroundings for fear they would soon eat all of the manhood out of me."[22] For instance, he resented those robber barons, the greedy, unscrupulous businessmen— "capitalists"—of the nineteenth century, who had allowed their wealth to render them soft and lazy. Such a lifestyle, according to Phillips, often resulted in self-complacency and weakened otherwise good strong men. He avoided culture because it suggested effeminacy and weakness. "If any symptoms of the artistic temperament appear, fight them to the death!"[23] In *The Reign of Gilt*, Phillips fantasized a strong, masculine. America contending against a decadent, cultural Europe. America would win out, he was sure, because Americans would not succumb to corrupt ideals. It was from this viewpoint that Phillips castigated the United States Senate as a millionaire's club, because it protected wealth rather than encouraged good character. In fact, the string of taboos in his novels and essays reflected Victorian morality about developing good character. For example, inherited wealth or marrying into wealth never produced a better man because inheritance was ultimately a sign of dependence. He resented automobiles because they made men fat, and Eastern colleges because they tended to emasculate their male students.[24] What mattered most to Phillips was that men be self-reliant, self-motivated, and self-confident, virtues any active, decisive man should possess. Phillips's concepts of the ideal man lay somewhere between the Nietzchean superman hero and the "Great Man as leader and inspirer" of Winston Churchill and the political philosopher Herbert Croly.

ROOSEVELT AND WHITE

One of Roosevelt's closest friends was William Allen White, editor of the *Emporia* (Kansas) *Gazette* and influential progressive Republican spokesman. White's attraction to Theodore Roosevelt reveals much about Roosevelt's profound psychological appeal to middle-aged men anxious about their status and their masculinity. White, born in 1868, was raised by his mother, a forceful, cultured woman who impressed on her son a keen sense of Puritan righteousness. White was fourteen when his father died, but the boy was not broken up at the time, although later he admitted that he should have been. "A boy of fourteen could not comprehend such a man as he was," White wrote in his autobiography, and added, "I have never ceased to sorrow that he did not stay with me for another twenty years, to help me."[25] White's boyhood was no constant frolic of adolescent playfulness and adventure, although, in one sense, young White wished it could have been. He hated fighting, probably because his mother taught him that it was unchristian and uncivilized. But as White matured, he began to suspect that he really was a sissy and a coward. His boyhood experiences provided the material for *The Court of Boyville*, a collection of short stories for boys. In these stories, latent tension exists between the naturally free primitive instincts of boyhood and the moral governance of stern parents, especially mothers, who restrain their sons from following their natural instincts. Mealy Jones's mother, for example, had been a "perfect little lady in her girlhood" (a perception of girls probably common to many little boys) who now was "molding her son in forms that fashioned her." The premise on which White based his stories was that boys should be free to run wild across the landscape to develop the individual ruggedness characteristic of strong-willed men. "There is a tincture of iron that seeps into a boy's blood with the ozone of the earth, that can come no other way," White wrote.[26] Natural instinct, not the artificial governance from a feminine, cultured viewpoint, was the key to the triumph of a new race of men. Boys needed a father's influence and example if they were to extend progress. But in White's case, and generally throughout the culture, as revealed in the literature of the period, fathers were absent. It was his mother's Republicanism, her yen for music, her theology, and her choice of books that surrounded him. When White went off to college, his mother accompanied him. After White got married, she lived in her son's house until he could afford to purchase the one next door for her.[27]

In June 1897, White found a new father. While in Washington, D.C., he was introduced to Theodore Roosevelt. The way White tells it, few first impressions could ever rival such a dramatic moment. "He sounded in my heart the first trumpet call of the new time that was to be. . . . [S]uch visions, such ideals, such hopes, such a new attitude toward life and patriotism and the meaning of things" made White ecstatic "with the splendor of [Roosevelt's] personality." White marveled at Roosevelt's masculinity, his hard-muscled frame, crackling voice, "the undefinable equation of his identity. . . . It was something besides his social status . . . quite apart from reason" that won White over.[28] To White, and men like him, who sensed a need for a forceful Christian reform movement at the dawn of the twentieth century, Roosevelt was an ideal leader. His masculinity contrasted sharply with the effeminate emotionalism of nineteenth-century reforms, the kind scorned by such men as the conservative Republican Senator Roscoe Conkling. On the other hand, Roosevelt was above boastful, exploitive paternalism. The strength of Roosevelt's masculinity lifted him above both the sentimental reformer and the crass politician. In *The Old Order Changeth*, a collection of political essays, White theorized that insofar as progressivism was instinctive and emotional it was feminine, but in its manifestation of power and dominance it was masculine. Roosevelt's great triumph was to supply and inspire a masculine power and dominance to make political and social reform appealing to a generation of men disturbed about the national trends towards plutocracy and an effeminate society and culture.[29]

White's concern that there be a restoration of masculine identity did not mean he categorically disapproved of American wives and mothers. They had provided their children, boys and girls, with valuable moral and cultural nourishment. But possibly mothers had succeeded too well, perhaps inadvertently, by shielding their sons from the harsh world. White himself, for example, was hardly Roosevelt's kind of man. He fainted at the sight of blood, was unathletic, and refrained from visits to such inner sanctums as the smoke-filled room. Although he spent his vacations at Estes Park, Colorado, a veritable hunter's paradise, he neither hunted nor fished.[30] White even fretted about the modern concept of Christ, writing to Roosevelt that it was essentially an effeminate one, portraying an image of a "pale, feminine, wishy-washy, other-worldly Christ [that] has grown out of the monkish idea of religion." Morally conscious women had brought Christianity to its present condition in the general absence of men, and White yearned for a new impression of Christ that was relevant to the age.[31]

In the same letter to Roosevelt in which White expressed a desire for a new interpretation of Christ, he praised Kathleen Norris's new novel, *Mother.* The story's heroine, little Margaret, lived with her family in New York, but, like many young girls of the age, she grew bored and restless with the dull routine of a young girl's life. ("Nothing ever happens to me. . . .") Ultimately she escaped from her family to become secretary to a prominent society woman. But it finally dawns on Margaret (and it pleased White immensely) that her mother's life of devotion to her family and the performance of her routine home duties is the most meaningful life for a woman. The commonplace life was, after all, the natural life, truly richer than the artificial existence of women who craved status, culture, and mobility. That White should praise such a novel indicates his own dispute with feminism, in that he felt that it tended to threaten the natural order of the world that he and many other males assumed was part of a sacred trust.[32]

Roosevelt was seen as the kind of virile male who was rescuing America from corruption without effeminizing American institutions in the process. By 1912, White was growing confident that American men were capable of sustaining their resurrected masculine identity; America's adolescence was over—the youth had been made strong thanks to Roosevelt's splendid example of male vigor and assertiveness. In 1912, William Allen White did not at first encourage his friend's renewed presidential aspirations. In the long run, the nation would benefit if the new, mature generation of men fended for themselves rather than follow Roosevelt for another four years. "We need a brother and not a master nor a servant," wrote White to Roosevelt, who had been a good father, but the sons were now experienced and adept, primed for their own manly heroics. Nevertheless, Roosevelt ran in 1912, and White supported him, as did four million other Americans, a million of whom according to White, were "Teddy votes—votes of men who had confidence in you personally without having any particular intelligent reason to give why; except that you were a masculine sort of person with extremely masculine virtues and palpably masculine faults."[33]

ROOSEVELT AND REFORM

White's comment reveals much of the emotional basis of progressive reform. In his autobiography, Roosevelt wrote that he had been unimpressed by the reformers of the 1880s. They had been handicapped because they were not real men; they had suffered from an overrefinement that rendered them unable to "grapple with real men in real life."[34] Yet Roosevelt perceived the political reform and economic change in America in the late nineteenth century that would create for white middle-class American males a new field of personal worth and accomplishment. According to Stuart Sherman, the Rooseveltian personality persuaded men "that there are a hundred more interesting things than making money, all 'worth while.' "[35] Traditionally, men had traveled, hunted, and gone to war, but now they were being urged to investigate reforming, governing, and organizing new parties. According to Roosevelt, the unimaginative plutocratic psychology of the Gilded Age following the Civil War had emphasized only material success. Mark Twain had said it earlier: "That government is not the best which secures mere life and property." Twain argued for "a more valuable thing—manhood," because it symbolized courage, decency, and forthrightness.[36] By the end of the nineteenth century, traditional concepts of manly success had helped produce a "psychology of efficient, militant, imperialistic nationalism."[37]

Roosevelt was both a fighter and reformer, a man who could and did blend the best of both worlds. He could fight well, but he demanded a fair fight for a moral cause. Roosevelt hated the bully and cheater because they were never manly. Such men were dependent, relying on means beyond their capabilities and power to achieve success. Roosevelt busted trusts, fought corruption, and championed conservation to promote equal opportunity for all men to succeed and realize a proud sense of masculine fulfillment. By 1912 the new emphasis of the progressives was on cooperation and togetherness, which varied considerably from the classic individualism that frontier America cherished. The heroes in popular magazine stories and novels were changing from strong-willed, powerful businessmen to socially conscious reformers and businessmen. In 1915 Edward Bok wrote that a man could no longer be evaluated only on the basis of the abilities he could demonstrate in making money but had to demonstrate his worth as he applied those abilities to the betterment of his fellow men.[38]

White qualified his emphasis on a renewed vigorous masculine identity for American men by observing still another aspect of Roosevelt's style. For all his action and gusto as a fighter and crusader, Roosevelt was, White reminded his readers, still a "Harvardian, a person of erudition who knew about music, painting, sculpture, history, poetry—the softer, finer things of life."[39] White perceived in Roosevelt two men gazing on the world. One was primitive, impetuous, and vigorous; the other was sophisticated, "not quite ever furtive, but often feline." Moreover, there was in Roosevelt a trace of deeply supressed femininity that sometimes "flicked catwise out of his subconscious," as the President "clicked his glittering ivory teeth while purpose was surging from impulse into measured words." When Roosevelt acted and spoke in his manly way, there was that hint of his great-grandmother's sternness hiding in the moustached smile. But, White assured his readers, "she was always a minority report," advising him on moral issues but never dominating the masculine side of his personality.[40] The Progressives were anxious about their virility in a changing social order but were not necessarily hostile to the influence of feminism and suffrage. It was masculine dominance that mattered, not the defeat of women's issues. One male writer noted in the *Independent* that women should keep to their own sphere of activity. Women had historically ordered society and defined the customs and services for human improvement. As government had become more organized and centralized, human services had improved, an indication that the process of government had moved closer to the women's sphere. While men were urged to participate in organizing society, Irving Bacheller wrote, they should not do so at the expense of women.[41] Yet women were told again and again to recognize their limitations. Suffrage still bothered some men more than any other issue because it threatened to upset the power of purely masculine institutions, such as the military. Henry Wood, president of the Aero Club of America, testified before a congressional committee that "it is a damnable thing that we should weaken ourselves by bringing into the war the woman, who has never been permitted in the war tents of any strong, virile, domineering nation."[42]

REFORM AND WOMEN

Roosevelt conveniently sidestepped the suffrage issue, saying that it really did not matter much. He had, however, written his senior dissertation at Harvard on equalizing men and women before the law. Roosevelt's New Nationalism in 1912 endorsed just about every social reform issue, including the suffrage. And why not? What the women's movement had done since the 1890s could be appreciated by progressive men on the basis of practicality, fairness, and the elimination of corruption and waste, objectives clearly within Roosevelt's reform framework. Andrew Sinclair noted, and correctly it seems, that a central feature of progressivism was the perpetuation of Victorian morality, that it was the woman's duty to help the unfortunate and solve the problems of an urban society. The woman who complained in the *Independent* that American men were guilty of "mammonolatry" was stating what many men and women had come to believe. That the American male was "losing his soul" and prostituting his manly vigor for material success helped promote the progressive ideal that American patriarchs had lost sight of the country's spiritual idealism and that women needed to help restore it.[43]

In one of the prosuffrage arguments was a demand for genuine personal and sexual equality of women in business or in bed. Seen in this perspective, the feminist contributions to progressivism were generally acceptable to progressive males, and, in fact, some welcomed the additional help women gave on some of the issues. Furthermore, many men were confident that they could control the female vote. Since sex roles were not basically changing, both the masculine mystique (of power over women) and the feminine mystique (of wife and motherhood), remained intact. Roosevelt, for example, believed explicitly that the race could be improved only by its mothers, and that motherhood was still the primary duty of women, just as men were to be the organizers and providers.[44]

Another point of view was that stronger and more vigorous women made for stronger and more vigorous men. Inherent in this attitude is the Victorian concept that women possessed the capacity to transform men through the sheer influence of superior moral attributes. This theme can be found in several novels by David Graham Phillips, Winston Churchill, William Allen White, and Frank Norris. In Norris's *Moran of the Lady Letty*, Ross Wilbur, a dignified businessman and Yale graduate, mysteriously disappears and winds up on a ship, *The Lady Letty*, upon which he experiences supreme adventure on the high seas with a mannish woman companion named Moran. She had "heavy brows . . . knotted over flaming eyes." In steering the ship and clearly assuming leadership, she makes Ross feel totally inferior. "I could never love a man," she confesses, and a distinct vision comes to Ross that this isolated female creature is beautiful in her own way: "as yet without sex, proud, untamed, splendid in her savage, primal independence—a thing untouched and unsullied by civilization."[45] It was a strong sensation to behold something so pure and to realize that to love Moran as Ross knew love existed would be a humiliation—a degradation to her. Her willpower and independence inspires Ross and transforms him. When Moran and Ross Wilbur are overtaken by some pirates, they have to fight for their lives. The struggle ignites the latent primal instincts in Wilbur, which becomes patently obvious when he kills one of the intruders. "All that was strong and virile and brutal in him seemed to harden and stiffen in the moment after he had seen the beachcomber collapse limply on the sand under that last strong knife blow."[46] Ross finds himself and from this point on becomes a dominant leader. Ross Wilbur, with Moran, makes it back to civilization, whereupon his identity is soon discovered by the prominent society men who had wondered at his disappearance. Ross tries to tell of his transformation and the prospects of a new life of adventure he now sees before him. But how can he explain it to stale city clubmen? When he discusses his plans, his friend Jerry is struck by the incredibility of it all and dismisses it as a passing fancy. But Ross Wilbur's masculinity has been restored: "Did you ever kill a man, Jerry? No? Well, you kill one someday—kill him in a fair give-and-take fight—and see how it makes you feel, and what influence it has on you, and then come back and talk to me."[47] The moral of this adventure tale seems to be that man's proper role is to be a man's man and that a woman must be a man's woman in order for him to achieve a proper masculine identity. Moran and Ross Wilbur discover this through their cathartic experiences together. *Blix*, written a year after *Moran*, is another tale about a mannish woman who has a significant effect on a man. In this novel, Blix strongly resembles Norris's wife, Jeanette. In the novel, Blix inspires Condy Rivers, a writer, to become more of a man.[48]

In his study of Phillips, McGovern carefully points out that a close reading of his novels reveals a similar theme in which power and freedom for women are essential for men to be happy and successful. The traditional women, who relied so heavily on their husbands for their life's needs, sapped their men's strength, drawing condemnation from Phillips, as they did from Robert Herrick. Phillips also despised pretentious, naive "crybaby" women because they fostered the worst form of weakness and sentimentalism among men. The women whom Phillips favored in his novels had hard characteristics and their homes were a secondary interest to them. They were independent and observed a single moral standard. Such strong women were highly functional because they could indulge their husbands' covert passivity and yet reinforce independence and an aggressive temperament. Taken to the extreme, several of Phillips's male characters even sought mistreatment from women. "I know I deserve any punishment you choose to give. . . . And I'll take it. Only I want to stay on here and have your friendship." Another male character, after being ridiculed by his fiancée, responds, "Your anger sets me on fire. You are superb! I never wanted you so."[49] As Elisabeth Woodbridge noted, "at certain periods and in certain moods [a man] strongly desires to meet the standards set for him by women," although he struggles almost all of the time to meet the expectations and standards of other men.[50]

REFORM AND CHRIST

It has been generally acknowledged that progressivism had many of the features of a Christian revival. One can even argue that progressivism might be considered the logical outcome of the social gospel movement of the late nineteenth century. It was moralistic and idealistic, and its spiritual energy was incendiary. To a leading theologian of the day, Walter Rauschenbusch, the high purpose of Christianity was to "transform human society into the Kingdom of God by regenerating all human relations and reconstituting them in accordance with the will of God."[51] Such a vision implied reform, but reform and reformers were not highly regarded in the nineteenth century. They were seen as artificial, effeminate, soft compromisers who could not successfully struggle with the world as it was and, therefore, wanted to change it. Roosevelt radically altered the perception of the reformer as a weak, unmasculine type into the image of vigorous, forceful manhood. The urban industrial environment was chaos and confusion that twentieth-century men would have to subdue and control just as their predecessors had subdued and controlled the wilderness. No true man would shrink from any conflict and strife that destiny had prepared him to face. Roosevelt's function as a historian and his participation in sports reminded American men of the bravery and courage they were expected to maintain. By 1912, Roosevelt was ready to lead the progressive Christian soldiers marching as to war.

Another aspect of the altered vision of the Christian reformer was the new image of Christ as manly and forceful. In 1880, Thomas Hughes, author of *Tom Brown's School-Days*, published *The Manliness of Christ*. Hughes, who had traveled widely in Europe and America, was disturbed by a popular contention that the kind of men who joined the Y.M.C.A. lacked manliness. Hughes stated that Christianity was considered a basically passive religion, appealing to the fears and timidity in men, but Hughes rejected this opinion, and the idea that Christianity was responsible for weakness. "The conscience of every man recognizes courage as the foundation of manliness, and manliness as the perfection of human character, and if Christianity seems counter to conscience in this matter, or indeed in any other, Christianity will go to the wall." Hughes emphasized that Christianity preached perfection of character. And as character was central to manliness, modern Christianity could hardly be considered by young men as something unmanly.[52]

In 1906, Carl Case wrote that the same feminine invasion into journalism, literature, and business had overtaken religion. In their church groups and club organizations, women had come to dominate the church and had effeminized Christianity. The female had become the arch priestess of religion, while many men had fallen away from close religious association during the nineteenh century. According to Case, a study of the Bible revealed tension between masculine and feminine forces, culminating with Jesus, who was seen as basically passive. Jesus was a meek and humble man who advocated a philosophy of turning the other cheek. Unfortunately, Case argued, the passive nature of Jesus had been exaggerated by excesses of sentimental altruism carried out in his name. Moreover, modern art portrayed a very mild-mannered Jesus, with dreamy eyes, long hair, and a resigned expression.[53] In a book about the training of boys, it was strongly advised that the church change the image of Jesus to a masculine and heroic one. Specifically, it meant that Jesus should appear to be emotionally volatile and domineering rather than be seen as a teacher.[54]

CHRIST AS HE-MAN

Together with Robert Conant, Harry E. Fosdick, Jason Pierce, and Alfred T. Mahan, Case asserted that modern man needed an image of a virile, energetic Jesus Christ. "The masculine military side of religion as portrayed in the Bible is too often overlooked because women are more religious than men."[55] Robert Conant argued that "Christian art and Christian preaching need a strong tonic of virility. . . . The men of a strenuous age demand a strenuous Christ." Conant criticized the art and painting responsible for shaping the modern image of Jesus. According to Conant, from every indication in the Bible it should be absolutely clear that Jesus must have had strong masculine facial features. Focusing upon the verse in the Gospel according to John that "Jesus increased in wisdom and stature," Conant's interpretation was that Jesus was a physically strong, robust individual, the very essence of manliness. He attributed to Jesus every kind of moral and physical courage. That Jesus was Jewish was dismissed by Conant, who claimed that Jesus was actually quite occidental, resembling the modern Anglo-Saxon.[56]

In the best tradition of nineteenth-century guidebook literature, Conant praised Christ's practicality and his natural, uncomplicated, straightforward style. Moreover, Jesus was a family man, even though he was never married, because upon his father's death he assumed leadership of his family. As Conant traced Christ's career, he made his subject conform to the self-made-man image, and even though Jesus ultimately died for his cause to redeem the world, Conant, of course, saw Jesus as the ultimate successful hero. For example, like all self-made men, Jesus had a plan of action that he pursued courageously and to which he steadfastly held, even though it alienated him from friends and family. Conant's theme was meant to appeal to many American men whose plans were not understood by their orthodox and tradition-bound mothers. Jesus never shirked his duty and confidently saw a struggle through.[57]

If Christ's true nature could only be understood, it would present modern man with a "splendid endowment of masterful virility." The tragedy of modern man was that the noble ideas of Christianity had been emasculated by women. It was even contended that the passive voice in writing and speech had become common, another indication of how passive modern life was. Twentieth-century man was left without a means of salvation because he had been denied a virile Christ to whom he could pray. Man's basic confidence in himself was undermined, replaced by what Conant called "fearthought," an attitude of conscious or unconscious inferiority, the opposite of self-reliance and self-confidence. Fearthought bred such common traits as "fear, dread, timidity, worry, anxiety, suspicion." These weaknesses formed the basis of discontent, unhappiness, egotism, conceit, servility, nervousness, indecision, inefficiency, pessimism, self-pity, failure, and even suicide. So afflicted was modern man that he no longer had an ability to master his environment and take charge of his life. But all was not lost to negativism and doubt. "Let the man of great physical vigor follow Christ by using his [Christ's] strength to help the helpless and protect the weak."[58] Putting into theological terms what William Allen White had expressed about the feminine and masculine aspects of progressivism, Conant wrote that "that Personality [Christ's]

presents to the world a marvelous blending of masculine force and initiative with feminine purity, a man's logic with a woman's intuition and delicacy—a perfect psychic cycle."[59]
Alfred T. Mahan focused his attention on the power of Jesus in a book he wrote for men, *The Harvest Within*. "Motive and Power; in these comprehensive words, which admit, and indeed in the end, require, large expansion, we have what Jesus Christ is to us."[60] What men needed was a reasonable assurance for practical action, a strong faith in Christ's power. For Mahan, the Resurrection was the most powerful act in history that could inspire such faith: that God had given Jesus this power and had created men to be powerful. That Jesus' body and spirit rose from the dead was evidence for Mahan that God wanted men to think in terms of unity. If man were going to extend the Christian mission, then, "it is necessary that the war-cry be one, that men speak with one tongue, and behold! they can!" Mahan perceived God as a strong masculine figure, capable of vengeful anger when necessary. The New Testament, with its preachment of love, had been misinterpreted, having been read as an argument against forceful action. Agreeing with other contemporary versions of Jesus, Mahan saw him as forceful, virile, and as proof that through struggle one gained strength and vitality to execute the Christian mission. The settlement of America was one high point on the whole course of human history in which strength and vitality had been determining factors. But the struggle was not over, because corruption threatened everywhere. As America was effeminized, did it have the power to withstand the infiltration of corrupting alien forces? Mahan's book reminded Americans of God's example for all people to fight to free the nation from corruption. Prayer was action, according to Mahan, and was necessary for all Christian men if they were to lead active, forceful lives.[61]

In 1910, there was a series of men-and-religion conferences that comprised representatives from the Y.M.C.A. and various church brotherhoods. From the meetings came the Men and Religion Forward Movement, the purpose of which was to recruit men and boys back into active church work, in which they might contribute manly leadership to the spiritual life of the nation. According to Fayette Thompson of the Methodist Brotherhood, there were too many men who felt no particular responsibility for the proper use of their manhood. The movement stressed "a sane, a virile, a Christian recognition of the place of social service in the new program" for getting men back into Christian activity. The rhetoric of the movement was not unlike that found in the guidebook literature of the nineteenth century. For example, much was made of good character and responsible individualism. Within the grasp of every nan was the power to overcome indifference and passivity in a society in which too frequently those qualities had become common.[62]

FATHERS AND SONS

Another significant dimension of the masculine progressive ideology was the new and serious attention given to fatherhood and the father–son relationship. Most fathers had become so deeply preoccupied with business concerns they had deserted sons and daughters, leaving their children's moral instruction to mothers. Concern was being expressed that too many American boys were being effeminized by overbearing mothers. As domestic discipline increased, one critic warned that a young boy would resist it like a "creeping paralysis and seek out those masculine hideaways where he can shed kid gloves, hide his white necktie in his pocket, and assert his manhood."[63] As early as the Civil War, it was noted that the industrial and business toll on the family was devastating, as "the weary came home to the weary," according to one account. The same author continued that "[t]here are fathers in our community who are almost strangers to their own children."[64] Foreign observers were struck by the estrangement of fathers in their own home. Fathers were mere "units" of the family, without any noticeable connections with other family members. Unlike his European counterpart, an American father felt fulfilled when his sons scattered. It was assumed that their removal from home, as soon as possible, was a positive sign of the sons' masculine maturity.[65]

When men began to feel the impact of serious social and cultural competition from women, concern about the father's role began to re-emerge. By spending so much of their spare time away from the home, at the lodge and club, fathers were depriving their offspring of some vital elements of character that they might have acquired from a closer companionship. Writing about child development from a medical point of view, H. L. Taylor pleaded for the assertion of a stronger paternal role, implying that a healthier child would result. Taylor called for fewer store-bought toys for children and more physical recreation, as provided by sports. Another author contended that if the roots of intimate contact with a father were not made during childhood, it would be impossible to achieve a complete father-and-son relationship.[66] Margaret Mead has taken this problem somewhat further by examining two types of fathers in the America of the

1880s who reflect two different social classes. For upper-class families who were wealthy or professionally well established, there was incentive for a son to strike out on his own, to be like his father. Fathers in this social class were very often estranged from their sons by the long hours they spent away from home, working at their businesses and keeping up social contacts. Usually they sent their sons away to the best prep schools and colleges when they came of age. Lower-class sons, on the other hand, had fathers whom they could not really respect because they often had low-paying, low-status jobs. In both family structures, however, sons were raised by mothers who protected them and warned of evil dissipations (e.g., the squandering of time on such pursuits as gambling and drinking) in the big bad world of their fathers.[67]

In some families, however, Victorian moral standards made fathers appear so righteous that they were alienated from their sons. Max Eastman recounted how his father's stature provoked a pathos that set him apart from the family and brought tears to his son's eyes. As a minister, his father was a very pious man with splendid moral courage, but his son sensed that he lacked toughness and the temperament of the rebel. Eastman's grandfather, however, was regarded as a real man who smoked and drank and had a genuine pioneer history, having tracked through the Wisconsin wilderness. But his grandfather was a remorseful figure who realized that the end of his way of life was near as industrialism encroached upon what had been the wild.[68]

The debilitating effect that business failure had on father–son relationships is graphically illustrated in Floyd Dell's autobiography. The conventional wisdom of the culture, learned from his mother, had conditioned young Floyd to assume that heroic men in America were materially successful. Dell's father had not been a success, although he had tried hard to do well for his family. Nevertheless, it disillusioned his son, who rejected his unsuccessful father as any kind of adequate model or mentor. One night in 1896, the Dell house caught fire, and father and son fought the blaze, doing something together for the first time. The son began to relate to his father after that, became interested in his Civil War stories, and began to see his father as a real man, although an unfortunate victim of economic circumstances. Dell began to blame the church and the conventional Christian respectability, as preached by his mother, for making a mockery of his father. Dell turned to atheism and eventually to socialism in a search for the true meaning of life, and to work out his masculine identity within a new frame of reference. He met Eugene V. Debs in

Chicago and wished that his father had been there to gain his inspiring insights into the evils of capitalism that were destroying men. "American respectability had taken my father away from me. Socialism has given me a chance to get him back."[69]

Business success or some form of material accomplishment had been an important indication of good masculine character. But it put American fathers on the spot, as was the case with Floyd Dell's father. American fathers were expected to provide for their children a life that was better than the one they had experienced. Children were supposed to be better educated and have more opportunities than their parents had had. It meant that fathers were in a perpetual state of trying to achieve more and often were frustrated at having to accept less when economic cycles turned against them or luck ran out. Geoffrey Gorer has argued that many young American men were upset by the realization, which came sooner or later, that their fathers were actually uneasy and dissatisfied with their stations in life. Moreover, the emphasis on "giving [their] children a better life" left fathers vulnerable to the implication of not really succeeding very well or well enough themselves. The groundwork was laid for a rejection of fathers. The problem can be seen to be particularly acute for immigrant fathers and sons; as immigrants had to adopt the ideals and customs of American culture, they had to reject Old World values and culture. In America, employment took men away from families and into factories and mines for long hours where they toiled without recognition and with minimal pay. Certainly a son could do better than "the old man." Even if a father owned a business, a son was expected to do better at something else or take the business over and expand it when a father retired. The pressure of never being satisfied with the way things were was not nearly so intensely felt in Europe. In America, sons seldom thought of their fathers as "great men." Often, sons failed to understand their fathers' frustration and low social status, which were held as marks against them.[70] Sons turned again to mothers, as they had always done, as Floyd Dell did when he doubted his father's manliness. Meanwhile, mothers continued to supply the emotional needs of their sons, while fathers suffered through their experiences in silence. It was one result of crass selfhood. In the case of the Dells and the Jameses (see discussion in Chapter 3), fathers and sons both struggled for masculine identity in a society highly confusing to them. The sharpness of sex-role differentiations that excluded love from fatherhood strained communication.

As the power and influence of women increased, one writer placed partial blame for the masculine-identity confusion on the inadequacy of the father in the lives of young daughters. The chief defect in rearing young girls lay in the fact that females matured in an atmosphere too intensely emotional. A father's experience in the world at large would help neutralize this emotionalism and reduce the feminine frivolousness accompanying it. Most of all, just as it was important for fathers to be heroic in their sons' eyes and set an appropriate model of conduct and accomplishment, daughters needed the same kind of reinforcement. Once a daughter understood her father, she would have a much better idea of what a "manly, honorable man" should be. She would be able to woo a better mate and blend together that "force and fire" that go into the making of a man.[71]

Most authorities still contended, however, that "to train children is primarily the mother's job." Mothers were at home, and it seemed only natural that they should make the decisions about clothes, health matters, manners, and the early rudiments of education. Male authority was seriously weakened because fathers had simply, without protest, conceded their wives' claim that they were responsible for the spiritual tone of the household. And because it had been left to the mother to set the spiritual tone, it meant that the father, like the children, was subject to her moral standards. In the larger context, during the Progressive era the absence of male authority was one reason why secondary institutions such as grammar school and Sunday school were assuming more and more responsibility for children. Arthur Calhoun agreed with an English critic of American fathers who saw them as tame cats, with their masculine role virtually eclipsed in the family. Many fathers were just around, leading a very passive existence in the household, while family members went about the business of daily living, planning vacations, and being sociable. The husband–father was usually generous, seldom denying what a wife claimed was necessary for the family's welfare.[72]

If it were true that mothers had taken over the family and the raising of children, then what was left for a father to do? In searching for an answer to this question, Edward Martin wrote that fathers were merely a convenience to have around, if only to enforce a mother's point of view—based upon father's experience gained beyond the front gate. Martin likened the father's role to that of a ship's captain. The mates do all the work aboard the ship; they boss the crew (comparable to the children), steer the ship, and get it through the storms. "Nevertheless, the habit of having a captain persists. What seems to be expected of them is, mostly, to think and to be on hand if they are needed." Martin continued, however, that a good father should be more than this, especially when children were passing from the age of tutelage to the age of emancipation. Boys especially needed a father as they reached their late teens, because fathers were experienced in the ways of men and could offer advice. Modern education introduced girls to concepts of independence. Their new hopes strained maternal patience and filial affection because the new thinking was at such a variance with tradition. A good father was needed to moderate these conflicts, to keep mother and daughter civil. After all, a father, according to Martin's analysis, was a "fellow subject" in the "beneficient tyranny" of the home, and, therefore, he was in a position to reach some understanding with the children. This view of fathers was hardly complimentary to men, who apparently dominated everything but their own homes. Revealed is a glaring inability of mothers and fathers to arrive at any sense of mutuality and shared responsibility for their children.[73]

ATTAINING MANHOOD

The absence of fathers from homes and the alienation from their sons, which many fathers had come to accept as the common pattern of American life, drew sharp criticism from many men interested in the welfare of the family, and especially that of boys. One study, by Thomas Clark, Dean of Men at the University of Illinois, surveyed high-school boys who had grown up between 1900 and 1920. Clark concluded that the sympathetic father who took his son into his confidence to talk frankly about the changes and issues facing his boys was "so rare as to be a negligible quantity in the discussion of the boy and his problems."[74] Ninety-five percent of the boys reported that they had had little or no discussion about sex with their fathers (which may have been true even for boys who had had close relationships with their fathers). Many boys, in fact, often identified with a sports hero, rather than with their fathers, as "the man" in their lives. The sports star demonstrated the qualifications necessary for manliness: full physical development, accomplishments, prowess, and courage. It was Clark's opinion that most fathers did not want their sons to follow their line of work, because, in most cases, it had been only hard labor without sufficient reward. It was common, however, for boys to want to mature quickly, in order to be accepted by their peers in school. If they got too involved with girls, they were usually "weakened," considered "soft and mushy." Associating with girls undermined interest in physical, masculine acitivities, and the boy would develop "feminine rather than masculine traits," a trend all fathers would surely deplore and seek to correct.[75]

Edwin Puller urged fathers to do their part in shaping the physical, mental, moral, and spiritual sides of their boys, to be active in what he considered God's noblest work, the making of a man.[76] Luther Gulick sharply contrasted the old forms of mother love and the passive form of father love. Modern times made it evident, according to Gulick, that a good father was as important as a good mother. During the war years, the role of fatherhood became more significant as a means of developing a son's strong, masculine inclination and, one suspects, one way of reasserting the power of men in the wake of female suffrage. T. W. Galloway was sad about the passing of the old ways: "Unfortunately for our ease and peace of mind, those good old days are gone, and we fathers have fallen upon bad times."[77] Yet a good father could still take the lead, for example, in helping his boys repress the natural sex impulses, but not as autocratically as mothers had done in the past. A good way for fathers to lead their sons through the troubling "sex questions" was to apply the substitution method. It was recommended that a father take his son camping and hiking and participate in other manly enterprises to "use up" the sexual energy of the young man. Most of all, because modern boys yearned for masculine models and advice after suffering generations of female domination in the home, modern fathers were advised to always be truthful with their sons. After all, they only wanted to be men, with "manly muscles, manly shape and proportions of body, manly voice and manner, manly spirit and courage, and manly ambitions."[78]

Gulick stressed that the modern boy should, more than ever, aspire to manliness and that the father was in the best position to advise and encourage good companionship and competition. The good father should help arouse a feeling of disgust and indignation for anything unmanly and help set an example of what it was to be a superior man. A boy should be told about the great men of his community, and emphasis should be given to the qualities needed to be a great man, such as bravery, honor, loyalty, fairness, and self-control. The boy should be given fiction full of vigorous heroes. Using all these examples, fathers could succeed in establishing what was manliness and help fashion the will of a young son to achieve it.

Gulick stressed that fathers would have to spend a greater portion of their time to act as fathers because the stakes were too high to neglect these duties any longer.[79]

Judging from the amount writtten on the subject, however, one can hardly be convinced that any of these recommendations was being successfully followed. Reports frequently cited the degeneracy and the effeminization of American boys. Behavior not in keeping with the Victorian preparation for a noble and virile manhood was commonly cited. Regardless of the truth of these charges, it is clear that many American parents and observers were anguished by the moral and physical condition of adolescent males.

Not all commentators accepted the doom-and-despair view of childhood behavior, however. Edgar Moon and George Fiske advised that boys be understood not so much in terms of deterministic moral precepts but rather in terms of their natural energies and inclinations. Fiske, a theology professor at Oberlin, conceded that Americans were losing their boys to something less than the manly standards of the past. American fathers were partly to blame for the waywardness of American boys. Because of the preoccupation with the order and rigors of business and success, fathers had no imaginative equipment to appreciate their sons' desires and yearnings. The contribution Fiske and Moon wanted to make was a reminder to parents that a boy's senses were basically savage, and that boys derived meaning from sensory experience. Fiske recommended that adolescent males be encouraged to recover their basic savage and barbarous instincts, a theme also articulated by Veblen, Norris, and others. Even if boys were occasionally crude, there was more harm to be done by repressing these instincts or showing alarm at them. Thus, in direct contrast to a nineteenth-century view, Moon argued that "the will should not be broken—that would leave the child a weakling; it should not be unreasonably suppressed." Unless boys had sufficient opportunity to vent their aggression, they would become passive, lack ambition and courage, and possibly damage their early manhood. Fiske contended that there was something wrong with any boy who grew up passive, hesitant, and reflective. More than likely such a boy would become eccentric and fail to achieve manly fulfillment. On the other hand, overactive boys, especially those who were aggressive, needed to be acquainted with older boys, who could humble the younger temperaments. But whether boys were aggressive or passive, Moon and Fiske agreed that great harm could be done by too much parental interference.[80]

SCHOOLS AND BOYHOOD

The public schools came under attack for interfering too often in the natural playfulness and activity of male students. Specifically, the problem was *"the overwhelming preponderance of women's influence in our public schools"*; many progressive reformers agreed. It was said that women were good at teaching facts but failed to understand the whole boy as well as men did.[81] Some critics complained that the women teachers were often more manly than the men teachers, creating confusion regarding models for the boys to follow. The conclusion of these writers was that there was not necessarily a need for more men in the schools "but more man" in the men who went into teaching. Thomas Davidson complained that American education was in chaos because educators had forgotten the fundamentals of freedom. The first step in educating American boys was to have them understand freedom, which was basically self-realization. Unfortunately, however, self-realization was being lost to the detriment of masculine development.[82]

A commission on education blamed the predominance of female teachers for the low average attainment by males in the schools. The report stated that although it might be possible to educate boys and girls together in the early years of school, "we must sooner or later come to admit that it is wrong to do so during the later years if the object be to develop a virile man." The report continued, with a note of regret, that "the boy in America is not being brought up to punch another boy's head or to stand having his own punched in a healthy and proper manner; that there is a strange and indefinable feminine air coming over the men; a tendency towards a common . . . sexless tone of thought."[83]

What to do about this "sexless tone," the loss of virility in schools as in society, was a major issue for progressive educators and reformers. Some urged segregation of boys and girls, Many, like William Allen White, urged that more men be attracted to public-school teaching through higher salaries and better incentives. The function of education, White believed, ought to be to "direct the conscience of the people toward wisdom" and "turn their hearts to that common sense . . . conduct known as righteousness." But women, because of their station in life, which was oriented towards culture and ideals, were too abstract, too theoretical, too artificial, that is, too void of masculine realism to be effective with young males. White argued, perhaps because of his personal lack of a strong male model as a youth, that young men desperately needed males with whom they could identify. How could a boy become aware of a man's world if he did not have firsthand experience with a man's ruggedness? Failure to provide a proper masculine example increased the chance of juvenile delinquency. The necessity of a proper masculine stimulation in education was all the more crucial in light of the vast immigration to the United States since 1880. White, Roosevelt, and numerous other progressives worried about race preservation if the virile Anglo-Saxon traditions were not properly protected and extended through education.[84] Some suggested having private tutors travel with the boys and show them the ways of the real (manly) world. Others sressed manual training and physical exercise so that boys would work with their hands and train their bodies to perform creative, manly tasks.[85]

The spate of books and articles on juvenile behavior, youth, and gangs around 1900 (along with "home in peril" pieces and essays on "the woman question") offers further evidence of a masculine-identity problem. According to a number of accounts, American boys were being influenced by bad elements, especially urban youth, who were literally living on the streets, in dance halls, and in billiard parlors. These were boys who apparently had nothing to do but spend idle time in unsavory places. Because the schools did not provide sufficient outlets for their natural energies and because Sunday schools were dominated by rather prissy men, these boys needed some place else to go or someone to turn to for manly guidance and direction. Some boys banded together in street gangs and groups for camaraderie and adventure. Often the result was mischief, occasionally petty crime, usually unknown to parents. Much of the mischief can be seen as boys' simply filling idle time while away from adult supervision. It cannot be doubted that an important component of gang life involved validating masculinity. To be tough, to be assertive, to defend personal honor, and to be able to successfully respond to an "I dare you" helped vouch for a boy's masculine authenticity and claim for respect.

BOYS' CLUBS

To counteract the ill effect of these associations, a number of boys' clubs and groups were organized to offer an attractive alternative to street life. These groups studied nature, did crafts, played games, discussed folklore and legends, were taught patriotism, and pursued many other pastimes, all with the purpose of arresting the drift and lack of manly direction in American boys. Even organizations like the Y.M.C.A., which had been in existence for some time, were criticized because they were too "high toned," and, most of all, they did not exist where the boys lived—in their neighborhoods. Some immigrant groups, mostly Catholic and Jewish, were already meeting the problems of their young men by sponsoring programs put on by older men who did not patronize the young men the way Protestant ministers did. The overall purpose of the boys' clubs was to build character. In a sense, the clubs sought to encourage the model of good character and conduct found in nineteenth-century guidebooks but to do it in a manner whereby the boy did not succumb to being a "goody-goody" boy, essentially an undesirable, effeminate image. Following the new premise that a boy's nature was bascially good, the clubs sponsored activities that were aimed at capitalizing on positive traits. The street-corner gangs were not viewed as essentially bad, but they were frowned upon because they did not have constructive ends.[86]

The most famous of all boys' organizations to emerge from the large number that existed after the turn of the century was the Boy Scouts. The Scouts were founded officially by Lord Baden-Powell in South Africa at the time of the Boer War (1899–1902), but there were several American men who had ideas for a similar movement in the United States. Daniel Beard's interest in American youth dated back to the 1880s, when he observed how little masculine guidance many boys received from their fathers. Beard's objective was to help boys accomplish manly tasks such as woodworking, blacksmithing, building tree houses, and flying kites, improvising their own amusement rather than playing with toys. As editor of *Recreation* magazine, he evolved a society known as Sons of Daniel Boone, which advertised and championed the strenuous life for American boys. In *The Boy Pioneers, The Book of Camp Lore and Woodcraft,* and *Buckskin Book for Buckskin Men and Boys,* Beard inspired his readers with tales of frontier and wilderness living by recounting the lives of Boone, Davy Crockett, Johnny Appleseed, and other frontier heroes. Behind these volumes was the commonly held view that a boy's character could be endangered by overcivilization. Boys should be allowed to exhibit their barbarian tendencies and learn the art of primitive survival to affirm their connection with the rugged, individualistic masculinity of the past.[87]

In 1902, Ernest T. Seton founded an organization for boys that he called the Tribe of Woodcraft Indians. The organization's guidebook and constitution, *The Birch Bark Roll,* spelled out the "tribe's" objectives, which included the promotion of the outdoor life and its preservation.

"The plan aims to give the young people something to do, something to enjoy in the woods, with a view always to character building, for manhood, not scholarship, is the first aim of education."[88] Seton was inspired to start a boys' organization because of what he felt was an unfortunate movement to cities and industries and the subsequent decline of farming and handcraft. Athletics was a noble effort to arrest the degeneracy of the nation's young men; yet Seton fretted that spectator games had divided the country into a few participants and a great passive crowd. Seton compared the American situation with that of ancient Rome. In the early history of both nations, every man was a soldier, but as the glory of Rome faded, there were only a few great gladiators performing in front of massive, jaded audiences. Thus, Seton saw the Woodcraft Indians as a way of combatting the loss of "our robust, manly, self-reliant boyhood" and keeping boys from being "flat-chested cigarette-smokers, with shaky nerves and doubtful vitality." In the early days of the movement he discovered that an ideal figure was necessary, reasoning that no philosophy had ever succeeded without a current example. "I needed an ideal outdoor man who was heroic, clean, manly, brave, picturesque . . . and already well-known." After considering Robin Hood and King Arthur, he took the James Fenimore Cooper Indian as an ideal. "I would have preferred a white ideal, but the Indian alone seemed to meet all the requisites," he wrote. To motivate interest and participation, the founder chose standards that were national, absolute, and not competitive, so that boys were striving not to defeat one another, but to accomplish objectives for which they strived.[89]

THE BOY SCOUTS

In 1904, Seton visited England, where he got advice from General Baden-Powell, whose movement to promote manly character in English boys had gained wide popularity. But it was William D. Boyce, a Chicago publisher, who came upon the Scouts performing their good deeds in England and was so impressed by their high regard for service that he dedicated himself to promoting the movement in the United States. In 1910, many separate groups—Beard's, Seton's, and others—came together to form the Boy Scouts. During the summer of that year, an experimental camp was set up in which boys lived in teepees, cooked, and camped out. The merit system and cooperation were emphasized, rather than competition, which characterized the tone of business and industry. The movement was founded with a sense of preserving many of the Victorian standards of personal conduct, honor, courage, and character, but it was also infused with the ideals of progressivism: fairness, efficiency, and an emphasis on the strenuous physical life as a way to masculine development. Americans interested in this movement agreed that the English Scout's oath had to be Americanized. Among the changes was the requirement that a boy keep himself "physically strong, mentally awake, and morally straight."[90]

Few movements swept the country as fast as the Boy Scouts did. According to William Murray, 300,000 boys had joined by the outbreak of the war and by the Fourth Liberty Bond Drive, there were 450,000 members. Explaining the movement to American mothers in *Good Housekeeping*, Thorton W. Burgess assured them that the Scout idea "comes to your aid as a powerful ally," because it relieved mothers of the sole responsibility for the moral training of their sons. The Scouts inculcated what mothers were trying to do in their homes for their boys, including the development of "manliness, chivalry, courage, honor, thoughtfulness for others, moral and physical stamina, integrity and independence in thought and deed." It was suggested to mothers that at a certain age a boy desired to be a man and search out a group and a new leader—a hero—to respect according to the laws of masculine superiority. Burgess contended that the Scouts made boys citizens of the world, "a world in which petticoats are scorned and an attempt at petticoat rule is resented."[91] Mothers had never been boys and therefore could not understand that boys resented a woman's interference on the ballfield and playground. Ths Boy Scouts offered a legitimate supporting structure to maternal influence, but one boys could fully accept because it appeared to emanate from their own initiative.

What is significant here is an important change of emphasis in the shaping of a masculine image. During the progressive years, in keeping with the instrumentalism of that era, it was argued that it was not abstract moral precepts of a mother's training that determined manhood; it was the struggle with temptations and ambitions, all of which had to be confronted in the breast of a noble-hearted boy. Strong, virile manhood could never again be produced in the sheltered home.[92] The new staging ground for the tests of young manhood was the Scouts, the boys' societies, or the gangs, sometimes consisting of little more than a group of neighborhood boys. Initiation into a gang or club tested the grit and tolerance of a young man, but often the real objective was to strengthen his spirit of loyalty to his comrades, which had always been the mark of moral manhood. Previously, the gang had been regarded the Achilles' heel of a growing boy, because gangs supposedly adulterated the boy's moral constitution. According to Fiske, the new emphasis on the positive features of the gang ought to stress the naturalness of boy-made societies, making them far superior to the adult organizations of the past in which intentions had been good but often produced a boy of less than manly potential.[93]

Many boys still preferred their own informal street gang instead of, or perhaps in spite of, the Boy Scouts, the Y.M.C.A., or other large organizations. Gangs had a unique appeal because they almost always tended to have action-oriented activities—games, adventure, the making of a certain amount of mischief, and even the possibility of an occasional fight. All of these activities built manly instincts, according to J. Adam Puffer, who surveyed a number of boys with gang associations. According to Puffer, eighty-six percent of gang activities centered on sports, games, and adventure, while only fourteen percent were of a passive nature, like reading and the collecting of things. He also found that boys most liked war stories and plays in which heroes killed villains. Not surprisingly, Puffer found that many young boys wanted to be firemen, athletes, prize fighters, and engineers.[94] Many of these activities reflected the basic desire to achieve distinction among other men. The gang and playing field, then, were crucial to both muscular and social education.

The Boy Scouts, boys' clubs, and gangs were in a very real sense part of a boys'-liberation movement, to free young males from women, especially from mothers. Puffer wrote that "between boys and women there is a solid wall," which may have something to do with the desire of all normal boys to run away from home, to literally escape what Senator Albert Beveridge called "their perfumed surroundings." The "new boy" of the Progressive years was not the Mama's boy he had been in the past, according to male writers, because the boy had an alternative to his mother. Her desire to keep him a child and his quest for masculinity were very often mutually antagonistic because her way of raising him to gentleness had made him a sissy. The gang, wrote Fiske, "saves the boy from lady-like fastidiousness, from effeminacy, from self-conceit." Fiske saw little that was common to boys and girls in childhood. Little girls, for example, were afflicted with "the homing instinct and the civilizing cares and responsibilities of a large family of dolls!"[95] Nature's way was to segregate the sexes to make their natures so completely different. Most boys usually wanted nothing to do with girls during the early teens. According to Fiske, boys recognized sex distinctions and followed nature's segregating pattern. Those exceptions of tomboys and girlish boys showed "very slightly the recapitulation tendency," i.e., the desire to reproduce. For the sissy boy with an effeminate nature, Fiske suggested a "good stiff dose of out-of-doors more than . . . parlor athletics."[96]

RANDOLPH BOURNE

From an intellectual perspective, Randolph Bourne brought together many of the nascent themes about masculinity in a couple of sharply focused books. Bourne was a progressive intellectual—influenced by John Dewey—and a strong nationalist. He was born in New Jersey and raised in a prestigious upper-class family, proud of its tradition and status, and quite Victorian. Randolph's father, Charles, a handsome and energetic man, deserted his family, forcing his wife and son to move back with the wife's parents. It is not certain what Randolph thought of his father, who is seldom mentioned in Randolph's writing, but it is quite possible that his barbs against the older generation were influenced by his father's behavior and commitment to the Protestant ethic, which Bourne viewed with contempt. More basic to Bourne's attitudes about youth were his physical handicaps. He was born with a facial deformity and at eleven contracted a disease that left him with double curvature of the spine. Nevertheless, in spite of his physical appearance (Theodore Dreiser called him "that frightening dwarf"), Bourne enjoyed skating, tennis, and especially hiking. At Columbia University, in which he finally enrolled after working to save enough money, he was a brilliant student, most impressed by the philosopher and educator John Dewey, the historian James Harvey Robinson, and the anthropologist Franz Boas. In 1911, he was encouraged to respond to an *Atlantic Monthly* article critical of the younger generation. His response marked him as an incisive spokesman for youth.[97]

In *Youth and Life*, Bourne's response, he portrayed the young men of America as apprehensive about life and resentful of old forms of discipline and restraint. Young men had extraordinary energy and enthusiasm, but they were accomplishing little because of inadequate leadership from middle-aged men, most of whom had been raised by stern, moralistic mothers. Caught up in a world of phrases and rhetoric, most male reformers had lost contact with life. What young men needed was a genuine heroic model who could feed the vital inner spirit of men. "There is a certain pathos in the fact that parents are so seldom the heroes from whom the children derive this revelation of their own personality," Bourne wrote.[98] Bourne considered hero worship youth's best defense against "cheapness of soul." To Bourne, hero worship was not to be a matter of imitation, as it may have been in the past. Heroes anticipated the doubts and fears of youth against the assaults of the world. To read about strong men was an education, and one important virtue gained from this education was the courage that American men of the past had always possessed. The crisis facing young men in America was that they were estranged from their families by the implicit pressures to be loyal to outmoded conventions and morals. Too often, love in past years had been shown by submission to these old morals and conventions, which the young generation now challenged. The old myth that elders had superhuman wisdom had nearly faded away, but youth had not yet found an adequate philosophy to follow. "Their seeming initiative was more animal spirits than anything else."[99] Lack of an essential vision was perilous even if young men were fresh, free, fearless, and aggressive.

Ironically, it was in the older men that youth found their most substantive counsel, according to Bourne. Old men shared with youth a strong lack of interest in life. They were possessed by no ulterior motives to evangelize their philosophy. Also, old men relished the past, but it was reality they idealized, by cutting away the superfluous. These old men distilled the "perfume of the past" and brought it to sweeten the present.[100] Such men had never grown old, and hence the charm and appeal of the older men, who seemed more genuine and more trustworthy than fathers and middle-aged reformers.

Unfortunately, for example, youth had been subjected to a misplaced emphasis on temperance that had usually meant restraint and repression. As a radical who believed in the freedom of expression, Bourne attacked the old attitude behind temperance and self-control—self-denial. Repression never eliminated latent desires, but, in fact, it usually strengthened those desires. Young men seeking to understand the mysteries of life were unable to speak freely with parents about their feelings and aspirations. This form of self-control, so common in the nineteenth century, dwarfed the spirit and guaranteed ignorance. It was even unwise, argued Bourne, to repress hatred and malice because neither went away if denied expression. A new meaning of temperance that Bourne suggested was "the happy harmonizing and coordinating of the expression of one's personality." Bourne envisioned a robust spirit of democracy that was rough and aggressive and stood people on their own feet. He looked to a time when forthright action would not be bound by tradition and men would take their own responsibility and cultivate their own powers. Men had been surrounded by too many moral hedges that smothered life. "Our liberation has just begun."[101]

Because he was physically handicapped, Bourne was extremely sensitive to assessment of individuals based on social gradations, which, he wrote, "so many of our upper middle-class women seem to have." It hurt Bourne to hear men described as failures or not amounting to much. Such proclamations seldom took an objective view of a person's circumstances, especially his luck in life. Perhaps because of his father's desertion, Bourne began at a very early age to seek out the cause of human unhappiness and unfulfillment, a search that took him to Henry George, a political economist, and a plan for human betterment. In addition to George, Bourne studied economic history and social psychology, establishing a belief in social progress as the primary interest of every thinking and true-hearted individual. Bourne accounted for his devotion to radical philosophy by explaining that his physical handicap made him want to excel in building an ideal of a militant character, "a new spirit of courage that will dare. . . . I want to give to the young men whom I see—who, with fine intellect and high principles, lack just that light of the future on their faces that would give them a purpose and meaning in life." To the young men of America, the physically twisted Bourne wanted to contribute a philosophy "that will energize their lives" and save them from unmanly timidity.[102] What tragic irony there was for a man so physically unmanly to nevertheless see his own life as a challenge and an arena in which to work out a militant philosophy for young men.

The greatest enemy young men faced was a weak will, not an inadequate body. For those who had disabilities, from whatever cause, Bourne set a marvelous example of striving for excellence. "Grow up as fast as you can," he advised, and cultivate every ability, preferably some artistic talent, because it was most durable.[103] His sense of urgency was well founded. Randolph Bourne died in December 1918, thirty-two years old.

NEW REFLECTIONS

Randolph Bourne's keen awareness of the problems confronting youth must be seen in the context of a whole range of problems faced by

American men before World War I. Bourne's concerns, coupled with the personal significance that men such as White, Root, Beveridge, and a host of others attributed to Theodore Roosevelt, make it apparent that the concern about virility in American life is crucial to an understanding of the whole progressive movement. While in no way refuting the "status revolution" thesis suggested by Richard Hofstadter, it is necessary to understand that status reputation had more than just the social and economic dimension that historians have usually emphasized.[104] Male progressives were anxious to redefine opportunity, achieve something noteworthy, and contribute to national greatness in the tradition of their manly predecessors. To this end they could thank Theodore Roosevelt, who helped American men understand the value and viability of revitalizing their masculine self-image. But the renewed sense of progress that came out of the boisterous years between 1900 and 1917 brought with it some disturbing conflicts to America's men, because it brought spiritual values into contention with the masculinity-validating processes of social Darwinism, and cooperation into contention with historic American individualism. It brought women into the national political and social consciousness after several decades of their restlessness's being condemned. It stressed regulation at the expense of freedom and recognized the complexity of life. As all of these changes slowly became apparent in one way or another to individual men, the myth of the masculine past took shape in the national consciousness. It consisted of a vivid set of images, recollections, and stereotypes against which men were to measure themselves in the future, be the image that of a Daniel Boone or a J. P. Morgan, or some combination of the two. In a variety of ways, through literature and, increasingly, through the popular culture, through sports and professional organizations, American men tried to maintain a connection with the past that would serve as an affirmation of their identity in the present. In the course of the twentieth century, the effort may have served a purpose some of the time, but in many instances it became a liability. The Boy Scout movement, for example, with its noble ideal of restoring the primitive past, in time became a huge bureaucracy in which there was conflict between the older romantics committed to handcrafts and the new, young executives who stressed urban social-reform programs. Nor did the Scouts entirely escape the "goody-goody" image, exemplified by their being seen—and ridiculed—as sissies in short pants doing good turns for old ladies. And while Scouts camped out and learned about honor, many books still stressed themes of hard work riveted to a background of physical labor and traditional rugged individualism as the sure road to success, but science and technology were rendering these celebrations of American masculinity less and less relevant.

It has been argued that many American males were filled with doubt and anxiety about women, the new woman's motives and aspirations being interpreted in terms of men's own fears about themselves. The old warnings about the voluptuous women who could emasculate the most manly of men were still taken seriously. But wasn't it a good possibility that the noble woman, the well-nurtured female from a wholesome background, was just as likely to make sexual demands as well as call for social recognition and economic security? From all that was being written about women and their changing place, it is not hard to understand why social feminism signaled the very real possibility that men were succumbing more than ever to the influence of women and female sexuality. How far would such new philosophies about sexuality have to go before disorder and chaos prevailed? Progressivism had not as yet gone so far as to raise this speculative premise to reality, but many men feared that the trend was headed in that very dangerous direction. For this reason also, the masculine mystique was important in serving to remind women, as well as men, of the masculine sense of progress, that America was, after all, man-made, with masculine objectives and achievements. Although men were willing to acknowledge the influence of women in all that men had accomplished and were even willing to grant them new rights and privileges, there were those who, in the same breath, praised the old days when everyone knew his or her respective place. And it was out of the very nature of the inconsistencies, ambiguities, and double standards of the old era that American men had shaped their ideal of success and advancement.

Notes

[1]Lawrence Abbott, *Impressions of Theodore Roosevelt* (Garden City, N.Y.: Doubleday & Co., 1920), p. 302.

[2]Theodore Roosevelt, *The Strenuous Life: Essays and Addresses* (New York: Century Co., 1900).

[3]Stuart P. Sherman, "Roosevelt and the National Psychology," in Morton Keller, ed., *Theodore Roosevelt* (New York: Hill and Wang, 1967), p. 45.

[4]Quoted in Carlton Putnam, *Theodore Roosevelt: The Formative Years, 1858–1886* (New York: Charles Scribner's Sons, 1958), pp. 44–45.

[5]Glenn Davis, "The Early Years of Theodore Roosevelt: A Study in Character Formation," *History of Childhood Quarterly*, II (Spring, 1975), 469–70.

[6]Ibid., 472–77.

[7]Theodore Roosevelt, *Autobiography* (New York: Charles Scribner's Sons, 1913), p. 22.

[8]Theodore Roosevelt, "The Essence of Heroism," *Youth's Companion* (April 18, 1901), 202; Theodore Roosevelt, *The Wilderness Hunter* (New York: G. P. Putnam, 1893); Theodore Roosevelt, *The Winning of the West* (New York: G. P. Putnam's Sons, 1900); Theodore Roosevelt, *The Hunting Trips of a Ranchman* (New York: The Review of Reviews Co., 1904); Theodore Roosevelt, *The Strenuous Life* (New York: Century Co., 1900).

[9]Owen Wister, *The Virginian* (New York: Macmillan, 1929), p. 399.

[10]Theodore Roosevelt, *Autobiography* (New York: Charles Scribner's Sons, 1913), p. 120; Theodore Roosevelt, "A Teller of Tales of Strong Men," *Harper's Weekly* (December 21, 1895), 1216.

[11]Theodore Roosevelt, *American Ideals* (New York: Putnam's, 1897), p. 40.

[12]Richard Fry, *Community Through War: A Study of Theodore Roosevelt's Rise and Fall As Prophet and Hero in Modern America* (unpublished doctoral dissertation, University of Minnesota, 1969).

[13]Theodore Roosevelt, *American Ideals* (New York: Putnam's, 1897), pp. 40–41.

[14]Lawrence Abbott, *Impressions of Theodore Roosevelt* (Garden City, N.Y.: Doubleday, 1920), pp. 3–4.

[15]Edward Bok, *The Americanization of Edward Bok* (New York: Charles Scribner's Sons, 1923), p. 267; George Douglas, *The Many-Sided Roosevelt* (New York: Dodd, Mead & Co., 1907), pp. 1–2; James Morgan, *Theodore Roosevelt: The Boy and the Man* (New York: Grossett and Dunlap, 1907), p. 278; A. Maurice Low, "Theodore Roosevelt," *Forum* (November, 1901), 259–67.

[16]Philip Jessup, *Elihu Root* (New York: Dodd, Mead & Co., 1938), pp. 36–37, 105–7.

[17]Elihu Root, *Men and Policies: Addresses by Elihu Root*, Robert Bacon and James Scott, eds., (Cambridge: Harvard University Press, 1925), pp. 7, 11, 14.

[18]Mark Sullivan, *The Education of an American* (New York: Doubleday & Co., 1938), pp. 273–74; Harold Ickes, *Autobiography of a Curmudgeon* (Chicago: Quadrangle, 1943), p. 217.

[19]Albert Beveridge, *The Young Man and the World* (New York: Appleton and Co., 1906), p. 216.

[20]James R. McGovern, "David Graham Phillips and the Virility Impulse of Progressives," *New England Quarterly*, XXXIX (September, 1966), 339.

[21]David Graham Phillips, "Restless Husbands," *Cosmopolitan* (August, 1911), 423.

[22]Quoted in James R. McGovern, "David Graham Phillips and the Virility Impulse of Progressives," *New England Quarterly* XXXIX (September, 1966), 340.

[23]Quoted in Ibid., p. 344.

[24]Ibid., p. 348; see also David Graham Phillips, *Old Wives for New* (New York: Appleton and Co., 1908); David Graham Phillips, *Susan Lennox* (New York: Appleton and Co., 1917); David Graham Phillips, *The Second Generation* (New York: Appleton and Co., 1909).

[25]William Allen White, *Autobiography* (New York: Macmillan, 1946), p. 85.

[26]William Allen White, *The Court of Boyville* (New York: Doubleday, 1899), p. 4.

[27]William Allen White, *Autobiography* (New York: Macmillan, 1946), pp. 137–38.

[28]Ibid., pp. 297–98.

[29]William Allen White, *The Old Order Changeth* (New York: Macmillan, 1910), pp. 165–68, 177–89; William Allen White, "Roosevelt, A Force for Righteousness," *McClure's Magazine* (February, 1907), 386–94.

[30]David Hinshaw, *A Man From Kansas* (New York: Putnam, 1945), pp. 34–35.

[31]Letter to Theodore Roosevelt, January 16, 1912, in Walter Johnson, ed., *Selected Letters of William Allen White* (New York: Holt and Co., 1947), p. 130.

[32]Ibid.

[33]Letter to Theodore Roosevelt, September 24, 1913, in Walter Johnson, ed., *Selected Letters of William Allen White* (New York: Holt and Co., 1947), pp. 112, 145; William Allen White, *Autobiography* (New York: Macmillan, 1946), pp. 345–47, 427–30, 472–74.

[34]Theodore Roosevelt, *Autobiography* (New York: Charles Scribner's Sons, 1913), pp. 86–87.

[35]Stuart Sherman, "Roosevelt and the National Psychology," in Morton Keller, ed., *Theodore Roosevelt* (New York: Hill and Wang, 1967), p. 38.

[36]John Sprout, *The Best Men* (New York: Oxford University Press, 1968), p. 68.

[37]Stuart Sherman, "Roosevelt and the National Psychology," in Morton Keller, ed., *Theodore Roosevelt* (New York: Hill and Wang, 1967), p. 38.

[38]Edward Bok, *The Americanization of Edward Bok* (New York: Charles Scribner's Sons, 1913), pp. 268–69

[39]William Allen White, "Theodore Roosevelt," in Morton Keller, ed., *Theodore Roosevelt* (New York: Hill and Wang, 1967), p. 30.

[40]Ibid., p. 19.

[41]Edward Ward, "Women Should Mind Their Own Business," *Independent* (June 22, 1911), 1370–71; Irving Bacheller, "What Women Know About Men," *Independent* (March 13, 1916), 378.

[42]Quoted in William O'Neill, *Everyone Was Brave* (Chicago: Quadrangle, 1971), p. 56.

[43]Andrew Sinclair, *The Emancipation of the American Woman* (New York: Harper, 1965), p. 321; "The Marriage Question," *Independent* (December 9, 1909), 1305; Peter Filene, *Him/Her Self* (New York: Harcourt Brace Jovanovich, Inc., 1974), pp. 63–66

[44]Theodore Roosevelt, *Autobiography* (New York: Charles Scribner's Sons, 1913), pp. 161–67; Theodore Roosevelt to F. M. Qvam, May 6, 1910, Carrie C. Catt papers, New York Public Library quoted in Andrew Sinclair, *The Emancipation of the American Woman* (New York: Harper, 1965), p. 325; Elisabeth Woodbridge, "The Unknown Quantity in the Woman Problem," *Atlantic Monthly* (April, 1914), 510–20; Corra Harris, "What Men Know About Women," *Independent* (March 13, 1916), 379.

[45]Frank Norris, *Moran of the Lady Letty: A Story of Adventure off the California Coast* (New York: A.M.S. Press, 1971), p. 91.

[46]Ibid., pp. 222–23.

[47]Ibid., p. 260.

[48]Frank Norris, *Blix* (New York: Doubleday and McClure Co., 1899).

[49]David Graham Phillips, *The Hungry Heart* (New York: Appleton and Co., 1911), p. 133; David Graham Phillips, *The Worth of a Woman* (New York: Appleton and Co., 1908), p. 89.

[50]Elisabeth Woodbridge, "The Unknown Quantity in the Woman Problem," *Atlantic Monthly* (April, 1914), 514.

[51]Quoted in David Noble, *The Progressive Mind* (Chicago: Rand McNally, 1970), p. 77.

[52]Thomas Hughes, *The Manliness of Christ* (Boston: Houghton, Osgood, 1880), p. 5; Thomas Hughes, *Tom Brown's School-Days* (Cornwall, Mass.: Cornwall Press, Inc., 1911), pp. 276–97.

[53]Carl Case, *The Masculine in Religion* (Philadelphia: American Baptist Publication Society, 1906), pp. 30–31, 46, 51, 115–16.

[54]John Alexander, ed., *Boy Training* (New York: Association Press, 1911), pp. 75–76, 111–14.

[55]Carl Case, *The Masculine in Religion* (Philadelphia: American Baptist Publication Society, 1906), p. 21.

[56]Robert Conant, *The Virility of Christ* (Chicago: published by the author, 1915), pp. 24, 51, 57.

[57]Ibid., pp. 59–61, 75, 86–95, 109–11, 224.

[58]Ibid., pp. 64–65, 90–91.

[59]Ibid., p. 91.

[60]Alfred Mahan, *The Harvest Within* (Boston: Little, Brown, 1909), p. 21.

[61]Ibid., pp. 85, 122–23, 146; see also Harry Fosdick, *The Manhood of the Master* (New York: Association Press, 1911); Jason Pierce, *The Masculine Power of Christ* (Boston: The Pilgrim Press, 1912).

[62]Fayette Thompson et al., *Men and Religion* (New York: Y.M.C.A., 1911), p. 8.

[63]George W. Fiske, "Boys' Normal Home Relationships," in John Alexander, ed., *Boy Training* (New York: Association Press, 1911), p. 41.

[64]Quoted in Arthur Calhoun, *Social History of the American Family*, Vol. III (New York: Noble, 1917), p. 187.

[65]Ibid., pp. 167–68; James Burn, *Three Years Among the Working Classes in the U.S.* (London: Smith, Elder and Co., 1865), pp. 86–94.

[66]H. L. Taylor, "American Childhood from a Medical Standpoint," *American Journal of Social Science*, XXX (1892), 44–55; C. P. Seldon, "Rule of Mother," *North American Review* (November, 1895), 637–40.

[67]Margaret Mead, "The Job of the Children's Mother's Husband," *The New York Times Magazine* (May 10, 1959), 7, 66.

[68]Max Eastman, *Enjoyment of Living* (New York: Harper, 1948), pp. 11, 16–17; Erik Erikson, *Childhood and Society* (New York: W. W. Norton, 1968), p. 312.

[69]Floyd Dell, *Homecoming* (Port Washington, N.Y.: Kennikat Press, 1933), pp. 55–56.

[70]Geoffrey Gorer, *The American People* (New York: W. W. Norton, 1964), pp. 26–28, 46–47, 56–57.

[71]Harry Peck, "What a Father Can Do for His Daughter," *Cosmopolitan* (February, 1903), 460–64; see also Charles Eliot, "The Part of the Man in the Family." *Ladies' Home Journal* (March, 1908), 7.

[72]Arthur Calhoun, *Social History of the American Family*, Vol. III (New York: Noble, 1917), pp. 157–60; Rose Young, "Men, Women and Sex Antagonism," *Good Housekeeping* (April, 1914), 487–90.

[73]Edward Martin, "Use of Fathers," *Harper's Magazine* (October, 1908), 764.

[74]Thomas Clark, *The High-School Boy and His Problem* (New York: Macmillan Co., 1920), p. 3.

[75]Ibid., pp. 6, 121, 156–57; see also H. W. Gibson, *Boyology: Or Boy Analysis* (New York: Association Press, 1922).

[76]Edwin Puller, *Your Boy and His Training* (New York: Appleton, 1916), pp. 277–81; "To Urge the Good to Marry," *Literary Digest* (March 28, 1914), 693–94.

[77]Luther Gulick, *The Dynamic of Manhood* (New York: Association Press, 1917), pp. 129–30; Thomas W. Galloway, *The Father and His Boy: The Place of Sex in Manhood Making* (New York: Association Press, 1921), p. 1.

[78]Thomas W. Galloway, *The Father and His Boy: The Place of Sex in Manhood Making* (New York: Association Press, 1921), p. 43.

[79]Luther Gulick, *The Dynamic of Manhood* (New York: Association Press, 1917), pp. 76–77; Philip E. Howard, *Father and Son* (Philadelphia: Sunday School Times, 1922).

[80]George W. Fiske, *Boy Life and Self-Government* (New York: Association Press, 1916), pp. 70–71; Edgar Moon, *The Contents of the Boy* (New York; Eaton and Mains, 1909).

[81]Soloman Schindler, "A Flaw in Our Public School System," *Arena* (June, 1892), 60.

[82]Thomas Davidson, "The Ideal Training of the American Boy," *Forum* (July, 1894), 571–81; David Porter, "An Ideal for American School Life," in John Alexander, ed., *Boy Training* (New York: Association Press, 1911), p.62.

[83]W. O. Thompson, "Character Development of Young Men When Subjected Largely to Female Instruction," *Ohio Educational Monthly*, LIV (July, 1905), 433.

[84]William Allen White, *The Old Order Changeth* (New York: Macmillan, 1910), pp. 177–89.

[85]Thomas Davidson, "The Ideal Training of the American Boy," *Forum* (July, 1894), 576–79; Henry Hetzel, "Manual Training in Mental Development," *Arena* (July, 1900), 93–98.

[86]Will Oursler, *The Boy Scout Story* (Garden City, N.Y.: Doubleday & Co., 1955), pp. 27, 35; W. Myron Forbush, *The Boy Problem* (Boston: Pilgrim Press, 1907), p. 145; Theodore Roosevelt, "Essence of Heroism," *Youth's Companion* (April 18, 1901), 202; Frances Maule, "Getting at the Boys," *Outlook* (December 2, 1905). 822–26; Charles Stelze, *Boys of the Street and How to Win Them* (New York: Fleming H. Revell Co., 1904), pp. 20–25, 37–38, 71; Edgar Moon, *The Contents of the Boy* (New York: Eaton and Mains, 1909); Lilburn Merrill, *Winning the Boy* (New York: H. F. Revell, 1908); John Rogers, "The Theory of a Boys Club," *Education*, XXX (September, 1909), 40–41.

[87]Dan Beard, Letter to *Outlook* (July 23, 1910), 696–97; Dan Beard, "The Scout Idea," *Outlook* (July 23, 1910), 607–08; William D. Murray, *The History of the Boy Scouts of America* (New York: Boy Scouts of America, 1937), p. 18.

[88]William D. Murray, *The History of the Boy Scouts of America* (New York: Boy Scouts of America, 1937), p. 16.

[89]Ernest Seton, "The Boy Scouts in America," *Outlook* (July 23, 1910), 630.

[90]William D. Murray, *The History of the Boy Scouts of America* (New York: Boy Scouts of America, 1937), pp. 15–23, 56–57; Dan Beard, "The Boy Scouts of America," *Review of Reviews* (October, 1911), 429–36.

[91]William D. Murray, *The History of the Boy Scouts of America* (New York: Boy Scouts of America, 1937), p. 101; Thornton W. Burgess, "Making Men of Them," *Good Housekeeping* (July, 1914), 3, 5; Ralph Blemenfeld, "The Boy Scouts," *Outlook* (July 23, 1910), 620.

[92]Thomas Davidson, "The Ideal Training of the American Boy," *Forum* (July, 1894), 572; James Rogers, "The Theory of a Boys Club," *Education*, XXX (September, 1909), 43–44.

[93]George W. Fiske, *Boy Life and Self-Government* (New York: Association Press, 1916), pp. 89–116.

[94]J. Adams Puffer, *The Boy and His Gang* (Boston: Houghton Mifflin Co., 1912), pp. 40–41, 64; Edwin Puller, *Your Boy and His Training* (New York: Appleton, 1916), p. 68.

[95]J. Adams Puffer, *The Boy and His Gang* (Boston: Houghton Mifflin Co., 1912), p. 3; George W. Fiske, *Boy Life and Self-Government* (New York: Association Press, 1916), pp. 112–14.

[96]George W. Fiske, *Boy Life and Self-Government* (New York: Association Press, 1916), p. 189.

[97]Carl Resek, ed., *War and the Intellectuals* (New York: Harper, 1964), pp. vii–ix; Henry May, *End of American Innocence* (Chicago: Quadrangle, 1959), pp. 326–28.

[98]Randolph Bourne, *Youth and Life* (Boston and New York: Houghton Mifflin Co., 1913), p. 78.

[99]Ibid., p. 266.

[100]Ibid., p. 96.

[101]Ibid., pp. 84, 86–87.

[102]Ibid., pp. 352–53.

[103]Ibid., p. 362.

[104]Richard Hofstadter, *The Age of Reform* (New York: Alfred A. Knopf, Inc., 1955), pp. 131–73.

6

FROM BATTLEFIELD TO BALLFIELD: THE RISE OF SPORT, 1880–1920

The organization and popularity of boys' clubs and gangs to provide outlets for youthful masculine instincts was accompanied throughout the
nation by the spectacular rise of sport and athletics. By 1917, baseball's
two major leagues were firmly established and the World Series had become a classic sporting event. Football games had become a prominent
feature of college life, accented by ceremony, ritual, and glorious praise
for hefty campus heroes who promoted the "school spirit." Athletic schol-
arships became a prize many young men sought. The first professional
tennis court was built in Boston in 1876, other cities soon following with
elaborate facilities; by the 1890s national-championship awards sparked
the competition. Basketball was invented in 1891; the American Bowling
Congress was formed in 1895; by 1890 the Amateur Athletic Union was
well on its way to becoming an established institution. Boxing became

one of the most popular sports of the period, with men such as James ("Gentleman Jim") Corbett and John L. Sullivan attracting national attention.*[1] More important than the games and leagues themselves is the significance of the rise of sport when many boys and men in America were concerned about achieving a vigorous masculine identity. American sport coincided with the emergence of urbanism and it is the psychological connection linking the two that reveals the extent to which sport became a masculinity-validating experience in America at the turn of the century.

SPORT AND MANLY CHARACTER

Mark Sullivan noted that as long as the frontier existed, a man with sons knew that when the urge to prove their manhood came, they could acquire a farm, start a business, or provide their own adventure by moving to the frontier.[2] But what happened when the frontier wilderness no longer existed and there were no new battlefields to test manly courage and perseverance? H. S. Williams commented that the "struggle for existence, though becoming harder and harder, is less and less a physical struggle, more and more a battle of minds." Williams observed that without the frontier, either as an inspiration or as a potent force, men saw themselves deprived of an arena that had always been used to prove themselves as men. The problem was especially acute because urban dwellers did not have the opportunity to acquire the physical culture necessary to sustain vigorous, healthy bodies. This deprivation encouraged "the introduction of calisthenics into our schools, the building of gymnasia for our colleges, the springing up of athletic clubs in our cities, the amazing popular interest in athletic games. . . ."[3]

Sports and games offered a release from modern tensions. For some men (see discussion in Chapter 5), sports became a convenient escape from women, as exemplified by the exclusion of females from many of the newly founded athletic clubs. In its own way, too, sport restructured a sense of social order through the elaborate rules, rituals, and planning that went into athletic events. This is not to say that athletic games were not often played just for fun by thousands of players of all types who simply desired exercise and recreation. A good case can be made, however, as Marshall McLuhan has already attempted to demonstrate, that then as

---

*Sport, in the context of this chapter, refers to the general social and psychological aspect of athletics. Sports refers to the specific games that grew in popularity.

now, the way sport was perceived by participants and spectators alike provides a fascinating and dramatic index of America's psychology.[4]

One of the most striking features about the rise of modern sport in America, however, was the extraordinary degree to which it was assumed that a manly character was shaped through sport. Precisely how this concept developed is not altogether clear, but there is sufficient evidence to support the thesis that the modern philosophy of sports had its roots in Victorian Christian morality. The Victorians maintained that a moral person was a good steward of mind and body. That is, one cultivated the moral instincts of both by guarding against sinful temptation and destruction. The Young Men's Christian Association, founded in England, had already caught on in America before the Civil War. A Y.M.C.A. convention in 1860 confirmed that one of the organization's goals was to protect young men "against the allurement of objectionable places of resort." To this end, gymnastic and athletic programs were set up at Y.M.C.A. facilities in many cities to advance the ideal of moral and physical culture.[5] The changing social conditions of the 1890s, however, began to render spiritual and moral stewardship harder to achieve and live by, while physical stewardship seemed more simple and direct and more likely to be within the range of a confident masculinity. The man of good character was more easily recognized as one who had a good physical appearance and could perform physical tasks. In time, sportsmanship became something of a new enlightenment and a quasi-substitute for the rule of Christian love, which seemed vague and passive and harder to implement in an age that generally followed the tenets of social Darwinism. For example, Lloyd Bryce described what he called "muscular Christianity" evolving out of "muscular heathenism through games."[6] Another enthusiast wrote that "athletics forbid almost everything that makes for the destruction of moral stamina."[7] Careful dieting, control of bad habits, and a knowledge of how the body functioned contributed to "the athlete's sum of practice and wisdom." It was stated that the athlete, more than any other person, knew the value of good health as the true basis of strength and that the training of his body and mind was another form of discipline. Physical examinations conducted at the time of the Spanish-American War revealed that tobacco, intoxicating drinks, and excessive and ill-directed physical exercises were the greatest enemies of manly development and strength. One author congratulated American colleges for giving prominence to athletics and for providing games in which muscular exertion with "a considerable amount of danger" were proving to be vastly beneficial to young men. Sports taught fairness and helped promote a great civilization. Michael Maccoby has touched on these trends in a book entitled *The Gamesmen*, a book not about athletes but businessmen and how they emulated jungle fighters in their quest for survival. Taking a theme from Tocqueville, Maccoby portrays the businessman as one who plays at life like a game of chance, and the man with superior strength and courage will win—or at least control the game.[8]

SPORT AND CITIZENSHIP

By the 1890s, magazines and newspapers frequently carried articles postulating the inherent character-building potential of spontaneous play. It was argued that sports were not only a matter of physical development but a valuable means of inculcating moral development and intellectual growth. The Y.M.C.A. was followed by many other organizations and clubs dedicated to fostering the masculine character-building values of fair and honorable play.[9] Numerous pieces of fiction dramatized the thesis that the struggle for Christianity was an inner spiritual one as well as a physical one. In *Tom Brown's School-Days*, for example, young Tom enriched his moral character by playing a sport and realizing that a good Christian was competitive and that, sometimes, even fighting was necessary in order to "prove" one's Christian character.[10] By 1900, many American authors used sports to help define their heroes, illustrate a central meaning to life, or to suggest a core of values for those who had left the relative freedom of the countryside and strained against the authoritarianism implicit in urban life. Children's magazines like *St. Nicholas* began to stress that athletics and training built strength and character and, therefore, ensured purity and temperance.[11] Casper Whitney, a popular journalist, extolled the virtues of sports building strong, decent men, the kind of men who had fought and won the war against Spain. "We have gone outdoors to engage in this stimulating, muscle-building play because our Anglo-Saxon instincts draw us toward it and we are outdoors to stay." He observed that no other people took sports as seriously as did Americans, whose intensity was explained by a commitment to always stand in first place.[12]

No one individual seemed as enthusiastic about the value of sports as Theodore Roosevelt, who never tired of extolling the virile virtues that produced great statesmen, soldiers, pioneers, and explorers. "The true sports for a manly race are sports like running, rowing, playing football and baseball, boxing and wrestling, shooting, riding and mountain climbing." Every boy brought up on these action sports "has by just so much fitted himself to . . . be a better citizen." Roosevelt made much of the fact that the best soldiers in the war against Spain were sportsmen, men who had trained their bodies for rugged tasks and had become accustomed to hardship and strain.[13] Judging from the many men who expressed this view in countless articles and essays around 1900, it is evident that, to them, the precious moral lessons and proof of masculinity discovered in that "splendid little war" far outweighed any other significance attached to it. "[T]he war has made startlingly clear how great a thing is physical health and strength. Probably no army and navy since the best days of the Roman Empire ever equalled ours man for man in the best results of athletic training." It was the polo, football, boxing, and baseball that created the "brawn, the spirit, the self-confidence and quickness of men" who filled the ranks of the army. "[T]here can be no doubting that the great wave of interest in manly physical exercises and training that has spread over the country during the past twenty years has wrought wonders in the way of preparing our young men for the important work they have recently done for their country." And the same author noted: "The greatest danger that a long period of profound peace offers to a nation is that of [creating] effeminate tendencies in young men."[14] Reaching the same conclusion, George Hibbard wrote that "there is a great deal of the spirit of sport in the spirit of jingoism," and that one had only to understand the attitude of the new woman to be convinced of the value of sports in maturing young men.[15] Some observers were hesitant to claim the virtues of sports along these lines, reasoning that the enthusiasm generated by sports and games detracted from higher and more noble causes. In some cases, this reservation can be explained by the long-standing concern about there being too much indulgence in anything that gave pleasure. Individual athletic exercises may have been favored because they kept attention properly focused on individual physical development, which was more in keeping with the doctrines about good stewardship of the body. But after carefully reviewing these factors and noting the place of sports and games in other nations, one skeptic encouraged sports because the nations that were good at games were inheriting the earth. The relationship was clear: athletics, masculinity, nationalism, and the American mission. In 1896, the Olympic games were revived, and when American athletes competed successfully against athletes from other nations, some authors took the outcome as proof of the superiority of the American male. W. R. C. Latson wrote that in everyday life, in man's continuing struggle for peace and power, athletics produced the rare building qualities of endurance, control, courage, and concentration. All of the great heroes of the past had possessed these qualities and it was the function of sport to instill the same qualities in young men.[16]

SPORT INSTITUTIONALIZED

Many guidebooks for young men had emphasized the virtues of having a strong body long before the strenuous-life philosophy became popular. German ideas about physical fitness related to national character and achievement contributed to this influence in the United States. In the 1840s, Pierce Egan's *Book of Sports* and Donald Walker's *British Manly Exercises* stimulated interest in sports by offering information about physical development, and James G. Bennett's *Herald* pioneered in sports coverage. During the Civil War one observer wrote of "dyspeptic men" with "puny forms, and the bloodless cheeks which characterized the population of our great cities at the present day."[17] The Civil War encouraged an interest in promoting the good physical condition of American men by placing a premium on the active man who could endure physical stress and strain. By the mid-1880s there were about three dozen colleges with physical-education facilities, and in 1885 the American Association for the Advancement of Physical Education was founded. Fitness tests administered to Harvard men in 1890 revealed that 250 men achieved better than the highest score in 1880. Many organizations advertised an active interest in promoting physical-exercise opportunities. The number of Y.M.C.A. gymnasiums increased from 68 to 168 between 1883 and 1887. Richard T. Ely and other civic leaders supported the establishment of playgrounds and parks, places where a young man's animal spirits might find full expression. Lillian Wald and Jacob Riis championed recreation facilities as a deterrent to gang activity. By 1903, New York City had a public-school athletic league and by 1904, 345 out of 555 major American cities had high-school athletic associations.[18]

A variety of explanations and rationalizations linked the rise of sport to the symbolic closing of the frontier and the muscling-up of American imperialism, each in its own way vitally linked to the masculine mystique. There were strong advocates of physical education in schools or in clubs, such as D. A. Sargent, who argued that athletics were needed to "counteract the enervating tendency of the times and to improve the health, strength, and vigor of our youth." American civilization had evolved and prospered with a very specific orientation about the importance of space. Frontier space had been integral to growth and vitality and was associated with youthfulness. One implicit assumption, therefore, about masculinity in America has been that younger men are the most manly—because they are more likely to be more active than other men. After conducting several studies of athletes and non-athletes, Sargent concluded that athletes were superior men, healthier and more vigorous. But Sargent warned that the physical qualifications of the athlete would be insignificant unless the individual developed an accompanying nervous system to supply "that almost sublime quality in man, courage." In addition, the athlete had to develop "coolness, presence of mind," responsibility, and sound judgment—all desirable in "the battle of life." Sargent believed that athletic activity should be encouraged in as many people as possible. Recognizing the growing popularity of football, Sargent registered a reservation about the brutality and violence of that game and some other sports and the objective to win at any cost. But Sargent pointed the way of the future when he admitted that, in spite of the roughness, sport furnished the best kind of "general exercise for the body, and develop[ed] courage, manliness, and self-control."[19]

By the 1890s, the assumption was explicit that there was a unique connection between physical development and the quality of mind and character a man possessed. Just what the body–mind–character relationship was and how it functioned, however, was never proved conclusively, and there were only a few attempts at a scientific explanation. According to Henry Williams, muscles and brain cells were mutually linked through the network of blood vessels and nerves. Muscular activity was a direct aid to the heart to keep up the circulation of the blood. The influence of the nerves, although not as tangible, was extremely important. The muscles and the brain were likened to the poles of a battery, the nerves being the connecting wires. Vital impulses traveled between the two poles, and the "integrity" of the impulses was directly dependent on the integrity of the brain and muscles at the poles as well as the integrity of the nerves connecting body and mind. Therefore, when exercising, a person was not just building the body; the mind and its integrity were also being enhanced. "The young man who appears to be bent only on grappling [with] a football is in reality helping himself to prepare his Greek lesson. The budding athlete as he measures his biceps and notes a fraction of an inch of increase is really measuring his mind also." And conversely, a person with a powerful mind possessed a sound body, potentially at least, if that individual only realized it and worked at developing his body. Williams's theory posed some problems, however. If the body and mind were so mutually dependent, the amputation of a limb had to have a serious impact on the brain and character of the individual. "His [the amputee's] nervous system is crippled as well as his muscular system, and this not merely in an imaginary way, but actually and demonstrably." In fact, Williams contended that "every other organ of the body also suffers to some extent since the body and mind were all so intricately linked."[20]

PHYSICAL FITNESS AND SOCIETY

Williams shifted from scientific analysis to social analysis when he promoted the value of physical exercise as a means of preserving the quality of civilization. Primitive peoples developed their bodies and minds naturally through the rugged, hard work of making a living and fighting human and animal predators. Modern tools and conveniences and sophisticated machinery had retarded the primitive instincts of self-development to a dangerous point of social disintegration. Only farmers had kept themselves in the kind of physical shape resembling that of primitive man. "Year by year the population of the civilized world masses itself into larger and larger communities, and lives on an average a more sedentary life."[21] The American city used to be stocked with new blood from the farm, but the new immigration from southern and eastern Europe after 1880 was swamping the cities with a progressively degenerative influence because less attention was paid to the physical factors of personal development. Finally, schools were awakening to the critical need to build sound bodies and introduce physical-development instruction into the curriculum. Country clubs, athletic games of all sorts, and the popularity of the bicycle attested to a "seemingly new interest in athletics," which was, however, "nothing new at all, but a return to nature." Engaging in calisthenics was the common way to develop muscle tone, improve the brain, and resist the degeneration of modern man. But Williams admitted that calisthenics and exercising were boring when done in one's own quarters. Competitive athletics furnished the elements of excitement and interest necessary to achieve not only strong bodies but good coordination basic to sports and a way to demonstrate courage. And mindful of the connection between mind and body, Williams reasoned that a well-coordinated body produced a well-coordinated mind.[22]

The yearning to participate in games and sports contests was occasionally attributed to a basic impulse in men to extend their primitive hunting instincts into modern times. This view is still held by those who argue the existence of a biological male imperative. Recent commentators describe work and war as male activities and suggest that sport came to emulate both. Throughout history, Lionel Tiger emphasizes, there has been a male bonding process from which females have been excluded. Sport seemed to reveal this process very clearly, in that male domination of sport has been virtually uncontested.[23] George Gilder writes that "athletics for men is an ideal of purity and truth," and that through sports, males learn cooperation and the valuable lessons of "struggle, toughness, and self-sacrifice."[24] Thus, sport is not only a matter of social evolution, according to Gilder and Tiger, but reflects qualities and impulses inherent in the human male.

In 1900, the economist Thorstein Veblen saw the sporting craze as an attitude of "emulative ferocity," the goal of which was the restoration of a lost sense of male prowess. Veblen believed that the temperament that inclined men to sport was essentially boyish in nature and was, therefore, a mark of an arrested moral development. Men and boys were attracted to sport because it conjured up a make-believe world in varying degrees, depending on the activity, by encouraging participation in the serious but lost art of human survival. Veblen noted the example of the typically mild-mannered and matter-of-fact men who seemed to radically alter their personalities when they went hunting. They outfitted themselves with an array of equipment as if to dramatize the importance of what they were about to do. These hunters were prone to a kind of histrionic behavior, a prancing gait and exaggerated motions emphasizing their intentions. Veblen also observed that athletic games were usually accompanied by a good deal of "rant and swagger and ostensible mystification—features which mark the historic nature of these employments."[25] Furthermore, Veblen noted, the language of sport resembled the terminology of warfare, again suggesting the presence of masculine aggression, which in modern times was finding a new form of expression. It had been the social elite in the past who had preserved certain leisure activity according to their codes of reputable living. But the kind of purposeless activity preferred by the leisure class served to perpetuate a make-believe world. What Veblen brought together, then, was an association of the ancient instinct of workmanship and survival and the modern purposeless activity (sports) through a subconscious desire of the leisure class to emulate the older latent instinct of male prowess and aggression. Probably most males of the leisure class did not fully comprehend their own desires, according to Veblen, and therefore they unwittingly manifested the requirements of the leisure class: the wastefulness of energy while trying to approximate through sport some kind of social purpose. In this way, according to Veblen, sports became popular among the leisure class.[26]

Athletic games were being justified, according to Veblen, on the basis that they were crucial to physical development and that they fostered a manly attitude. This attitude could be understood best in the context of modern competition, which all men seemed to relish. The unique qualities sports developed were ferocity and cunning, traits highly relevant to a philosophy of economic individualism and crucial elements of the ancestral predatory instincts of man. With varying degrees of potency, Veblen observed, these instincts remained available "for the aggressive shaping of men's action and sentiments."[27] These instincts could be forcibly asserted as long as no other special activity interrupted the individual's interests and desires. This, explained Veblen, is why sports and the sporting influence were appealing. The result was the attainment of manly virtues. But more than that, from Veblen's economic view of man, sport furthered or advanced that ancient instinct of workmanship, the very essence of human activity. That instinct had been destroyed by the decadence of modern civilization. Most apologists for sport, he explained, never got far enough in their analysis to see that through sport there was an emulative predatory impulse taking man back to his true primitive nature. That impulse was often exploitive, often manifesting itself in force or fraud, which Veblen claimed existed in modern sports and games. These characteristics were "the expressions of a narrowly self-regarding habit of mind."[28] While Veblen chafed that these values were of little consequence to the collective life he personally favored, he was certain in his analysis that sport did provide an emulative situation in its real and imagined dimensions.

G. STANLEY HALL

From another perspective, G. Stanley Hall, the German-trained psychologist, wrote that "we inherit tendencies of muscular coordination that have been of great racial utility. The best athletic sports and games are composed of these racially old elements, so that phylogenetic muscular history is of great importance." Hall maintained that play was a process of "rehearsing racial history," and, therefore, the best exercise for young men was the kind that developed the "basal powers old to the race." Physical development should be directed toward cultivating and enforcing these inherent masculine powers.[29] Hall paid tribute to Father Jahn, a German physical-culture pioneer of the early nineteenth century, whose motto was "only strong muscles can make men great and nations free." Jahn realized that many of man's former activities that required various kinds of muscle activity had lapsed into disuse, and it was his objective to rescue these acitivities and restore them to the benefit of modern men. Jahn had made gymnastics a special art, and by having his pupils practice his theories he established the basis for a noble and virile patriotism in Germany. Hall was impressed that by 1870, Germany had become the greatest military power since ancient Rome, a remarkable development considering the dispirited state of Germany in the early 1800s, when Jahn began his work. The ideals of the Christian religion had been added to the training so that the soul of man might have "a regenerated somatic organism," establishing "exercise [as] a form of praise to God and of service to man."[30] Hall's goal was to extend Father Jahn's work, combining it with the very best physical-culture practices from other Anglo-Saxon countries in order to help men become "soldiers of Christ" and promote a higher level of progress through powerful muscularity.[31] Obviously, Hall enthusiastically supported physical education through gymnasium and athletic programs that prepared man's physical frame for the needs and challenges of the twentieth century. Hall believed, as did Roosevelt, that through physical fitness young men would become more efficient and better able to express their virility. He was particularly impressed with new track-and-field records constantly being set since the 1870s, which, to Hall, indicated better athletes and better men.[32]

Through an evolutionary process, human beings had developed naturally, and as with animals, Hall theorized, play had been basic to that development. Some play was functional while other forms were less significant, but all animals instinctively knew they had to exercise or they would cease growing and die. Weakness made men miserable but strength gave a sense of joy and glory. "[Strength] gives a sense of superiority, dignity, endurance, courage, confidence, enterprise, power, personal validity, virility, and virtue in the etymological sense of that noble word. To be active, agile, strong, is especially the glory of young men." Activity in the form of play was actually a form of pleasure and served as a reminder of the life history of the race. Hall saw much modern play activity as a recapitulation of ancestral chores. For example, running, dodging, and hitting a ball with a club were throwbacks to the hunting and fighting stage of man's history. The resemblance to modern baseball was obvious to the student of these ancient feats. Other men enjoyed fishing in the same respect because they were unconsciously re-enacting their past through that activity.[33]

According to Hall, based on his study of race history, good exercise for young men should include not only physical activity but "psychic" exercise as well. The best psychoneural forms of exercise took advantage of a man's interest, zest, and spontaneity. Efforts to block off these emotions would cause great harm. For example, spontaneous anger might be gross and repulsive but should not be eliminated. Anger, in fact, was interpreted as a positive part of moral education for a growing boy seeking manhood. If he were prevented from acting on his anger, his masculinity would not ring true. To develop into a powerful and virtuous man required the challenge of enemies so that the real man could indulge in noble strife, which sanctified great causes. However bad pugnacity might seem, a scrapping boy was better than a boy who "funks a fight" and turns sentimental. Healthy boys needed to be taught boxing early in life even though the prize ring was considered degrading and brutal. Hall felt that boxing needed to be rescued from the bad connotations it aroused and hence forward seen as a manifestation of true manliness in action.[34]

Hall also had a theory about the female influence on the young male athlete. It was necessary for young men to show off in front of admiring girls just as male birds and beasts paraded their charms in courting gestures before females of their species. "The presence of the fair sex gives tonicity to youth's muscles and tension to his arteries to a degree of which he is rarely conscious." Suffering defeat in front of female spectators constituted a serious humiliation no young man wanted to face. Being able to demonstrate force and skill and, above all, a victory made a hero and invested him with a romantic glamor that, though concealed, "makes the winner more or less irresistible." While men might appreciate the approval of their teammates and other men, "the applause . . . of ladies is ravishing." The presence of cheering females at an athletic contest, then, actually served a very functional purpose in that it acted as an incentive for physical refinement and good form. The modern woman was serving the same role as the woman who had spurred the medieval knight toward an honorable and civilizing state of chivalry. In a theme consistent with his theory of racial recapitulation, Hall wrote that modern woman was "still engaged in this work as much as ever, and in his dull, slow way man feels that her presence enforces her standards, abhorrent though it would be to him to compromise in one iota his masculinity."[35]

REORIENTING A SOCIETY

By the 1890s, America had gone sports crazy. The arguments for pure athletics continued to emphasize specific body-building techniques; however, there was more attention being focused on team sports, the big game, and the spectator aspect of sports. Theodore Roosevelt, for example, was one who warned against the trend toward professional athletics. He argued that the object of indulging in athletics was to build strong men *throughout* society, not just within a limited group of players. Reading the debates about the value and place of sports in America at that time reveals that the sporting impulse came to have much more significance when it was related to the masculine impulse to display prowess and virility. The sociologist Franklin Giddings made a direct connection between the primitive instincts of man to fight and endure and the modern sporting impulse. The author argued that in spite of the evolution to modern industrial civilization, there was still a demand for the primitive virtues in men. "Consequently it is not among primitive men only that physical prowess is valued above all other gifts. . . . The prize fighter, the athlete, the military hero, the imperturbable leader who can withstand the assaults of malignity, these are the popular idols."[36] Athletic contests, then, began to furnish society with new heroes to worship at a time when genuine contemporary frontier heroes were disappearing. Francis Walker, president of Massachusetts Institute of Technology, claimed that the nation was painfully in need of a new popular amusement, something that would get men out into the open air again and interest them in something besides money. Others, like John Jay Chapman, criticized America's stultifying conformity, and the condescending habit of always trying to please, and "the lack of passion in the American."[37]

John Higham has referred to what was happening at the turn of the century as "the reorientation of American culture." In part, it was a reaction to the social restraint and control of the Victorian era. The sons of Civil War veterans were thirsting for their own adventure and action in order to validate their own claims of masculine fulfillment. New terms came into vogue, decrying effeminacy, such as "sissy," "pussyfooter," "cold feet," and "Miss Nancyish." At the Chicago World's Fair in 1893,

Bernarr Macfadden became a popular attraction with his weight-lifting and muscular demonstrations. Several years later he brought out a magazine called *Physical Culture*, which carried as its slogan *"weakness is a crime."*[38]

Thousands of people were witnessing sports events, especially on college campuses where cheers and fight songs were supposed to spur participants on to victory. Dartmouth's new fight song, written by Richard Hovey in 1894, combined a sense of the old pioneer virtue with the insurgence of masculinity in the 1890s:

> *They have the still North in their hearts*
> *The hill-winds in their veins.*
> *And the granite of New Hampshire*
> *In their muscles and their brains.*[39]

The crucial question that aroused a storm of controversy well into the twentieth century was whether the physical-education movement in colleges and high schools initiated to promote manly bodies had been subverted into something quite different. What had started out to promote better physical development among young men, especially those in the city, had evolved into a pervasive spectator-sports boom by 1900. Some critics argued that "house exercises" (calisthenics) would prove to be much more beneficial to health than the games between teams from different institutions.[40] One camp supported physical education, which tended to reflect health and fitness values, and the other camp supported after-school games, which catered to the social and psychological needs of producing masculine heroes. One educator stated it would be disastrous to make the play hours "as dully disciplined as school hours." There had to be a consciousness of the "robust community" to sustain a boy's growth and enthusiasm for success that the old methods of teaching had not always done:

> From a health point of view there can be no comparison between a good healthy game—in which every muscle is suitably exercised, and brain and lungs join in the complete happiness of the honest laugh and the careless shout—and the "dead alive" military drill, or formal gymnastics, which, while developing many muscles abnormally, leave the brain torpid and the spirit depressed.[41]

Games had to be regulated, of course, and unselfishness emphasized at all times. The weak had to be helped by the strong to become better; team selection had to be based only on merit; pride of success had to be encouraged without conceit. Because all of these goals were possible through team sports, the assumption became widespread among many American educators and parents that the playing field was, in its own way, an unwalled schoolroom. Ancient lessons about justice and honor were learned while masculinity was being confirmed. Who could ask for a better system?

The fast-paced trend of the sports boom epitomized the dominance of the physical rather than the intellectual criteria of masculine validation. It was acknowledged by proponents and critics alike that scoring a touchdown or hitting a home run was a much more direct way of gaining recognition than by doing so "intellectually." One skeptic who disagreed with the sports-builds-character proposition maintained that the sentiment for sports had "seriously crippled even the appreciation of the delight of mental growth." According to one teacher, the pressure to participate successfully at a sport had become so intense that if he tried to encourage boys to enter different activities, his influence as a teacher would be jeopardized. Some boys, it was charged, were so caught up in competitive sports that they ruined their "intellectual curiosity." American culture was quick to dispense notoriety to the active man, the athlete, rather than to the man whose accomplishments, however worthwhile, were passive and, therefore, not considered manly. And the individuals awarding notoriety were older men, alumni of a college or university, who perhaps experienced a vicarious lift from the victories and heroic feats of the young men from their alma maters.[42]

Charles Eliot, the president of Harvard, was convinced that football dulled the senses—restricted the intellect from developing. And he pointed out that team sports certainly did nothing for the physical welfare of the spectators. Nevertheless, Harvard was one of the first colleges to build a large football stadium. The Big Ten Conference was drawing more than a million spectators a season to football games by early in the century. There were serious protests registered about the competing interests of intellectualism and athleticism on college campuses. At Yale, for example, the alumni raised $180,000 for a memorial to honor the great sportsman Walter Camp, while admirers of Josiah Gibbs, one of America's greatest physicists, failed to raise $12,000 for a modest tribute.[43] N. S. Shaler, a Harvard geologist, was another educator who concluded that athletic interests had increasingly encroached upon the academic interests of the male student to the extent that physical activity postponed mental maturity. In addition, he regretted that so many of the young athletes suffered injuries, especially those who played football. The extent of intercollegiate competition worried Shaler and others, as did the exuberant celebrations that often accompanied victory. To a reflective professor devoted to cultivating the mind, the mob hysteria surrounding the sports hero was distressing.[44]

The clamor for what was called athleticism, however, was too powerful for even the most stalwart defenders of the American educational institutions to ignore. Even Shaler recognized a certain value of physical training for young men and admitted that house exercises by them were not very interesting to the student who wanted to match his strength and skill against those of an opponent. The risk of injury was counterbalanced by the opportunity sports provided the athlete to learn to master his rage as "a kind of moral training." Shaler saw sports as a deterrent to the consumption of alcohol and tobacco, which he saw as two distinct corruptors of manliness. And so, Shaler, while critical of sports for its uncivilizing aspects, could still argue that America could risk the ill effects of sports "for the better reason that the world needs . . . the swift reaction of man against his surroundings which the athletic habits favor."[45] Frederick Taussig, an economist and tariff expert, wrote that the maintenance of intellectual standards was essential but that sports had to be given a place of recognition too. "We have not too much of pleasure and romance in our everyday American life and can welcome everything that gives it a brighter and happier aspect." Walter Camp, "the father of American football" and the man said to have developed the first forward pass, agreed that boys needed to get out of the classroom and onto the athletic field where they could learn courage and self-reliance.[46]

ESCAPING WOMEN

By 1914, college sports had achieved recognition and enthusiastic support from virtually every quarter of American society, certainly not the least of which was from the White House. There were, however, additional vital forces propelling the rise of sport in American society. Sports offered a seemingly safe retreat for the male establishment from feminine influence. One writer noted that it was time more attention be given to the ego development of adolescent males. Fathers were so engrossed in businsss that they were cut off from their sons, the undesired result being that boys were usually left with their mother, "whose affections are so curiously set on sons [that she] is apt to interfere with the father's ideas." Tensions between fathers and mothers over their sons was a serious issue, and, accordingly, one way out of this situation was to enlist a boy's interest in sports, in which the proper environment was offered to develop manly skills and manners, free from feminine interference. Even though some authors confessed that athletics might be carried to an extreme in America, sport was accepted as a necessary antidote to feminine influence.[47]

E. D. Cope stated his fear that masculine power would be significantly diminished if women were successful in abolishing boxing, as was being proposed in several states. In protecting men from the emergence of women, Cope concluded that "the popularity of athletic sports at the present time will prove most useful to us as a race."[48] An editorial in *Independent* rationalized that American men were not cultured because they had an entirely different motivation from the one that women had. Women had been left in charge of culture, meaning music, art, and literature. Women had succeeded quite well in promoting the elegant arts, it was observed, and had carried their refinement over into education. With the widening gulf between men and women in education and with women trying to impose their refinement, "boys have been driven from the classroom onto the football field by force of feminine competition. It [the football field] is the only place where masculine supremacy is incontestable."[49]

Before World War I, many considered the football player to be the most manly of men because of the courage required to play the game— especially so in its early history when protective gear was primitive or nonexistent. Football itself came to have a tremendous appeal because, as the sports writer Tom Dowling has stated, "the game . . . was cut along the lines of the American grain; it was savage, violent, militaristic in its meticulous organization, moralistic in its celebration of performance and high purpose, remorseless in its contempt for failure and its adulation for success."[50]

In the 1870s, American football evolved from rugby, incorporating several new features, the most significant being the scrimmage line. Offside playing was outlawed so that, in effect, a battle line of sorts advanced downfield as the offensive team moved the ball toward the goal line. The defined scrimmage line made possible certain offensive maneuvers requiring plays that had to be practiced.[51] Innovations made by such coaches as Alonzo Stagg at Chicago and Henry Williams at Minnesota required special skills of their players that added to the action of the game. By 1896, football had become so popular that on Thanksgiving Day of that year there were thousands of football games across the country. At these games enthusiastic crowds cheered their teams to heroism and victory. In 1887 Alexander Johnston praised the game for the courage it brought out of the players under conditions remselbing warfare. "Across the field stretched the football infantry," with the "artillery" (or fullback) ready to go to work. Johnston concluded, "One who gets the full force of the military nature of the American game of football will have comparatively little difficulty in following intelligently the real course of the game." No game could rival football in advancing manliness as a unique American value. The game was, however, really just a manifestation of a larger force in America, and for Alexander Johnston, there was a "satisfaction in knowing that this outdoor game is doing for our college-bred men, in a more peaceful way, what the experiences of war did for so many of their predecessors in 1861–65."[52]

MANLINESS AND MORE

Lazy men and slackers were the ones most likely to change their ways if they went to a college with a good football program. Membership on a football team forced boys to organize their time carefully and cut out worthless dissipations of male energy. Football could force young men with little observable athletic skill to develop what skill they possessed. Because of football, "the hopelessly unathletic student thus gets less mercy every year."[53] It is not surprising that Theodore Roosevelt became one of the greatest advocates of football in its early years, but not necessarily because football promoted good physical conditioning in American youth. Roosevelt saw football as a means of transforming youth from wealthy homes, who were usually considered effeminate, into tough, aggressive men. "A coward who will take a blow without returning it is a contemptible creature. . . . In short, in life as in a football game the principle to follow is: Hit the line hard; don't foul and don't shirk, but hit the line hard."[54]

Price Collier, a commentator who thought highly of the game, wrote that football, more than any other sport, had advanced the goal of achieving manliness among American men and was, therefore, unique in advancing civilization. Collier welcomed any proof that would confirm his belief that American boys were more manly than they once were.[55] Many critics thought that football exacted too high a price when it came to vouching for manliness. Newspapers chronicled the injuries players suffered while executing the flying wedge and other open-field plays. By the turn of the century the injury situation had reached crisis proportions, as stories of permanently maimed and injured players were widely reported. Twelve fatalities were reported in 1902 and eighteen in 1905, prompting a storm of indignation from men like Shailer Mathews, Dean of the Divinity School at Chicago University. "Football today is a social obsession—a boy-killing, education-prostituting, gladitorial sport. It teaches virility and courage, but so does war." Several colleges suspended football operations, and groups were organized to abolish the sport in other schools, not only because of injuries but because football had virtually taken over campus life.[56]

There were those who supported the game precisely because it was rough and brought out virility. Speaking to the Harvard Alumni Association shortly before the Spanish-American War, Henry Cabot Lodge let it be known that he was in favor of rough sports. He argued that the time given to athletics and the injuries that players sustained in trying to win were "part of the price the English-speaking race has paid for being world conquerors." The individualism conveyed through the tame house exercises was not nearly as valuable to the Anglo-Saxon race as the more valuable sense of efficiency taught through the fierce athletic competition of football. "A nation must have that spirit to succeed in the world, and a college must have that spirit to succeed in the nation." Harvard's President Eliot was not so sure. Football did indeed encourage combat, but was there not a more serviceable strength for society associated with gentleness and courtesy? Father Cavenaugh of Notre Dame probably summarized the feelings of most football advocates, however, when he asserted, "I would rather see our youth playing football with the danger of a broken collarbone occasionally than to see them dedicated to croquet."[57]

Charles Thwing, president of Western Reserve, wrote that although football might have some evil aspects, the game was ideally suited for instilling positive values in young males. Football illustrated all that was positive, and it emphasized an "aggressive putting forth." The game embodied Thomas Carlyle's "eternal yea" Thwing wrote, and "it stands for the perpendicular," suggesting to him at least a certain phallic quality about the game, perhaps alluding to the fullback's repeated thrusts into the defensive line.[58] A letter-writer to *Outlook* emphasized that football helped a young man overcome any hesitancy he might have toward life.

After all, America had no room for meek, mild fellows who suffered from nervous strain over doubts about their identity. Football was an ideal antidote to counteract such strain.[59] One writer defended football's effect of bringing out a young man's fighting instinct by quoting G. Stanley Hall: "An able-bodied young man who cannot fight physically can hardly have a high and true sense of honor and is generally a milk sop, a lady boy, or a sneak. He lacks virility, his masculinity does not ring true, his honesty cannot be sound to the core."[60]

Winning had always been a logical aspect of the male image of success in America, and to win at football became a grave matter for dedicated coaches and players. Between 1907 and 1915, the emphasis on winning for the sake of the school's reputation as a tough, manly insitution led some coaches to use "tramp athletes," players who traveled between schools to help produce a winning team. These athletes often registered for only one course, giving rise to the *prima donna* student athlete, often caught up in the self-image of athlete-hero, the ultimate campus he-man. The player often lacked self-discipline and had a negligent attitude about his studies, what little was demanded. Worst of all, he tended to have an unrealistic picture of himself. Unless he was a superb performer, his varsity athletic career did not guarantee future success, regardless of how manly he may have appeared when he had been making savage tackles or running the ball into the enemy's line.[61]

CHANGING THE GAME

Even the game's most ardent supporters began to accept that rule changes were essential to save football from being abolished because of its brutal nature. One observer noted that too often players came off the field sobbing from exhaustion, which, it was noted, was not in line with the best tradition of Anglo-Saxon men. The appetite for manly success was so keen that football had been transformed into a brutal enterprise. *Nation* railed against the win-at-any-price spirit in college football. This attitude had permitted moral deterioration and corruption to take over the undergraduate mind. Americans were far from understanding the English philosophy of playing for fun. In America, *Nation* argued, winning was so important that losing was a disgrace, a psychological death for the losing team. A game that had originally been justified as part of a nation's character-building efforts had become a sickening national moral tragedy.[62]

In spite of the criticisms leveled against it, in 1905 a survey showed that out of 555 American cities, 432 had football teams. Of those same cities, 360 had baseball teams and 213 had basketball teams. By 1909 almost all of the seventy-five largest high schools in Nebraska played football. Rule changes finally did reform the game in 1910 after strong encouragement from Theodore Roosevelt, who thought it would be a great loss to the growth of American men if football were abolished. Walter Camp, who played a significant role in the rule revisions, praised the game for having made such fine progress during the first decade of the twentieth century. The game had become an integral part of American life, he maintained, because it stood for vitality.[63]

To many young men growing into manhood during these years, participation in sports provided a means of compensation. In his early days at West Point, Dwight Eisenhower was a socially reticent youth, but sports provided an opportunity for personal accountability. Athletics made him self-confident, truculent, and game for anything. The promising young halfback weighed 175 pounds but was listed at 190. However, the gridiron career that Eisenhower anticipated was terminated by a knee injury that had a profound effect on him. "I was almost despondent," he wrote. "Life seemed to have little meaning; a need to excel was gone." While Eisenhower was at West Point, Ernest Hemingway was trying to make the football team at Oak Park High School in Chicago. He worried about his puny stature and tried to compensate for it by practicing his shooting marksmanship, but that proved an inadequate substitute because of deficient sight in his left eye. When his growth suddenly spurted between his freshman and sophomore years, it left him clumsy and slow, and he could only make substitute tackle. Hemingway took up boxing in 1916 and found that there was a streak of the bully in his nature when he discovered the power in his fists.[64] Through boxing, at least, Hemingway could lay claim to a praiseworthy manliness because of the inherent pain and challenge, factors certain to eradicate any taint of femininity.

H. Addington Bruce summarized the psychological theories about football by assessing the various arguments, most of which were along the lines of man's search to revert to the primitive life in which, by inference, there had been a more genuine masculinity. More than any other sport, Bruce concluded, football with its relentless furious action dependent on brute strength and fleetness of foot recalled that stage of man's development. Men and women assembled at football games "to let off steam" in a constructive manner. "It is the game of games" to "take a man out of himself." Unlike baseball, tennis, or golf, in which there was tedious waiting, football proceeded on a course of action far more stimulating to the imagination. Bands, the waving of colors, and cheers all penetrated to the subconscious and brought out even the most reserved man's true sentiments. Football, then, had become one of the most valuable forces in America by stimulating the nation's young men to adopt the ideals and behavior characteristics of their ancient forefathers. It also acted as a moral safety valve to a nation of people filled with the energy to renew the race. And, ultimately, football helped the coward overcome his weaknesses by stressing the value placed on team play and self-sacrifice.[65]

SPORT AND WAR

During World War I, the relationship between sport, manliness, and soldiering came into sharp focus. Percy Houghton, Harvard's football coach, contended that the instinctive action of his men on the playing field was attributable to the army-style discipline he employed. All of Houghton's players had to endure hard work, sacrifice, and strain much as they would in the military. Dean Briggs of Harvard agreed that "this war has come nearer [to] justifying our methods in inter-collegiate athletics than we had thought possible."[66] The war was teaching a valuable lesson of spiritual togetherness in politics and sports. A young man could glorify his alma mater with a victory in sport. After all, the school's ideals were embodied not only in academics but also in the development of manliness. And so it was that victory in war would bring to men another crown of manly accomplishment and enhance the nation's power and patriotism. By 1917, many Americans felt confidently prepared for war because of the rise of sport. Excellence in sport meant that America would never lack sufficient fighting instinct. Sports also provided the country with a new set of heroes to help confirm certain verities about the American experience. "War cements a nation," according to one writer on the subject, and "clarifies a national ideal, brings common hopes and fears, gives cohesiveness, tests fidelity and loyalty and involves all in some great and common destiny." And "play does [on a lesser scale] exactly what war does on a larger scale."[67] By pursuing sports, the nation's men could test their strengths through athletic combat and simultaneously maintain a fine martial capacity.

Some years after the war, Lotus Coffman, the president of the University of Minnesota, praised football because it gave young boys heroes to respect in an age when heroes were hard to find. Football was valuable because it embodied the fighting spirit and upheld clean sportsmanship. And "the same kind of red blood qualities are required on the football field that animated the men on the battlefields of France and Belgium."[68]

Many of the proponents of sports assumed that the kind of action that made men physically masculine helped those men become self-confident and assured them of success no matter what they did later in life. It was assumed that this attitude made men complete and content with themselves. Optimally, sports offered the sort of challenge missing in an over-civilized society, challenges that had once helped men define themselves. As Myron Brenton, among others, has pointed out, this strategy was bound to fail in several important respects. The more men looked to the past for a confirmation of their identity, trying to act out those rituals again, the more disadvantaged and confused they were going to be. The mystique of traditional manliness made men participate in sports with motives that jeopardized self-enjoyment if a game were lost. To lose at sports became disgraceful to many American men and boys.

The truth was that there was a startling gap between optimistic projections about the quality of masculinity and the reality of physical fitness and military preparedness. The shock came in December 1917 when it was announced by the Provost Marshal that one-third of the three million men drafted into the armed forces were physically unfit for service. All the effort and emphasis that supposedly contributed to the buildup of muscle and character in American men had failed to produce very distinguished results in terms of good physical health. One survey concluded that boys from wealthy homes and young men who had been surrounded by women much of their life were the least physically fit for military duty. The highest percent of physical rejections came from the Northeast, whereas the best record for passing the physicals came from the Midwest. Overall, the results were disappointing to a society that had boasted about its virile young men and their capability of demonstrating collective eagerness for manly action.[69] Greater efforts would have to be made involving more men more intensely in sports if the nation's physical health were to be upgraded. In spite of the dismal results, there was little questioning that participation in a sport was a prime indicator of masculinity. For a boy to be considered "a man" he needed to at least try out for a sport. Being truly physically fit in terms of muscle development, posture, and diet, however, seemed less important. What received the most publicity was heroic manhood and the reputation of masculinity, which squared with the myth and folklore of the heroic American manhood of the past.

THE HEROES

It is not the intention here to condemn the trend toward competitive sports but rather to suggest how the ideal of traditional masculinity and hero worship influenced the growth of competitive team sports at the college level after 1920. Newspapers and radio, and later television, provided a heavy diet of coverage that helped publicize the virtues of manly heroes. A writer in *Commonweal*, for example, had much to say about Christy Mathewson, baseball's winningest pitcher between 1900 and 1917:

> No pitcher loomed so majestically in young minds, quite overshadowing George Washington and his cherry tree or even that transcendent model of boyhood, Frank Merriwell. . . . Such men have a very real value above and beyond the achievements of brawn and sporting skill. They realize and typify, in a fashion, the ideal of sport—clean power in the hands of a clean and vigorous personality, a courage that has been earned in combat, and a sense of honor which metes out justice to opponents and spurns those victories that have not been earned.[70]

The aspect of power was what seemed most important to sports fans. The man who could hit the hardest, be his target another man or a ball, was certain to be ranked with the great men of history. Power suggested domination and control, symbolized by men like Ruth and Grange, who were to dominate their respective sports in the 1920s. Even for sports like tennis, in which finesse was as important as power, it was not until power play took over the game that it became popular. Maurice McLaughlin helped transform tennis with his powerful serves and ground strokes. As John Betts has observed, fans across the United States only had to "read of his thundering service to be convinced of the new tone of masculinity in tennis." McLaughlin's cyclonic play was something that the common man preferred to identity with. The game was no longer associated with the refined etiquette of the social elite. The elements of brawn and power that McLaughlin's furious play brought to tennis made it such that "no longer did the man in the street or the boy in public school regard it disdainfully as a sissy sport." Soon rivals emerged who invigorated tennis even more. Yet some skeptics criticized the game as still not he-man enough, a few especially objecting to the term *love* used in scoring games![71]

Extending masculinity through sport coincided with and complemented many of the values of progressivism. Sport offered the potential of an invigorated manhood in which power, efficiency, and fairness ideally blended together. The box scores and score columns presented a daily accounting of just how things were going that no other index of success or failure could quite provide except perhaps the Stock Exchange. The togetherness theme of Progressive reform was promoted through sport by a sense of solidarity that males felt as teammates or as spectators cheering for a common cause. Team sports offered a unique opportunity for males to demonstrate physical strength and power, the core of masculine identity. At the same time sports brought men together, it helped them to differentiate themselves from one another, which, in effect, augmented individualism. Sports also helped distinguish men from women just at a time when feminism and women's rights appeared most threatening. In retrospect, sports can be seen as limiting as well as liberating for men to the extent that they had to base their identity on power and winning. Such an identity was misleading in that it had nothing necessarily to do with good health. It certainly could not guarantee success or even a manly character for young men trying out for a team. In fact, the broad invocation of "good character," which was so generously employed during the progressive era, may have been a cover for many behavioral ambiguities and inconsistencies. Yet the record suggests that the rise of sport in America and its subsequent popularity after 1920 had much to do with preserving the masculine mystique.

Notes

[1] John Betts, *America's Sporting Heritage* (Reading, Mass.: Addison-Wesley Publishing Co., 1974); Robert Boyle, *Sport: Mirror of American Life* (Boston: Little, Brown, 1963); Roger Callois, *Man, Play, and Games* (New York: Free Press, 1961); John T. Talamini and Charles H. Page, eds., *Sport and Society* (Boston: Little, Brown, 1973); Charles Merz, *The Great American Band Wagon* (New York: Garden City, 1928).

[2] Mark Sullivan, *Our Times*, Vol. I (New York: Charles Scribner's Sons, 1935), pp. 141–42.

[3] Henry W. Williams, "The Educational and Healthgiving Value of Athletics," *Harper's Weekly* (February 16, 1895), 166.

[4] Marshall McLuhan, "The Extensions of Man," in Mabel M. Hart, ed., *Sport in the Socio-Cultural Process* (Dubuque, Iowa: Brown, 1972), pp. 146–48.

[5] John Betts, *America's Sporting Heritage* (Reading, Mass.: Addison-Wesley Publishing Co., 1974), pp. 107–8.

[6]Lloyd Bryce, "A Plea for Sport," *North American Review* (May, 1879), 519; Lyman Bryson, *Science and Freedom* (New York: Columbia University Press, 1947), pp. 131–32.

[7]Maurice Thompson, "Vigorous Men, A Vigorous Nation," *Independent* (September 1, 1898), 610.

[8]Michael Maccoby, *The Gamesman* (New York: Simon and Schuster, 1977).

[9]Frederick Cozzens and Florence Stumpf, *Sports in American Life* (Chicago: University of Chicago Press, 1953), pp. 99–100.

[10]Thomas Hughes, *Tom Brown's School-Days* (New York: Harper, 1870).

[11]Samuel Scoville, "Training for Boys," *St. Nicholas* (June, 1899), 638–44.

[12]Casper Whitney, untitled article, *Independent* (June 7, 1900), 1362–63; Casper Whitney, "Amateur Sport," *Harper's Weekly* (November 4, 1893), 1067; Gamaliel Bradford, "The American Out of Doors," *Atlantic Monthly* (April, 1893), 452–58.

[13]John Betts, *America's Sporting Heritage* (Reading, Mass.: Addison-Wesley Publishing Co., 1974), pp. 183, 194.

[14]Maurice Thompson, "Vigorous Men, A Vigorous Nation," *Independent* (September 1, 1898), 610.

[15]George Hibbard, "The Sporting Spirit," *Outing* (September, 1900), 601.

[16]Hjalmar H. Boyeson, "The Most Athletic Nation in the World," *Cosmopolitan* (May, 1904), pp. 83–86; W. R. C. Latson, "The Moral Effects of Athletics," *Outing* (December, 1906), 389–92.

[17]John Betts, *America's Sporting Heritage* (Reading, Mass.: Addison-Wesley Publishing Co., 1974), p. 173.

[18]Ibid., pp. 107–8, 179–80.

[19]D. A. Sargent, "The Physical Proportions of the Typical Man," *Scribner's Monthly* (July, 1887), 3–17; D. A. Sargent, "The Physical Characteristics of the Athlete," *Scribner's Monthly* (November, 1887), 541–61.

[20]Henry S. Williams, "The Educational and Healthgiving Values of Athletics," *Harper's Weekly* (February 16, 1895), 166.

[21]Ibid.

[22]Ibid.

[23]Lionel Tiger, *Men in Groups* (New York: Random House, Inc., 1969), pp. 148 ff.

[24]George F. Gilder, *Sexual Suicide* (New York: Quadrangle, 1973), p. 231. Copyright © 1973 by George F. Gilder. Reprinted by permission of Quadrangle/The New York Times Book Co. from *Sexual Suicide* by George F. Gilder.

[25]Thorstein Veblen, *The Theory of the Leisure Class* (New York: Modern Library, 1931), pp. 246–75.

[26]Ibid.

[27]Ibid., p. 264.

[28]Ibid., p. 275.

[29]G. Stanley Hall, *Youth: Its Education Regimen and Hygiene* (New York: D. Appleton, 1909), p. 80.

[30]Ibid., p. 55.

[31]"Christianity and Physical Culture," in Charles Stickland and Charles Burgess, eds., *Health, Growth and Heredity* (Richmond, Va.: William Byrd Press, 1965), pp. 155–62.

[32] G. Stanley Hall, *Youth: Its Education Regimen and Hygiene* (New York: Appleton, 1909), pp. 68, 62.

[33] Ibid., pp. 78–79.

[34] Ibid., pp. 78–79, 94–95.

[35] Ibid., pp. 102–04.

[36] Franklin Giddings, *Democracy and Empire* (New York: Macmillan Co., 1900), p. 317; John Betts, *America's Sporting Heritage* (Reading Mass.: Addison-Wesley Publishing Co., 1974), p. 212.

[37] John Higham, "The Reorientation of American Culture," in Eugene Drozdowski, ed., *American Civilization* (Glenview, Ill.: Scott, Foresman and Co., 1972), p. 266.

[38] Ibid., p. 267.

[39] Ibid., p. 265.

[40] Eugene Richards, "College Athletics and Physical Development," *Popular Science Monthly* (April, 1888), 731–32; Arlo Bates, "The Negative Side to Modern Athletics," *Forum* (May 1901), 287–97; John Betts, America's Sporting Heritage (Reading, Mass.: Addison-Wesley Publishing Co., 1974), p. 212; Robert Boyle, *Sport: Mirror of American Life* (Boston: Little, Brown, 1963), p. 39.

[41] Frances H. Tabor, "Directed Sport as a Factor in Education," *Forum* (May, 1899), 321.

[42] Arlo Bates, "The Negative Side to Modern Athletics," *Forum* (May, 1901), 287–97.

[43] Robert Boyle, *Sport: Mirror of American Life* (Boston: Little, Brown, 1963), p. 39.

[44] N. S. Shaler, "The Athletic Problem in Education," *Atlantic Monthly* (January, 1889), 83; "Common Sense Athletics," *Current Literature* (March 5, 1900), 234–35.

[45] N. S. Shaler, "The Athletic Problem in Education," *Atlantic Monthly* (Janurary, 1889), 88.

[46] Quoted in John Betts, *America's Sporting Heritage* (Reading, Mass.: Addison-Wesley Publishing Co., 1974), p. 214; Walter Camp, "Base-ball for the Spectator," *Century Magazine* (October, 1889), 831.

[47] Joseph Rogers, "Educating Our Boys: Athletics and Sentiment," *Lippincott* (May, 1908), 633.

[48] E. D. Cope, "The Effeminization of Man," *Open Court* (October 26, 1893), 3847.

[49] Editorial, "The Uncultured Sex," *Independent* (November 11, 1909). 1100.

[50] Tom Dowling, *Coach: A Season With Lombardi* (New York: W. W. Norton and Co., 1970), p. 16.

[51] Alexander Johnston, "The American Game of Football," *Century Magazine* (October, 1887), 889–90.

[52] Ibid., p. 898.

[53] Ibid.

[54] Theodore Roosevelt, "What We Can Expect from the American Boy," *St. Nicholas* (May, 1900), 574.

[55] Price Collier, "The Ethics of Ancient and Modern Athletics," *Forum* (November, 1901), 309–18; Casper Whitney, "Development of Athletics in the United States," *Fortnightly Review* September, 1893), 412–24.

[56] John Betts, *America's Sporting Heritage* (Reading, Mass.: Addison-Wesley Publishing Co., 1974), pp. 126–28.

[57]Ibid., pp. 129, 195, 212.

[58]Charles Thwing, "The Ethical Functions of Football," *North American Review* (November, 1901), pp. 627-31.

[59]"Correspondence," *Outlook* (March 11, 1905), 655-56.

[60]H. Addington Bruce, "The Psychology of Football," *Outlook* (November 5, 1910), 544.

[61]Harry Edwards, *Sociology of Sport* (Homewood, Ill.: Dorsey, 1973), pp. 28-29.

[62]"Athletics and Character," *Nation* (February 5, 1914), 126-27; Paul Van Dyke, "Athletics and Education," *Outlook* (February 11, 1905), 389-93.

[63]Walter Camp, "American Sports," *Century* (November, 1909), 61-73; Casper Whitney, "Brain Defeats Brawn," *Outing* (January, 1907), 534-37.

[64]Peter Lyon, *Eisenhower* (Boston: Little, Brown and Co., 1974), pp. 43-45; Carlos Baker, *Ernest Hemingway* (New York: Charles Scribner's Sons, 1969), pp. 18, 22.

[65]H. Addington Bruce, "The Psychology of Football," *Outlook* (November 5, 1910), 543.

[66]L. B. R. Briggs, "Intercollegiate Athletics and the War," *Atlantic Monthly* (September, 1918), 304.

[67]George E. Johnston, "The Fighting Instinct," *Survey* (December 4, 1915), 248.

[68]"Football or Baseball the National Game?" *Literary Digest* (December 6, 1924), 61-66.

[69]J. H. Beard, "Physical Rejection for Military Service," *Scientific Monthly* (July, 1919), 5.

[70]*Commonweal* (October 21, 1925), 579.

[71]John Betts, *America's Sporting Heritage* (Reading, Mass.: Addison-Wesley Publishing Co., 1974), pp. 157-58.

The only thing eternal about morality is man's desire for the better. But what the better is, time and circumstances redetermine from situation to situation.

Sidney Hook, 1936

The ideal of the internationally famous good American husband is an ideal of male submission.

Alice Kelly, Harper's, *1931*

WAR TO DEPRESSION: PRESERVING MASCULINE CONTROL

The Progressives placed their hope for the future in America's youth, especially its young men. "The word *boy* is still another term for opportunity—opportunity for the prevention of degenerate and wicked men; for the building up of character in righteousness; for the saving of the individual, the nation, and the world."[1] To those ends, American men during the first twenty years of the twentieth century had campaigned to instill a more militant Christianity in the nation's youth. Many men agreed that the public schools were too effeminized and urged that more male teachers be hired. Randolph Bourne pleaded for a stronger masculine leadership. Natural, aggressive, and forthright male models like Tarzan and Owen Wister's Virginian were popularized through literature. A host of youth organizations, the Boy Scouts among them, sought to preserve and teach traditional manly arts, skills, and the outdoor life.

Through sports, the sense of competition, with all its combined forms of aggression, courage, and physical prowess, gave rise to the image of powerful, virile males who gave the impression that they knew what they were doing and did it well by winning.

Such was the stuff upon which traditional manly behavior and performance depended. Then came a war in Europe (which the United States entered in 1917), putting to the ultimate test the strength and endurance of young American males, about whom so much had been proclaimed. In Theodore Roosevelt's words, "No nation can be great unless its sons and daughters have in them the quality to rise [to a] level to [meet] the needs of heroic days. . . . We can leave our heritage undiminished to those who come after us only if we in our turn show a resolute and rugged manliness in the dark days of trial that have come upon us."[2] But there would be more "dark days of trial" to face in the years after Versailles. The peace and the "new times" of the twenties, followed by a devastating depression, put a severe stress on American men, especially those who idealized the masculine past and who felt compelled to live up to the tenets of a masculine image that stressed aggressiveness and domination.

GUTS AND GLORY

During the fall and winter of 1914–15, Roosevelt became deeply disturbed that President Woodrow Wilson lacked the manly will that all good American men were supposed to possess to defend their convictions. His indignation at Wilson's refusal to take a strong stand against Germany escalated sharply during 1915 and 1916 on the basis that it was a righteous nation's obligation to fight. Roosevelt raged that the pacifists "represent what has been on the whole, the most evil influence at work in the United States for the last fifty years. . . . Wilson has done more to emasculate American manhood and weaken its fiber than anyone else I can think of. He is a dangerous man for the country, for he is a man of brains and he debauches men of brains."[3] Roosevelt believed that Germany harbored a disrespect for the United States because Americans seemed willing to submit to outrages against their shipping on the high seas. He asserted that there was a growing sentiment in Germany that the United States was cowardly and effeminate. Any nation bearing those characteristics did not deserve respect. Considering the best interests of the entire world, Roosevelt believed it better for America to have "a policy of blood and iron" rather than of "milk and water."[4]

Roosevelt saw the war as rescuing the nation's youth from the bad habits of cowardice and weakness. Each generation had proven itself to be a forthright defender of the nation's best values. Destiny had called forth the best efforts of the men of the 1770s to successfully fight for a revolution, to another generation to win the West, and to another to fight the Civil War. "We inherit as free men this fair and mighty land only because our fathers and forefathers had iron in their blood."[5] To Roosevelt, the Spanish-American War had been a useful if only a short excursion, hardly of the magnitude that loomed ahead for American soldiers in 1917. One of Roosevelt's great disappointments was that he never got to the trenches of France, where "the fighting was the hottest," although he made an exhaustive effort to recruit an army of his own and train and lead it into battle. His view of war as the supreme test of moral and physical manhood suggested a romantic vision, compared with the real situation of 1917. Roosevelt believed that every nation needed heroes, but that the only true heroes were military heroes, those who actually manned the guns and faced danger. "The rest of us are merely supplementing their work."[6]

Roosevelt was not alone in believing that military training protected and helped maintain the nation's manhood. One theme running through wartime rhetoric was that men were not really made for the soft office life of modern times and that the noticeable loss of self-respect could be overcome by donning military uniform. It made men feel especially manly in the eyes of women. And the sight of women serving as nurses gave relief to the suffering soldier and glorified women in the eyes of men. Such a vision coincided with a historic sex-role definition of woman submissive and domestic in the service of man. According to the literature, the drilling and preparation for a war put virility on a high moral plane and induced a sense of swelling strength characteristic of maleness. The horror of war did not detract from this idealism. Four thousand miles from the battlefront, death and destruction were so abstract that there was a heroic romanticism in their training.[7]

There were repeated pronouncements about how the war brought out the most masculine and, of course, best virtues in the people. Although the war was no "pink tea" it was still "worthwhile," according to the novelist Arthur G. Empey. One thing Empey learned was that anticipation was far worse than realization. As in civilian life, he noted, frequently a man wondered how he could ever be worthy to fill the shoes of a man ahead of him whose strength and courage he admired. But when the time came to act, there was a certain relief to feel that "the interest of the walk grips him . . . and that the best sort of happiness . . . comes from duty done."[8] This was the great lesson the war was supposed to teach. Quoting private letters, Peter Filene relates the account of a young soldier's telling his mother that he did not dread the trip across the ocean because he, like all true Americans, thought it an honor to be there and to fight for America. Another young man wrote in a letter home, "You know, I think soldiering makes real men."[9]

Given the positive attitude about the effect of military training on the nation's young men, it is not surprising to read arguments rationalizing conscription. Undersecretary of the Navy Franklin Roosevelt urged that all boys, however pacifistic their philosophies, must be prepared to fight and that they would be better men as a result of their training.[10] Henry Stimson praised military service as a deterrent to the decadence of youth. The passing of the frontier life, in which men had had to be physically alert and prepared at all times to overcome obstacles and defend against threats to life, was a serious problem. Stimson was certain that the softness of urban living could not help but have a deleterious effect upon young men. He stated that in Germany, life expectancy was five years longer for those who had had military training in peacetime. For this reason, he praised the Plattsburgh Plan as having a positive effect on youth, and suggested that the United States should provide some military training in schools.[11]

As Theodore Roosevelt had so emphatically stated on many occasions, willingness to exert and sacrifice was a mark of the true patriot, and no true man could ever be anything less than a full-blooded patriot. Books like *And They Thought We Wouldn't Fight* by Floyd Gibbons, a war correspondent for the *Chicage Tribune,* praised the vigor and vitality of the doughboys. Gibbons, who went "over the top" and was wounded, characterized Germany as a bullying, unmanly nation willing to strike from behind to overcome an opponent.[12] Gibbons's book took on a dramatic appeal because of the time that elapsed before the United States abandoned its pacifism to participate in the war.

Even one of the war's greatest heroes, Sergeant Alvin York, was initially opposed to killing other human beings. York was a special type of man, though, raised in the Tennessee mountain country. Tom Skeyhill, linked the war hero to the Boone–Crockett–Jackson image. York was brave and strong, a man of rugged, natural instincts. He was void of "book larnin'," and like Boone, York liked to be left alone. After his father died in 1911, his mother tried to control and direct her son. Although he was a rugged individualist in the mountain-man tradition, he was pacifistic. Finally, when York realized the duty to his country and himself to defend his kind of free-spirited individualism, he was ready to join the army and take his place in the trenches.[13]

BRINGING OUT THE BEST IN A MAN

Young Ernest Hemingway could not wait for America's declaration of war to get into the fighting. He enlisted in the Italian army, became an ambulance driver, and, thus, got his wish to be close to the action. Although there is danger in generalizing on the basis of Hemingway's feelings, there are some aspects of his background that help explain the masculine impulse and the associated patriotic sense of duty during war. Hemingway grew up in the Midwest at a time when Progressivism was attempting to revitalize American institutions. He had been influenced by the ideas of the strenuous life and physical exertion. Hemingway was bothered by a protective and cultivated mother who scolded her son and wanted him to come to his senses and enter proper manhood. Both parents, in fact, reflected the values and passivism of Victorian times. From his father, for example, Ernest learned to fear that masturbation was somehow either the cause or the result of mental sickness. The sentimentalism and idealism of Hemingway's parents left their son with many quandaries, but like Alger and many boys a century before, he had a serious desire to see for himself what life was all about. For Hemingway the war seemed to fulfill that desire.[14]

When the war came, the young generation plunged into it, said Harold Stearns, because it was something they understood. It was an opportunity to "do something." Restraint, sentimentalism, and oratory were now obsolete when the time of action arrived. Fighting poverty and courageously reforming institutions may have been a satisfactory moral equivalent of war, as William James had suggested, but it was unconvincing to young men like Hemingway. After Hemingway was wounded on one of his rescue missions to the front, he wrote from his hospital bed, "It does give you an awfully satisfactory feeling to be wounded." It gave Hemingway a feeling of accomplishment to be able to say that all the heroes of this war were dead and that dying was, after all, a very simple thing. To survive and get through it, to avoid death, if you could, with dignity and grace was the mark of a man. "I've looked at death and really I know," he professed. But if need be, it was better for a man to expire, to go out in a blaze of light, "than to have [his] body worn out and old illusions shattered."[15] John Dos Passos was another young American with incendiary feelings who enlisted in a foreign army to get into the action. In the midst of the horror of battle in France in 1917, Dos Passos confided in his notebook that "I must experience more of it. . . . When one shell comes I want another, nearer, nearer, I constantly feel the need of the drunken excitement of a good bombardment—I want to throw the dice at every turn with the old roisterer death . . . and through it all I feel more alive than ever before—I have never lived yet."[16]

There would be some, notably the poets, scholars, and college men, who might not possess the fighting qualities other men possessed. "I think we are a pretty milky lot," Dos Passos wrote, with "tea-table convictions." What made the difference was the old asumption that scholarship and intellectualism were characteristics of a softer kind of man who could not take the rough military life and would falter during the fighting. "And what are we fit for when they turn us out of Harvard?" complained Dos Passos. "We're too intelligent to be successful businessmen and we haven't the sand or the energy to be anything else," were words perfectly conveying one of the basic attitudes of masculinity in America.[17] Yet, when the poet Joyce Kilmer died in the fighting, *Delineator* magazine expressed a special admiration that even this man, whom one would not consider a warrior, "could think of but one thing—that he must, with his own hands, strike a blow at the Hun. He was a man!"[18]

For such had come to be the mark of a true man in wartime: To be a success as a writer or poet was insufficient to prove one's manhood, but the will to kill was the distinguishing feature that resolved all doubts. Noting the discussion about the softness of the literary man during the Civil War, Charles Thwing, president of Western Reserve University, wrote that college life did not lessen the spirit and quality of democracy or a desire to serve for the cause of democracy. Thwing stated that the kind of individual who came to college was usually adventurous and curious and believed in having experiences that truly tested his character. To support his argument, Thwing pointed out that many young college men enlisted in various foreign field-service organizations that took them close to the fighting long before the United States entered the war. When war was declared, colleges developed military-training programs. In the process, the college man became more industrious and obedient. Most of all, the liberal learning that the college man brought to the military effort made him especially adaptive to the conditions of war.[19]

To Theodore Roosevelt, Hemingway's philosophy would have been commendable. "Woe to those who invite a sterile death," Roosevelt had said. He saw the combat experience as a great purging of weaklings, illusionists, materialists, and faddists. The war would surely cure America of these effeminate maladies and bring Americans face to face with the eternal verities that were "manfully faced by our fathers in the days of Lincoln, [and] by our forefathers in the days of Washington." It followed that Roosevelt assailed the peace movement and those parents who did not teach their young men the necessity of fighting for their country. He advised against exemptions and castigated those sentimental Americans who did not want to see their sons go off to war.[20] He could respect fathers like John R. Mott, General Secretary of the International Committee of the Y.M.C.A., who saw the war as a great boost for fathers because they could appreciate the war's effects vicariously. The "war has sounded new depths in the hearts of the fathers of America," Mott observed, and he predicted that out of this war would come "worthier fathers of nobler and manlier sons."[21]

LIBERALISM REVIEWED

In the same year in which Theodore Roosevelt died and Woodrow Wilson's peace treaty was defeated in the United States Senate, Harold Stearns published a book that reviewed the liberal Progressive period in terms of the outcome of the World War. Stearns saw the liberalism of the years after 1900 as an essential quest for action. Before the war, Americans had been unprepared and even unwilling to take vigorous action because of the softness of Victorian culture and transcendental thought. America had become rudderless and needed a rallying cry, a cause, a great moment, a leader to believe in to reawaken its virile nationalism. The war was the last best effort to restore purpose in the national life. "Here was something we understood—*doing* something."* No more unpleasant spiritual introspections. "Better still," he observed, "it seemed plausible to wrap our activity in the midst of a vague, yet genuine idealism. Thus the cycle was complete; we disliked self-analysis, the war gave us our chance to return whole-heartedly to action."[22]

Stearns rebuked liberalism because even though men's calling themselves liberals might have brought young men back from idealism to

*Emphasis added.

action, the ideals of Progressivism had not been a very good preparation for the realities of war. The old liberals were, after all, a bloodless lot. They did not have in them the robust zest for life they claimed; in fact, "they are just a trifle too self-consciously good and pure." When freedom was on the line at home while the soldiers were overseas fighting for freedom, the old liberals gave in to Prohibition. Liberalism in America had succumbed to "perverted Puritanism." Fanatics who were carried away with their own emotional self-righteousness drove the liberal intellectual into silence. The field of political and social action had become impotent. Woodrow Wilson, most of all, embodied this travesty. His precepts were sterile and, therefore, his idealism, fed by "a sentimental pacifism and moral love of peace," prevented his directing forthright action after the war. Instead, Wilson had been captured by events. His Fourteen Points were a *re*action to a situation, not an action based on a realistic assessment of the facts. In a nation that had praised generations of heroes for their courageous active spirit and control of events, Wilson's peace embodied the mistaken ideas of the "college-bred internationalists" who were willing to jeopardize America's independence, which underscored the masculine vision of the world. Such a policy was taking America down the path that was leading to moral emasculation.[23]

It has become something of a cliché for historians to write that America was different after 1920, and, more specifically, that the war was responsible for changing things the most. Given the concepts of masculine identity, which assumed virility and action and the persistent search for noble causes on the part of American youth, the war years did signal an important shift in American culture with regard to masculinity-validating criteria. From all that has been observed about the masculine style throughout the nineteenth century, it will be remembered that American men seemed to be, or thought they were, in control of things. Men tended to see themselves successfully forcing their will on their environment, their communities, their families, women, and institutions. A great deal was said about manly character, courage, and action, hallmarks of all truly masculine men. Manly men had always made things happen; they got results, moved on to a new frontier where they would be brave, work hard, and, it was hoped, triumph again. But after 1920 there was a subtle but noticeable shift in the perception of the hero. His masculinity was no longer evaluated quite as much on the basis of his ability to control situations and life generally, as it was now measured by his ability to withstand experiences and events that happened to him. This is not to suggest that all the former images and moral guidelines for a strong manhood had vanished. Rather, it was still only a dim awareness that perhaps the world of modern times was beyond the ability of any man, however manly, to shape and control. Now things happened to him as luck and fate would have it.[24]

WARRIORS AFTER THE WAR

Whatever impact the war alone may have had in altering the masculine sense of self and society after 1920 is an open question. No doubt other factors played a part too, but the war experience took its toll on many traditional beliefs and customs. Several writers in the popular periodicals warned that it would be a different man coming home from France. The greatest difference would be in temperament caused by a "pathos of distance," a Nietzchean term, suggesting that some experiences were so intense that they were beyond the apprehension of those who had not experienced them. The roar of battle, the shell shock, the gas, the mud and vermin, the loneliness, the fear of death were leveling experiences. When the war finally lurched to a halt, there was no great sense of expected glory in the triumph of masculine energy or even nationalistic idealism as had been the case in the Civil War and the Spanish-American War. Dos Passos confessed that the war drained his "sentimentalizing over action." In his *Three Soldiers*, the mood was somber and cynical toward war, fighting, heroism, and causes.[25]

At the end of Hemingway's *A Farewell to Arms*, Frederick Henry sat before the fire watching the ants on a burning log trying to escape the inferno. He thought it a wonderful opportunity to be a savior to the ants and lift the log off the fire. But he did no such thing. He tossed water on the fire, emptying his cup to put whiskey in it, and the water on the fire "steamed" the ants. Such was the futility of heroic action.[26] So it was with the soldier's experience, Willard Sperry wrote. The soldier fought only to survive and was most of the time bewildered and inarticulate. "He understands clearly neither his world nor himself. He knows only that he has been living intensely. And he feels vaguely that the proffered systems of religion and politics and economics by which the civilian would help him to self-knowledge are not founded on a discipline as drastic as his own." The old system of masculine discipline that had demanded a man take charge of things and act according to the dictates of his conscience had been revised. "Their life has depended, not on their ability to force any rigid system upon the facts, but rather on their infinite adaptability to fact." Herein lay a crucial reality in determining the direction masculine energy would take in the future. To fully appreciate this new temperament of the soldier was a task that had to be seriously considered by society.[27]

Returning soldiers would still desire action, but they wanted action that would count for something substantial. They would be willing to assume risks based on a new sense of confidence in the method of their approach to life. The veteran would demand efficiency and competence without emotionalism, as his military training had stressed. Most of all, Sperry maintained, the returning veteran did not want to experience the same dullness of routine experienced by the Civil War veterans. In retrospect, it seemed as if the generation that had fought in the Civil War had failed to sustain the active life. To the men who had fought in World War I, it seemed that society after the 1870s had grown soft and effeminate. It had been only through the leadership of an exceptional man like Roosevelt that the nation's men had rediscovered masculinity. Now, in the 1920s, the lasting effect of the European war was that it would prove again the value of the physical life over the contemplative life. The question was whether sufficient action could be found for the men who had experienced the sensations of war.[28]

The quest for the active life and the search for the new heroes, which many historians have noted about the 1920s, explains, in part, the observation that the generation of the 1920s had no interest in politics. Why should there be an interest in politics? All the rhetoric of Progressivism had not altered America or the world very much, just as the political and emotional rhetoric of the 1850s had failed to solve the sectional crisis over slavery. It had finally taken the courage of brave American men in the heat of battle to resolve the crisis. In the final analysis, it had been masculine strength and physical power that got results, and not the words of politicians, intellectuals, and moralizers. Results justified soldiering and the military life as the best exemplification of the masculine ideal in the national mind.

Searching for adventure and a cause drew many young veterans to the revived Ku Klux Klan, which seemed to epitomize manly virtue. The Klan was, in fact, different things to different men. Whereas it was well known for its Negrophobia during Reconstruction, the Klan in the twenties emphasized one-hundred-percent Americanism. To some members this meant a vigorous support of Prohibition. To others it meant a campaign against immorality, immorality that undermined and cheapened American manhood. The Klan campaigned against the black and the whore, denounced pacifism, and advocated a strong navy. The Klan even took issue with the portrayal of America's history in school books by demanding a more militant and aggressive tone to describe the nation's past.[29] In his analysis of the motives for the Klan's revival, Frank Bohn wrote that "our American youth in general never had quite enough excitement out of the experience of the recent war." The Klan appealed to the "hard-minded" youth, many of whom had just been mustered out of the army, and many of whom had never had a chance to actually fight. Recognizing the challenge of the Klan, one young Klansman proclaimed, "We propose to do the deed. . . . This is a military organization. We are under discipline and command."[30] Bohn wrote that Americans needed to understand this aspect of our national psychology if they were to correctly interpret the motives and appeal of the K.K.K. In *The Kluxer,* the organization's weekly newspaper, one could read that Klancraft was a science of character building, a science that Klansmen feared was being disregarded. To them it was a science that could operate only for Anglo-Saxons, a unique heritage handed down from the virile forefathers. They were alarmed by the fact that native Americans were having fewer children while lesser breeds of men and women seemed to propagate more profusely. Thus, the Klan was a unique attraction to many young American men raised in a culture that had always proclaimed the ideal of a strong manly character, patriotism, and courage. Through such an organization as the Klan, the myth of masculinity was sustained.[31]

THE SPECTATOR

The extraordinary popularity of sport during the 1920s, built on the foundation prepared for it before the war, offers another striking example of the perpetuation of the masculine impulse to train, fight, and win in the heroic fashion of the forefathers. Sports writers and observers of American culture began to psychoanalyze sports, and what emerged was a trend toward relating American sports and games to those aspects of American history that vouched for masculine achievement. Sports coverage became more extensive, making it possible for young and old readers alike to have modern heroes to follow and a vicarious sense of accomplishment in their successes. Since the real frontier where men had adventured and tested their courage and bravery was closed, sports offered the possibility of a surrogate frontier and battlefield where modern men could vouch for their masculinity.[32]

A. A. Brill, a noted psychoanalyst, explained that the insurgence of sports was linked to the ancient "mastery impulse" in men. This theme, touched on earlier by Thorstein Veblen and others, was more obviously true during the 1920s, but, according to Brill, that participation was becoming more passive and vicarious. For one thing, the softness of modern times had rendered inadequate the ability of most men to be physically active. Nor was it possible that any significant number of men could play football or baseball because most men did not possess the talent, and there were insufficient teams and facilities to accommodate all who may have wanted to play. Nevertheless, according to Brill, every man still felt the need to "triumph and surpass" and be heroic. Therefore, vicarious involvement substituted for real participation. Brill reasoned that "through the operation of the psychological laws of identification and catharsis, the thoroughgoing fan is distinctly benefited mentally, physically, and morally by spectator participation in his favorite sport."[33]

From a psychoanalytical viewpoint, the aggressive component in sports is what attracted many men as spectators and participants. Athletic contests were seen as substitutes for warfare, in which the contest was always one of potency. Like Veblen before him, Brill believed in the necessity of the cathartic experience for every animal. As life had become more completely organized by the 1920s, it easily became monotonous and routine and "the ancient and unyielding itch for supremacy" often took over. If not allowed some degree of expression, these internal forces could break out in dangerous ways, Brill warned. For example, he suggested that Klan violence and lynchings most often occurred in more remote sections of the country, where sports were scarce.[34] The need for catharsis, which Brill discussed, drove many adolescents to compete in sports even though they may have had a more natural artistic or musical talent. It was necessary for a young boy to exhibit enough physical prowess "to offset any possible suspicion as to his virility." Arnold Beisser contended that many young men were motivated towards sports because they saw in the coach a father figure who could indicate goals and standards real fathers seemed unable to provide, especially as the consequences of the Depression set in. Knute Rockne, for example, who encouraged his players to win one for "the old man," was one such father figure who could inspire great achievements from his boys.[35] It was agreed by most critics that it was significantly valuable for society to have heroes like baseball's Babe Ruth, boxing's

Jack Dempsey, and football's Red Grange and coaches like Knute Rockne, because these individuals helped men and boys appreciate the high standards of manly achievements.[36]

Through the promotional efforts of men like Tex Rickard, boxing attracted an enormous following during the 1920s. Interest in the sport significantly rose during the war, when it had been a main feature of camp athletics and training. Rickard, who had tramped the wilds of the Yukon in search of gold and had ranched in South America, had been successful in staging some prize fights. He perceived that there was a commercial future in boxing and found a fighter, Jack Dempsey, who aroused national interest with his savage punching ability and killer instinct. At first the crowds were cool toward Dempsey, accusing him of being a slacker during the war. But once he proved he could fight like a man, or better than any man who challenged him, the hostility waned and Dempsey became one of the real masculine heroes of his time. In 1926, Dempsey was upset by Gene Tunney, a former marine and American Expeditionary Force boxing champion during the war. A handsome man and a good boxer, Tunney should have been the heir to Dempsey's popularity. But Tunney did not make the grade because he was a different kind of man, in some respects unmasculine. He read books, liked poetry, and even talked to Yale students about Shakespeare. None of this was the mark of a masculine hero. ("He probably hadn't opened a copy of the *Police Gazette* in years," remarked one observer.) When Tunney left professional boxing to pursue his interest in the "highbrow world," it was regarded as no great loss to sports, considering that he had never been the genuine manly type that a heavyweight champion was expected to be.[37]

American men sought in their sports heroes men whose individual actions and behavior personified what American life had always been about, and, somehow, whose efforts might prove that those qualities still existed. Babe Ruth, for example, had been orphaned and fought his way through life to ultimate success by accomplishing some extraordinary feats playing baseball. He was a hard individual to manage, however. He was defiant of authority, demonstrating a common component of the masculine ideal in American culture. Even though baseball was a team sport, Ruth excelled as an individual star, suggesting one man alone against the opposition, fighting hard to win acclaim for himself as much as for the Yankees. Heywood Broun wrote that the fascination with Ruth was in his intense concentration on victory. There was never a moment when he was not trying. "One feels that no crusader has ever been more firmly convinced of the righteousness of his cause. . . ."[38] In recognition of Ruth's individual accomplishments, Yankee Stadium, opened in 1927, was nicknamed "the house that Ruth built." (One should compare fans' attitudes toward Ruth with fans' moods in the changed social climate of the 1930s and '40s, when heroes were recognized as much for their team efforts as they were for their individual feats.) When the public lauded models like Ruth and Grange, they also praised sports for bringing fathers and sons together in the never-ending attempt at making men out of boys.[39]

As American life became more sedentary and civilized, as social and economic reality became more complex, men were going to need a lot more than manly muscles and manly voice and manners to survive. The necessary adjustments men would have to make in their masculine identity during the twenties and the thirties required a much different set of perceptions if men were to retain their composure and cope with change.

EFFECTS OF WOMEN'S SUFFRAGE

Many articles written by men in popular journals and magazines suggested rather strongly a deep concern about the effeminization of American culture and society. Some men interpreted women's suffrage—achieved in 1920—as a lethal blow to masculine predominance. Even though significant changes for women did not immediately result from the suffrage (nineteenth) amendment, there persisted the view that in the little things there were ominous signs of petticoat government.[40] Before the vote was given to women, one writer conceded that female politicians might not be so bad, that clergywomen could be tolerated, and that women stockbrokers would be fair and honest. But what about the old masculine privileges? Some men saw women's getting the vote leading to an invasion of men's private lives, the new voters denying them cigarettes and enforcing Prohibition, actions that would certainly qualify many of the old symbols of masculinity. Even the male diet was expected to come under siege from women.[41]

Feminine fashions and etiquette symbolized a freedom for women in the 1920s. Part of the flapper look was short hair, which made women appear more masculine. Women were going to the barber shop, "the last refuge of masculinity in America," the only spot that had not become "coeducational." Even bars had been invaded by women. Many women now smoked in public. Swimming pools were crowded with women.

Men's clubs now had ladies' nights. But little had changed visibly for men. Their fashions and manners remained about the same. One of the more defensive antifeminist positions was that a rising divorce rate and a declining interest in getting married among some young people was attributable to the masculinization of women. As women's conversation, dress, manners, and leisure-time activity became more like men's, some critics charged that women had lost their feminine interest and capacity for romance.[42]

FEMINISM AND SEX

As part of what some considered a sexual or moral revolution, many stage plays, movies, pop music, and novels borrowed freely from Freudian psychology to dramatize the hidden motives and aspirations of human behavior, in such a way as to suggest that sex explained everything. Eugene O'Neill's plays *Strange Interlude* and *Desire Under The Elms,* movies like *Up in Mabel's Room* and *Her Purchase Price,* and songs like "There's Yes Yes in Your Eyes," "Runnin' Wild," and "If You Knew Suzie Like I Know Suzie" marked an era of flirtatiousness and dialogue about intimate, and what had previously been considered private, matters.[43] Men and women raised according to Victorian moral precepts were shocked to hear about what girls expected—and said they did—on dates with young men. Confessed one very respectable coed about her feelings while on a date: "I don't particularly care to be kissed by some of the fellows I know, but I'd let them do it any time rather than think I wouldn't dare." Another girl reported that "it is natural to want nice men to kiss you, so why not do what is natural?" But did this mean that coeds were now willing to "go all the way" with their dates? Some girls only necked, usually described as kissing and hugging, while others petted, implying a considerably more advanced titillation, but not necessarily resulting in intercourse.[44] Such behavior, and the implications arising from it, were used to document the case for a sexual revolution, which, in reality, centered primarily on the image of the flapper and female sexuality.

But what of the young men who drove the women around in their automobiles, only to park somewhere to experience the sensations of sexual arousal? One thing that became clear during the roaring twenties was that the old distinction between the virtuous-woman-mother-wife image and voluptuous-seductive-indulgent woman that many men had made only a few years before was now quite blurred. Instead of a young man honoring all the well-known platitudes about not insulting a young lady's virtue and being told to treat her as a "frail vessel," he now could find himself in a situation with a young woman who might not only want to indulge in some degree of sexual excitement but might even expect satisfaction from it. The folklore of the jazz age insisted that women could be "fun," but how much fun was an open question. To establish himself as an irresistible he-man among his peers, a young man developed a "line," a combination of light, suggestive chatter with insinuations of sexual action.[45] But what were the consequences if a man expected more than he got from his date? Evidence concerning male premarital sexual attitudes after the war is obscure, but it does seem safe to conclude that the newly professed sexual freedoms and frankness did not result in a new feeling of mutuality and sociability with women. Many girls often brought things to an abrupt halt by resorting to cries of virtue, consistent with their historic role of keeping men pure. Conceivably, young men may have exited from such a situation confused, possibly feeling rejected or even guilty about their performance. Some men, no doubt, had to lie a bit in relating the episode to male peers, in order to be properly recognized for their "masculine achievement."

By 1930, "to become a man" among male peers implied having a sexual experience in spite of parental and social admonitions against promiscuity and the fear of getting a girl pregnant. Compromises with conscience and risk of being caught produced a situation bound to cause its share of problems, not to mention the confusion that resulted from what appeared to be a society overwhelmed by sex obsession, but one that acknowledged traditional morality as the best way to behave.

The availability of birth-control devices added to the problems men had. When Margaret Sanger campaigned for the distribution of birth-control information, she did so not only to protect women from unwanted babies but also to improve the quality and quantity of sex for women, which she maintained was "the most important of all." Sanger interpreted Freud's work as an endorsement of virtually unlimited sexual indulgence. Old repressions and inhibitions had to be overcome, and once they were, Sanger predicted women would achieve a highly rewarding sexuality. In accord with Havelock Ellis and George Carpenter, Sanger viewed sex as a new avenue of mutual expression and self-development. Historically, sex had been a male privilege endured by females, but the new ideology stressed the unique nature of female sexuality and encouraged women to understand and develop it. They were now advised to think of themselves as equals who could lead and give for the sake of their own fulfillment as well as their mates'. Birth control made possible the romanticization of sex, extending it beyond a biological function necessary to preserve the race.[46]

The implications of Sanger's philosophy put men on the spot. Birth control made it possible to have intercourse more frequently, and the condom, when properly used, removed fears of unwanted pregnancies. Now men had to perform up to a standard of satisfaction determined by women's as well as men's pleasures. Marriage manuals began to instruct couples on simultaneous orgasms. All of this threatened to expose males as good lovers or bad. Evidence suggests that even men who considered themselves quite virile were disturbed by the new standards. There was no longer the plea for moderation to protect them from sexual scrutiny. As a result, male neuroses and nervous breakdowns became more frequent, according to psychiatrists treating males upset by their sexual performance.[47]

Antifeminists protested that women were seeking too much. Their emancipation was a man's loss. Progress had depended on masculine productivity and domination. The critics argued that the most recent phase of the revolution had made American women freer than American men, who still felt compelled to live up to the standards embodied within the framework of traditional masculine identity. A contributor to *Forum* wrote that American women had successfully fashioned a new caste for themselves, one clearly superior to the male caste. From this position, women were running American institutions and extending a wide range of influence over everybody. Some of the new freedom women found came as a direct result of the war. Although it did not approach the movement into "men's jobs" of World War II, a trend of more women entering the labor force was evident. Women were claiming they could support themselves, a fact that those men who took very seriously their breadwinning role could not help but worry about.[48]

NEW IDEAS ABOUT MARRIAGE

One of the most startling scenarios was spun out in Dorothy Canfield Fisher's *The Happy Homemaker*. The happy homemaker turns out to be a man who has failed at business and decides to stay home and raise the children while his wife goes into business.[49] A more complex relationship was developed between Fran and Sam Dodsworth in the Nobel–Prize-winning novel *Dodsworth* by Sinclair Lewis. Sam had forsaken the lure of being "a Richard Harding Davis hero" to marry and settle down with the tantalizing Fran and invest his life in the automobile-manufacturing business, knowing "he would be caught for life." But Sam's life was incomplete and unfulfilled, and he was made aware of it by Fran, who "had the high art of deflating him." She persuaded him to go to Europe, experience culture, and have new friends, an education that Fran believed would restore zest to their dull life. But, the trip deepened Sam's self-doubt and sense of inadequacy. He could not help but appear as a boob American, trapped by his conventional behavior while feeling personally unfulfilled even though he was a man of considerable business success.[50]

The novelist Fanny Hurst announced that she and her husband were taking up separate living quarters in order to lead more contented lives—but they would remain married. She charged that marriage had failed to respond to the modern temper of both sexes. The companionette marriage, in which each partner retained a strong sense of individuality, had the advantage of lending privacy to both husband and wife, the kind of privacy traditional marriage did not permit. If monogamy were to survive, it would require some sophisticated pampering to appear more appealing than it really was. "A woman must be new to her mate, a man must be a not altogether known quantity to his. Neither can afford to let all the barriers fall." In the companionette marriage, Hurst believed, it would be easier to preserve a sense of spontaneity and vitality. "Yet men are afraid to build it and women are afraid to live in it. Fear, fear of living, that is the cause of the slow step of progress in all avenues of life." Regardless of the logistical and moral issues in Hurst's proposal, her point about freedom touched sensitive nerves. Although America was a free society, marriage and the social sanctions supporting it had not done a very good job of protecting personal freedom and enhancing the growth and maturity of husband and wife. Hurst assumed people had to be free to be creative and that only creative people could be truly happy and successful in their personal relationships—however those relationships were structured. Freedom, not the fears and restraints of the past, was the path to feminine as well as masculine fulfillment.[51]

A NEW SELF-IMAGE

The changes affecting the nature and substance of masculinity were becoming more perceivable by the late twenties and were especially noticeable with the onset of hard times. In the nineteenth century, the self-made man, through the sheer force of his energy and personality, had made things happen. According to the mystique surrounding these individuals, they had achieved their goals in life precisely because they were physically and mentally fit as men. They had gone through all the tests, perhaps even war, and triumphed in the tradition of all true and worthy men. During the twenties, however, success seemed to happen to individuals because of mere luck. Forces and events beyond human control were often more in charge of life than men were themselves. In his revealing content analyses of popular biographies in magazines, Leo Lowenthal has found that beginning in the twenties individuals were no longer described as possessing a boundless energy that had made for success and had shaped progress. Successful men seemed to be more often the ones who were able to adjust appropriately to events.[52]

The Depression forced almost all Americans to adjust as best they could to events absolutely out of the average person's control. A survey of many writers who described the impact of the Depression and diagnosed the difficulties men experienced in coping with hard times reveals a general agreement that the Depression helped trigger an acute masculinity-identity crisis. Never before had American males suffered as emotionally as they did when they were confronted by situations that rendered obsolete many of the old symbols and standards of virile masculinity. In fact, many of the changes in contemporary American sex roles that have received wide attention by historians and sociologists can be dated from the 1930s. Essays and short stories abound in which it is argued from many perspectives that the mastery of the masculine component had become just an illusion. One woman wondered how men could ever expect to regain their lost hegemony when "the inevitable march of events diminishes every year and every day the value of brawn and muscle."[53] Other women and even some men noted how "puny" men had become, how fragile and easily hurt they were, producing a mixture of warnings and complaints that tended to undo the masculine image. "Just as woman has needed to cloak the hard realism of her present position with a certain philosophic glamour, man, in an effort to recapture his old social value, must continuously find fresh excuses for the loss of his old prestige."[54]

Sherwood Anderson's *Puzzled America* documented the loss of manhood in the wake of joblessness and pleaded for a sincere understanding of the identity crisis facing American men. He found that although the Depression certainly was economic, it also had an enormous psychological impact. "The breaking down of the moral fiber of the American man, through being out of a job, losing that sense of being some part of the moving world of activity, so essential to an American man's sense of his manhood—the loss of this essential something in the jobless can never be measured in dollars."[55]

A British visitor, Shaw Desmond, had reached the same conclusion in 1932, observing that American males saw their personalities reflected in their bank balance, and when the balance dwindled, they were often overcome by remorse and self-doubt. Because European culture did not tend to associate business success with masculinity, European males were not as susceptible to ravaged egos during economic difficulties. Sherwood Anderson agreed that American men were not as well prepared as European men to withstand the depression.[56] In *Hard Times*, Studs Terkel wrote of his interviews with several psychiatrists, among them Nathan Ackerman of Columbia University, who observed miners in Pennsylvania during the Depression. According to Ackerman, some of the laid-off miners were reluctant to head home to report on their joblessness. "The women punished the men for not bringing home the bacon, by withholding themselves sexually, by belittling and emasculating the men, undermining their paternal authority, and turning to the eldest son." David Rossman concurred that, in spite of the numerous and complex factors causing the economy to turn bad, there was a distinct tendency to blame one's self for being down and out.[57]

Several empirical studies made during the 1930s generally verify Anderson's observations and those of the psychiatrists quoted by Terkel. Mirra Komarovsky studied fifty-nine families of lower-middle-class background. Generally, the status of the male was more precarious with the loss of his job, particularly so in the eyes of his wife. There seemed to be a crystallization of personal inferiority touched off by unemployment. Those men who saw other members of their families get jobs, even if only menial tasks, were put in the humiliating position of having to tap the family kitty for tobacco money. Some admitted to nervousness and a decrease in intercourse. Some felt their wives showed open contempt for them. Men who had traditionally held an authoritative position in the family and in their society because of their breadwinning role now found themselves disgraced by the loss of earning power. Of the families studied, it was concluded that in very few cases did the husband successfully accommodate himself to a subsequent realignment of power and prestige.

Such an emotional impact could only happen in a society in which the male ego was so completely dependent upon concepts of "success" that were implicitly tied to productive employment and virility. Even after tireless efforts to find employment under economic conditions over which they had very little control, the men in Komarovsky's study still adhered to the old work ethic that bringing home a paycheck was "up to the man." Some engaged in self-recrimination and withdrew from friends and church, apparently preferring not to run the risk of exposure as a failure.[58] Winona Morgan's study, not as detailed or as convincing but covering more families, found that twenty-seven percent of the fathers questioned reported that a personal sense of failure was the most serious effect of the hard times. Twenty-one percent ranked a lowered income as the specific reason.[59]

COPING WITH HARD TIMES

Another valuable study, of one hundred Chicago families, reveals much about Depression-era problems and attitudes and remains quite instructive to subsequent generations seeking to construct new sex-role patterns. Conducting the study in the mid-1930s, Ruth Cavan and Katherine Ranck were as interested in observing problems of status, especially masculine status, as they were the specific effects of a loss of income. Although it is difficult to generalize from their study about the overall effects of the Depression and adjustment to it, the patterns shown by the Chicago families nevertheless suggested that men had a worse time coping than women. But there were men who adjusted to the unsettling nature of the Depression because they were able to be philosophical about it and understand that economic ups and downs were not altogether uncustomary. Where established patterns of sharing and interchanging of sex-role functions around the house had existed before, there seemed to be an easier adjustment to austere living. But the men who tried to live as before and maintain an impression of invulnerability were the most vulnerable of all to emotional problems caused by an eclipse of their masculine self-image. The study reported cases of insomnia, nervous breakdown, estrangement from children, excessive drinking, and in extreme cases even suicidal tendencies. But again, a significant aspect of the study is that much of this behavior is traceable to a decline in status, the kind of status that had been associated with the masculine mystique of invincibility and high self-esteem based on the premise of financial well-being. When men considered their masculine roles more liberally, the better they were at enduring the impact of the Depression.[60]

The Robert and Helen Lynd study *Middletown in Transition* supports the conclusion of the empirically based studies that women withstood the pressures of the Depression better than men. The study also emphasized the status quo with regard to the traditional masculine image. The authors revealed an American community in which the people believed and trusted the average man of character more than they did the man with great intelligence. They believed that hard work was the key to success and defined success almost exclusively in economic terms. They believed that college men were no better off than non- college men, and that the college man was less practical and had to learn about life through experience to counteract his tendency to quote theory. And, like many Victorians who had subscribed to social Darwinism, the people who were questioned believed that a man was better off for having gone through the school of hard knocks and that there was no such thing as a "youth problem." The Lynds were told that "men should behave like men, and women like women," that women are better ["purer"] than men," that men were more practical and efficient than women, and that women could not understand public problems as well as men. Middletown citizens believed that fathers did not understand children or women. They saw and valued "red-blooded" physical sports as normal recreation for men rather than art, music, and literature, which were seen as womanly things. And it was more acceptable for men to smoke and drink than it was for women to do the same. And so on, the point being that the values found by the Lynds in Middletown suggest that these men and women had not moved very far from the sex-role configurations of Victorian culture. These findings suggest that a diversifying of sex roles and willingness to relinquish old images would not be very likely to happen in helping men and women cope with Depression-related problems.[61]

Examining the popular periodical literature, one can find numerous authors who acknowledged that serious tensions existed between American men and women. Those authors traced the roots of that tension far back into American history and noted that sex-role distinctions had become blurred through time. The harsh reality of an austere existence during the Depression quickly brought those tensions to the surface in many cases. In the first year after the crash, Lillian Symes gravely observed that "just as woman has needed to cloak the hard realism of her present position with a certain philosophic glamour, man, in an effort to recapture his old social value, must continuously find fresh excuses for the loss of his old prestige." As a result, some men, according to contemporary spokesmen, became obsessed by female assertiveness and sought to pull their rank and restore their status.[62] Or, as one anxious male confessed shortly before the 1929 crash, "The only great kick I get out of my life any more, my greatest fun, is my business." For him, American life had become too closely monitored by the new woman to be considered "free" any longer. He wrote of fantasizing an escape to the seashore and then fleeing again when his wife caught up with him there. He confessed that women were inherently tougher than men, implying that if they only realized it, they would lessen their demands on their "boob husbands." If pressure were not lessened, divorce would continue to increase because of the masculinization of women, that is, women's rising to the level of men in all areas: having common male habits like smoking, playing at sports, taking part in political conversation, and even dressing like men.[63] D. H. Lawrence summarized the situation by complaining that women had become so assertive since getting the vote that they had lost all perspective and had rushed headfirst into sports, public welfare, and business. "She is marvelous, outmanning the man."[64] *Time* described the state of marriage and family affections in 1940 as a "grim panorama which gives the impression that Americans are an irritable, aggravated, dissatisfied people for whom marriage is an ordeal that only heroes and heroines can bear."[65]

SOCIETAL CHANGES

John Erskine lamented the passing of male influence and the physical as well as emotional dislocation many men experienced with the rise of the new woman. Worst of all, the new woman had so completely effeminized culture and religion that Erskine anguished at the prospect of one day having to compete with the people of the East and their vigorous, male-oriented religion. According to Erskine, American women were having a disastrous effect on the nation's politics by criticizing some of its cherished beliefs. The New Deal had, in effect, surrendered to women and had adopted feminine techniques of administering social justice. The best example of this was the process of taking wealth from one group and distributing it to the needy, representing, to Erskine, a manifestation of rampant feminine sentimentalism. It was the very antithesis of the masculine idea of progress in America and was contrary to natural law, which recognized the inequality of talents just as Christ had done. "The vision He tried to set before us was of heroic manliness." Erskine predicted a major shift in world power from Western societies to Japan, where the men had not allowed creeping effeminization to undermine their traditionally masculine institutions. Those nations still aggressive and powerful would in time overtake the more passive nations of Western civilization. Erskine prescribed a massive revitalization of the masculine image to offset the feminine encroachment. Men were even advised to avoid romantic love because, when taken too seriously, it made a virtue of surrendering their hearts to women, thus making men maudlin and submissive. Fathers needed to get to know their sons better and drive out of their lives all that was artificial and sterile.[66]

Another Erskine recommendation concerned the schools. If true manliness were to be salvaged, male teachers should replace females in the public schools. The woman teacher had become a symbol of authority— one more instance in which young men were forced to obey women.[67] Robert Rogers, an M.I.T. professor, agreed that American schools had been completely emasculated by overzealous female teachers who were too anxious to shape things: "her husband, her sons, her community." Single-minded female teachers discouraged the development of natural manly attributes for the sake of artificial discipline and learning. Tough-minded, pragmatic, nonidealistic male methods had become items of scorn for the more intense, less patient modern woman. Rogers went so far as to claim that women were chiefly responsible for revolutions and wars—products, he wrote, of feminine moralistic idealism and dogma. Female teachers were critical of men and the way they raised their sons because a father's goal never appeared sufficient. As one father put it, as his son approached junior high, "I am about to be weighed in the balance of modern education and found wanting." In contrast, males conditioned by experience knew that truth was relative and variable in application. Men could, therefore, accept the reality of a pluralistic existence attuned to nature rather than the artificial cultural platitudes articulated by women.[68]

The unemployment and underemployment caused by the Depression meant that many husbands, fathers, and sons spent more time around the house and crossed paths frequently with wives and mothers. It was difficult for these men, who cherished the "manly tradition of activity," to be content at home. If they read, sipped tea, or cooked, things they had time to do, they compromised the concept of male virility that assumed an action-oriented life. They were constantly scrutinized by women who picked up after them and even laid out their clothes. Home became a new realm for the "bewildered man of affairs," according to an *Atlantic Monthly* article. A man found himself confined in a restless exile, in a house where as often as not he was in the way of a wife's routine. "A husband is a puny thing against such an avalanche."[69] In effect, men felt estranged in their own homes because they had always been the women's domain. One review of the "helplessness" of modern American males contended that some women actually relished having their psychologically bruised husbands around to mother. It was reflected in their desire to help care for "their boys," The author Corine Lowe suggested, however, that this attraction to the suffering male might really be a manifestation of female "power in helping somebody weaker than ourselves." The American male once praised by many as the international ideal of manliness, had come to typify submission and defeat.[70]

The *American Mercury* published numerous articles in the late 1930s about the beleaguered condition of American men. Stewart Holbrook lamented that the old he-man had changed irrevocably after Theodore Roosevelt and was now reduced to a check-writing eunuch. No longer did Americans even seem to cherish the heroic moments of war as they had in the past. The change, of course, was due to the effeminate, pacifistic nature of modern times. As gadgetry was making Americans docile, more and more husbands slept in single beds, gaining access to their wives only if suppliant. Gone were beards, the old badge of nineteenth-century American virility, as well as the tough cop whose brute strength was well known and respected, replaced now by more "civilized" law officers. Decreasing in number were the old all-male bars, now infiltrated by females who sipped their brew, triumphantly contemplating the new world that belonged to women. Like other conservatives, Holbrook believed that the government, through social security, was undermining the older, more masculine world by legally declaring its concern for the welfare of American citizens. What a long way man was from the masculine cut-throat competitiveness of the nineteenth century. Holbrook recognized that the "disappearing manhood of the Yankee male" had been predicted before, but now terrified at the prospect, Holbrook admitted that the pattern was unfolding. Amram Sheinfeld called it "one of the greatest upsets of all time." Males were found to be weaker than females, less resistant, more defective and more likely to collapse under adverse conditions.[71]

Several unscientific opinion surveys suggest how many men apparently felt about being overthrown by women and the subsequent eclipse of the once-proud male status as dominant provider. Ninety percent of the men questioned in a *Ladies' Home Journal* survey in 1939 said that women should not take a job after marriage. Fifty-nine percent said women were doing too much outside the home in the way of club activities, parties, and going to sports events. Fifty-five percent of the men thought women were spoiled or overindulged by men who were only trying to keep them happy. Forty-two percent listed "nagging and jealousy" as the most common faults of women. Thirty-six percent said women tended to be too extravagant and thirty percent blamed women for being too bossy. Thirty-eight percent blamed the increase of divorce directly on women, while only fourteen percent of the men said it was the men's fault. Thirty-nine percent of the men answered "yes," that men alone should be boss at home. Two years after this survey, a University of Tennessee professor reported that one out of three husbands was unhappy with his marriage and two out of seven women were discontent with their marriages. Men were hard pressed to escape the feminine influence.[72] One sympathetic woman observed that "by following the men from the schoolroom and the home into his working fields, for that matter his playing fields, his club, his bars, his barbershops, we have stolen from him his last retreats. Now he never gets away from our sex."[73]

FATHERS AND SONS

Floyd Dell urged that America's men quit being so depressed by the hard economic times because fathers were inflicting debilitating effects on their sons. Recalling his youth, when his own father had faced hard times, Dell recalled that his father had worried mostly about his life insurance and felt that he really could not do much for his children. Dell's father believed in success and, like most men, defined success and fulfillment in very narrow economic terms. But, Dell noted, the really important thing was not the money "but the human actuality of my father himself." Even though his father had been out of a job, Dell remembered fondly in 1934 that "he was still the bulwark of my childhood adolescence." And the same lesson applied to men of the 1930s who felt sorry for themselves because they were failing in their breadwinner role. It was time for American men to stop whimpering about their strained status and depleted savings, time to help their sons develop courage and acquire a sense of power and a "belief that [they] can help reshape this sorry scheme of

things."[74] Dell's socialism provided the basis for his advice to fathers, b
from the evidence available, that advice does not seem to have been
followed. A man interviewed by Studs Terkel recalled how shocked,
confused, and hurt many boys were about their fathers' condition of not
being able to better provide for the family. Often quarrels that were bitter
erupted between fathers and sons over the lack of financial support. One
result was the deepening of a split attitude regarding parents as fathers
seemed more remote than ever and mothers increasingly became the
source of love and emotional support.[75]

In spite of all the advice to fathers, dating back to the nineteenth
century, and the occasional efforts exerted, as in the Progressive era, to
bring American fathers into the mainstream of family life, especially into a
closer relationship with their children, the evidence suggests that this
objective never really succeeded. Admittedly, the time fathers had to
spend away from children and the exhaustive nature of their work undoubtedly militated against a closer association between fathers and children. But there were other causes of patriarchal estrangement that had to
do with the very nature of sex-role functions throughout history and specifically with the masculine image. Floyd Dell's analysis provides a good
example. Men seemed to lack the capacity to love, be affectionate, and
relate to children, especially in time of financial hardship or when social
status was in a state of flux. Men, especially fathers, were always expected
to be confident, strong, and in control, someone to look up to as an
authority figure. Many fathers found it hard to project such an image at
home (if indeed they ever had). One result was that mothers remained
clearly at the center of family life in the wake of a father's silent, moody
behavior and found themselves in a position to exert more influence and
be more assertive than ever. Problems developed when mother love became too egotistical, emotional, and possessive, according to Lois Boyliss.
The problems created at home by such a mother were so acute that Alice
Kelly contended that she knew of college students who dreaded going
home for vacations to face their mothers. Emotional refuge was sought by
keeping children tied to the mothers' apron strings. They often shielded
their children from normal social interaction with other young people,
apparently resenting any joy or affection their sons and daughters might
have had with anyone else. Because the father's role was so nebulous,
there was an increasing likelihood that children were going to assume that
women were naturally the bosses. Boys needed a strong man in their lives,
but it was more difficult in the 1930s than ever for boys to identify with

many dads had become little more than "star board-
.n homes. Too many mothers were spoiling their sons,
.., who registered a strong appeal for the return of male
"We are sick to death of pansies," she wrote.[76]

.alaise of fatherhood was blamed for the patterns of deviancy
, adolescent males during the Depression. Mothers had been negli-
ge. . and even deceptive, most often evasive, in dealing with sex matters.
The result, it was charged, was very often an immature young man, prone
to have sexual problems and even commit sexual offenses. "For every
man in prison there are usually two women—a mother and a wife—who
should be there with him for contributing to the infantilism of male
adults," wrote Gordon Shipman.[77] It was argued that the woman in the
average man's life had diminished his self-confidence by careless remarks
or overly protective care, all administered in the name of love and affection.

Philip Wylie found, some years later, that when these "over mothered"
men went into military service in World War II, they were the ones most
likely to have adjustment problems. Their increased use of profanity was
interpreted as an emotional attack on the shackles of matriarchy, which
had entrapped many boys in their teens. The way they met social challenges and faced the dangers of war reflected a sense of immaturity and
personal doubt about their past and their masculine identity. Wylie
scrutinized educational institutions and, most of all, American mothers,
finding them scandalously deficient in purpose and responsibility. "The
male is an attachment of the female in our civilization," he complained,
the result being a disastrous psychological disturbance of American males
in the 1940s.*[78]

THE DISPLACED MALE

How individual men coped with the anxiety caused by the Depression
is still mostly an untold story. Some men simply escaped by hitting the
open road, perhaps to find work somewhere else, but in some cases, one
suspects, to avoid having to face the humiliation over the loss of their
masculine dignity. Some men apparently escaped into alcohol or chewed
more tobacco to relieve tension, but also because alcohol and tobacco had

---

*The implications of Wylie's thesis are discussed in greater detail in Chapter 8 of this
book.

always been associated with the image of a hard-driving, hard-living man. At least one female critic castigated men for this foolish behavior, claiming they were activities designed to conceal self-consciousness about failings.[79] Some men moved their entire family, like the Joads in John Steinbeck's *The Grapes of Wrath*, in which, it is interesting to note, it is Ma Joad who keeps the family organized, maintains morale, and preaches self-control to young Tom. Symbolically, at the novel's end, Rose of Sharon, following the stillborn birth of her baby, gives her breast to a transient male, keeping him from starvation.[80]

When a man lost his job, he tended to avoid his friends, whom he could not face because of the psychological wounds caused by joblessness. He preferred to endure the crisis alone rather than admit failure to a friend or a loved one. Caroline Bird, a Vassar graduate of 1935, estimated that the Depression postponed some 800,000 marriages. Some young men wanted nothing at all to do with women because courting involved at least some degree of expense they were not capable of meeting. What a young man had to spend on a girl was often interpreted as an indication of his character, and quite an embarrassment if there wasn't enough money to make a date happy. "Childish as it sounds," complained one young man, "I keep away from girls for fear I'll fall in love and make matters worse."[81]

To David Cohn, a frequent contributor to *Atlantic* and *Saturday Review*, the tension between men and women came as no surprise. The calamity of the Depression catalyzed certain social and sexual mores and private aspirations that had been in latent conflict between American men and women for a long time. What had been suggested earlier by Junius Browne and Floyd Dell, among others, Cohn developed further in a book titled *Love in America*. The main point of his analysis was to explain the failure of Americans to achieve a mature understanding of love. One obvious culprit was the business-and-success syndrome that had made slaves of American men and robbed them of their sense of adventure. From the vantage point of the Depression, Cohn pointed out the differences between American and European businessmen. According to Cohn, the business existence of the average European male seldom disturbed the emotional center of his life. He was able to love, whether his wife or mistress, regardless of the goings-on at the office or shop. Love was important to him and because he had a sense of historical continuity with his community and home, the European did not segment his life the way Americans did. Perhaps even worse, the business culture compelled American men to relate to things and people in terms of possession because they could only relate to life through their acquisitions. What the Depression did was reveal some glaring faults in these patterns. When success hung in the balance, or if failure confronted a man, he usually was without emotional anchor since he had never taken the time (because American men were always in a hurry) or the care (because American men eschewed sentimentality) to make loving a part of living. Cohn had contempt for women too, because many of them had become so accustomed to being pampered that they had no other expectations from their men. Women had become the classic consumers—devouring the goods and enjoying the services and luxuries of an economy that had achieved a remarkable record of growth and productivity.[82]

A central question emerging from Cohn's book was whether men continued to work so hard because their wives demanded so much from them or because men did not know how else to impress their wives or know what to do for them. Like men, women believed things could be like they were before, when, according to their nostalgia, success came easy and the middle class had money to spend and spent it. The fact that women's magazines tended to ignore the Depression indicated to Cohn that women did not understand or have an interest in the socioeconomic process and its related problems. Cohn urged women to finally do what they had always promised: civilize American men. To help break the fetish of practicality and the business-culture fixation men had, women were advised to enter politics and higher education to help men re-examine their traditional interests and values in order to create diversity and relieve them of their desperation. Advice-to-the-lovelorn columns became popular reading during the 1930s, perhaps because they served as a universal confessional or a way to reach out for information and communication available in no other place.[83]

FINDING DIVERSIONS

Some men turned to prostitutes for a release of pent-up emotions or just to communicate with a woman who had no expectations or demands to be met, except the payment of a fee. Polly Adler, a famous New York madam, is said to have claimed that her business nearly doubled during the Depression. Many men visited her establishment just for conversation, even if it meant spending up to thirty dollars for liquor. One frequent customer said he found Adler's parlor the only place he could go to cry without revealing his shame of having been defeated. There were cases, however, of unexplained violence: One customer, a regular patron, suddenly turned brutal and beat up one girl. The next day he shot himself while sitting at his desk.[84] Shaw Desmond viewed turning to prostitution as a matter of retaliation: "For the American man tends to get so frightened and so tired of his lawful spouse, that he is apt to face solace in the arms of dangerous attractiveness. It is the revenge of the harassed male for years of suppression." Burlesque theatres catered to a poorer clientele, offering escape, relaxation, and fantasy while "broads," "floozies," or "chippies" entertained them. These women complemented the attitude about sex of the men who watched them. There was no commitment—to marriage, to family, or to anything. Strippers teased the men by seductively removing their garments solely for the purpose of erotic arousal, but with absolutely no promise of sexual engagement. Geoffrey Gorer viewed the men attracted to such performances as basically unsure of their masculinity, wanting no personal involvement of any kind for fear that they would have to account for themselves.[85]

Sports, on the other hand, conjured up refreshing images of masculine activity and, as always, offered some involvement to capable participants. Even though team sports were popular, Joe Louis, as an individual, electrified the boxing world with his dynamite punching ability. That a black man, always the underdog, could rise to the top of a sport seemed encouraging even to whites. And there was farmboy Dizzy Dean, whose unpredictable behavior was the subject of many stories on and off the baseball diamond. The St. Louis Cardinals, dubbed the "gas-house gang," caught the imagination of American sports fans with their aggressive style of play. The very frenzy of such forceful competition in sports gave the fan an inner exhilaration and restored a sense of confidence that at least somewhere men were still men in a time when there were grave doubts about masculine dominance.[86] But even athletics showed signs of creeping effeminization, or, more bluntly, according to Eliot Spalding, America's athletes were becoming a bunch of crybabies who could no longer take physical punishment as they had in the days of Theodore Roosevelt. In the thirties, complaints of ailments and pains were much more frequent than before. College and professional sports had grown soft, and Spalding held sportswriters responsible because they played up to the modern trend that it was no disgrace to enjoy a good cry at misfortune rather than fight it out in the old true competitive style. Only hockey, he said, was free from the psychiatrist and the pill bottle.[87]

Beyond the attraction of sports, there existed the world of make-believe, in which masculine figures were etched in absolute terms, unabashed and uncompromised. One popular character of the thirties was the tough detective, as created by Dashiell Hammett, whose heroes usually drank a lot and had sexual relations with four or five exciting women but never became emotionally involved. In Hammett's *The Maltese Falcon*, Sam Spade has an affair with a woman who turns out to be his partner's killer. Without hesitation, Spade takes her to the police. Superman and Tarzan appeared in movies and comic books as popular masculine images during the twenties and thirties. Tarzan lived in the wild, a timeless character always able to cope with his hostile environment. Superman, like Tarzan, defied the harsh realities of his environment—even gravity—to maintain order. Both represented exaggerated extensions of frontier heroes in that the superheroes lived by simple social codes. Tarzan left his jungle home for England, where he learned English, but he secretly yearned for the jungle and eventually returned, suggesting that perhaps man was not suited to civilization at all.[88]

Cowboy heroes like Tom Mix and the Lone Ranger became household names as they successfully captured a sense of the Old West, in which the sheer power and grit of one's masculinity were the best and only defenses against disorder and chaos. In 1934, the cartoonist Alex Raymond launched Flash Gordon with all the necessary ingredients to make him a great masculine hero. Gordon, a handsome specimen of a man, educated at Yale and a polo player, had a beautiful female companion, Dale Arden. Along with the insane Dr. Zarkov, who had kidnapped and taken them to the planet Mongo, the trio faced a yellow race led by Ming the Merciless. Constantly the subject of intrigues and seduction by beautiful women, Gordon, nevertheless, remained faithful to all the old values of his childhood and the rules of fair play, a testimony to the strength of his manhood. Meanwhile, Jack Armstrong, "the All-American boy," led Hudson High to glory and battled bad guys whenever they intruded upon progress and decent living. In the midst of the Depression, it must have been reassuring to all Americans when a Tibetan monk told Jack that the world belonged to the boys and girls of the United States—if they had "hearts of gold" and were honest and kind.

Heroes on the screen and in comic books entertained as well as inspired many people who were down and out. American males could identify with John Wayne's forcefulness and courage in *Stagecoach* and laugh at Charlie Chaplin's attack on industrialism and technology in *Modern Times*. Some men may have secretly relished the sight of Carole Lombard being slapped by Fredric March in *Nothing Sacred* or applauded James Cagney in *Public Enemy* when he smashed a grapefruit into Mae Clarke's face. And surely, among the most famous lines uttered on the screen came from the masculine Clark Gable in *Gone With the Wind* when, confronted by adversity, he proclaimed, "I don't give a damn." It was all very entertaining, but it also provided an exciting, if vicarious, striking-back at unsettling times.

REINVIGORATING THE MALE

But all was not doom and gloom for men. The well-known critic Gilbert Seldes cited several examples in which masculinity was being restored. Household furniture and fixtures were returning to functionalism, replacing the feminine daintiness of previous years. Natural (masculine) foods were coming back after their temporary eclipse by processed and packaged (feminine) foods. But to Seldes, the real triumph of masculinity came with the repeal of Prohibition. Once again men could retreat to their sanctuaries of masculine preference at least to those still reserved for men, to tell stories and nurse damaged egos. In the long run, however, Seldes believed that it would take another war to prompt the real return of American males back to full esteem and credibility.[89]

Two publications, Dale Carnegie's *How to Win Friends and Influence People* and Napoleon Hill's *Think and Grow Rich*, also outlined the return of male success and domination.* Both, however, followed assumptions similar to nineteenth-century guidebooks, that success was possible if one would only *be a man*. The authors spelled out no new techniques to ensure success. No new theories of business enterprise or masculinity abounded. Instead, as John Cawelti has noted, the suggestions for success and personal fulfillment in business were mostly recapitulations of old ideas. Another book, by Russell Henderson, that pictured Superman on the cover, was dedicated to the neurotic, nervous American male who wanted to restore his virility and reassert his masculinity. The book covered diet, grooming, and exercise suggestions and offered counsel on sex matters. Throughout, the emphasis was on "toughening up" the male, restoring him to prime physical and moral condition.[90]

---

*The Carnegie and Hill books are comparable to nineteenth-century guidebook literature, which is expertly summarized in both John Cawelti's *Apostles of the Self-Made Man* (Chicago: University of Chicago Press, 1965) and Irvin Wyllie's *The Self-Made Man in America* (New York: Macmillan Co., 1954).

The impact of the Depression on male consciousness demonstrates that the masculinity stereotype was at best a troublesome asset. The bread-winning role in American civilization assumed masculine activity, success, courage, and accomplishment. Throughout American history, to be considered manly and receive the status associated with rugged manliness called for a total investment of energies and resources. Perhaps, in an earlier period, when the nation's economic development was more primitive, the spatial distance between individuals greater, and the question of survival more direct, the standards of masculinity may have been more relevant. On the basis of these standards, the male role had been defined and the expected behavior of men established. In several important ways, the stereotype that emerged from that era was bound to imprison men and leave them without adequate resources to survive the stress of hard times. For example, men had assumed that their status in business and their success on the job endeared them to wife and family. But to their families, men were virtual strangers whose importance revolved around activity away from home. Once the paycheck was deposited, it was a common feeling that family responsibilities had been met. When the paychecks stopped coming in or decreased in amount, a man was suddenly accountable and scrutinized as to *his* failure and *his* problems. Instead of home being a place where a man could find comfort and love in a time of need, a man often found that home had its own routines and relationships quite unknown to and very separate from him.

THE MYSTIQUE AS HANDICAP

Many men who survived the Depression could look back on it as one of the best of times, or at least a time in which their manhood was tested and proven. Because they survived and, in some cases, did well, the masculinity of those who failed was questioned. It was easy for the successful to see individuals at fault, which was quite in keeping with the association of good character and success in American thought, rather than see the victims' tragic condition as the breakdown of an economic system. It was easy to blame the jobless, the ghetto dweller, or the welfare recipient for not having the drive, courage, or whatever was seen as the ingredients of true manhood. And it was easy to reject legitimate explanations and criticism about how the *system* may have failed an individual. Those men who believed in the masculine mystique of success and status and still failed often resorted to self-ridicule or took out their frustrations on others who they believed were the cause of failure. Women, minorities, education, the company, the children—any one or all—were blamed for holding back what would otherwise have been a successful man. In success or failure, the masculine mystique had become a prison, a genuine barrier to creative and productive thinking and living. Instead of being an inspiration for achievement, the mystique cut men off from reality and limited their spontaneity, crucial prerequisites for surviving with peace of mind and dignity in a complex world.

Notes

[1] Edgar Moon, *The Contents of the Boy* (New York: Eaton and Mains, 1909), p. 259; Richard J. Beamish and Francis A. March, *America's Part in the World War* (Philadelphia: The John C. Winston Co., 1919), pp. 19–33, 238–58.

[2] Theodore Roosevelt, *The Great Adventure* (New York: Scribner's, 1918), p. 33.

[3] Robert E. Osgood, *Ideals and Self-Interest in America's Foreign Relations* (Chicago: University of Chicago Press, 1953), pp. 144–45.

[4] Ibid., p. 144; Theodore Roosevelt, *The Great Adventure* (New York: Scribner's, 1918), p. 35.

[5] Theodore Roosevelt, *The Great Adventure* (New York: Scribner's, 1918), p. 33.

[6] Ibid., p. 10; Harold Ickes, *Autobiography of a Curmudgeon* (Chicago: Quadrangle Books, Inc., 1969), p. 217; John Holme, *The Life of Leonard Wood* (Garden City, N.Y.: Doubleday, 1920), pp. 29–30.

[7] William E. Hocking, "Morale," *Atlantic Monthly* (December, 1918), 721–28; see also Charles Bird, "From the Charge: A Psychological Study of the Soldier," *American Journal of Psychology*, XXVIII (July, 1917), 315–48; Ira W. Howerth, "The Great War and the Instinct of the Herd," *International Journal of Ethics*, XXXIX (1919), 174–87; "Training Under Fire," *Literary Digest* (January, 19, 1918), 50–53; "Thrilling Moments in History's Greatest Battle," *Literary Digest* (May 4, 1918), 42–50.

[8] Arthur G. Empey, *Over the Top* (New York: G. P. Putnam's Sons, 1917), p. 280.

[9] Peter Filene, *Him/Her Self: Sex Roles in Modern America* (New York: Harcourt Brace Jovanovich, Inc., 1974), pp. 111–12.

[10] Franklin D. Roosevelt, "On Your Own Heads," *Scribner's Magazine* (April, 1917), 413–16.

[11] Henry Stimson, "The Basis for National Military Training," *Scribner's Magazine* (April, 1917), 408–12.

[12] Floyd Gibbons, *And They Thought We Wouldn't Fight* (New York: George Doran, 1918).

[13] Tom Skeyhill, *Sergeant York: His Own Life Story and War Diary* (New York: Doubleday, 1928), pp. 48, 136 ff, 144, 168.

[14] Carlos Baker, *Ernest Hemingway* (New York: Scribner's, 1969), pp. 1–37, 52.

[15] Ibid., p. 52.

[16]Peter Filene, *Him/Her Self: Sex Roles in Modern America* (New York: Harcourt Brace Jovanovich, Inc., 1974), pp. 112–13.

[17]Ibid.

[18]Editorial, "To Joyce Kilmer," *Delineator* (January, 1919), 3.

[19]Charles Thwing, *The American Colleges and Universities in the Great War* (New York: Macmillan Co., 1920).

[20]Theodore Roosevelt, *The Great Adventure* (New York: Charles Scribner's Sons, 1918), p. 5; Theodore Roosevelt, *Average Americans* (New York: G. P. Putnam's Sons, 1919), p. 31; Theodore Roosevelt, *The Foes of Our Own Household* (New York: George Doran Co., 1917), pp. 15–30.

[21]John R. Mott, "When I Saw My Boy in France," *American Magazine* (November, 1917), 1–4 ff; see also L. W. Standish, "My Son," *American Magazine* (November, 1917), 1–4 ff.

[22]Harold Stearns, *Liberalism in America* (New York: Boni and Liveright, Inc., 1919), p. 62.

[23]Ibid., pp. 68–70, 133; Theodore Roosevelt, *The Great Adventure* (New York: Charles Scribner's Sons, 1918), pp. 81–82.

[24]Roderick Nash, *The Nervous Generation* (Chicago: Rand McNally & Co., 1970), pp. 126–36.

[25]Peter Filene, *Him/Her Self: Sex Roles in Modern America* (New York: Harcourt Brace Jovanovich, Inc., 1974), p. 156.

[26]Ernest Hemingway, *A Farewell to Arms* (New York: Charles Scribner's Sons, 1929), pp. 327–28.

[27]Willard L. Sperry, "Bridging the Gulf," *Atlantic Monthly* (March, 1919), 313–14.

[28]Harold Hersey, "The Soldiers' Idea of the Folks Back Home," *Scribner's Magazine* (November, 1918), 611–14; Willard L. Sperry, "Bridging the Gulf," *Atlantic Monthly* (March, 1919), 318; Oswald Knauth, "Reflections After Discharge," *Nation* (July, 12, 1919), 42; Walter Lippmann, "The Basic Problem of Democracy," *Atlantic Monthly* (July–December, 1919), 616–27.

[29]Preston Slosson, *The Great Crusade* (New York: Macmillan, 1930), pp. 308–9.

[30]Frank Bohn, "The Ku Klux Klan Interpreted," *American Journal of Sociology*, XXX (January, 1925), 397–98.

[31]Ibid., 400–6.

[32]Lotus Coffman, "Football or Baseball the National Game?" *Literary Digest* (December 6, 1924), 66; Preston Slosson, *The Great Crusade* (New York: Macmillan, 1930), pp. 272–81.

[33]Abraham A. Brill, "The Why of the Fan," *North American Review* (October, 1929), 430.

[34]Ibid., 432–34.

[35]Arnold Beisser, *Madness in Sports* (New York: Appleton-Century-Crofts, 1967), p. 201; Pringle Barret, "The Emancipation of Men," *Atlantic Monthly* (June, 1934), 665–72.

[36]Abraham A. Brill, "The Why of the Fan," *North American Review* (October, 1929), pp. 432–34; see also John R. Tunis, "The Great God Football," *Harper's Magazine* (November, 1928), 742–52.

[37]Henry W. Clune, "Palookas and Plutocrats," *North American Review* (January, 1929), 45–55; Preston Slosson, *The Great Crusade* (New York: Macmillan, 1930), p. 279.

[38]Heywood Broun, untitled article, *Collier's* (April 29, 1922), 12.

[39]Thomas W. Galloway, *Father and His Boy* (New York: Association Press, 1921), p. 43.

[40]Henry I. Brock, "Mussing Up Mama's Boy," *Unpartisan Review* (July–December, 1919), 283–93.

[41]L. L. Jones, "When Women Run Things," *Vanity Fair* (January, 1918), 40, 102.

[42]George Nathan, "Once There Was a Princess," *American Mercury* (February, 1930), 242–44.

[43]William Leuchtenburg, *The Perils of Prosperity, 1914–1932* (Chicago: University of Chicago Press, 1958), pp. 158–77; Loren Baritz, *The Culture of the Twenties* (Indianapolis: The Bobbs-Merrill Co., 1970), pp. 251–93.

[44]Eleanor R. Wembridge, "Petting and the Campus," *Survey* (July 1, 1925), 593–95.

[45]Frederick Lewis Allen, *Only Yesterday* (New York: Harper and Row, 1931), pp. 92, 290; Peter Filene, *Him/Her Self: Sex Roles in Modern America* (New York: Harcourt Brace Jovanovich, Inc., 1974), pp. 136–37; "Virgins for Husbands," *American Mercury* (July, 1938), 466–68; Ernest W. Burgess, *Predicting Success or Failure in Marriage* (New York: Prentice-Hall, Inc., 1939).

[46]David M. Kennedy, *Birth Control in America* (New Haven: Yale University Press, 1970), pp. 127–40.

[47]Peter Filene, *Him/Her Self: Sex Roles in Modern America* (New York: Harcourt Brace Jovanovich, Inc., 1974), pp. 164–165; Regina L. Wolkoff, "The Sex Revolution Revisited: Ideas About Male Sexuality in America, 1890–1930" (paper delivered at the seventy-first meeting of the Organization of American Historians, New York City, April 12–15, 1978); James Reed, "A Necessary Compromise: Male Attitudes Toward Contraception, 1830–1975," (paper delivered at the seventy-first meeting of the Organization of American Historians, New York City, April 12–15, 1978).

[48]Herman Keyserling, "Caste in America," *Forum* (July, 1928), 103–6; Preston Slosson, *The Great Crusade* (New York: Macmillan, 1930), pp. 60, 131; E. W. Howe, "These Women," *Forum* (April, 1930), 244–46.

[49]Dorothy Canfield Fisher, *The Homemaker* (New York: Harcourt Brace Jovanovich, Inc., 1924).

[50]Sinclair Lewis, *Dodsworth* (New York: The Modern Library, 1929), pp. 13, 29, 103.

[51]Fanny Hurst and Rose C. Feld, "Eight Years After a Novel Marriage," *The New York Times* (December 9, 1923), Sec. 4, p. 1, col. 1.

[52]Leo Lowenthal, *Literature, Popular Culture, and Society* (Palo Alto, Cal.: Pacific Books, 1961), pp. 109 ff.

[53]Mabel Ulrich, ed., *Man, Proud Man* (London: Hamish Hamilton, 1932), p. 33.

[54]Lillian Symes, "The New Masculinism," *Harper's* (June, 1930), 103.

[55]Sherwood Anderson, *Puzzled America* (Mamaroneck, N.Y.: P. P. Appel, 1935), p. 46.

[56]Shaw Desmond, *Stars and Stripes* (London: Hutchinson and Co., 1932), pp. 20, 180; Sherwood Anderson, *Puzzled America* (Mamaroneck, N.Y.: P. P. Appel, 1935), pp. 159 ff.

[57]Studs Terkel, *Hard Times* (New York: Pantheon Books, 1970), p. 229. Reprinted by permission of Penguin Books Ltd.

[58]Mirra Komarovsky, *The Unemployed Man and His Family* (New York: Dryden Press, 1940), pp. 23–43.

[59]Winona Morgan, *The Family Meets the Depression* (Minneapolis: University of Minnesota Press, 1939), p. 63; Thomas Uzzell and V. E. LeRoy, "The Decline of the Male," *Scribner's*

Magazine (December, 1936), 19–25; Studs Terkel, *Hard Times* (New York: Pantheon Books, 1970), pp. 85, 105–8.

[60]Ruth Cavan and Katherine Ranck, *The Family and the Depression: A Study of One Hundred Chicago Families* (Chicago: University of Chicago Press, n.d.), pp. 76 ff.

[61]Robert Lynd and Helen Lynd, *Middletown in Transition* (New York: Harcourt Brace Jovanovich, Inc., 1937), pp. 410–12.

[62]Lillian Symes, "The New Masculinism," *Harper's* (June, 1930), 103; see also D. H. Lawrence, "Cocksure Women and Hensure Men," *Forum* (January, 1929); "Why I Rebelled Against My Wife," *American Magazine* (June, 1929), 48–49; George Nathan, "Once There Was a Princess," *American Mercury* (February, 1930), 242–44; Sherwood Anderson, "I Want to Work!" *Today* (April 28, 1934), 10–11, 22; Thomas Uzzell and V. E. LeRoy, "The Decline of the Male," *Scribner's Magazine* (December, 1936), 19–25; U. V. Wilcox, "New Deal Females," *American Mercury* (August, 1936), 417–23; Struthers Burt, "Our Feminized United States," *Forum* (May, 1937), 266–71; Margaret Fishback, "Are Men Mice?" *Forum* (July, 1938), 17–21.

[63]W. O. Saunders, "I'm One of Those Boob Husbands," *American Magazine* (April, 1929), 165; "Why I Rebelled Against My Wife," *American Magazine* (June, 1929), 48–49.

[64]D. H. Lawrence, "Cocksure Women and Hensure Men," *Forum* (January, 1929), supp. L.

[65]Quoted in David Cohn, *Love in America* (New York: Simon and Schuster, 1943), pp. 10–11; Mary Day Winn, "Submerged Husbands," *North American Review* (October, 1929), 405–9.

[66]John Erskine, *The Influence of Women and Its Cure* (Indianapolis: The Bobbs-Merrill Co., 1936), pp. 89, 124, 131; see also Struthers Burt, "Our Feminized United States," *Forum* (May, 1937), 266–71.

[67]John Erskine, *The Influence of Women and Its Cure* (Indianapolis, The Bobbs-Merrill Co., 1936), pp. 70–74, 78–84, 89, 110–14, 121–31; see also U. V. Wilcox, "The New Deal Females," *American Mercury* (August, 1936), 417–23.

[68]Robert Rogers, "Feminization of Our Schools," *Pictorial Review* (September, 1930), 68–70; Frederick Van de Water, "A Father Falters," *Parents' Magazine* (December, 1935), 48.

[69]John Coleman, Jr., "Home for the Day," *Atlantic Monthly* (December, 1932), 778.

[70]Corine Lowe, "The Lure of the Helpless Male," *Pictorial Review* (July, 1932), 4, 28; Alice Kelly, "These Downtrodden Men," *Harper's* (April, 1931) 565; Pringle Barret, "The Emancipation of Men," *Atlantic Monthly* (June, 1934), 665–72; David Bates, "A Husband Turns Housewife," *Forum* (January, 1939), 8–10; "Getting Along with Women," *Harper's* (October, 1935), 614–23; Ida Tarbell, "Domesticating the American Male," *Woman's Home Companion* (June, 1931), 13–14.

[71]Stewart H. Holbrook, "The Vanishing American Male, *American Mercury* (March, 1937), 270–79; Amram Sheinfeld, *Women and Men* (New York: Harcourt Brace Jovanovich, Inc., 1943), p. 58; Caroline Bird, *The Invisible Scar* (New York: David McKay, Inc., 1966), pp. 56–58.

[72]H. F. Pringle, "What the Men of America Think About Women," *Ladies' Home Journal* (April, 1939), 14 ff; B. Davis, "Are Husbands Happy?" *Ladies' Home Journal* (October, 1941), 84; Mary Cookman, "What Do the Women of America Think About Men?" *Ladies' Home Journal* (January, 1939), 19 ff.

[73]Elisabeth Cushman, "Office Women and Sex Antagonism," *Harper's* (March, 1940),

356–63; Rose W. Wilder, "Woman's Place is in the Home," *Ladies' Home Journal* (October, 1936), 94, 96.

[74]Floyd Dell, "A Father Speaks His Mind," *Delineator* (November, 1934), 34, 57; H. I. Phillips, "Fallen Fathers," *Collier's* (May 6, 1933), 21 ff; Terence Croyn, "To Fathers of Sons," *Parents' Magazine* (September, 1941), 31 ff.

[75]Studs Terkel, *Hard Times* (New York: Pantheon Books, 1970), pp. 106–9.

[76]Lois Boyliss, "The Vanishing American Female," *American Mercury* (August, 1937), 503; Alice Kelly, "Too Much Mother," *Atlantic Monthly* (September, 1931), 353; Katherine Winant, "Problem Mothers," *Forum* (December, 1937), 279–82; Anna Wolf, "The Forgotten Father," *Parents' Magazine* (December 15, 1940), 30 ff; W. L. Chase, "Fathers to the Rescue," *Parents' Magazine* (February, 1941), pp. 24 ff.

[77]Gordon Shipman, "How to Make Your Son a Misfit," *American Mercury* (March, 1938), 288.

[78]Philip Wylie, *Generation of Vipers* (New York: Rinehart and Co., 1942); see also Frances Strain, "The Nagging Mother," *Hygeia* (February 1929), 144–47; Paul Marcus, "Unfair to Fathers," *Parents' Magazine* (December, 1942), 46.

[79]Susan Ertz, "Man as Pleasure Seeker," *Harper's* (September, 1932), 418–25.

[80]John Steinbeck, *The Grapes of Wrath* (New York: The Viking Press, 1939), pp 618–19.

[81]Caroline Bird, *The Invisible Scar* (New York: David McKay, Inc., 1966), pp. 283–85.

[82]David Cohn, *Love In America* (New York: Simon and Schuster, 1943), pp. 30, 39, 46–51, 54–57, 72–74.

[83]Ibid., pp. 56–57, 141, 200 ff; Gertrude Atherton, *Can Women be Gentlemen?* (Boston: Houghton Mifflin, Co., 1938), pp. 49, 66–70: "Warning to Wives," *Ladies' Home Journal* (October, 1936), 14, 15 ff.

[84]Richard Ellis, *A Nation in Torment* (New York: Capricorn, 1971), pp. 95–96; Geoffrey Gorer, *Hot Strip Tease and Other Notes on American Culture* (London: Cresset Press, 1937), pp. 49–50, 55, 61, 76; Alan Devoe, "Any Sex Today?" *American Mercury* (June, 1937), 175–78; see also Theodore Dreiser, *Hey Rub-a-Dub-Dub* (New York: Boni and Liveright, 1920).

[85]Shaw Desmond, *Stars and Stripes* (London: Hutchinson and Co., 1932), p. 244; Geoffrey Gorer, *Hot Strip Tease and Other Notes on American Culture* (London: Cresset Press, 1937), pp. 50–55.

[86]Arnold Beisser, *The Madness of Sport* (New York: Appleton-Century-Crofts, 1967); Abraham A. Brill, "The Why of the Fan," *North American Review* (October, 1929), 429–34; Paul Gallico, "The American Goes to the Game," *Transatlantic* (September, 1943), pp. 28 ff.

[87]Eliot Spalding, "America's Cry Baby Athletes," *American Mercury* (September, 1937), 65–75.

[88]Leo Gurko, *Heroes and Highbrows and the Popular Mind* (Indianapolis: The Bobbs-Merrill Co., 1953), pp. 173–85.

[89]Gilbert Seldes, "The Masculine Revolt," *Scribner's Magazine* (April, 1934), 279–82.

[90]Russell Henderson, *Man of Today* (New York: Books of Merit, Inc., 1940); Dale Carnegie, *How to Win Friends and Influence People* (New York: Home Institute, 1941); Napoleon Hill, *Think and Grow Rich* (Meriden, Conn.: The Ralston Society, 1937).

We frequently misplace Esteem by judging Men by what they seem.

Benjamin Franklin

We are not going around looking for opportunities to prove our manhood.

Henry Kissinger

Women have no idea how much men hate them.

Germaine Greer

PERILS OF THE MASCULINE MYSTIQUE SINCE 1940

Two weeks after Japan attacked Pearl Harbor and the United States plunged into another world war, Jonathan Daniels, who was to become President Roosevelt's administrative assistant, wrote with great joy that America had become "magnificently male again. The twenties are gone with self-indulgence. The thirties have disappeared with self-pity. The forties are here in which Americans stand on a continent as men—men again fighting in the crudest man terms." To Daniels it was an hour of elation, rather than fear or hesitation, because the war was a time when "a man can be what [being] an American means."[1] Others saw the war as another testing of America's character, perseverance, and courage. "Guts" became the new code word for manliness, and the rough talk and strident behavior within any company of soldiers was supposed to help take "the chicken" out of the weaker ones.[2] The legendary General George S. Patton, "Old Blood and Guts," proclaimed that all American men loved to fight; no *real* man did not. And, furthermore, they loved to win, or in Patton's own eloquence, Americans didn't "give a hoot in hell for a loser." Patton's attitude can be seen in the famous "slapping" episode of 1943. During the Sicily campaign, in which casualties were extensive, the general had occasion to visit a field hospital and was deeply touched by the sight of the wounded men. As he was about to leave the tent, he noticed a young man who on initial appearance gave no indication of being wounded. When Patton inquired about his ailment, the soldier responded that he guessed he just couldn't "take it." Patton flew into a rage and slapped and then kicked the young soldier. The general shouted to a colonel nearby that he wanted the soldier removed from the hospital. "I don't want yellow-bellied bastards like him hiding their lousy cowardice around here, stinking up this place of honor." Patton yelled that he did not give a damn whether the man could take it or not and ordered him back to the front at once.[3]

The common code by which a combat unit was judged and that applied to individuals as well, as General Patton made evident, had roots deep in American culture and boiled down to a basic commandment: Be a man. Manliness during the war encompassed the traditional attributes of courage, endurance, toughness, and a lack of squeamishness when confronted by the dangers of a raging battle. Other features of the masculine image during World War II were a reticence about emotional or idealistic matters and a high regard for sexual competence. Compared with the prevailing attitude during World War I, there was much less covert community pressure on individuals to enlist in military service to demonstrate their manliness. People agreed after 1941 that there was a grave job to be done and that all worthwhile men and women, because they were loyal citizens, would do their part. It was not necessary for an individual to stick his neck out as did the bellicose Theodore Roosevelt or as the idealistic Hemingway had wanted to do in World War I. The real test of manliness during the 1940s was how well a person filled whatever role he chose, regardless of what he did. Combat obviously presented the situation that still tested manliness most severely and in the most revealing ways, as it had done in all wars. During World War II, soldiers expressed fear of the censure that would result if they did not do their jobs competently. An additional fear was that a soldier might be thought of as less than a man and unsuitable for soldiering if he did not perform well. Army and civilian

vocabulary contained a whole list of terms applicable to such a person: "sissy," "weak sister," "chicken," "yellow," "gutless," "old maid," "bastard," "fuck-up," and "lacy-drawers," among others.[4]

An interview with an infantryman wounded during the North African campaign illustrates clearly the distinctions soldiers made on the basis of the masculinity code:

> One time me and another guy were in a hole. The guy says, "Let's get out of here." I talked to him (tried to calm him down) but he never was a soldier—did typewriting, ran errands for officers. He was a suck-ass for a colonel, not a real soldier. A real soldier is a guy—he'll drink and swear—but he relies on himself; a guy that can take care of himself.[5]

A survey taken of a division that had fought in North Africa and Sicily also showed some variations of the attributes of masculinity according to rank. Leadership was ranked as the highest attribute for officers, even higher than aggressiveness and courage; aggressiveness and courage (guts), the heart of the masculine code, were the most cherished characteristics attributed to the manly private. There was also a feeling reported among some soldiers at the front that their masculinity was superior to that of those soldiers in the rear or those with noncombat duties. There was a special pride in being thought of as an "old beat-up Joe," one who had been tested, endured the worst, and somehow survived. The key element in this variation of the masculine image was that for "old Joe," things were going just about as badly as he had expected.[6] Another aspect of this image, captured so well by the cartoonist Bill Mauldin, was the grizzled veteran's sardonic regard for the army's spit-and-polish regulations. What difference did it make if a soldier was clean shaven, had polished boots, or even if one was a good physical specimen? The harshness of war seemed to render all of those qualities irrelevant and artifical, which raises another perspective about masculinity and soldiering. Some novelists, Robert Lowery, for example, depicted army life and routine, which had always been praised for "making men out of boys," as a monstrous fraud. The army faked everything, he wrote, valor, heroism, and even duty. It broke men down, deprived them of their will, while hypocritically rewarding unintelligent but prestige-seeking officers who thought only about themselves.[7]

World War II did produce its share of brave American heroes whom a Patton would admire and a Jonathan Daniels would no doubt associate as the epitome of true Americanism. *Esquire* ran a series, "Esquire Hall of Fame Heroes," about the exploits of men like Joe Foss, who was credited with shooting down twenty-six Japanese planes. "Tough Joe, the Dakota farm boy turned flier, won in a gigantic poker game of pure bluff where you held a fist full of nothing and made the other guy lose his nerve," was the way Paul Gallico described Foss's outwitting a Japanese maneuver. According to another *Esquire* story, young David Waybur weighed 150 pounds, and while his wounded buddies lay helplessly nearby, David single-handedly held off the new Goliath, a twelve-ton German tank. There was the cool and efficient Reinhardt Keppler, who fought a raging fire aboard the *San Francisco* to save the ship's explosives.[8] A superhero of the war most Americans learned about was Lieutenant Audie Murphy, who was decorated fifteen times. One of his most valiant exploits came when he ordered his men to take cover from an advancing tank group while he remained in a forward position to direct over his telephone the artillery assault from the rear. When the tanks overtook his position, Murphy climbed aboard a burning tank destroyer and used its guns against the enemy, holding off enemy tanks and support infantry that got as close as ten yards. All of this, written up in his war memoirs, was made into a movie starring Murphy playing himself. Few men during the war matched Murphy's extraordinary accomplishments and lived to tell their stories. Murphy's survival seemed to attest to his heroism and masculine strengths.[9]

The journalist Ernie Pyle brought the home front fact to face with the war through the feeling of the men he wrote about in his stories. Pyle himself was a war hero, as Stephen Crane and Richard Harding Davis had been, because he put himself on the front, exposed to enemy fire, regardless of the personal danger. He was killed during the Okinawa campaign.

Hollywood also did its share to promote a view of the war in which American servicemen were gallant, brave, and, above all, had guts. *Air Force* depicted the adventures of a mythical B-17, the *Mary Ann*, and the plane's brave crew. In *Sands of Iwo Jima*, John Wayne portrayed a hard-driving sergeant who led his men ashore in the thick of desperate fighting, only to lose his life when he was bayoneted from behind by an enemy soldier. Most major battles in time were portrayed in a movie version, often simplistic, and, in most cases, the star attraction was the tough masculinity demonstrated by American fighting forces, which no doubt contributed to the films' popular appeal. Very few war novels surpassed the celebration of nationalism and traditional masculinity found in Vincent

McHugh's *The Victory*. Jason Crane is a Westerner, likened to Daniel Boone, possessing the best qualities of manhood American culture could produce. Even in the army he affirms a vigorous expansionism, coupled with a belief in brotherly love reminiscent of liberal progressivism. Crane, in fact, has a mission to bring together the natives of a South Pacific island to appreciate progress, symbolic of what American male culture had done throughout history.[10]

These stories of individual valor and heroism can be, and were, compared with stories of wartime bravery in previous periods of American history, when battle, sacrifice, and honor had vouched for the ultimate patriotism and masculine qualities in a man. Such comparisons, however, miss some crucial points of difference in terms of explaining the continuity and changes within the masculine mystique. One significant difference is that World War II was not as universally considered by the soldiers as The Great Cause the way other war experiences had been. In large measure, the outcome of World War I, which appeared in retrospect to be rather inconclusive and was remembered more for its ghastly horrors than its great heroes, took much of the glory out of war.[11] According to a navy captain, the soldier fights because he is involved in a job that has to be done. "In past wars this philosophy might have been summarized as a determination on the part of every man to do his duty. They don't use any high flown words that smack of heroics or sob stuff." Even Audie Murphy felt anxiety about his heroism. He was praised, paraded, and stared at when he returned to the States. No matter how much he sought to tell the exact truth about his service career, it always seemed to come out bigger than life, which bothered Murphy. He eventually gave away his fifteen medals and was criticized for his action, but Murphy explained that he never felt that the decorations entirely belonged to him. The exemplary modern hero, Murphy thought his whole unit deserved to share them.[12]

Any grand desire to be a combat hero usually dissipated when the battle heated up. The hero role, then, was something that ensued mostly from fortuitous circumstances. This is not to imply that the G.I.s were mediocre soldiers or had a negligent attitude toward battle. What it does suggest, as Ray Grinker and John Spiegel reported, is that stories of past military valor, as told by friends and relatives, seemed unimportant to the soldier in the field. Individual accomplishment and being a hero were secondary to the vast majority of soldiers, who fought more for self-protection rather than for personal glory or adventure, the kind of quest for action that had characterized a Hemingway and Dos Passos in 1917. Some undoubtedly did look forward to battle in the abstract, or for personal reasons, perhaps for vindication or revenge, as did the young veteran of the North African campaign who exclaimed, "I want to go back and get those dirty Nazi bastards. I want to show them we're not yellow. They think we're just playboys." But the indications are that this attitude did not represent a primary motivation.[13]

BLOOD AND GUTS

Even covert displays of patriotism were rarely expressed during World War II by combat soldiers. Whereas slogans, high ideals, and demonstrations of partriotism had inspired American war psychology in the past and had often been associated with masculinity of the finest quality, enunciation of such sentiment now seemed too emotional and inconsistent with masculinity. Men who believed they were tough and prepared to do the job of fighting believed that action spoke louder than words. Surveys show that the more combat action a soldier experienced, the greater his self-confidence grew and the less he talked about the war (just as in the adage "those who talk about it [sex] the most do it the least"). Some soldiers, however, did experience anxiety that their actions were not significant enough. Some of these cases were studied by Grinkler and Spiegel and revealed a feeling of helplessness when it came to limiting casualties in combat. An individual experiencing such anxiety, whatever his combat record may have been, had a tendency to come home not a conquering hero but a physically and psychologically depleted person.[14]

Saying that a soldier "had guts" often conveyed the misunderstanding that there were soldiers who had their courage honed to such a fine point that they were anxious to plunge into battle and fight on sheer instinct alone. But not even Patton believed in that kind of soldiering. In fact, the nickname "Blood and Guts" was a reporter's invention, although the general liked it because "it served its purpose." But according to Patton, it took more than blood and guts to win battle. It took "brains and guts." During the Battle of the Bulge, Patton reiterated this theme in a conversation with his staff. "All you've got to use is *brains* and guts. That wins polo games and it wins battles."[15] It took more intelligent soldiers to follow complex orders and use the sophisticated equipment of modern warfare, which tended to reduce the premium on brawn and mythic individualism in heroes who would expose themselves to an enemy for the sake of supreme personal adventure. Modern warfare, like many other aspects of

modern life, had been altered by technology and science so that cooperation, coordination, and strategic execution were extremely important.
Swashbuckling, individualistic performances were, in fact, dangerous because they could threaten the lives of fellow soldiers and undermine the
success of a mission. No doubt Patton did love the romantic adventures of
war. His personal egotism stands out in sharp contrast to that of other
generals, such as Omar Bradley, who once said that the difference between him and Patton was that Patton fought because he loved to fight
and he (Bradley) did it because he was trained to do it. General Dwight
Eisenhower represented an even sharper contrast as a modest, unassuming
man with basically decent impulses, a deep sense of moral responsibility,
and an unflinching attention to technique and detail. Eisenhower was less
bouyed by the possibilities of heroic masculinity; he was more attentive to
the subtle realities of war and peace, as evidenced by his accommodating
sensitivity toward the Russians as political allies.[16]

WAR AND THE INDIVIDUAL

In a very significant way the military offered a unique form of security
by stressing "team philosophy" and cooperation and in defining the job to
be done. The soldier was provided with all he needed and was only
expected to carry out his orders, accommodate the bureaucracy, and accept
his assigned station. There was even a form of security after the war,
extended through the GI Bill, which helped many servicemen buy homes,
start businesses, and obtain an education. These incentives and opportunities and the necessary cooperation demanded, however, sharply contrasted with a past in which the individual had to take advantage of an
opportunity, whether in peace or in war, and then capitalize on it. Thus,
the wartime demands upon men and women marked a significant further
revision in the perspective about individualism, as had the New Deal
measures of a decade before.

To accomplish the cooperation and organization to get the maximum
gains from the technology and strategy and save as many lives as possible
required a higher level of physical and mental training than had been
known before in the armed forces. Accepting a bureaucracy and submit-
ting to authority and discipline were exigencies bound to conflict with
some of the traditional attributes of the American character, especially the
celebrated freedoms of traditional masculine behavior. Results of studies
made of servicemen during and shortly after the war indicated some

severe adjustment problems for many American youths entering military service during the 1940s. Generally, the studies showed that many recruits were repeatedly forced to alter their values and social patterns to conform to army regulations. Those who did submit were "well adjusted." To many other servicemen, the demands of the military life depreciated the ideal of freedom and individualism. They became G.I.s—general issue—complete with "dog tags." There was little in modern military service that could be compared to the ideal of soldiering in a nation in which, through legend and symbol, military heroes had received a special kind of recognition and attention.[17] One interpretation attributed difficulties of adjustment to a masculinity-and-virility ideal derived from peer-group gangs. Many young men had gloried in exhibiting their toughness and aggressiveness in school and in the neighborhood, occasionally offering proof of their manhood by beating up a bookish sissy. After induction, however, they had to shape up, conform, and regiment their lives according to commands of drill sergeants and other authority figures. Instead of dishing out the punishment, now the recruits were the ones who had to take it. It meant that they were unable to live up to their prevailing, idealized views of their personalized masculine standards of control, domination, and aggression. Off duty they frequently resorted to a variety of release mechanisms that were often rowdy and rebellious.

Some of the most popular fiction about the war vividly centered on the concept of submission. Red Valsen, a Thoreauvian idealist, is "broken" by his superiors in Norman Mailer's *The Naked and the Dead*. Jack Mallory and Robert Prewitt fight the regimentation and authoritarianism in James Jones's *From Here to Eternity*. Their stubborn resistence to military authority not infrequently provokes brutal retaliation in which traditional masculine behavior and patterns of independence face a certain demise. Once they are off duty, their maverick tendencies reassert themselves. But Prewitt, who struggles against army discipline, also realizes that he liked army life, with its opportunities to drink and screw and party as part of the normal routine.[18] Rejection of anything that seemed orderly, moral, and practical was common. The boy-scout image was now considered sissified because it implied a moral standard that bordered on being effeminate.[19]

SEX AND THE G.I.

The intention here is not to attempt a full accounting of this behavior. The reasons for it are undoubtedly complex. Battle fatigue, loneliness, tension, homesickness, remorse, and revenge all intertwined in varying degrees to trigger certain reactions of servicemen against their unique environment. Authorities who made studies of G.I. behavior suggest that the old masculine image of the powerful and aggressive American male had much to do with influencing his behavior. According to Henry Eikin, who studied troops from a number of countries in his travels during the war, the domination of boys by women in the homes, churches, and schools of America resulted in many young men's feeling a constant pressure to prove that they were really "red-blooded boys." There was a tendency for some to feel that they had not really achieved manhood because of the restrictions placed on them by mothers and female teachers. "Hence they are impelled to adopt an image of manhood which, like all compensations for inadequacy, exaggerates and distorts the dominant, aggressive quality that is a natural sign of virility." Such overreaction implied that they were capable of overthrowing anything associated with femininity or accepted moral standards. The availability of prostitutes offered an easy and cheap sexual release, although a visit to a whorehouse was probably also important because it would be recounted to buddies as an adventurous experience that "never failed to do credit to the subject's virile capacities." Because his basic response to sexual matters was so egocentric, the young recruit could even identify with the prostitute and believe she liked her work and that perhaps he was somehow special to her. That she took money was a credit to her own good practical sense. It was said that German girls were especially desired because of their alleged preference for excitement and submission to anything masculine.[20] Alfred Hayes indicted American G.I.s for their crass and mean treatment of Italians, especially the women. Hayes described scenes of sex-hungry American men making out with whores amidst the ruins of the Colosseum. How ironic it was to Hayes that American men were portrayed as strong and moral liberators from a society that had honored womanhood, but in Italy they defamed women and even mocked life itself, as symbolized in the author's novel by one American who forced his Italian mistress to go through with an abortion.[21] For many servicemen, just having a pinup of a sexy woman was important not only for decoration but as a confirmation to buddies that here was a virile man who could recognize a "good-looking broad."[22]

And yet, Dixon Wecter reminded his readers, the American woman at home still ruled by proxy through her long-standing and deep influence on her sons and husband. In fact, bombardiers used the names of wives and sweethearts as a code signal for bombs away; many soldiers and pilots carried pictures of wives and sweethearts into battle. From all this, Wecter concluded, "Once more a war is being fought for the American Girl, and the right to return to her with honor."[23] American men had always maintained this very contradictory conceptualization of women, viewing them either as sacred angel-mother beings or as sex objects. Perhaps the insecurities of war and the live-for-today philosophy put the emphasis more on the latter concept. However, it was possible that in order to live up to an image of sexual competence, the former image of woman had to be attacked.

The occurrence of profanity in the language of American servicemen offers another indication of social and moral rebellion based on a sense of endangered virile masculinity. Much of what was blatantly derogatory to women has been interpreted as a form of retaliation or rebellion against a female-controlled culture. The language conveyed an attitude that sex was dirty and degrading but something that red-blooded men enjoyed, and through it advertised their masculinity. Drunk G.I.s were known to threaten to "tear a place apart" or "beat the hell out of somebody" if those present did not keep their place or say the right things. Looting provided the necessary tangible evidence that G.I.s had been somewhere and had made their mark. Many Europeans soon rejected the premise that the American occupation forces were always composed of good, responsible boys. "Being good" implied a feminine influence, and if one were able to scrutinize more closely subconscious impulses, one might find that American servicemen were loath to subscribe to such a code. Many authorities conclude that the soldiers wanted to leave behind, with the allies and former enemies alike, an impression that American men were tough, conquering heroes with a swaggering masculine style that would forever be dominant.[24]

THE ATTACK ON MOMISM

Philip Wylie attacked American culture and the extraordinary influence throughout history that American women had over their sons, husbands, and lovers. They had taken over for the men, Wylie complained, possessed them and devoured them with their insidious feminine charm and penchant for organization and moral causes. "Thus the women of America raped the men, not sexually, unfortunately, but morally, since neuters come hard by morals." American culture had evolved a cult of momism whose goal, as Wylie saw it, was to personify moms as *the* history of the United States. Hence, all patriotic fervor was really a whooping up for mom. "I cannot think, offhand, of any civilization except ours in which an entire division of living men has been used during wartime, or at any time, to spell out the word 'MOM' on a drill field." The tragic element in all of this was that mom protected her sons to such an extent and so carefully shielded their development through childhood that they either became barbarians as adult males or exhausted themselves denying that barbarism. Moreover, boys were not able to enjoy any other kind of love for any other female because American mothers so effectively redirected it to themselves. "The process has given rise to the mother problem, and the mother-in-law problem."[25] Edward Strecker, chairman of the Psychiatry Department at the University of Pennsylvania, agreed with Wylie, and claimed that momism loomed as a large factor in the mental health of a large number of men, some three million, who were rejected or were lost to the service for neuropsychiatric reasons. Many of those rejected had never been emotionally weaned or even allowed to toughen physically because of their mother's dominance. The result was immature men, a problem diagnosed by Strecker as critical. He viewed momism as the product of a complex set of cultural forces that had always been associated with a strong matriarchial influence. Political considerations dictated that the young men being called into military service be treated in a less than strictly military fashion because of civilian sensitivities, registered mostly by moms. Training camps became homelike, and draftees were granted frequent leaves or it was made possible for wives and mothers to follow along. According to Strecker, one of the chief ingredients of momism had been possessiveness, an unwillingness to let sons develop a sense of masculine independence, a firm basis for growing into powerful and confident men. In many of the case studies, the mother had objected to the games her son played, the way he cut his hair, the friends he had, and his choices of activities around the house. Fathers were not blameless either, because a "lack of interest on the part of the husband often brings momism to the fore."[26]

Strecker followed others who blamed progressive education for assuming an effeminizing, protective role over young men. Most notably it had aimed at limiting aggressive competiveness, which progressive educators thought brought out the worst in the child. To this end, progressive education had gone too far, in Strecker's view, because it militated against a basic masculine instinct of wanting to be aggressive and dominant. Strecker's point was that so many men, schooled according to a progressive education philosophy, were unprepared for the rigors of the real world. That education and other "soft" influences in the lives of adolescent boys rendered them not tough enough, mentally *or* physically, to cope successfully with life. The result was immaturity and, frequently, a behavior pattern of overcompensation for a felt lack of masculinity.[27]

What then were some of the most telling revelations and lasting effects of the war on the American male's consciousness and behavior? According to the study by Grinker and Spiegel, men were put in a more dependent position then ever before because of the wartime needs for cooperation and submission to authority. Submission did not always mean humiliation because in the bureaucracy there were always "those below" over whom a certain amount of authority could be extended. Those on the bottom, who were able to adjust to the military life, as most did, could project their feelings of abuse against the enemy. Hence there was a bonding process, manifested among soldiers who frequently used the names "Mac" or "Joe" to refer to men they did not know. To submit to authority and belong to a team that had an objective that required everyone to do his part meant that a process of adaptation was necessary and that basically it was undemocratic. In this sense the system was quite similar to that of the fascist state the men were fighting against.[28]

The crucial question about war experience that many researchers asked was: Once conditioned to a more passive and dependent position, could American males regain the independence and free spirit associated with American history, or did the discipline of military life forever negate that quality in American men? The rather astonishing discussion (astonishing for 1946, perhaps), based on the investigations of Grinker and Spiegel, suggests that American men were not as independent as many men had thought and often proclaimed they were. Even granting that obvious dependent factors existed in all animals and human beings, the two psychiatrists concluded that "certain factors within our American culture, however, seem calculated to prolong this dependence beyond its usual biological duration. Among these factors, the most important are overprotection and spoiling, and their opposites, deprivation and frustration." Throughout American society there were many instances in which masculine independence and mature judgment had been obstructed. For example, without denying that good cases could be made for such laws, boys, nevertheless, were prohibited from working at many jobs until they reached the age of sixteen and could not marry without their parents' consent until twenty-one, even though they might have been biologically mature long before that age. Schools, colleges, and religious institutions had, over the years, prescribed behavior patterns through *loci parenti* rules in an effort to help bind a child more closely to norms preferred by parents. Parental emphasis on "safety first" had resulted in a depletion of the child's independent spirit by making him more cautious than necessary in situations not necessarily demanding such caution. What these observations reveal, as brought out in the context of wartime, is that, while society continued to maintain as its "theoretical ideal for the free, independent individualistic man of its frontier days . . . the strong dependent needs of the boy [were] in serious conflict with the forces pushing toward aggressive, independent, masculine and competitive existence."[29]

How the conflict between cherished ideal and frustrating reality in America was to be met would have a lot to do with the nation's politics, economic future, and interpersonal relationships. Grinker and Spiegel were concerned that any group or individual who might easily seem to reduce or resolve these conflicts could gain the attention and loyalty of men frustrated with their identity. They urged caution and understanding of the returning serviceman's need for dependence and support. When the trends toward independence seemed to be evident, Grinker and Spiegel urged that society should facilitate these efforts by furnishing satisfying outlets. Once self-confidence was restored, the irrational complaints and behavior would tend to disappear and "the veteran would again fit himself into his normal social groove.[30]

THE COMPANY MAN

What came to be recognized as the "normal social groove" after the war and in the fifties, however, was the absorption of many individuals into very large organizations, businesses, industries, and colleges. Individuals were expected to accept the company line because the company, with all of its collective wisdom, really knew what was best. What followed was a further erosion of individualism and the establishment of a conforming and standardizing atmosphere. Harold Rosenberg saw it as "the flattening of personality," caused by interrelated economic and social pressures. David Riesman claimed that the inner-directed man of the nineteenth century had been replaced by the other-directed man of the postwar era.

Contemporary men had a much stronger orientation toward situational rather than internal goals and were said to be much more sensitive to peer-group pressure than had been their nineteenth-century counterparts. Modern man was more likely to conform on the basis of external values, had less of a personal-achievement orientation than earlier Americans, and, hence, had less of the classic individualism associated with masculinity. Vance Packard explained the trends of behavior in America's mass society in terms of status, how people were anxious to impress others because they so desperately needed to be accepted and liked. The flight to suburbia was described by A. C. Spectorsky as the achievement of a mode of life exemplified by such conformity and sameness that it could not help but trigger a comparison to the days of a frontier. Meanwhile, positive thinkers like Norman Vincent Peale, a latter-day Russell Conwell, urged men to see the possibilities of self-improvement and advancement within their own jobs. In the popular play *A Man Called Peter*, God really liked best the nice, regular guy, who just worked hard without complaining.[31] The popular culture, at least on the surface, seemed to stress the preference for the "good guy," who did not rock the boat. Consensus prevailed. Old conflicts and issues seemed to be pushed aside by an attitude of cooperation and reconciliation. Big companies, big universities, mass media, suburbia, and pronouncements about togetherness suggested security and contentment for all.

Any hope, however, that a climate of consensus would resolve long-standing sex-identity problems for men and women soon vanished. Increasingly throughout the 1950s, there was reference to the masculine fulfillment problem—the trouble men were having defining themselves in social and economic relationships with women, especially at home. Helen M. Hacker noted that men had always been associated with the more general problems and goals of mankind. In American history the idea of progress was assumed to be chiefly the work of men. In the 1950s, men still believed in progress, but the cold war and corporatism made a much different national and international climate in which men had to sustain progress. The emphasis on the breadwinning role, the patterns of being individualistic, aggressive, successful competitors, and controlling and shaping events had always been indicators of masculinity. Much of the literature about men in the postwar era discussed how these traditional indicators of masculinity had trapped men into a rather narrow frame of reference. The new demand, then, was for men to view their masculine identity more broadly. For the most part, the record suggests that men had great difficulty facing this challenge. Oscar Handlin noted, for example, that for those Americans brought up on the ideal of progress and youthfulness, the colleges of the early 1950s provided only modest ambitions and clouded dreams of the future.[32]

Edith Stern thought that man's primitive state was frustrated virtually beyond repair. Men made pathetic attempts to find satisfactory substitutes, like golf, for traditional emotional and physical needs once fulfilled by activities like hunting. While Stern's determinism may have led to some extreme conclusions about male behavior, she correctly perceived the conflict between the myth of traditional masculinity and the reality of the modern times. Professional responsibilities and the pressures of the success syndrome of an action-filled life, a happy wife, nice home, well-adjusted children, and respectable status put the modern man at the mercy of a company to use or abuse his talents as long as it produced the paycheck. And yet, Stern wrote, when the man finally got to his suburban home to relax, he found it full of feminine furnishings and items that made him ill at ease, even resentful. "Not only does modern man suffer from many frustrations but also he has anxieties from which his ancestors were free. For the first time his status as a member of the dominant sex is jeopardized."[33]

VERTIGO

A veteran of World War II and author of four novels, Robert Lowry expressed concern about the mental health of the middle-class success-striving American male. In spite of having all the right possessions to help make him acceptable, the right clothes, enough money, a good wife, and the right liquor in his cabinet, "He is serious. And nervous," and he was discontented without understanding why. His opinions were acceptable and predictable, reflecting the harsh realities of domestic and international politics of the 1950s. When Lowry questioned a man he knew who was trying to sort out his anxieties, as was Lowry, the man described himself as an "underground man." According to Lowry, the man felt a deep dissatisfaction with the present generation of men because all the old idols from Hemingway to Henry Wallace (Franklin Roosevelt's Secretary of Agriculture and later his second vice president), who had inspired belief and urged men on to action, had vanished. The young men of the postwar years did not know what they believed in anymore; and the old men had forgotten or did not care any more about their former causes.

Amidst the plenty of the fifties and the conformity of corporatism, the stunning, sickening conclusion of men at peace was that they were incapable of solving their problems alone.[34]

Few authors got to the core of the problem affecting men in postwar America as perceptively as William Whyte in *The Organization Man*. There was little doubt that the "American Dream," that of freedom, individual initiative, and success, which had shaped manliness and masculine achievement, was being seriously altered. What Whyte called the new "social ethic" stressed the group as the source of creativity and belongingness as more desirable than individualism in coping with complexity. The new ethic also stressed the application of science and scientific methodology as a way to achieve success, again discounting individual brawn and will.[35] In describing some of the forms and techniques embodied in the social ethic, it is clear that Whyte was skeptical of the new trend. He admitted organizations were permanent fixtures, and that for survival and security men would have to cooperate and adapt themselves to the big organizations, just as the G.I.s had learned to cooperate with the army bureaucracy during the war. What makes Whyte's book especially worthwhile in terms of studying the ever-changing masculine image is that the author was cognizant of the culture and history that had always emphasized individualism and personal independence. Whyte was not only nostalgic for the old ethic of the rough-and-tumble days but seemed ideologically committed to it as the best environment for the making of strong-willed, dedicated men and from their efforts, a more viable America.

THE NEW ETHIC

Whyte eulogized America's past when young men had possessed keen ambition and had desired to make it to the top to become heads of firms or presidents of businesses, or perhaps engineers building bridges. By contrast, college men of the 1950s did not have such high goals or make such extravagant claims for themselves. Perhaps it was because the percentages were against making it big and it was futile to try. But Whyte lamented that goals being set in modern America were minimal. In fact, his research suggested that the very idea of success had acquired a negative connotation because of the sacrifices and exceptionally hard work involved. The preferred goal was to get to a middle management level at which there would be sufficient security and some status. Promotions would come in terms of lateral movements, at least giving the impression of mobility within a company. The new organization man, in fact, could not even be considered working, in the traditional sense of the term. What he did best was attend meetings and conferences to keep things going within the company's vast scheme of organization. But what was being created? And where was the real action? Whyte said a dangerous trend toward human manipulation in which the instinct for individual excellence was being thwarted was evident. The new social ethic was breeding normalcy and sterility—in effect, a robot man. Teamwork was promoted to facilitate integration and to give men a sense of the big picture, but all at the expense of their individuality. How futile, how destructive is this solution, Whyte concluded, and, therefore, "We must *fight* The Organization." In the appendix of *The Organization Man*, Whyte offered suggestions on how young men could defeat the personality tests used by companies to select the "right" employees.*[36]

One only had to consider the plight of the executive to appreciate the negative consequences of the new social ethic. The price was his individualism, sometimes his health, but most often his overall sense of manhood. Work dominated his life; even his leisure was converted into "company time": Dining out and family vacations were often business trips paid for by company expense accounts. One ex-president of a large conglomerate, who had been in corporate business since the 1940s, admitted that his life had been one of fear and insecurity even as he reached the top of the ladder: "You're always fearful of the big mistake. You've got to be careful when you go to corporation parties. Your wife, your children have to behave properly. You've got to fit in the mold." He likened the executive to a lonely animal in the jungle, aware of being dominant but also aware that others were preying on his position. "To give vent to his feelings, his fears, and his insecurities, he'd expose himself," a sure sign of weakness. In a corporate career, one "always saw signs of physical afflictions because of the stress and strain. Ulcers, violent headaches." To "stick it out" was the only manly thing to do.[37] Whyte maintained, as did others, that the executive struggled within himself much of the time because even though he may have been very talented, had risen to the top, and had apparent power, there was a great likelihood that the organization, with all its coordination and vast committee structure, would, in

*Daniel Bell, in *Work and Its Discontents* (Boston: Beacon Press, 1956), adds that the value of work itself was depreciating, even though being part of a team was enjoyable.

the long run, dominate him. An ever-increasing number of corporate obligations, guidelines, ethical standards, government regulations, and, most important, government contracts promoted subservience from business men to a degree unheard of in American history. In 1961, a Boston judge taunted Roger Blough, then chairman of U.S. Steel, that compared with past chairmen of that great company, "Mr. Blough has far less power. . . . He is a constitutional monarch with the diffused power of the Queen [of England]." Blough did not disagree.[38]

By the mid-1950s, the great American success story, the American dream, had become an unsettling experience. There was a certain irony to this ominous situation. "Businessmen rarely suffer nervous breakdowns from overwork alone," wrote Richard A. Smith in *Fortune*. "The real dangers lie not merely in failure but in success; and the executive who has climbed high on the ladder is often the most vulnerable." The very qualities of an individual's rise to success were cited as the basis for some serious weaknesses. Businessmen were highly organized, neat, and precise, but no matter how successful they were, they still had to survive mergers and competition from outside as well as within the company.[39] Thus a higher position in the company did not necessarily mean the road to easy street and invulnerability. Because some men who arrived at executive status had expected more from it in terms of comforts and opportunities, they would often resort to the myth of eternal youth, living with an illusion of more freedom, believing they were more virile than they really were. Of course, part of this dream life can be associated with aging, not just business success, but because American men had always tended to see themselves through their businesses, equating personal success and comfort with business success and comfort, the two merged so that often family and personal life became miserable when things were snarled at the office.[40]

REALITY AND FICTION

In 1958, *Look* published a series of articles on the plight of American males, bluntly attributing much of the problem to the emphasis on group conformity. Males had virtually lost contact with their individuality because of the trend to consensus thinking and behavior. Decisions were made in committees by men who increasingly put aside personal convictions and instead tuned in their radar to pick up the moods of others in the group. In fact, according to *Look*, in applying for jobs that required taking a battery of personal-inventory tests, men often answered questions the way they were sure the company wanted them to answer. The evidence was clear: Big American companies were more interested in well-adjusted people than in men who might contribute ideas at variance with company norms and policy.[41]

In the popular culture, however, there were times when teamwork and organization broke down and individualism was asserted. In *High Noon*, one of the most popular western movies of the decade, the hero sheriff realizes the virtue of cooperation, but when an evil gang threatens the town and support vanishes, the sheriff has to overcome his own fear and confront the gang alone. When the grateful citizens offer congratulations, he rejects them and rides off unforgiving, reminding the audience that individualism and bravery had, in fact, won the day. The popular *Caine Mutiny* is another good example of an organization's facing a crisis and how individuals find ways to protect themselves without questioning the system. Lieutenant Maryk is a solid, hard-working navy man, devoted to the institution. But what happens when things go wrong and there is a crisis and a breakdown in organization (when, for example, Captain Queeg loses his senses and becomes a babbling fool as the ship faces a typhoon), and decisive action that conflicts with established order and military procedure becomes necessary? The man of moral action, described in the old guidebooks and typified by a Theodore Roosevelt, might not have hesitated as long as Maryk to decide that Queeg was incompetent and had to be relieved. Maryk is acquitted at a court martial for his mutiny. But his lawyer, at a party afterward, argues that Maryk and his comrades were the real villains. Queeg was, after all, a regular officer, and where would the system or any organization be without someone in charge? In *Cash McCall*, a novel by Cameron Hawley, a shrewd operator remains uncontrolled by an organization. Although he is extremely shrewd and manly, he adopts a proper balance of social values. In all of these instances cited above, the organization itself is incapable of coping with reality, thereby serving as a refreshing reminder that the actions of individual men still matter. The masculine mystique, even if encumbered by many modern realities, survives.[42]

William Attwood, *Look*'s foreign editor, observed that the pursuit of success and upward mobility had become such a passion that it had rendered many men immature and had deprived them of relaxation. The rat race was paying off in alcoholism, neurosis, and a general decline in good mental and physical health.[43] Lemuel McGee wrote that one reason men were dying at a younger age than women was that "the practice of manliness has become a curse—a lethal curse." The very fact that so many men thought they needed to be physical in a fairly sedentary age, and that they should not be emotional or reflective because to do so would be unmanly, left them strikingly discontented. Men were cut off from sources of relief that may have been highly beneficial. The ideal image was epitomized by Humphrey Bogart, on screen neither successfully, expressive or emotional, grunting his way through complex situations with a celebrated masculine coolness and skill.[44]

WOMEN AND WORK

The other problem affecting the masculine image in the postwar era was defining (or redefining) the place of men with regard to women. Men had always held the reins of power in the nation's political and economic institutions, which meant that they controlled other people. Since 1920, especially after the onset of the Depression, more and more women were working, some for economic reasons, but others because they desired a career. The prospect of female employment's increasing and becoming a permanent part of America's life style was strengthened by the war emergency. Although many old attitudes about women's working were revised during the war, there was a persistent opposition to careers for women that was based on traditional concepts of male and female sex roles. The question after the war became whether or not women would finally settle down and return to the home where they belonged and once again be satisfied to raise a family as they had always done. In short, would women once again be women so that men could be men?

Richard Malken posited the widely held opinion that the war, while disruptive of family life, also provided some genuine benefits for men by restoring their roles. It clearly revitalized the role of male protectiveness, a basic male function throughout history. Draft deferment based on family size was seen as a good inducement to have more children, certainly a step toward restoring the appearance of male virility.[45] Also, in spite of concentrated efforts to throw the best possible light on female employment during the war, there were reports that women might not be suited for the strenuous jobs men had held. *Newsweek* reported that women were less well-muscled, could not do heavy lifting, fatigued sooner, had a faster heartbeat, and were not as emotionally stable on the job. *Time* reported that women did not withstand the bombings in England as well as men and did not take to employment without adjustment problems. The conclusion was that women were most successful at home or wherever they could make the most of their special gifts of sympathy, kindness, and human warmth. Servicemen also did not like what they saw as the intrusion of women into their domaine. They saw WACS as too aggressive and complaining, characteristics unnatural to their female role.[46]

Charges were made that women had "forgotten their place" during the war and had endangered the home and their children's lives because they had worked. Frederick Crawford, head of the National Association of Manufacturers, praised women for their excellent performance during the war but added that "from a humanitarian point of view, too many women should not stay in the labor force. The home is the basic American institution."[47] There were many women, as well as men, who believed that a sharp division of labor, based on sex-role distinctions, should be established once the war emergency ended. Men had the experience and insight to make the big decisions, it was argued; therefore power should be firmly restored to them. Many others believed that even if women appeared qualified and wanted to work, they should not enter a labor market in which they would compete with men. "The American spirit fell into a strange sleep" during these years, according to Betty Friedan, in which substantive, worthwhile social change for women seemed arrested. Women were captured by a feminine mystique, she argued, an irresistible force that brought many women back to submissiveness and domesticity.[48] Men had their mystique too, rooted deep in American social history. There had always been the assumption that a basic state of harmony should exist between men and women. Unfortunately, women had not always kept their place as the submissive partner and things had consequently gotten out of hand, producing domestic disharmony when women had tried to break away from their submissive domestic roles.

Viewing the problem from England, the anthropologist Eric Dingwall concluded that American women were suffering from having feminized American men through subtle female tactics of influencing American society. Unlike Phillip Wylie, Dingwall charged that men were partly to blame for their own malaise and subjection. Men did not adequately understand or use their virile powers or know the meaning of love. Dingwall presented evidence dating back to colonial America to illustrate the confusion about love and sex and the subsequent guilt it produced. American males still had two concepts of women, the motherly image associated with morality and propriety and the image of the beguiling woman who had fallen from grace because of her sexuality. The former strained masculine identity by having men toe the moral mark while the latter encouraged adventure and pleasure. The two views were in obvious conflict.[49]

NEW STANDARDS

Helen Hacker observed that many men harbored resentment against women as evident in many plays, novels, and films in which women were portrayed as castrating Delilahs. Women seemed to be constantly testing men and then eagerly criticizing them when they failed the test. What did women really want? Did they want to come down off the pedestals, on which they had been so proudly placed by American men throughout history, to become a part of the masculine, sexual world? Or did women want to retain the privileged sanctuary of their traditional role? Either way, men and women faced a critical situation of adjustment. Hacker noted, for example, that virility used to be thought of as a unilateral expression of male sexuality, but in recent times it was beginning to be regarded as an ability to evoke a full sexual response from women. Hacker, as well as several other observers, indicated that this new burden of masculinity might be too much for some men to cope with, driving them away from women, away from heterosexuality, in order to maintain their "social distance" from women.[50] "According to cocktail folklore," wrote Amory Clark, "the American male is a sexual disaster, a blundering bull moose in the fragile china shop of feminine emotion." The social changes of the last three decades had left men so confused that many wished women did not exist at all, said Clark.[51]

David Cohn described the American home as devoid of intimacy, friendship, and mature affection between men and women. American men were simply retarded adolescents whose ideal of femininity remained the girl in a bathing suit, "Men of this kind are neither adult nor adequate in their relations with women." American men, Cohn concluded, really did not know American women at all because of the psychological and social distance that had come between men and women. Citing the conventional dinner party, he noted how frequently men felt trapped, bored, and uneasy in the formal setting, proving to Cohn that, although the social dynamics of group interaction apparently brought people together, "we are perhaps the loneliest and most bored peoples." Cohn predicted increasing divorces and incompatability between the little woman in the kitchen and the boy in the overstuffed easy chair. There was little in common between them that seemed likely to draw out a strong positive relationship. To feel manly, men had to go off to the club, drink, and tell off-color stories "on the theory [that] this is virile." On occasion, Cohn noted, a husband might even take up with another woman and share his frustrations with her. How ironic! Men who did not understand or communicate with their wives could find companionship with other married women who they claimed had husbands who did not understand them.[52]

Through the war years and after, Cohn wrote, a historical process was simply paying dividends after more than a century of investment in which several ideals finally came into conflict. Men had recognized the value of marrying a woman who could help them get started in a business or a career and help them to realize the ideal of being successful. The payoff for women came when, once established, men (not knowing what else to do) put women on a pedestal to enjoy the good life. In the twentieth century, men seemed to indicate through their behavior that they did not desire any interference from women. Men wanted the freedom to capitalize on another ideal, that of behaving like the proverbial "red-blooded American boy." More than ever, man needed the freedom, i.e., noninterference from women, to drink what and when he wanted to with the boys. His speech contained four-, nine-, and twelve-letter words that not even his father or grandfather had used. He needed to feel adventurous, perhaps why the typical convention and out-of-town visit became so important. In short, nothing had happened during or after the war to create a basis upon which men and women might get together to understand each other better. Many men continued to indulge in a behavior pattern that exemplified what to them were masculine traits. Women, meanwhile, became more neurotic and frustrated living in the suburbs, telling themselves that they were happy when they knew they were not. According to Cohn's analysis, here were the makings of a divorce rate that could only increase.[53]

The classic postwar statement about women and their changing role was furnished by Marynia Farnham, a sociologist, and Ferdinand Lundberg, a historian. They traced the feminine neurosis of modern times to the futile desire of women to compete with men. Employed mothers had been bad for the children and had produced devastating consequences for men, who had been breadwinners and knew no other role. The whole feminist movement had perpetuated a great illness in which women had been encouraged to repudiate their natural sex instincts. Farnham and Lundberg argued that Mary Wollstonecraft, the founder of the feminist movement, embodied what was wrong with the new woman. She had experienced a frustrated childhood and had a cruel father and mother who had not responded to the child's real needs for affection. Her older brother had been treated more generously by her parents, and out of jealousy and frustration Mary rebelled and started her own incessant search for happiness and fulfillment. Portrayed this way, Wollstonecraft could be viewed as little more than a lovesick woman in search for sexual gratification. More generally, the Farnham–Lundberg thesis served to illustrate just how unnatural the basis of the woman's movement really was. Freud had called it a manifestation of penis envy, but whatever it was called, feminism was seen as an abnormal condition, abnormal not only because it contradicted the true place of women, but because it fundamentally altered traditional sex-role concepts, upon which traditionally secure masculinity depended.*[54]

The conventional wisdom advertised the joys of just being a woman and the thrill and anticipation of motherhood. Ashley Montagu represented the consensus that "being a good wife, a good mother, in short a good homemaker is the most important of all occupations in the world."[55] During the same period, American males, many assisted by the G.I. Bill, started businesses, went to school, bought homes, and joined big companies, attempting to fulfill their historical mission as protector, provider, and breadwinner. The social trends, at least on the surface, pointed to a rather remarkable recovery of man as the head of the household, the boss once again after several decades in which his role in the family and the image of manliness had been confused.

UNDER HER THUMB

The popular journals, novels, and movies, however, depicted American man as harrassed by women. Fathers appeared to be sniveling adolescents at home, basically incompetent when it came to children and family matters. In a movie about three returning servicemen, *The Best Years of Our Lives*, the men are uncertain, almost weak and inept, while the women are capable and assertive. One senses that the army may have provided the best years, when status depended on a uniform rather than on a woman or

---

*Other antifeminist arguments can be found in *McCall's* and *Ladies' Home Journal* from 1930 to 1970.

a bank account. The editor of *Coronet* conceded that women had won the day, that only a few strongholds of masculinity were left. But still women were pushy and unsatisfied, "demanding a staggering tribute of sympathy from the very people [they have] conquered!" An anonymous contributor to *Rotarian* wrote that men simply were not free any more in America— that the entire social spectrum of food, fashion, music, and entertainment had been captured by women. J. Fisher claimed that never before in history had society seen such a high proportion of "cowed and eunuchoid males." Men had dedicated their lives to pampering women while, in return, women had pursued the task of reforming men, and "the measure of their success is the number of Walter Mittys in our society."[56] From the female point of view, American men in their gray flannel suits were a bore, an old charge heard many times, voiced many years before by women complaining that men lacked culture and sophistication. Most of all, they did not understand women because men did not read and had not kept up on social changes, according to Dorothy Kilgallen. Men were practioners of the double standard, unwilling to grant to women the freedoms they (men) enjoyed. And while they loathed their wives' keeping up with the Joneses, men still went out of their way to impress the hat-check girl.[57]

In 1957, Robert Moskin reported that a number of authorities known for their studies of human behavior had concluded that women clearly dominated the American male. Moskin stated bluntly that "these scientists worry that in the years since the end of World War II, he has changed radically and dangerously; that he is no longer the masculine, strongminded man who pioneered the continent and built America's greatness." Quoting David Reisman, Moskin bemoaned the fact that only from age six to ten could a boy be sure of his masculinity. "Beyond those years, a boy is unsure of his maleness, torn by his mother's sometime love, afraid to fail in front of girls. Can his masculinity take it?"[58] The explanations for the plight of contemporary males varied from girls' "being taught more sex know-how" to the "woman's new rank in the family." Much of the difficulty men had in maintaining their position regarded money, making enough to support the desired lifestyle of a wife. Women were beginning to voice the complaint that men were inadequate lovers or were insensitive to the sexual needs of women. The alarming consequences did not auger well for the future. Trends suggested that women would increasingly enter into authority-wielding executive jobs. The number of women who already owned securities had increased more than thirty-five percent between 1954 and 1958. Women owned $100 billion worth of stocks (sixty percent of the individual shares of A.T.&T., fifty-five percent of Du-Pont, and fifty-four percent of General Electric). *Fortune* credited women with making sixty percent of all consumer purchases and a Gallup Poll showed that wives participated in managing seventy-one percent of the funds of the American households.[59] To American males who had always been accustomed to measuring the quality of their lives through quantitative evidence, who had assumed that their happiness depended on maintaining their traditional power, which meant domination of women, such figures were upsetting.

RE-EXAMINATIONS

Morton Hunt explained the crisis of American masculinity in terms of a classic confusion between a particular conception of the male social role and the actuality of his biological role.

> The biological role cannot change (as yet) without extinguishing the human race, but the social role is hardly more fundamental than the form and style of a suit of clothes. The particular cut of the suit in this case is the ancient western model, especially as adapted to the Victorian era, but many a man regards any attack on the clothing as an attack on the man inside.[60]

The common opinion as to what constituted the fundamentals of masculinity still assumed a high degree of male independence and physical activity. The social climate sanctioned assertiveness and success in terms of domination and winning, being on top, and having status. In fact, one suspects that some of the masculinity-validating criteria were so important that the Victorian shibboleths about moral manhood, which Theodore Roosevelt had championed during the Progressive era, were now demoted in the placement of values. A great number of slogans emphasized winning during the 1950s, implying that the ends justified the means, an ethos not inconsistent with the cold-war mentality. Hunt criticized American males for failing to understand that times had changed and that, in fact, many men were deceiving themselves about America's past when they sought to identify with it for whatever benefits they hoped to derive. What modern men failed to understand was that social masculinity "does not consist of one unalterable cluster of traits and abilities." Anthropologists had proved that what was considered masculine and feminine differed greatly from one culture to another, and they suggested that a realistic study of American history would show that there had come to be a wide variation of masculine conduct and style within American society.[61]

Hunt's understanding of history led him to conclude that men and women were no longer held together by economic necessity and self-preservation, as had been the case in the nineteenth century. Contemporary men and women expect marriage to provide not goods and services, but love, companionship, and happiness—and if it does not, it has no other cement to keep it from falling apart. This new-relationship situation, however, called for a new mutuality and intimacy rarely known before. In the very process of adjusting to the relationship, modern man found himself "stripped of his former sturdy independence, and dragged into a sharing of 'womanly' activities" to the point of making him uncertain about his masculinity. Confronted by this sexual ambiguity, men fretted about their personal lives as much as they did about their professional lives, wondering whether the former were normal and well adjusted. Obviously, many men had grave doubts, doubts existing among American males since the nineteenth century. Hunt, anticipating future sex-role changes, called for a new definition of manliness, suggesting that the "new idea of masculinity will probably be subtler." Men would not be able to claim exclusive rights to learning, legal dominance, or business promotions. They needed to worry less about the externals, he wrote, because the essentials of biological manhood, built into the bones, glands, and nerves, would affirm a man's claim of manhood.[62]

The anxiety many men felt about their masculine identity meant that they were less prepared than ever to establish themselves as strong and capable fathers, respected by their sons and daughters. The absence of fathers from the home was not new, of course, but it was a problem that persisted and intensified as more men spent more time away from home, leaving children in the care of mothers. A *New York Times Magazine* article, summarizing some case studies of fathers and the concepts of fatherhood, concluded that one of the only things American fathers were good at was instructing their sons how to be aggressive in business. Fathers did not relate to emotional and intellectual issues because, as another analyst put it, given the he-man ideal, fathers thought they would be regarded as a psychological failure if they seemed too reflective, loving, and gentle.[63]

SETTING GOOD EXAMPLES

A *Parents' Magazine* article told of an anxious couple, worried sick about whether their son was a sissy. Because he did not seem to enjoy doing "boy things," the parents questioned whether he was normal. For example, when the father took him to the movies to see westerns, the boy did not come home all enthused and act out the plots in his play. What could be done? The boy's school teacher assured the parents that their son was normal, and that many boys liked "girl things" for a time—it was a stage. What a relief! But this article, and many like it, concluded on a somber note, reminding parents how important it was for a son to grow up and be like a man. The overriding fear of homosexuality (which many thought to be a serious disease) in such cases was obvious, especially in light of the Kinsey Report's finding that as many as thirty-seven percent of American males had at one time or another engaged in homosexual activity. How could parents be sure of developing manly qualities in their sons? The response was that fathers needed to take more responsibility for their sons' activities, a well-worn suggestion. In a subsequent issue of the same magazine, Marynia Farnham expressed regret that many boys and girls were brought up to be alike, playing with the same toys and even dressing alike. Farnham scolded parents for not doing a better job in helping children understand what was feminine and what was masculine.[64]

The problem of the father and the child's perception of him had gotten more complicated within the confines of the masculinity syndrome. Children knew that fathers were the breadwinners, but many had no idea just what their fathers actually did (although children were well aware of what their mothers did). Many fathers, however, retained the job of disciplinarian, making them occasionally unwelcome interlopers into their children's worlds. In the nineteenth century, noted Morton Hunt, fathers had an aura that demanded respect from children. Many sons even followed their fathers into their line of work or business, often out of a sense of loyalty. But all of this had changed. "Father's decline has been sharp and steady, bringing him to his modern status as a simple biological necessity and wage earner. His is a sorry plight indeed."[65]

On television, in movies, and in comic strips of the 1940s and '50s, fathers were often made to appear as fumbling incompetents, "a kind of living fossil, a creature trying to ape some of the manners of a bygone era." Dagwood Bumstead, for example, blustered and fussed in front of Blondie and the kids, but the reader knew that Dagwood could not control anything, not even the family dogs. On television, Bill Bendix presented the American dad as one whose plans never seemed to work out. Other favorite plots were those in which Dad was left in charge of the kitchen or household for a day, with disastrous results, or he attempted to interject his wisdom into the romance of son or daughter only to see his advice come back to haunt him or to find out just how ridiculous it (and he) was. TV fathers were involved in a contest of potency, trying to buttress their masculinity. When they failed they were portrayed as less than "real men" whereas women could appear unfeminine but still be real people. Meanwhile, on "Gunsmoke" and "Bonanza," Matt Dillon and Ben Cartright had no wives to counteract or confuse their masculinity.[66]

Many scholars saw the decline of fathers and the struggle for male social potency in a cause-and-effect relationship pertaining to many other problems. Without adequate masculine models, the argument went, America would be sissified and homosexuality would increase. Pitirim Sorokin saw the crisis of fatherhood as one of the real causes of contemporary juvenile deliquency, drug addiction, and other troubles.[67] As the number of urban gangs and street hoodlums became an object of great concern, many scholars began to agree. While the evidence is sketchy, it is not hard to understand how teenage boys, under the cover of urban anonymity, found appealing masculine models in gang leaders and participated in games of chicken that to them vouched for masculine toughness. Inner-city gangs engaged in turf (territorial) wars that were carried on in a climate of power and violence that was part fantasty and part real. The number of teenage murderers was up twenty-six percent from 1955 to 1956, and auto theft among teens was also increasing. Movies like *The Wild Ones*, *Teen Age Doll*, and *The Blackboard Jungle* focused on themes of teenage rebellion against a society that obviously had lost the respect of the teen generation. Asked what he was rebelling against, Marlon Brando, chief of the Black Rebels Motorcycle Club in *The Wild Ones*, replied, "Whaddayagot?" The leather jackets, switch-blade knives, motorcycles, and hot cars were evidence of a new, hard-shelled masculinity among many youths. The movies also helped popularize a tough, threatening street lingo designed to put down any weakling or call any bluff. "You got thirty-two teeth, wanna try for none?" asked a young hood in *High School Confidential*.[68]

Accepting the risks in suggesting a connection between the demise of fathers as masculine models and the existence of juvenile delinquency and violence in the movies, one still cannot help but ponder the cast of male characters that showed up in films like *Running Wild*, *The Lawless Breed*, *Lone Gun*, *The Gunfighter*, *Gunpoint*, *Love Me Madly*, *Blood Alley*, and *The Man With the Golden Arm*. Although the characters varied in these films with regard to plot and situation, they tended to be individualistic, anti-authority, and cunning, the very attributes that had come to be associated with the most red-blooded masculine men. Paradoxically, at a time when many professional men and women in counseling positions were encouraging men to revise their behavior, to be more sensitive, tolerant, and more democratic, the popular media offered countless examples of situations, plots, and characters demonstrating a masculine stridency and combativeness that helped to authenticate again the traditional myths.[69]

The motorcycle hoodlum experienced his masculinity through his machine; by making it roar, he was always guaranteed attention, and by keeping on the move he was less vulnerable. Occasional brushes with the law made for a sense of adventure that put him in touch with the romantic role of the outlaw. The girls accompanying the street gang motorcycle pack were part of the contested territory. An insult to one of the chicks from another gang was cause for a rumble, not just to clear the reputation of the girl, but also to uphold the honor of the gang. Women were sex objects, around to satisfy the warrior class. According to Harrison Salisbury, it was a mark of genuine virility to get a girl pregnant (to "knock her up," in street lingo). If the girl insisted on a contraceptive, holes were pricked in the end of it to get the job done.[70]

BOYS AND GIRLS

The large doses of sadism and violence in movies and paperback books reflected what one psychiatrist termed " 'frustration diseases,' the twisted products of sexual desire denied fulfillment." At the center of the problem was the average boy's ignorance about sex and his struggle to conquer his fear of the opposite sex. Like their fathers, who had not understood women very well, many adolescent males fared poorly with the girls they knew, as enticement and rejection constantly haunted the growing boys. Usually they were inarticulate around girls, unsure of what girls wanted in life or how they felt about things. The only other relationship in which boys felt they could "score" was the sexual one, in which they pressured girls to "give out" in the heat of passion. Some boys preferred to reject the girl scene altogether, not wanting to run a risk of an ego-shattering put-down. In any event, both aggression and avoidance provided evidence that youth was profoundly confused about sex.[71]

Since the twenties, the problem of how to grow up and be popular with girls and have a sufficiently active sex life to impress the boys has been a crucial part of developing a satisfactory masculine image for a boy. In recent years, men's consciousness-raising sessions have produced confessions that graphically document the humor and the tensions of some of these early adolescent sexual encounters. One male related how he felt when he perceived that to be considered tough, he would have to seduce girls "like the cool guys did." But for many middle-class boys like him, there was a part of him that said the whole thing was repugnant, yet, another part of him urged that he get on with it—to win the acclaim such an accomplishment generated. This high-school boy had to decide whether to try it with popular girls, who might not yet want sex, or date a local whore, who would not present much of a challenge but whose conquest would not induce as much respect from the boy's peers. And so he says:

> I tried to solve the conflict by dating the popular girls and working toward fucking them, too. . . . From the first date on, I tried ceaselessly to go as far as possible—parking, feeling the girls up, bare tits, into their pants, fingering, etc. I can see how I never related to the person I was with. I didn't feel anything particular toward her, except the challenge, not even sexual excitement. My first goal was to go out with even more popular girls; my second was to go as far as possible sexually.[72]

Since he was not involved in sports, this man recalled how he felt compelled to get into other activities at school to achieve the desired popularity. He was lucky enough to get into a popular high-school fraternity, which helped him get to know a more popular group of students. But the obsession with sex remained, as it did for many high-school boys, a frustrating problem. By the end of his junior year, he still had not experienced a sexual conquest. "But," he remembers, "there was always this ethic to insinuate that a guy had gone farther than he really had, although not to outright lie about it." And so his plan of attack continued under the pressure that to be masculine and to be popular around the boys and girls, he had to appear to have scored. "There was also an ethic," he added, "very strong in me, to never go steady—not to be 'pussy whipped.' No girl could ever hold me down. I wanted freedom to fuck around with lots of girls." In his senior year, he did ask a girl to go steady and had sex with her. Growing restless with the relationship, he terminated it without regard for any pain or remorse he might have inflicted.[73]

College started off with a similar effort to achieve the Big Man on Campus rating. But the competition with so many cool fraternity men for the attention of sophisticated sorority women was so intense that it made him fearful and frustrated. He discovered that the women he met at mixers turned him down for dates. He tried to repair his damaged ego by joining a singing group and putting a lot of emphasis on looking immaculate: trenchcoat with umbrella, sweaters, the latest suits, and sportswear. With still no luck, the anxiety of being a loser gradually overcame him. Meanwhile, he had to face all that "authoritarian bullshit—the paddle beating, senseless make-work . . . the endless petty humiliations" of the fraternity, just to be considered a man. Fortunately, the individual who told this sexual–social tale of woe was rescued by a counselor. The next year he transferred to another college, began to take academics seriously, became a beatnik, and was "saved from the straight American success story" his father had assumed he would pursue.[74]

That many American men were engulfed by desires, expectations, and feelings similar to those described above cannot be denied, although some of the deeper reasons and motives still elude a full understanding. Sex, love, and a Saturday-night tumble in a whorehouse all became horribly tangled as Jack Nicholson's film *Carnal Knowledge* vividly depicts. Some might argue that young men of the fifties and sixties were far better off free of Victorian restraint and able openly to explore sexuality, but the record hardly warrants saying that they were happier, better adjusted, and confident men because of it. As there was cold war in politics, there was a psychic war between the sexes, and within men themselves, revolving around what it took to have a secure sex identity. How could one achieve peace of mind coupled with the assurance that one could love and be loved according to each individual's understanding of his or her moral code?

JAMES DEAN AND ELVIS PRESLEY

Few individuals captured the sense of identity frustration of American youth as well as James Dean. Orphaned early in life, Dean was raised by his uncle, worked on a farm, and attended a university for a while, but drifted off eventually expressing his rebelliousness with rare clarity in three movies, *Rebel Without a Cause*, *East of Eden*, and *Giant*. Even Dean's appearance—blue jeans, sweater, open collar, leather jacket, a kind of deliberate sloppiness—expressed that his individualism and silent pride could not be compromised by a momistic society. In *Rebel Without a Cause*, the young rebel goes to his father for advice regarding his having to play a game of chicken to verify his masculinity. But his father has been completely effeminized, appearing in a bibbed apron carrying a meal to the boy's sick mother, and can only recommend that his son draw up a list. Dean stomps out, plays the game in which another boy is killed, and then recognizes the need to tell the police. But his uncomprehending mother restrains him, fearing exposure and reprisal. In *Giant*, the Dean character's rebelliousness against traditional norms becomes full blown as it turns into bitter hatred in a role that Dean said was "a part for me." Dean struggled to possess life, to be denied no experience. This struggle dramatically colored his life and brief movie career; the same kind of compulsion could be seen in the young Hemingway. In the end, Dean's quest turned to speed, which claimed his life when his racing Porsche crashed. He left behind an extraordinary legacy and cult.[75]

Shortly after Dean's death, a truck driver-turned-popsinger, Elvis Presley, expressed an interest in playing the lead in the James Dean story if and when Hollywood got around to such a production. Because Presley was the other—some said the only other—true teen idol during the fifties, he felt qualified to play the role. Both young men were often seen as rebels against middle-class, middle-age pretensions, tastes, and values: Dean had been sullen and brooding, holding it all in until the right moment to unleash his emotions; Elvis was explicit and direct. His song titles and lyrics—"You Ain't Nothing but a Hound Dog," "Don't Be Cruel," and "Love Me Tender," for example—got right to the point, and his gyrating and thrusting motions while performing, earning him the nickname "Elvis Pelvis," even stimulated the imaginations of twelve-year-olds, said one alarmed critic. What makes Elvis fascinating, however, is that in spite of his style he had a high regard for his family and church and the ideals exemplified by the manly heroes of America's past. (In fact, it was reported in 1978 that Elvis had been outraged by the anti-war and other "radical" activities of some members of the entertainment industry and had offered himself to the F.B.I. as a spy to help put a stop to this.) He loved to play football, and even after he was a recording star he rented football fields, organized teams (Elvis usually played end), and bought equipment so that he and his friends could play during off-hours. In school, he liked shop and R.O.T.C. best. But his long hair and loud clothes, the pink and black, caused Elvis trouble, especially with the football coach, who may not have appreciated what to him was the sissy look.[76]

What Elvis brought to popular music was an expression of sexuality that was troubling to many Americans because it was so direct and obvious. It could hardly be claimed that Elvis originated a new sexuality, or even a new music, yet he certainly was considered responsible for encouraging young Americans to express their feelings through a different kind of music and dance. According to an admiring biographer, Elvis came when kids were "worrying about saltpeter in the school-cafeteria lunch and whether or not the rubber was going to come off at the crucial moment." His style, which many considered outrageous, encouraged many youngsters to express their feelings the way Elvis apparently did when he seemed so relaxed and so much in touch with the hysterical crowd listening to him sing. Soon, longer hair and bright-colored clothes, formerly associated with femininity, began to be accepted as manly and cool. For many, Elvis became a new model of manners and success, a symbol of a changing time, different from dad's ideas of success and certainly at variance with his notion of good music.[77]

DIFFERENT TYPES OF COOL

In 1957, Norman Mailer summarized the case for male survival in his description of the hipster, who knew how to swing, how to be cool, how to really make it so that he would not "flip out" and lose control:

> To be cool is to be equipped, and if you are equipped it is more difficult for the next cat who comes along to put you down. And of course one can hardly afford to be put down too often, or one is beat, one has lost one's confidence . . . one is impotent in the world of action and so closer to the demeaning flip of becoming a queer or indeed closer to dying.[78]

The hipster was a hero because he did not capitulate to the dehumanizing struggles of a complex totalitarian order. Throughout Mailer's writing there is a procession of males, including Mailer himself, who seek confidence and fulfillment in a society that increasingly wants to deny their identity. In *An American Dream*, Steve Rojack, an accomplished television personality, professor, and congressman, saves himself from a spiritual death by murdering his domineering wife, a bitch-goddess of American power. The act galvanizes Rojack's deep sense of masculine will to survive, and he triumphs over fear and fatigue to arrive at new intensities of masculine experience. "Murder offers the promise of vast relief. It is never unsexual," Mailer tells us. In *Advertisements for Myself* and *The Presidential Papers*, Mailer carries into the sixties the countervailing emotions of dread, a near-fatalistic outlook, and the determination to triumph and not to flip out. How a man keeps his cool depends on the understanding he has of his true nature. In *Why Are We in Vietnam?*, D. J. Jethro discovers his masculinity on an Alaskan hunting trip. The real male is a truly virile male, the hunter of animal flesh and the pursuer of sex. To do both well is to achieve and fulfill the American success story, the success of grace and salvation in finding one's manhood.[79]

Certainly Mickey Spillane never flipped out (in Mailer's terms, at least). The Brooklyn-born writer rode the crest of a popular wave that sold almost thirty million paperbacks about the adventures of the tough private detective Mike Hammer. The physically powerful leading character in these murder mysteries is a street-wise, decisive man who throws caution to the winds to capture evildoers. Hammer is irresistible to all the women he meets and they all want to snuggle into his protective arms. ("No dame can take care of herself," Hammer says.) Curiously, he refuses to have sex with either of the two women to whom he was engaged at one time or other, Velda, his secretary, and Charlotte in *I, The Jury* (whom he shoots in the stomach), although both plead with him to do so. What makes Hammer super-masculine and heroic (and impossible to believe) is that nothing deters him from accomplishing his job. Not even when he is reprimanded and disarmed by the F.B.I. and has his private-eye license suspended in *Kiss Me Deadly* does Hammer quit. He plunges into the night hunting two killers, and when he finds them in a bar he hits one from behind "like a kid snapping worms" and kicks the other's face so hard that "the things that were in Charlie's face splashed all over the floor."[80] It was all part of a night's work, done with cool precision, followed by a respite in bed with another passionate dame.

The idea that a man who was not physically inclined was not truly a man was graphically illustrated in a small scene with no dialogue in it from the 1967 movie *Genghis Khan*, a fictionalized account of the life of the Mongol ruler. Preparing to go to war for the Chinese, Khan feels he must test his men's suitability for war and combat; in an earlier scene in which he and his men are invited into the Chinese nation, he warns that they cannot allow themselves to become fat and lazy and soft. Khan decides to test his troops' manhood. After having his men strip to the waist, he lines them up in a row and punches each one in the stomach. A man who cannot take the punch and doubles over is deemed unsuitable for combat and is probably not a man in Khan's eyes. Khan passes him over for having failed the test. However, those who are able to take the punishment are rewarded by being allowed to fight in the war. The scene from this movie graphically depicted the traditional test of manly courage and vitality in the face of war just at a time, coincidentally, when thousands of American boys were about to be tested for their combat readiness in America's war in Southeast Asia.

Through the 1950s and 1960s, then, various expressions of masculinity appeared in print, film, and even music. The substance of the image was rooted in the traditional masculine style of earlier times. Robert Luce observed that the male feels a need to consolidate his identity and prove himself against whatever threatens his identity. Throughout American history the boy who wanted to be a man felt he had to at least *look* like one. In the social climate of the fifties and sixties there was a greater emphasis than ever on appearance and image. But as Luce also noted, "Manhood is not pretending," but committing oneself to a course of action. The lack of commitment, evident in many of the popular images, could only serve to stunt maturity and lessen the chances of genuine creativity.[81] Orrin Klapp registered a concern that masculine models had sharply diverged from the traditional ones extolling achievement and accomplishment to ones who compensated for failing to achieve success. Even the bum was a cultural hero. "Good character," which in the nineteenth century was assumed to mean high moral, spiritual, and physical qualities, now seemed to mean sympathy and understanding for mediocrity and failure. The popular stereotypes of masculine heroism, seen or portrayed in various media, were really marginal beings, as seen from the normative viewpoint, in that they lacked a vital center, a core of values and commitments that related to the consensus vision of American progress. The cowboy gunfighter, the beat-hipster-folksinger, the motorcycle hoodlum, the playboy, the wheeler-dealer, and the warrior hero were seen as cardboard figures without authentic feeling. These masculine stereotypes usually lacked a feeling for anything other than what fulfilled and complemented their own narrow identity. Such types often categorized reality into polarized extremes, providing an unhealthy pattern to those boys and men seeking models to emulate. Klapp even suggested that the government subsidize the publicity of biography, fiction, or drama that focused on a masculine character of the "good type," who exemplified consensus social ideology. Equally concerned, Luce asked, "How can we inject into the bloodstream of American popular culture the notion that masculinity grows through commitment. . . .?"[82]

COMMITMENT AND RELATEDNESS

Pioneers, tycoons, and professional men of the previous century had the commitment Luce referred to, or at least that is the commonly held impression. They had reached out, moved forward, affected people by the very direction, action, and energy of their commitment. But by the 1950s, as Rollo May, Karl Bednarik, and others have documented, a condition existed in which men found it much more difficult to define commitment and gain recognition. Some failed absolutely in their efforts to have meaningful lives. Consolidation and bureaucracy made it less likely for individuals to reach the top or make an impact. Economic complexity and specialization left many men confused and bewildered when they realized that they had to decide about their professional training and place in life. This crisis of relatedness (May's term) to a cause and lack of commitment contributed to the apathy of the 1950s, and, according to May, a dialetical relationship existed between apathy and violence, as evidenced in the 1960s. "Violence is the ultimate destructive substitute which surges to fill the vacuum where there is no relatedness."[83] Various forms of violence ranged from degrees of obscenity, pornography, temper tantrums, riot, and assault to wife- and child-beating. When a man's life had seemingly dried up, the potential of violence increased. May observes that

> to inflict pain and torture at least proves that one can affect somebody. In the alienated state of mass communication, the average citizen knows dozens of TV personalities who come smiling into his living room of an evening—but he *himself is never known*. In this state of alienation and anonymity . . . the average person may well have fantasies which may hover on the edge of pathology. The mood of the anonymous person is, If I can not affect or touch anybody, I can at least shock you into some feeling, force you into some passion through wounds and pain; I shall at least make sure we both feel something, and I shall force you to see me and know that I also am here.[84]

It is not to be construed that this situation applied only to lower-class males or minorities or to the have-nots of society. Studies suggest that a surprising number of middle-class males also engaged in violence in coping with the anxiety of nonrecognition. Does anyone notice what I am achieving for the company? Does anyone care? are aspects of the same apathy problem. A man taunted by such doubts may compensate by asserting his masculine authority at home by becoming a tyrant, a veritable lord of the manor, in which his wife and children are expected to serve him. Yet he seeks work and achievement as the only real means to status and success. Little value is seen in mastering a skill or in cultivating an outside interest, because men are basically interested in what any effort will get them in terms of success symbols. Unlike lower-class males, the middle-class striver often resorts to advertising masculinity through possessions (wife and children included), which he assumes will earn recognition from others, thereby inflating his self-esteem. But all of this is a dangerous illusion, according to Bednarik, because in the long run, acquisition does little to alleviate the anxiety such men feel about their circumstances. The commitment is often only to an *appearance* of success, which American culture has conditioned men to value. The humanistically creative side of the personality remains sterile.[85]

HUGH HEFNER AND PLAYBOY

Several other notable masculine images emerged to help redefine manhood in terms calculated to do away with any hint of sterility. With the advent of *Playboy* in 1953, the sexually aggressive masculine image was underscored by a philosophy contributed by Hugh Hefner. Ostensibly, Hefner's magazine rebelled against Victorian prudery and the norms of male (and female) conduct that had been used to judge ideal masculinity. What Hefner proposed through *Playboy* was "to give the American male an identity and the right frame of reference."[86] Hefner's mission was founded in the wake of the Kinsey report on the sexual behavior of American males, which Hefner read as a student at the University of Illinois. The revealing statistical report provoked Hefner to write for a campus magazine an indignant attack on the social and moral prerequisites of male sexuality. "Our moral pretenses," he wrote, "our hypocrisy on matters of sex, have led to incalculable frustration, delinquency and unhappiness." After his graduation from college and several jobs in journalism, Hefner launched *Playboy*. From the start, *Playboy* was a different kind of man's magazine, catering to the needs of the more educated, sophisticated, urban, middle-class white male, the young man in college or just out of college heading into the company organization. There is less of the robust, physical masculinity in *Playboy* than there is male fashion and furnishing, food and drink, intellectual discussion, and, of course, sex. "We plan to spend most of our time inside," said the first issue. "We like our apartment."[87]

Hefner placed himself in the vanguard of the attack on Puritanism, which he claimed had repressed sex and had been a major cause for moral confusion among American men for so long. Hefner's playboy philosophy, which appeared in twenty-five installments during the 1960s, argued the case for experiencing good, healthy heterosexuality as a means of achieving a healthy mental outlook. One gets healthy sex not by ignoring it, as nineteenth-century Americans had done, but by emphasizing it, as Hefner now hoped to do. Sex was the best means of expressing the innermost, deepest-felt longings and desires in a person, married or not. When sex served those ends, apart from reproduction, it was good and above the animal level, according to Hefner. To that end, Hugh Hefner, the Horatio Alger success story of the 1950s, established an enormous publishing empire built around a magazine built around a center gatefold.

The ideal playboy enjoyed his life because he had money. He had money because he was a success, which implied he also had some degree of power. The essence of the image can be found in a classic advertisement for That Man cologne in *Playboy*'s tenth-anniversary issue in 1964. The ad shows a man standing behind his desk, confidently viewing the city from his window high up in a modern office building. The ad copy reads that here is a man who has "the will and wherewithal to do as he pleases. When he talks, men unconsciously hunch forward to listen. When he looks at a woman, she feels *all* woman. You may admire him; resent him. But no one can be indifferent to him."[88] The strong ingredients of independence and virility are basic to the masculine mystique, which could now even be scented with the lusty tang of lemon. Reality was kept at a fair distance. The magazine's advertising director, Howard Lederer, explained in 1967 that *Playboy* deliberately "takes the reader into a kind of dream world. We create a euphoria and we want nothing to spoil it. We don't want a reader to come suddenly on an ad that says he has bad breath. We don't want him to be reminded of the fact, though it may be true, that he is going bald."[89]

Hefner himself set the pace for the image by confining his life and work almost exclusively to his famous Playboy mansion in Chicago. There, surrounded by art treasures, expensive furnishings, swimming pool, game room, and beautiful women, Hefner worked and played, more or less isolated from the social tensions erupting in the 1960s.[90] Divorced, Hefner confessed no desire to marry again. "Variety, vitality and adventure are more meaningful to me than the security of marriage." Hefner has been known to have a special girl, one who he liked to think depended on him. But a former girl friend, Cynthia Maddox, observed that it was always a one-sided relationship. "I'd think to myself that some day I would have a discussion with Hef when I'd come out on top and he wouldn't devour my words."[91]

The nature of the relationship to women says much about the playboy and about male sexuality of the 1960s. Like his car and hi-fi, the playboy's women are status possessions, generally, depersonalized objects of pleasure to show off to other males. It has been argued that the playboy lacks personal commitment as an aspect of mature manhood. Some critics characterize the playboy as a "subvirile man" who wants to be no closer to women than the centerfold of *Playboy*. Basically, he is afraid of the girls. *Playboy*'s playmates appear aloof in their poses, suggesting they neither want nor expect sex. William Hamilton has said that Hefner rightly affirms the goodness of the body but misses "the beauty and mystery of sexuality." Others saw the playboy of the sixties as only half a man because of his devotion foremost to appearance.[92]

Myron Brenton has argued that *Playboy* could literally pass as the "bible of the beleaguered male." *Playboy*'s philosophy, the articles and attitudes that run through its pages, depend on and reinforce clearly distinguished sex roles. Women have their place: for the purpose of serving men. *Playboy*'s ideal woman had a small brain and big breasts. The rabbit was a well-chosen symbol for those men who identified with the magazine's values, wrote Brenton, because while the rabbit stood for profligacy, it was also one of the most timid of animals. In the presence of the *Playboy* bunny, the rabbitty male did not need to worry about intelligence because none was needed. Qualities of humanity or companionship were unnecessary because it was strictly a look-but-don't-touch proposition guaranteed to preserve sex-role dichotomies along the most traditional lines. It surely must be one of the greatest of all anomolies in American society that the image of the uncommitted, cool male was considered to be one of the most masculine.[93]

SPORTS AND THE JOCK MENTALITY

What the playboy image did not offer in terms of physical exertion, the athletic image supplied in abundance. Many men combined the two: a tough, hard-driving tennis or golf player under the sun by day, a suave cool man with a winning way around the ladies by night. Games have been a great part of modern American life, but during the twentieth century (as discussed in Chapter 6), games and recreational activities acquired elements that helped inflate the masculine mystique. Athletic games were no longer just character-building exercises but had become contests of potency in which winning meant a great deal because it represented successful masculinity. It became an axiom of American culture that any respectable father would urge his son into competitive athletics, and the sooner the better, so that the magic of character-building could begin early. David F. Aberle and Kasper Naegele found that only one out of twenty middle-class fathers did not want his boys to be good athletes.[94] Little League, Biddy League, junior-high and high-school coaches took their respective turns in helping boys understand what life was about through the competition of sports. Football was given special attention, according to the sportswriter Roger Kahn, because "like no other game in America, football has become a ritual for coming of age. Such rituals are as old as history: to tread glowing coals, swim a rapids, spear a lion. Always, when a young man seeks to proclaim himself, one finds excitement, violence, danger, courage, pain."[95] The ritual was repeated in thousands of American towns every Friday night. In Tracy, California, the freshman game began at five P.M., followed by the sophomore game, and finally the varsity competition. "People don't think of these kids as teenagers," a Tracy newspaper reporter said. "They're men. . . . Put a uniform on a kid and he turns into John Brodie."[96]

Behind all the hoopla loomed the image of the professional athlete, who, because of his size, skill, and salary, became one of the nation's most powerful symbols of masculinity. Football offered an abundance of action as compared with the standing around and waiting for something to happen in baseball. And the action involved tests of muscular strength and the courage to hit another person hard, get up, and hit again. These basic features led Murray Ross to argue that football's popularity in the 1960s rested on the fact that football had become a heroic game, whereas baseball was largely a pastoral game, a reminder of open space. In space dramatic things can happen: the double off the wall, the spectacular catch, and the home run, which transcended the boundaries of space. Baseball players seemed more human, more boyishly happy and expressive. But football players were bigger, less boyish (and therefore more manly), and expressionless behind the cagelike face mask. "Football converts men into gods and suggests that magnificence and glory are as desirable as happiness."[97] In an era of social turmoil and foreign-policy controversy, when personal as well as national excellence seemed in doubt, sports (and especially football) could be seen from the Woody Hayes perspective as "the last look at what's right with America." Fred Exley described football as an island of directness in a world of circumspection, a world unclouded by leger domain and subtlety.[98]

On the personal level, the *Time* essay of November 1, 1970, beautifully captured the mystique of pro football:

> There is no Mittyism about this. I could never for an instant imagine myself performing the feats of these uniformed supermen; yet thinking about Sunday's heroes does offer relief from mundane cares. When I fall asleep, however, I begin to dream middle-aged dreams. I dream that I am old eggbald Y. A. Tittle in high-top shoes, running a bootleg into the end zone on my weary legs. Or I dream of being Sonny Jurgensen, proudly puffing out my potbelly as if it were a chest, fading back and letting go with the most accurate arm in the game. And when I wake, I feel somehow fit and fresh and ready to go. . . . In short, I am a pro-football nut. And I share my insanity with thousands—nay, millions—of others who have turned a weekend entertainment into a mystique, an obsession, and a secular religion.[99]

To the racing fan, virility was achieved through the automobile. Like football fans, stock-car fans sensed that they had little control over what was happening to them, so they identified with a driver who personified control. "Look at Petty out there in his Dodge, controlling it, passing cars at 180 miles an hour . . . the fan puts himself in Richard's Petty's place and it makes him feel like a man."[100]

The corollary of the Roosevelt–Lombardi–Hayes view of football (or any sport, for that matter) was that it was not enough to play the game; one had to win. "Jesus!" Woody Hayes exclaimed. "We just don't talk about losing," and the oft-repeated "winning isn't everything, it's the *only* thing," drove many a sports fan to forget about "it's not whether you win or lose, it's how you play the game."[101] This philosophy is driven home in part by the fear that if one loses, one appears less of a man or less of a university, exposing weakness and inviting talk among peers (and opponents) that so-and-so lost his control. To always be in control, to be cool, to be on top, and be number one ranks high in the hierarchy of values for those living according to the orthodox masculine image. Winning means sacrifice, punishment of self with little doubt that it is all worth it in sports as in war. To the Green Bay Packers of the sixties, it meant grueling hours of conditioning and no complaining because "fatigue makes cowards of us all," as Lombardi told his players. "When you're tired, you rationalize. . . . Then you're a coward."[102] One could argue that, for the Packers, this attitude paid off in a string of winning seasons. For the amateur jock, however, who modeled his intense desire to win after the Lombardi method, it jeopardized not only his health but the basic enjoyment of recreational games. Because the jock proclaimed himself a winner, *he had to be one* or produce excuses for failure: lousy racquet, poor set of clubs, biased umpire, a chronic injury, and so on. Winning was the only way he could enjoy playing.

Upon his retirement from football, George Sauer, all-pro wide receiver for the Jets, explained that the whole value structure of winning at all cost put such pressure on a player that "it's no longer any pleasure to compete." Reflecting on the system of rewards used to induce quality performance, Sauer concluded that a "true athlete doesn't need any incentive beyond himself." Sauer's point helps understand the jock mentality. The real emphasis is to *appear* athletic, whether the jock has genuine skill or not, because he is driven by the incentives of social recognition and acclaim, which are perhaps even more important and pleasurable to him than just playing and competing. Sauer, who was one of several players to speak out critically about football in the early 1970s, maintained that the war analogy was responsible for diminishing the appeal of football. It encouraged hating an opponent and thereby dehumanized one's values while competing against other human beings. In no way did Sauer demean the desire to win or deny the value of competition. Rather, he attacked the absurd means employed by some coaches and players to get the job done. "When you're full of hate, you are always less than what you can be; you are always dangerous not only to other people, but to yourself." While believing that football was a beautiful and worthwhile sport, Sauer suggested that a comprehensive evaluation of its impact on youth and society be undertaken.[103]

One serious effort to evaluate the role of sports was undertaken by two psychologists, Bruce Ogilvie and Thomas Tutko, who studied the effects of competition on personality. Over an eight-year period, they tested some 15,000 athletes in high schools, colleges, and in the pros. They found no empirical support for the traditional belief that sports builds character. In fact, they produced some evidence that athletic competition obstructed maturity and growth in some situations. When it came to character-building, which was so intrinsically linked with the masculinity syndrome, athletics had no more beneficial effect than other endeavors, be they playing the violin or building model airplanes. It was just that a society caught up so completely in the mystic implications of the action-oriented masculinity syndrome had rested its case long ago that to be masculine and a success, a boy must be involved in some form of athletic competition. Horatio Alger's success, according to the study, in sports or elsewhere, comes to those who already are mentally fit, resilient, and strong. The study did find that those who made it in the star-oriented sports system had personalities that reflected the traditional male stereotype, which, no doubt, helped to advance the character-building myth. They had a high need for achievement, respected authority, were dominant in peer-group situations, and were basically self-centered, all traits recognized as masculine. What about those who did not make the team or were not good enough to play? Marc Fasteau noted that many took a "psychological beating" and developed depression and anxiety because they saw themselves as failures if they did not make the team or did not play regularly, even though a team could put only a fixed number of players on the field at a time. Fasteau called for a broader range of opportunities for potential participation, so that playing would become an option rather than a compulsion, free of the limitations and restrictions of the masculine mystique.[104]

Until the 1960s, competitive sports were such a part of the masculine establishment that they were virtually untouched by women. Since late in the nineteenth century, occasional male voices have been heard denouncing women's meddling in athletics. Few aspects of the women's movement of the 1970s stirred up as much ire as the feminine march into the male sports arena. At the Little League level, several court cases have been argued with the thesis that girls would get hurt more easily than boys. In 1974, New Jersey Little League fathers and managers threatened to cancel the whole season if they had to comply with a civil-rights order permitting girls to play. A statement by Charles Mass, Secretary of the Indiana State Coaches Association, gets to the heart of the matter: "There is the possibility that a boy would be beaten by a girl and as a result be ashamed to face his family and friends. I wonder if anybody has stopped to think what that could do to a young boy." A dramatic manifestation of the same sentiment occurred in 1972 when Ellen Cornish, an Olympic distance runner, entered a two-mile high-school event on an exhibition basis. At the end of the seventh lap, Cornish, fighting for the lead, was pulled off the track by the coaches, who, by previous agreement among themselves, had decided to do so. *Sports Illustrated* said it was done "to protect the male runners from the morale-shattering possibility of being beaten by a girl, a possibility that was probable."[105]

POLITICAL FOOTBALL

During the 1960s, events from Selma to Saigon forced many Americans, mostly the young, to attack traditional racial and sexual stereotypes that had been part of the national consciousness. There were new civil-rights acts, open-housing legislation, and a renewed effort to pass the Equal Rights Amendment, guaranteeing sex equality. The ideals of the masculine establishment—the mystique of the potent white American male, always dominant, always winning, always in control—began to disintegrate, which may be one of the most significant developments in recent American social history. The Vietnam War has already been interpreted by one new-thinking male as the colossus of the masculine-power ethos. Marc Fasteau, who worked on Senator Mike Mansfield's staff, remembers American intervention predicated on the domino theory. To him, "the feeling that the United States must at all costs avoid 'the humiliation of defeat' " demonstrated the faults in the cult-of-toughness attitude and the mentality behind prolonging the Vietnam War. While this interpretation does not suggest the continuity-of-toughness thesis as the only rationale for 1960s foreign policy, Fasteau's analysis, nevertheless, likens attitudes that Theodore Roosevelt espoused to some of the Kennedy–Nixon expressions and actions. John F. Kennedy was a cold warrior, hating to lose at anything. Once embarrassed in Cuba in 1961, he determined not to lose again in the missile crisis of 1962 and suffer the stigma of having been "soft on communism." Reflecting on his meeting with Nikita Khrushchev in 1961, shortly after the Bay of Pigs, Kennedy commented that his adversary had a low opinion of him. "So I've got a terrible problem," he told James Reston of the *New York Times*. "If he thinks I'm inexperienced and have no guts, until we remove those ideas we won't get anywhere with him. So we have to act . . . and Vietnam looks like the place."[106]

As a child, Lyndon Johnson had to struggle to achieve independence from a domineering mother. According to Harold Lasswell, Johnson grew up trying to decide whether to accept domination or rebel against it "to reassert [his] independence and masculinity and sense of adequacy." Lasswell concludes that Johnson's "subsequent political career—with his demand to make his own decisions, and his demand to *control* a situation has these very deep roots." Johnson hungered for power, for control over others to manipulate situations and people in order to get things done, because getting things done was the mark of a "real man."[107] And as President, Lyndon Baines Johnson got a lot of things done, but as it was for Teddy Roosevelt, *machismo* was no small part of his style. In the Dominican crisis of 1965, during which Johnson ordered Marines into the Dominican Republic because of its Civil War, he sent word through McGeorge Bundy to Colonel Deno, the rebel leader: "Tell that son of a bitch that unlike the young man who came before me I am not afraid to use what's on my hip." But Johnson never seemed quite certain that others were taking him seriously and was, therefore, haunted by the prospect that he would be judged "insufficiently manly" for the job of President.[108] Thus, ironically, Lyndon Johnson, winner by a huge margin in the election of 1964, felt insecure, needing to have the genuine respect of *real* men around him, the tough men who were doers and not doubters.

VIETNAM

There were some, like Joseph Alsop, who felt that Johnson was too weak to take decisive action and who said so in print, deeply irritating the President. Johnson confided to Bill Moyers that if he pulled out of Vietnam, it would just prove the weakness thesis being advanced by some of his opponents. He feared that men like Robert McNamara, the "Mr. Tough" of the Kennedy Administration, would think him less of a man and tell stories about him. "They'll push Vietnam up my ass every time." Johnson feared. The situation obviously played into the hands of the military men who could gain Johnson's support by advancing what they labeled the "manhood positions," referring to the alternatives as the "sissy positions." Doubt was a feminine quality, in Johnson's view of things, and, hence, the doves, with a few exceptions like George Ball, who still advocated an activist power position, were considered effeminate. When word got to Johnson that a member of his administration was going dovish, he retorted, "Hell, he has to squat to piss." When Senator George

McGovern sought to caution President Johnson about allowing the military too much latitude in conducting the bombing, Johnson assured the Senator that he was in control. "I don't let those guys bomb so much as a shit-house without my personal approval," he said. To the dovish McGovern, Johnson used language indicative of his earthy aggressiveness, as if to emphasize the difference between him and the passive Senator. According to McGovern, "At one point he said [with reference to the militarists], 'I'm sneaking up their knee an inch at a time, and I'll grab their snatch before they know it.' And I said, 'Mr. President, sometimes, when you start going up a skirt, you get your hand slapped.' He didn't like me saying that, but he finally said, 'Well, I'm watching that.' "[109] And so it was that the political and social scene in the last half of the sixties was divided between the men and the boys, between the hawks and the doves, between the short-hairs and the long-hairs, between the *macho* types, like the Green Berets, and the flower children. By raising the ante, by conducting the bombing, by sending in the troops, President Johnson was riding tall in the saddle, thinking himself secure in history, enhancing America's power and status in the eyes of the world.[110]

The cult of masculine toughness, as Marc Fasteau has observed, often meant overlooking reality, especially in Vietnam when indications pointed toward something less than an American victory. There is evidence suggesting that Richard Nixon himself did not think the Vietnam War could be won. "But we can't say that, of course," he is quoted as saying in 1968.[111] In Nixon's case, the philosophy underlying the cult of toughness is manifest in his own *Six Crises*. The book deals with six episodes in Nixon's career and how he responded to pressure in each situation. In every crisis there "is the period of indecision—whether to fight or run away."[112] But what self-respecting man could run away? The very choice of words is revealing; "running away" connotes cowardice. Again, as Fasteau and others who have analyzed Nixon's character and actions have suggested, the substance of issues often became less important to Nixon than how Nixon looked to himself and to the world. He desperately wanted to be liked, not as a do-gooder or a glad-hander but as one of the boys, which helps to explain Nixon's frequent cursing and sports talk. No one was more painfully aware than Nixon himself, however, that he was not liked by many in the press corps. "You know, a lot of people think I'm a prick, but I'm really not," he said. Failing to be tough in Vietnam would risk undermining America's credibility everywhere and encourage America's enemies to capitalize on that weakness. This was the logic of the Nixon–Kissinger position. But many historians and foreign-policy experts doubt the validity of the "macho" theory. Much more research needs to be done on the relationship of personality and decision-making, but a case can be made, it seems, that Nixon continued the war so that he could find "a peace with honor." Such a concept, however, had much more to do with arbitrary, masculinity-first principles than it did in pursuing a rational course of action that would have brought the fighting to an end sooner. When Nixon ordered the Cambodian invasion, he explained that "it is not our power but our will and character that are being tested tonight" adding with a grim intonation that the United States will not behave like "a pitiful, helpless giant."[113]

From the soldier's point of view, there was little pride of masculine accomplishment in fighting the Vietnam War. Robert Lifton notes that, from the outset, the goals and objectives of the war were confusing to soldiers and the Vietnamese. Much of the time soldiers had to search for the enemy among the civilians and, too often, found that the enemy *was* the civilian population. How could one feel masculine destroying the homes and villages of innocent people and even "wasting" some of them to secure an area from the enemy? Even in the old American West, it had been considered cowardly to shoot innocent or unarmed people. It was not a case of American soldiers' having no "feeling" for the war; they had tremendous feelings—feelings of rage and violence at the enemy and within themselves, emotions that many brought home with them. In Vietnam "you're mad all the time—you wake up mad—you're mad when you eat, mad when you sleep, mad when you walk, mad when you just sit—just mad all the time."[114] It was not the kind of rage or meanness expressed by Croft in Mailer's *The Naked and the Dead*. Croft's meanness was a product of his environment (Texas), where he had been taught to hate weakness. The anger in Vietnam was rooted in a sense of guilt about the war, guilt that could bring a young soldier who had killed a Viet Cong with a knife to confess, "I felt sorry, I don't know why I felt sorry. John Wayne never felt sorry." The guilt brought another young man to a confirmation of a different kind of self-identity: "I was somebody with feelings who had done something wrong and I—I was not an animal or some kind of killing machine."[115] The government made efforts to advertise, through the Green Berets, a traditional military strength and courage (guts), the strong-man ideal. Yet for many millions of Americans, those who had been there and those who stayed home, the archetypal military hero was a notable casualty of the war. The long-awaited "peace with honor" was finally achieved and America was out of the war, but for Richard Nixon, another crisis, again testing his character as a man, was already engulfing him and America.

WATERGATE

Few examples in modern times illustrate the crisis of the masculine mystique as does Nixon's handling of Watergate. Again Nixon's *Six Crises* sets the background. In every crisis situation, Nixon was obsessed with maintaining his identity and coolness. As Bruce Mazlish has pointed out, it was never a case of Nixon's finding his true self, but, rather, a testing of his already formed self.[116] At work in Nixon's seventh crisis was an overriding sense of paranoia, a feeling that forces were constantly out to get him, to do him in, to embarrass him by forcing him to change policy, which would have amounted to an admission that his initial actions had not been right. Men can change their minds, of course, but to maintain masculine cool, the reasons for change must appear to come from within. To accept, even partially, opposition arguments or to recognize a point offered by the demonstrators would have suggested unmanly vacillation. James David Barber has maintained that Nixon's greatest fear was public exposure of personal inadequacy. To play it safe, Nixon removed himself to "a cleared circle, an emotional DMZ, space razed and defoliated, so he [could not] be 'got to' unexpectedly."[117]

From 1970 on, and especially after the Pentagon Papers were published, Nixon became obsessed with getting back at the opposition, to keep the space around him perfectly clear, as embattled males are wont to do. Even if one accepts the national-security argument and the natural inclination of any person to defend one's own policy, it is difficult to justify Nixon's enemies list of 1971. On this list were many names of persons who could hardly be considered a threat to government policy or national security. These people were just *personally* irritating to Nixon. What James Barber wrote in 1973 about Nixon seems even more plausible in the light of subsequent events. "What moves and excites [Nixon] is not principle or policy or result, but an endless struggle for control. First to control himself. . . . Then to control others. . . . But above all to control doubt . . . doubts of his manliness."[118] On the basis of what has been learned about Nixon's personality, few observers would suggest that he could have come to grips with the mistake of Watergate, admitted it, and apologized. To have done so would have been a confession of weakness and having lost control. Instead, the "hang-out route" was taken, in which scenarios were spun, making it appear that Nixon really was in control and that Watergate was the work of some overzealous supporters. "The tougher it gets, the cooler I get," Nixon said in response to a 1973 press-conference question on Watergate. Right to the end, Nixon was concerned about how his manliness would be perceived. After the tearful session with Henry Kissinger the night before his resignation, Nixon got back to the Secretary of State on the phone imploring him not to mention the episode, for fear that anyone might think he was not strong. And the next day, in a rambling farewell, Nixon identified with Theodore Roosevelt: "As an ex-President, he served his country, always in the arena, tempestuous, strong, sometimes right, but he was a man. And as I leave, let me say that's an example I think all of us should remember."[119]

WHEN MEN WERE MEN

Examples of tough manliness from America's history were plentiful and appealed to Richard Nixon, who found a model in Teddy Roosevelt. Millions of other American males nostalgically looked to the past and yearned for the good old days, or an idealized version of them, when men had been dominant in sex, politics, war, and work. In spite of changes, contradiction, and confusion pertaining to the masculine ideal, it was the *myth* of the masculine past that kept the old stereotypes alive and fashioned the mystique of masculinity, which assumed that men could go on living, working, and acting very much as they had always done. Like most myths, a grain of truth, or at least a viable aspiration, provided the core, as Norman Mailer succinctly stated in 1963 in describing the plight of mass man. "America was . . . the country in which the dynamic myth of the Renaissance—that every man was potentially extraordinary—knew its most passionate existence." And when the frontier space was settled and the old field of heroism became occupied, Mailer noted "the expansion turned inward, became part of an agitated, over-excited, super-heated dream life." In the twentieth century, it became a function of Hollywood to salvage

> the romantic possibilities of the old conquest of land turned into a vertical myth, trapped within the skull, of a new kind of heroic life, each choosing his own archetype of a neo-renaissance man, be it Barrymore, Cagney, Flynn, Bogart, Brando or Sinatra, but it was almost as if there were no peace unless one could fight well, kill well

(if always with honor), love well and love many, be cool, be daring, be dashing, be wild, be wily, be resourceful, be a brave gun. And this myth, that each of us was born to be free, to wander, to have adventure and to grow on the waves of the violent, the perfumed, and the unexpected, had a force which could not be tamed no matter how the nation's regulators . . . would brick in the modern life with hygiene upon sanity, and middle-brow homily over platitude; the myth would not die.[120]

Although the masculine myth provided material for much entertainment through the popular media, for some men, especially, that myth has been a source of exasperation. The myth has inspired a variety of identities or adaptations of identities: the jock who cannot stand losing, the playboy who sees women as sex objects, the tough guy who defines masculinity through violence, the wheeler-dealer who is always seeking to cash in, the workaholic who has no time for fatherhood, and still others, most often resting on a vision of youthfulness. Myron Brenton observed that a significant number of men wanted to restore some sense of the past, when there had been more freedom and less tension in being male. Did it work? In part, yes, according to Brenton. The masculine images and the myths these men generated could and did provide wonderfully therapeutic release from the fenced-in feeling of modern times. There was nothing wrong with physical activity, or being aggressive, or winning, but problems arose when men discovered that these qualities did not make them more manly. Such behavior did not enhance their value to a company, alleviate marriage tensions, turn them into adequate lovers, or raise their status in any substantial way. So-called masculine activity simply did not create an attitude or style that could make any man successful.[121] In every period of American history, especially since the 1920s, the more men tried to build an identity based upon an idealized masculine vision of the past, more problems were left unresolved than solved.

WORK

Achieving and validating their masculinity had always meant that sooner or later men had to contend with their feelings and reactions toward work and women. There is evidence that, by 1970, many men, for many reasons, were becoming disillusioned with their work. Even a casual reading of Studs Terkel's *Working* reveals a great deal of status anxiety, a lack of fulfillment, and boredom, all of which can often be traced to an identity concept rooted in the masculine mystique. Consider the spot welder in an automobile plant who wonders why "more guys don't flip." The first thing the bosses try to do, he says, "is break your spirit" and turn workers into machines. Another auto worker complained that the quest for efficiency made for monumental boredom. An older worker talked about a boss he had had some years earlier who was "a real bull of the woods. Tough guy." He was poor at communicating and his style had gone out of fashion. "The old days of hit 'em with a baseball bat to get their attention—they're gone." The generational differences were reflected by yet another man, aged thirty. "Fathers used to show their manliness by being able to work hard and have big, strong muscles and that kind of bullshitting story. The young guy now, he doesn't get a kick out of saying how hard he can work. I think his kick would be just the opposite: 'you said I had to do that much, and I only have to do *that* much' . . . It isn't being manly to do more than you should." Speaking about his father, the son recalled that his father worked very hard on an incentive-pay basis, but the son disavowed this attitude, commenting that there was more to life than the almighty dollar. Now it is "how I'm treated" as a man that counts. A garbage worker said he liked what he did because he was more free than a man who worked in an office. A policeman professed a liking for his job because it gave him authority, and he suggested that many white males were attracted to the job because of that factor.[122]

Terkel interviewed a stockbroker who remembered how he dreamed of hitting it big as a kid. He sold cakes in an open market when he was twelve and later caddied, all the while believing in his earning power. "I felt that somewhere along the line someone would recognize that I had that special gleam. Horatio Alger—which is a crock of shit. . . . People like me start out with a feeling that there's a place for them. . . . They see it destroyed. . . . I felt I could really buck this machine. When I began, I was sure I could win. I no longer have that confidence." Most troublesome to this broker was not that he had failed to make money, but that he was being demeaned as a human being. He saw himself trapped between moral concerns and the operations of the market machine. Somehow he thought he would be able to cope, but coping, too, was an illusion for him. "Oh I'd like one morning to wake up and go to some work that gave me joy. If I could build houses all over again I would do it. Because when it's finished, somebody's gonna live in it, and the house is gonna be built and it's gonna be there after I'm gone. (Pause.) Ahhh, fuck it!"[123]

Not even supposedly prestigious careers offered the assurance that an individual would be treated like a human being. A banker who wanted to be recognized as a human being, "not as a million-dollar piece of machinery," said there was no thrill in banking. "I didn't run home and say, 'Ma, I'm working for a bank now. . . .' I'm still searching." A factory owner spoke of his "need to work." His whole being was invested in his work, and he claimed that he would go crazy if he retired. The ex-president of a large conglomerate described the corporation as a jungle. "You have the tremendous infighting of man against man for survival and clawing to the top. Progress." As a boy, during the Depression, he had heard about the great tycoons, "the men of power, the men of industry. And you kind of dream that, gee, these are supermen." He had believed that these men were so powerful that they were beyond human emotions and the insecurities everybody else had. But once at the top of the corporate structure, this executive found that fear, loneliness, stress, and neurosis were the common features of his peers. What made it worthwhile? It was not money. "It's the power, the status, the prestige." But suddenly one day, the power and the status were empty, and the executive came to the realization that "it [wasn't] worth it."[124]

Another Terkel interviewee was a thirty-seven-year-old English teacher, the son of a board member of a large corporation. His father had "the successful American life. . . . But I wouldn't trade places with him for a million dollars." And why? "In the business world . . . you have to become ruthless . . . stab your competitor in the back." One cause of youth's dissent was a disillusionment with the corporate rat race and the alleged valuelessness associated with it. Kenneth Keniston found sons describing fathers who, despite public success, were "failures in their own eyes . . . apostates," disappointed, frustrated, and disillusioned men. Many fathers were seen as once having had ideals that for one reason or another became lost. They had become reserved, lonely, withdrawn men who often appeared weak and uninteresting. Many factors contributed to this condition, but whatever the explanation, rebelling youth wanted a different lifestyle. As one hippie put it, "I want to be a frontiersman of the spirit where work is not a drag."[125]

At the heart of the social consciousness of the sixties was a feeling that the masculine mystique was based upon assumptions of success and status that turned men into robots. Warren Farrell and many other authors have taken note of this discovery. Men who thought they had to live up to the masculine ideal became harsh and vindictive in their struggle to succeed. Failure triggered insecurity, self-doubt, and fault-finding, often at the expense of minorities, women, and other men who were thought to have been given an unfair advantage. Usually insecure men were the ones most prone to become intensely involved in proving their manhood—by any means. The insecure have always been the most easily manipulated. And there have always been people willing to manipulate them. It is here that Norman Mailer's superheated dream life takes over. The insecure are susceptible to image-projecting and advertising claims (like preventing baldness or fast weight reduction). They became more vulnerable to corruption, were willing to commit acts of violence to stay in control, and appeared in control when things, especially their ideal of masculinity, are completely out of control.[126]

NEW IMAGES

Many professional athletes recognize the limits of the masculine mystique, which they, perhaps more than any other class or group, are expected to fulfill. The hockey player Eric Nesterenko said that "being a physical man in the modern world is becoming obsolete." Industrialism and modern business operations do not call for brute strength and so man has become more passive and conforming. Even on the ice, the old drive to "really put it" to another player has left him. "I don't want to be anybody any more in those terms." Nesterenko regretted that the pattern of his life, dictated by an early desire for success at hockey, had limited his horizons, cutting him off from the arts. The great ego trip of being a champion, like the businessman who wanted to dominate the market, had unfortunate side effects, limiting human awareness: "The things I like now are more soft." Describing a trip into the wilds, which he took with a professional football player, Nesterenko said he became aware of a great aesthetic feedback. "It's soft and comforting and sweet."[127] Even Joe Namath, still considered by many a super-jock-playboy-stud, suggests a different perspective on masculinity. Namath brought white shoes to the N.F.L., let his hair grow, wore mink coats, advertised popcorn poppers and panty hose. "What's he turned into?" steel-mill workers wanted to know. "A fag or something?" Kathy Keeten explained that Namath gave the impression "that masculinity didn't have to be a threatening thing." Although a strong competitor, Namath never implied that he wanted to kill anybody to win. His strength, as a player and as a human being, was in just wanting to be himself. He proved, as Martin Ralbovsky has stated, that courage "was more of an inner quality than an outer one."[128]

It would be an overstatement to conclude that all of this, symbolized by Namath's famous panty hose, marked a sweeping social revolution in American history pertaining to male identity and sex-role functions. Yet, in the early 1970s, many factors pointed to change along these lines, not the least of which was a spin-off from the women's liberation movement. With increasing militancy during the 1960s, women attacked the role concept that had restricted them in the past. They formed new organizations like the National Organization for Women, wrote manifestos, distributed literature, and worked at consciousness-raising. A new corps of authors contributed powerful books like *Sexual Politics, The Female Eunuch,* and *The Dialectics of Sex.* The language, some of it painfully direct and personal, was aimed at the heart of the male establishment, which had denied women equality on the basis of biology. While some men remained cynical and others expressed reactionary outrage, there were indications that a few were beginning to critically evaluate masculine roles and the behavior patterns that the masculine mystique had forced upon them. Some men were emotionally and intellectually prepared for the women's arguments, after years of the uninspiring role that they led as breadwinners, holding down a job they found neither rewarding nor stimulating. Others came to the liberation attitude through opposition to the Vietnam War or from efforts made on behalf of civil rights for minorities and homosexuals. Pleas were heard for male liberation, which called for "men to free themselves of the sex-role stereotypes that limit their ability to be human."[129]

Warren Farrell and others made the logical point that it was impossible to realistically discuss women's liberation without discussing corresponding changes for men. Not to do so, Farrell asserts, "feeds the male tendency to avoid introspection." Out of liberation can come freedom, he argued, freedom to select from a variety of alternative lifestyles and commitments. America's social history provides much evidence to support Farrell's thesis about male polygamy, "a man married to his job and wife (but barely to the latter)." The peculiar influences that evolved with American capitalism and free enterprise motivated many men into an unswerving devotion to the breadwinner role, thinking it would guarantee love and happiness, only to have it bring misery and alienation from those they loved. At a time in American history when sex-role myths bewildered many husbands and wives, consciousness-raising efforts toward redefining the whole family unit seemed entirely appropriate as one means to a better life.[130]

Harvey Kaye raised the specter of the physical and mental toll the masculine mystique has exacted. To work was noble, he emphasized, but to stake one's moral worth and whole sense of being on one's work has proved to be a physical and psychological catastrophe. Men needed to freely examine sources other than their work to support individual identity and validate claims of personal worth. Liberationists offered the possibility that the breadwinning role could be comfortably shared between men and women, much to the relief of both, once men overcame their fears of competing against women and the prospect of having a female boss.[131]

SHARING

Logically, it followed that sharing the breadwinning role led to sharing the domestic role. While most men had some limited experience with domestic chores, it was not something "respectable males," caught up in the masculinity syndrome, would do voluntarily, much less admit to, because such duties had always been stigmatized as the undignified work of the "weaker sex." Men were urged to understand that it was not a matter of turning woman's work into man's work, but a creative means toward more efficient household organization.[132] Liberationists also asserted that, after decades of being prodded without results, fathers finally needed to assume a much more qualitative involvement in the lives of their children. With more time available through shorter work periods and longer vacations, the old excuse of no time or energy for kids was not convincing. Dad should no longer stand by, watering the grass, "wooden as a dead post," as Stephen Koch put it, "while inside the household lived that real life in which he didn't count." The old perception of a manhood of constant achievement, of being feared, or ignored or pitied or dispised or even hated, had to end.[133] But to relate effectively to children, to understand them and earn their respect in return, meant bringing oneself to the level and developing the imagination of children. For many American men, worried about being or appearing feminine rather than tough, rugged, and always cool, the ways of children were irritating and even intimidating because children did not respond predictably to fatherly discipline and authority. To men who operated out of the old stereotype, it was better not to get too close to children for fear of being unmanly. However, men liberated from the masculine-power stereotype could find in children an enthusiasm that fathers could develop and further nurture in their children—and help renew spontaneity in themselves.

Most importantly, male liberation encouraged men to shed chauvinistic attitudes and behavior, resting on assumptions of superiority and power, that have prevailed throughout American history. Male liberationists maintained that these perceptions, defining women as nursemaids and housekeepers by day and sex objects by night, not only demeaned women but equally restricted and demeaned men. The liberationists called for an end to terms like "broads," "chicks," and "dolls." More seriously, they emphasized that men should assume a much greater responsibility for birth control.[134] Unlike the feminist movement preceding it, women's liberation stressed more of the personal aspects of human freedom, the freedom to be spontaneous, creative, and aggressive sexually. Men had to be more open and sensitive, and aware of the subtleties of female responsiveness during intercourse. Those who attacked the chauvinistic "wham-bam-thank-you-ma'am" style of sex maintained that male gentleness and sensitivity could be as rewarding for men as it was for women. The freedom of being truly aware of another person heightened individualism.

MEN'S LIBERATION

By the mid-1970s, men's conferences were being held and organizations formed to respond to a growing list of male concerns, ranging from divorce and alimony rights, parenting, and job situations to sexual fulfillment and, especially, gay rights, which dominated the early movement. A men's liberation movement had been born. The basic focus was a recognition of the shortcomings of playing the traditional masculine role of always getting ahead and staying cool. Men were thinking about how they treated associates, competitors, and women and how they chose to spend their leisure time. Men were encouraged to evaluate their physical and mental health in a new light. Although the movement was mostly campus based, it appealed to men everywhere who felt the need to discuss their masculine identity. Robert Gould stated that the liberation movement was just beginning, and he predicted that it would have far-ranging consequences comparable to the civil-rights movement.[135]

Most critics agreed that the masculine mystique would be hard to overcome. "Man, it's heavy," said one male in response to the liberation idea.

"Like you gotta build a whole new way of seeing her and yourself. . . ." One slip these days and "wow, bam it's over. That's living in terror, man."[136] Many men would no doubt share Norman Mailer's skepticism about sex discussions and role evaluation. In a letter to Farrell, Mailer confided, "it's a way of digging too close to the source of one's work. . . . [M]an is verily a bag and when he blows out in one place, [he] caves in at the other."[137] In extensive interviews with sixty-two college men, Mirra Komarovsky found that "despite some changes, the traditional ideal of masculinity was still the yardstick against which the seniors measured themselves." While some males questioned the *machismo* elements of masculinity, "the ideal man was still an 'assertive,' 'strong,' 'courageous,' 'aggressive' man."[138]

Charles Winick argued that the liberation idea was desexing American men, and he too remained apprehensive about the results. Allowing that liberation from traditional sex roles and functions regarding work and sexuality would mean a greater flexibility, Winick, and other critics of liberation, argued that flexibility would lead to ambiguity and uncertainty about one's basic identity. To make his point as to how extensive this social trend had become, Winick examined everything from the movies (today's younger male movie stars have an ambiguous masculinity unlike John Wayne's) to home furnishings (whatever happened to sturdier, rugged, masculine furniture?) to names of children (he does not care for genderless names) to modern music and dance (today's young people do not even touch one another when they dance). Patricia Sexton claimed that society had effeminized males, mostly through elementary and secondary education, in which women dominated the field. Boys who got good grades in academic subjects and went on to college were the ones who tamed or repressed their innate aggressiveness. Other boys who were aggressive and mechanically oriented got lost in the shuffle because educational institutions could not deal with masculinity. The wordiness and bookishness of modern education gave males a false sense of reality and insufficient means of coping with their instinctive aggressiveness.[139]

Steven Goldberg presented the thesis that sex differences and role functions had to survive if culture were to survive and progress to continue. Relying on anthropological and biological evidence, Goldberg concluded that males were aggressive, not out of bad habit, but because natural evolution had made them the dominant sex. Evolutionary processes allowed them to lead and fight and protect women and children, not oppress them, as the liberationists mistakenly assumed. Women, Goldberg believed, had not been designed to compete with men and were doomed to inevitable defeat if they did so.[140]

"The liberationists have no idea where their program would take us," wrote George Gilder. ". . . They are promoting in the United States an epidemic of erotic and social disorders." Gilder observed that male nature ranged from ferocity and strength to apathy and weakness. In Gilder's range of experiences, males were basically driven by a sexual urge related to creativity. Gilder expressed a view common in the nineteenth century: It was up to women to help tame and civilize men, to civilize male instincts and passions according to the innate capability of the gentler female biology. To do this, women had to retain their domesticator role as wives and mothers. For Gilder, there could be no "open marriage" or any other alternatives to the traditional family that came with liberation. In the family situation, males were motivated to work at being providers and protectors, guaranteeing human progress. A male's socialization and his sense of community were shaped by work and women. "If he finds work that affirms his manhood and a girl who demands that his sexuality be submitted to hers—submitted to love and family—he is likely to become a valuable and constructive citizen." Liberation, whether personal, political, sexual, or economic, was viewed by Gilder as an erosion of the proper conditions for male socialization. The liberated condition and the freedom it encouraged would lead to sexual frustration and violence, pornography, increasing homosexuality, and divorce.[141]

DOUBTS

The controversy over sexual liberation has generated wide discussion on radio and television talk shows and has inspired many books, articles, and surveys presenting a wide assortment of views and statistics on almost every phase of the topic. Was there widespread assimilation of liberation ideals, as some claimed, or was there more often than not a rejection of them, based on a preference for familiar patterns that seemed more stable than the uncertainties of liberation?

In Komarovsky's study of college males, there is an undertone of sentiment that sex roles should not change. Some men stated they felt threatened by intellectual women and said that women should not pursue "unnatural careers" like medicine. Clearly, the men did not want to compete against women, which bears out Gilder's assumption of a male imperative to be the dominant provider. One college senior explained that "my girl often beats me in tennis. . . . Now losing the game doesn't worry me. It in no way reduces my manhood. But being in a lower position than a woman on a job would hurt my self-esteem." Failure to live up to the ideal of masculine strength produced psychic strain to the extent that some men avoided women rather than risk being thought of as weak and unmasculine. One student asserted that "[b]iology makes equality impossible." He wanted to marry a woman who wanted children, and he assumed that it "would be the happiest thing she [could] do. After we have children, it will be her career that will end, while mine will support us."[142] Once married, many men resented their wives' working—and not always because it meant frozen dinners or sharing household chores. A Chicago man confessed that after his wife went back to teaching, he felt "it was a form of competition for her to work anywhere, and when I saw others interested in her as an individual, it created terrific insecurities in me."[143] How far has such an individual progressed from the 1930s, when modifications of behavior and role consisted of "tolerated exceptions" rather than "clear alternatives"? Individuals, then as now, were caught up in "conflicting patterns, none of them wholly condemned, but no one of them clearly approved and free from confusion."[144]

Komarovsky discovered a considerable amount of role strain, defined as "felt or latent difficulty in role fulfillment or the experience of low rewards for role conformity." Eighty percent of the men interviewed experienced mild to severe difficulty in fulfilling masculine-role obligations in one or more of the areas encompassed by the study. Seventy-two percent said they had trouble with sex, including twenty-four percent who were distressed because they were still virgins and forty-eight percent who had had sexual experiences and had one or more specific difficulties with sexual performance. Forty-three percent of the men had painfully ambivalent father–son relationships and twenty-six percent had ambivalent mother–son relationships. Forty-five percent of the men felt deficient in their relationship with women in other than the sexual sphere, and fifty-three percent had significant worries about their future as workers.[145]

A survey of 28,000 *Psychology Today* readers revealed that traditional masculinity was no longer much admired by either sex. Men and women are reaching toward the androgynous ideal but have not reached it yet. The survey showed that both sexes support the ideal of men's liberation. It also reveals that men want to be more sensitive and loving and that women want men to be more gentle and expressive. Masculinity has been harder for men to define than it has for women, according to the survey, but both sexes agreed that daring and aggressiveness were no longer necessary to prove one's manhood. Violence was repudiated, although sixty percent of the men had struck another man in anger, and forty percent said they had struck a woman. Most of the respondents did not believe masculinity required frequent sexual conquests, but they were divided on whether it required heterosexuality. Seventy percent of the heterosexual men thought that homosexual men were not entirely masculine. Overall, the data indicated that men expressed a much different idea of what constituted masculinity from that which Theodore Roosevelt espoused or John Wayne provided a model for. Even so, one respondent noted that although he expressed liberated ideals, his gut feelings still reveled in feats of physical strength, aggressiveness, and an awareness of being masculine.[146]

HOW IT IS

The Hite report pictured males as insensitive, blundering beasts, likely to support liberation if it was to their advantage to do so. However, Anthony Pietropinto and Jacqueline Simenauer came up with findings more complimentary to men. The research, based on 4,000 interviews with males from different regions, classes, and age groups, suggests that men do care about women as human beings and for their needs as sex partners. According to the authors, the iron-fisted, macho male of Mailer's superheated dream life does not reflect the real American male. Many of the men interviewed in this study confessed a need to be loved and to feel secure in their relationships with women. In fact, thirty-eight percent of the men said that love and female companionship were *more* important to them than sex. Yet only fifty percent of the men said that marriage with one's wife as the only sex partner was the ideal sex life. Twenty percent said the ideal sex life was to be married and have other sexual activity. And while love and security were important to men, being faithful to one woman was sanctioned by a mere forty percent of the men under thirty, and only fifty-one percent of the men between thirty and thirty-nine.[147]

As in the past, many men expressed a belief that American women did not really understand them at all, not a surprising allegation, perhaps, in light of the women's reporting men as emotionally withdrawn and reticent about expressing themselves. The Pietropinto and Simenauer survey sustained a time-worn conviction that men felt women were often illogical and inconsistent. The one serious source of contention was still the question of male domination. Many men felt their dominance was so integral to them personally and such a part of American culture that women should simply accept it and even gratify men's need for it although some men did see the desirability of modifying it.[148]

The *Psychology Today* survey found that in spite of all the emphasis on physical prowess and appearances that the masculine mystique has historically celebrated and advertisers have spent fortunes in selling to the American people, the successful man was most sought after and admired by women, rather than the handsome man or the jock who could only boast of physical abilities. Success still came through one's work, especially financial affairs; therefore, career ambition was highy valued.[149] Other studies have corroborated the thesis that whether or not a man's work was seen as a function of a man's biology or a product of his culture and environment, many American men still work very hard, in part at least, to validate their masculinity.[150] American capitalism and the values inherent in it, dating back to colonial times, have helped shape capitalism into a predatory system that demands victories over tough competitors and clients. Those men who achieve a high success rate in terms of sales or management are customarily thought of as tough, hard-nosed, persistent individuals, a view consistent with a legacy of the manly male. Unfortunately, it has left many of these same men psychologically unable to relax or enjoy leisure. Peter Chew has described the world of the middle-aged man as one in which men worry a great deal about having sufficient clout, sex appeal, energy, and an ability to dominate given situations. An older man who delegates certain responsibilities to younger associates or slows down his pace a bit runs the risk of having his actions interpreted as a sign of giving up, not being able to take it as a man any longer. For such an individual, the relentless drive for success is lethal, a fact that many medical doctors treating high blood pressure and heart problems know all too well.[151]

The sexual and career-related problems and crises many men have confronted in their own lives, based on evidence gathered by numerous researchers, make a good case for understanding the potential of liberation. But just how is it to come about? Liberation as advanced by Betty Friedan, Warren Farrell, and others seems to be most applicable to middle-class men and women, especially those with some higher education or those with some viable economic and social means on which to base a sophisticated assessment of sex roles and altered lifestyles. What are the chances for those without such a base? What are the realistic possibilities for consciousness-raising in which men bare their souls to one another when it has always been a common notion that men just do not do those things? Can male liberation broaden its base to really make a difference in the way the majority of heterosexual males judge themselves? Is it not just as likely that liberation will emerge out of fortuitous and pragmatic circumstances? Yet, all qualifications and reservations aside, the evidence suggests that sex roles are changing in America, which helps to confirm the significance of the social and cultural upheavals that began in the 1960s. Many men have found they can work alongside women who, with affirmative action behind them, have taken their place in business and the professions. Men have found women to be competent colleagues, or at least as competent as many other male colleagues. Meanwhile, men have had to take over more domestic responsibilities and have concluded that it is not such a great inconvenience in order to have a second income in the family, a necessity for many middle-income homes in an era of inflation and expensive leisure activities.[152] Consideration of lifestyle has been as important as salary and advancement for many young men ready to launch careers. While work is still the key to success, there is an awareness that freedom and peace of mind are important, too.

Finally, the most desirable frame of reference for sex-role discussions may be in the context of seeing such changes as objectives for self-improvement, whether in the "know thyself" Emersonian sense or as part of a broader existential philosophy. All too often, participants in consciousness-raising efforts, causes, and reform movements throughout history (including E.R.A. militants and some gay liberationists) have been victimized by their own crusading zeal, romantic expectations, rhetoric, fault-finding, and occasional ill-mannered tactics, which encumber the noble ideals of justice and dignity those efforts seek to achieve. There is always the danger that theorists who advocate solutions to critical problems, such as the ones fostered by the masculine mystique, will become so idealistic they cannot succeed. The resulting frustration and disillusionment can only make people more miserable. An open marriage, as recommended by the O'Neils, may be a worthy objective, but not possible, at least in any total sense, for all couples. What is ultimately at stake, in terms of a better quality of life, is not the success or failure of a liberation movement but how to be better parents, how to be more creative individuals, and truly loving and fair men and women. These are personal objectives that challenge men and women to rethink the meaning and practices of competition, aggression, success, sex, and how men and women together may more intelligently integrate these insights into their lives and overcome the rigid sex-identity distinctions of the past.

Notes

[1]Quoted in Richard Hofstadter et al., *The United States*, 4th.ed. (Englewood Cliffs, N.J.: Prentice-Hall, Inc., 1976), p. 602.

[2]Dixon Wecter, *When Johnny Comes Marching Home* (Westport, Conn.: Greenwood Press, 1944;), p. 486.

[3]Ladislas Farago, *Patton: Ordeal and Triumph* (New York: Obolensky, 1963), pp. 144, 324-27.

[4]Samuel A. Stouffer and Arthur Lumsdaine, *Studies in Social Psychology in World War II: The American Soldier, Combat and Its Aftermath* (Princeton: Princeton University Press, 1949), pp. 131-32; Frederick Elkin, "Soldier's Language," *American Journal of Sociology*, LI (March, 1946), 414-22.

[5]Samuel A. Stouffer and Arthur Lumsdaine, *Studies in Social Psychology in World War II: The American Soldier, Combat and Its Aftermath* (Princeton: Princeton University Press, 1949), p. 133.

[6]Frederick Elkin, "Soldier's Language," *American Journal of Sociology*, LI (March, 1946), 418; *This Fabulous Century, 1940-1950* (New York: Time-Life, 1969), p. 136.

[7]Robert Lowry, *Casualty* (New York: New Directions, 1946).

[8]Quoted in *This Fabulous Century, 1940-1950* (New York: Time-Life, 1969), pp. 108-12. Reprinted by permission of Harold Ober Associates Incorporated. Copyright © by Paul Gallico. Renewed.

[9]*This Fabulous Century, 1940-1950* (New York: Time-Life, 1969), pp. 40-50, 108, 110, 112, 117; Audie Murphy, *To Hell and Back* (New York: H. Holt Co., 1949).

[10]*This Fabulous Century, 1940-1950* (New York: Time-Life, 1969), pp. 184-85; Vincent McHugh, *The Victory* (New York: Random House, 1947); Ernie Pyle, *Brave Men* (New York: H. Holt Co., 1944).

[11]Ray Grinker and John Spiegel, *Men Under Stress* (Philadelphia: Blakiston, 1945), p. 45; Robert Clark, "Aggressiveness and Military Training," *American Journal of Sociology*, LI (March, 1946), 423-32.

[12]C. G. DeFoney, "What Makes a Man Brave?" *American Magazine* (February, 1944), 94; *This Fabulous Century, 1940-1950* (New York: Time-Life, 1969), p. 117.

[13]Dixon Wecter, *When Johnny Comes Marching Home* (Westport, Conn.: Greenwood Press, 1944), p. 486.

[14]Samuel A. Stouffer and Arthur Lumsdaine, *Studies in Social Psychology in World War II: The American Soldier, Combat and Its Aftermath* (Princeton: Princeton University Press, 1949), pp. 150-51, 156; Ray Grinker and John Spiegel, *Men Under Stress* (Philadelphia: Blakiston, 1945), p. 449; S. K. Weinberg, "The Combat Neuroses," *American Journal of Sociology*, LI (March, 1946), 465-82.

[15]Ladislas Farago, *Patton: Ordeal and Triumph* (New York: Obolensky, 1963), pp. 144-45.

[16]Leo Gurko, *Heroes and Highbrows* (Indianapolis: Bobbs-Merrill, 1953), pp. 190–92; John Gagon, "Physical Strength Once of Significance," in Deborah S. David and Robert Brannon, eds., *The Forty-Nine Percent Majority* (Reading, Mass.: Addison-Wesley, 1976), 169–78.

[17]Henry Elkin, "Aggressive and Erotic Tendencies in Army Life," *American Journal of Sociology*, LI (March, 1946), 408–13; August Hollingshead, "Adjustment to Military Life," *American Journal of Sociology*, LI (March, 1946), 446–47.

[18]Norman Mailer, *The Naked and the Dead* (New York: Holt, Rinehart & Winston, 1948); James Jones, *From Here to Eternity* (New York: Charles Scribner's Sons, 1951).

[19]August Hollingshead, "Adjustment to Military Life," *American Journal of Sociology*, LI (March, 1946), 439; Henry Elkin, "Aggressive and Erotic Tendencies in Army Life," *American Journal of Sociology*, LI (March, 1946), 409; Orrin Klapp, *Heroes, Villains, and Fools* (Englewood Cliffs, N.J.: Prentice-Hall, Inc., 1962), p. 167.

[20]Henry Elkin, "Aggressive and Erotic Tendencies in Army Life," *American Journal of Sociology*, LI (March, 1946), 410, 412.

[21]Alfred Hayes, *All Thy Conquests* (New York: Howell, Soskin, 1946); Alfred Hayes, *The Girl on the Via Flaminia* (New York: Harper, 1948).

[22]Henry Elkin, "Aggressive and Erotic Tendencies in Army Life," *American Journal of Sociology*, LI (March, 1946), 412–13.

[23]Dixon Wecter, *When Johnny Comes Marching Home* (Westport, Conn.: Greenwood Press, 1944), p. 498.

[24]Renwick C. Kennedy, "The Conqueror," *Christian Century*, LXIII (April 17, 1946), 495–97; Henry Elkin, "Aggressive and Erotic Tendencies in Army Life," *American Journal of Sociology*, LI (March, 1946) 411; Frederick Elkin, "Soldier's Language," *American Journal of Sociology*, LI (March, 1946), 414–22; Norman Longmate, *The GIs* (New York: Charles Scribner's Sons, 1975), pp. 110–16, 247–61, 281–84; Orrin Klapp, *Heroes, Villains, and Fools* (Englewood Cliffs, N.J.: Prentice-Hall, Inc., 1962), p. 167.

[25]Philip Wylie, *The Generation of Vipers* (New York: Pocket Books, Inc., 1955), pp. 185, 190, 197; see also Estelle Brown, "Down With Wylie! Up With Mom!" *Saturday Review of Literature*, XXX (May 31, 1947), 7 ff; for a scholarly overview, see Richard LaPiere, *The Freudian Ethic* (New York: Van Rees Press, 1959), pp. 81–84.

[26]Edward Strecker, *Their Mother's Sons* (Philadelphia: Lippincott, 1946), p. 71.

[27]Ibid., pp. 164–66.

[28]Ray Grinker and John Spiegel, *Men Under Stress* (Philadelphia: Blakiston, 1945), pp. 452–54.

[29]Ibid., p. 458.

[30]Ibid., p. 459; Editorial "Soldiers and Civilians: Why Are They Growing Apart?" *Life*, XVI (April 17, 1944), 32.

[31]Harold Rosenberg, *The Tradition of the New* (New York: Horizon Press, 1959); Vance Packard, *The Status Seekers* (New York: D. McKay Co., 1959); Vance Packard, *The Hidden Persuaders* (New York: D. McKay Co., 1957); A. C. Spectorsky, *The Exurbanites* (Philadelphia: Lippincott, 1955); Catherine Marshall, *A Man Called Peter* (New York: McGraw-Hill, 1951); Norman Vincent Peale, *The Power of Positive Thinking* (New York: Prentice-Hall, 1952); David Reisman, *Individualism Reconsidered* (Glencoe, Ill.: Free Press, 1954).

[32]Helen M. Hacker, "The New Burdens of Masculinity," *Marriage and Family Living*, XIX (August, 1957), 227–33; Oscar Handlin, "Searching for Security," *Atlantic Monthly*, CLXXXVII (January, 1951), 25–27.

[33]Edith Stern, "The Miserable Male," *American Mercury*, LXVII (Nov., 1941), 541.

[34]Robert Lowry, "Is This the Beat Generation?" *American Mercury*, LXXVI (January, 1953), 16–20.

[35]William H. Whyte, Jr., *The Organization Man* (New York: Simon and Schuster, 1956), p. 7.

[36]Ibid., pp. 26, 495 ff.; Daniel Bell, *Work and Its Discontents* (Boston: Beacon Press, 1956).

[37]Studs Terkel, *Working* (New York: Pantheon Books, a Division of Random House, Inc., 1972; London: Wildwood House Ltd, 1976), pp. 406, 408; see also Reinhard Bendix, *Work and Authority in Industry* (New York: Wiley, 1956).

[38]William H. Whyte, Jr., *The Organization Man* (New York: Simon and Schuster, 1956), pp. 141–56; John Brooks, *The Great Leap* (New York: Harper and Row, Publishers, Inc., 1966), pp. 60–61.

[39]Richard A. Smith, "The Executive Crack-up," *Fortune*, LI (May, 1955), 108.

[40]Ibid., pp. 108–12, 177, 180; Peter Chew, *Inner World of the Middle-Aged Man* (New York: Macmillan Publishing Co., 1976), pp. 89–90, 91, 92–95.

[41]George Leonard, "The American Male: Why Is He Afraid to Be Different?" *Look*, XXII (1954), 95–98.

[42]William H. Whyte, Jr., *The Organization Man* (New York: Simon and Schuster, 1956); Orrin Klapp, *Heroes, Villains, and Fools* (Englewood Cliffs, N.J.: Prentice-Hall, Inc., 1962); Herman Wouk, *The Caine Mutiny* (Garden City, N.Y.: Doubleday, 1951); Cameron Hawley, *Cash McCall* (Boston: Houghton Mifflin, 1955); *High Noon* (United Artists, 1952); H. J. Friedsam, "Bureaucrats as Heroes," *Social Forces*, XXXII (1954), 269–74.

[43]William Attwood, "The American Male: Why Does He Work So Hard?" *Look*, XXII (March 4, 1958), 70–75.

[44]Lemuel McGee, "The Suicidal Cult of Manliness," *Today's Health*, XXXV (January, 1957), 28–30; Ruth and Edward Brecker, "We Must Take Better Care of Our Boys," *Parents' Magazine*, XXXI (April, 1956), 52–53; Myron Brenton, *The American Male* (Greenwich, Conn.: Fawcett Publications, 1966), pp. 15–40.

[45]Richard Malkin, *Marriage, Morals and War* (New York: Arden Book Co., 1943); Ernest W. Burgess and Harvey J. Kocke, *The Family* (New York: American Book Co., 1945), p. 518.

[46]"Yes, Women Are Different," *Newsweek*, XXI (June 21, 1943), 105–06; "Male and Female," *Time*, XLIV (October 23, 1944), 55; Victor Dallaire, "The American Woman? Not for This GI," *The New York Times Magazine* (May 10, 1946), 15; *This Fabulous Century, 1940–1950* (New York: Time-Life, 1969), p. 176; "The War of the Sexes: An Interim Report," *Saturday Review of Literature*, XXXIII (April 22, 1950), 22.

[47]William H. Chafe, *The American Woman* (New York: Oxford University Press, 1972), p. 176.

[48]Betty Friedan, *The Feminine Mystique* (New York: Dell Publishing Co., Inc., 1963), p. 178.

[49]Eric Dingwall, *The American Woman* (New York: Rinehart and Co., 1956), pp. 241–42.

[50]Helen Hacker, "New Burdens of Masculinity," *Marriage and Family Living*, XIX (August, 1957), 227–33; Eric Dingwall, *The American Woman* (New York: Rinehart and Co., 1956), pp. 245–50; Joseph Furst, *The Neurotic and His Inner and Outer Worlds* (New York: Citadel Press, 1954); Amory Clark, "The American Male and His Sex Habits," *Cosmopolitan*, CXLII (May, 1957), 31–32.

[51]Amory Clark, "The American Male and His Sex Habits," *Cosmopolitan*, CXLII (May, 1957), 31.

[52]David L. Cohn, "Do American Men Like Women?" *Atlantic Monthly*, CLXXVIII (August, 1946), 72–74.

[53]Ibid., 74.

[54]Marynia Farnham and Ferdinand Lundberg, *Modern Woman: The Lost Sex* (New York: Grossett and Dunlap, 1947), pp. 144–59; see also Agnes Meyer, "Women Aren't Men," *Atlantic Monthly*, CLXXXVI (August, 1950), 32–36; Lynn White, *Educating Our Daughters* (New York: Harpers, 1950); Margaret Mead, "What Women Want," *Fortune*, XXXIV (December, 1946), 172–75.

[55]Ashley Montagu, "Triumph and Tragedy of the American Woman," *Saturday Review of Literature*, XLI (Sept. 27, 1958). 13–15.

[56]Eric Dingwall, *The American Woman* (New York: Rinehart and Co., 1956), p. 226; Claude Bowman, "Are Husbands Slaves to Women?" *Coronet*, XXVII (April, 1950), 111; "Freedom's a Fraud," *Rotarian*, LXXX (February, 1952), 11 ff; "The Loving Care of Determined Women," *Harpers Magazine*, CCXI (August, 1955), 20.

[57]Dorothy Kilgallen, "The Trouble With Men," *Nation's Business*, XXXIX (July, 1951), 30–32; Romona Barth, "What's Wrong with American Men?" *Reader's Digest*, LV (November, 1959), 23–25; G. T. Mayes, "The American Male is OK, But. . . ," *The New York Times Magazine* (May 12, 1946), pp. 18 ff; Aline Loucheim, "Now the Booing is Done in Soprano," *The New York Times Magazine* (September 4, 1949), 17; Lauren Bacall, "I Hate Men," *Look*, XVII (November 3, 1953), 36–37; Cameron Shipp, "Men Are the Sucker Sex," *Nation's Business*, XL (October, 1952), 32–33 ff.

[58]Robert Moskin, "The American Male: Why Do Women Dominate Him?" *Look*, XXII (February 4, 1958), 77.

[59]Ibid., 76–80.

[60]Morton Hunt, "Our Manly Men," *Cosmopolitan*, CXLVII (July, 1959), 36.

[61]Ibid., 33–37.

[62]Ibid., 37.

[63]Dorothy Barclay, "The Overlooked Parental Influence," *The New York Times Magazine* (June 15, 1952), 47.

[64]"Was Our Boy a Sissy?" *Parents' Magazine*, XXVI (April, 1951), 44–45; Marynia Farnham, "Helping Boys to be Boys and Girls to be Girls," *Parents' Magazine*, XXVIII (January, 1953), 34–35; Charles Winick, *The New People* (New York: Pegasus, 1968).

[65]Morton Hunt, "The Decline and Fall of the American Father," *Cosmopolitan*, CXXXVIII (April, 1955), 23; O. S. English and Constance J. Foster, "Father's Changing Role," *Parents' Magazine*, XXVI (October, 1951), 44–45 ff, Dorothy Barclay, "The Overlooked Parental Influence," *The New York Times Magazine* (June 15, 1952), 47.

[66]Bill Gale, "TV Makes a Fool of Dad," *American Mercury*, LXXXIV (February, 1957), 33–39; Bill Iverson, "Love and Death of the Hubby Image," *Playboy* (September, 1963), 94, 192 ff.

[67]Morton Hunt, "Decline and Fall of the American Father," *Cosmopolitan*, CXXXVIII (April, 1955), 23.

[68]Quoted in *This Fabulous Century, 1950–1960* (New York: Time-Life, 1969), p. 234.

[69]Orrin Klapp, *Heroes, Highbrows, and Villains* (Englewood Cliffs, N.J.: Prentice-Hall, Inc., 1962), p. 148; Sergeant Cuff, "The Toughie Submerged," *Saturday Review of Litera-*

ture, XXXIII (December, 24, 1955), 14; Sergeant Cuff, "Prime Crimes of '56," *Saturday Review of Literature*, XXXIX (December, 22, 1956), 14; Will Wright, *Six Guns and Society* (Berkeley: University of California Press, 1975).

[70] Harrison Salisbury, *The Shook-Up Generation* (New York: Harper, 1958), p. 34; James Short Jr. and Fred L. Strodbeck, "Why Gangs Fight," *Trans-action* (September/October 1964), 25–29; Robert Luce, "From Hero to Robot: Masculinity in America," *Psychoanalytic Review*, LIV (1967), 67.

[71] T. F. James, "Dangerous Years," *Cosmopolitan*, CXLII (May, 1957), 26–29.

[72] John W. Petras, *Sex: Male Gender: Masculine* (Port Washington, N.Y.: Alfred Publishing Co., 1975), p. 195.

[73] Ibid., pp. 195–96; Jerome Kagan and Howard Moss, *Birth to Maturity* (New York: John Wiley, 1962).

[74] John W. Petras, *Sex: Male Gender: Masculine* (Port Washington, N.Y.: Alfred Publishing Co., 1975), p. 198.

[75] Sam Astrachan, "The New Lost Generation," *New Republic*, CXXXVI (February 4, 1957), 17–18; *East of Eden*, (Warner Brothers, 1955); *Rebel Without a Cause* (Warner Brothers, 1955); *Giant* (Warner Brothers, 1956).

[76] Jerry Hopkins, *Elvis* (New York: Warner Books, Inc., 1971), pp. 42, 48, 181.

[77] Ibid., pp. 143–44; Richard Gehman, "Toupees, Girdles and Sunlamps," *Cosmpolitan*, CXLII (May, 1957), 39–43.

[78] Norman Mailer, "The White Negro," in Gene Feldman and Max Gartenberg, eds., *The Beat Generation and the Angry Young Men* (New York: Citadel Press, 1958), p. 357.

[79] Norman Mailer, *An American Dream* (New York: Dial Press, 1965), p. 8; Norman Mailer, *Advertisements for Myself* (New York: Putnam, 1959); Norman Mailer, *The Presidential Papers* (New York: Putnam, 1963); Norman Mailer, *Why Are We in Vietnam?* (New York: Putnam, 1967).

[80] Frank Morrison (Mickey) Spillane, *Kiss Me, Deadly* (New York: E. P. Dutton and Co., 1952), pp. 86, 140; Frank Morrison (Mickey) Spillane, *I, the Jury* (New York: E. P. Dutton and Co., 1947); Christopher La Farge, "Mickey Spillane and His Bloody Hammer," *Saturday Review of Literature*, XXXVII (November 6, 1954), 11–12, 54–59; Richard Johnston, "Death's Fair-Haired Boy," *Life*, XXXII (June 23, 1952), 79–95.

[81] Robert Luce, "From Hero to Robot: Masculinity in America," *Psychoanalytic Review*, LIV (1967), 64.

[82] Orrin Klapp, *Heroes, Villains, and Fools* (Englewood Cliffs, N.J.: Prentice-Hall, Inc., 1962), pp. 155–56; Robert Luce, "From Hero to Robot: Masculinity in America," *Psychoanalytic Review*, LIV (1967), 65.

[83] Rollo May, *Love and Will* (New York: Dell, 1969), p. 30; Karl Bednarik, *The Male in Crisis* (New York: Alfred A. Knopf, Inc., 1970), pp. 14–15, 62.

[84] Rollo May, *Love and Will* (New York: Dell, 1969), pp. 30–31.

[85] Lucy Komisar, "Violence and the Masculine Mystique," in Deborah David and Robert Brannon eds., *The Forty-Nine Percent Majority* (Reading, Mass.: Addison-Wesley, 1976), pp. 201–15; Myron Breton, *The American Male* (Greenwich, Conn.: Fawcett Publications, 1966), pp. 22–24, 60–61; Harvey Kaye, *Male Survival* (New York: Grosset and Dunlap, 1974), pp. 18–19; see also Philip Slater, *Pursuit of Loneliness* (Boston: Beacon Press, 1970); Robert Gould, "Measuring Masculinity by the Size of the Paycheck," *Ms.* (June, 1973).

[86] Diana Lurie, "In Hefnerland, Women Are Status Symbols," *Life* (October 29, 1965), 68.

[87]"Think Clean," *Time* (March 3, 1967), 77; "Hugh Hefner Faces Middle Age," *Time* (Feb. 14, 1969), 69–70.

[88]*Playboy* (January, 1964), p. 29, reprinted courtesy of Revlon, Inc., New York.

[89]"Think Clean," *Time* (March 3, 1967), 78.

[90]"The Playboy Mansion," *Playboy* (January, 1966), 105 ff.

[91]Quoted in Diana Lurie, "In Hefnerland, Women Are Status Symbols," *Life* (October 29, 1965), 70–73.

[92]William Hamilton, quoted in "Think Clean," *Time* (March 3, 1967), 80; J. Claude Evans, "The Playboy Philosphy," *Catholic World* (October, 1964), 42–48; Karl Stern, *Flight from Women* (New York: Farrar, Straus and Giroux, 1965), Harvey Kaye, *Male Survival* (New York: Grosset and Dunlap, 1974), pp. 20–22.

[93]Myron Brenton, *The American Male* (Greenwich, Conn.: Fawcett Publications, Inc., 1966), pp. 73–74; see also Cynthia Proulx, "Sex as Athletics," *Saturday Review of Literature, Society*, I (May, 1973), 60–66.

[94]David F. Aberle and Kasper Naegle, "Middle-Class Fathers' Occupational Roles and Attitudes Toward Children," *American Journal of Orthopsychiatry*, XXII (1952), 60.

[95]Roger Kahn, "Why Football?" *The New York Times Magazine* (October 7, 1973), 42.

[96]Diane Divoky and Peter Schrag "Football and Cheers," *Saturday Review of Literature* (November 11, 1972), 59; see also James Michener, *Sports in America* (New York: Random House, 1976); Joe Pleck "My Male Sex Role—and Ours," in Deborah S. David and Robert Brannon, eds., *The Forty-Nine Percent Majority* (Reading, Mass.: Addison-Wesley, 1976), pp. 253–64; James Coleman, "Athletics in High School," *Annals of the American Academy of Political and Social Science*, 338 (November, 1961), 33–43.

[97]Murray Ross, "Football Red and Baseball Blue," in John T. Talamini and Charles H. Page, eds., *Sport and Society* (Boston: Little, Brown, 1973), p. 106.

[98]Fred Exley, *A Fan's Notes* (New York: Harper and Row, 1968); Lucy Komisar, "Violence and the Masculine Mystique," in Deborah S. David and Robert Brannon, eds., *The Forty-Nine Percent Majority* (Reading, Mass.: Addison-Wesley, 1976), p. 205.

[99]Reprinted by permission from TIME, The Weekly Newsmagazine; copyright Time Inc. November 9, 1970, p. 36.

[100]William McIlwain, "Speed, Sex and Heroes," *Atlantic Monthly* (June, 1973), 72–79; see also John Copp, "Why Hunters Like to Hunt," *Psychology Today* (December, 1975).

[101]Joe Soucheray, "Woody Hayes, Anachronism," *The Minneapolis Tribune* (October 20, 1974), Section 1C, p. 1, col. 1; George Leonard, "Winning Isn't Everything: It's Nothing," *Intellectual Digest* (October, 1973), 45–47.

[102]Quoted in Jerry Kramer, *Instant Replay* (New York: Signet Books, 1968), p. 31.

[103]Interview with Jack Scott, "The Souring of George Sauer," *Intellectual Digest* (December, 1971), 52–53.

[104]Bruce C. Ogilvie and Thomas A. Tutko, "Sports: If You Want to Build Character, Try Something Else," *Psychology Today*, V (Ocotober, 1971), 61–63; Harry Edwards, *Sociology of Sport* (Homewood, Ill.: The Dorsey Press, 1973), pp. 317–30.

[105]*Sports Illustrated* (June 11, 1973), 60.

[106]Marc Fasteau, *The Male Machine* (New York: McGraw-Hill, 1974), p. 167; quoted in David Halberstam, *The Best and the Brightest* (New York: Random House, Inc., 1969; London: Barrie & Jenkins), p. 97.

[107]Quoted in David Halberstam, *The Best and the Brightest* (New York: Random House, Inc., 1969; London: Barrie & Jenkins), pp. 537, 541.

[108]Ibid., p. 644

[109]Marc Fasteau, *The Male Machine* (New York: McGraw-Hill, 1974), p. 173; David Halberstam, *The Best and the Brightest* (New York: Random House, Inc., 1969; London: Barrie & Jenkins), pp. 643, 645; Robert Sam Anson, *McGovern: A Biography* (New York: Holt, Rinehart and Winston, 1972), p. 159.

[110]David Horowitz et al., *Counterculture and Revolution* (New York: Random House, Inc., 1972); Theodore Roszak, *The Making of a Counter Culture* (Garden City, N.Y.: Doubleday and Co., 1968); Norman Mailer, *Why Are We in Vietnam?* (New York: Putnam, 1967); Norman Mailer, *The Armies of the Night* (New York: New American Library, 1968); Norman Mailer, *Miami and the Siege of Chicago* (New York: World Publishing Co., 1968).

[111]Marc Fasteau, *The Male Machine* (New York: McGraw-Hill, 1974), p. 177.

[112]Ibid.; Richard Nixon, *Six Crises* (Garden City, N.Y.: Doubleday and Co., 1962), p. xv.

[113]James David Barber, *The Presidential Character: Predicting Performance in the White House* (Englewood Cliffs, N.J.: Prentice-Hall, Inc., 1972), pp. 435–36; Chalmers M. Roberts, *First Rough Draft* (New York: Praeger Publishers, Inc., 1973).

[114]Robert J. Lifton, "Home From the War: The Psychology of Survival," *Atlantic Monthly* (November, 1972), 66.

[115]Ibid., 69.

[116]Richard Nixon, *Six Crises* (Garden City, N.Y.: Doubleday and Co., 1962); Bruce Mazlish, *In Search of Nixon: A Psychohistorical Inquiry* (New York: Basic Books, 1972), pp. 87–88.

[117]James David Barber, *The Presidential Character: Predicting Performance in the White House* (Englewood Cliffs, N.J.: Prentice-Hall, Inc., 1972), pp. 416–19, 441–42; Garry Wills, *Nixon Agonistes: The Crisis of the Self-Made Man* (Boston: Houghton Mifflin, 1970), p. 409.

[118]James David Barber, *The New York Times*, November 8, 1973, p. 47.

[119]Bob Woodward and Carl Bernstein, *The Final Days* (New York: Simon and Schuster, 1976), pp. 422–24; *Time* (August 19, 1974), 68; Marc Fasteau, *The Male Machine* (New York: McGraw-Hill, 1974), pp. 190–95.

[120]Norman Mailer, *The Presidential Papers* (New York: G. P. Putnam's Sons, 1963), p. 47. Reprinted by permission of the author and the author's agents, Scott Meredith Literary Agency, Inc., 845 Third Avenue, New York, New York 10022 U.S.A.

[121]Myron Brenton, *The American Male* (Greenwich, Conn.: Fawcett Publications, 1966), pp. 16–19.

[122]Studs Terkel, *Working* (New York: Pantheon Books, a Division of Random House, Inc., 1972; London: Wildwood House Ltd, 1976), pp. 105, 137, 162, 181, 189; Mirra Komarovsky, *Blue Collar Marriage* (New York: Random House, 1962), p. 281; Arthur B. Shostak, *Blue-Collar Life* (New York: Random House, 1969).

[123]Studs Terkel, *Working* (New York: Pantheon Books, a Division of Random House, Inc., 1972; London: Wildwood House Ltd, 1976), pp. 333, 339, 340.

[124]Ibid., pp. 369–99, 400, 408, 412.

[125]Ibid., pp. 446, 564; Kenneth Keniston, *Youth and Dissent* (New York: Harcourt Brace Jovanovich, Inc., 1971), pp. 173–88.

[126]Warren Farrell, *The Liberated Man* (New York; Random House, 1974), pp. 90–97; Marc Fasteau, *The Male Machine* (New York: McGraw-Hill, 1974), pp. 144–57.

[127]Studs Terkel, *Working* (New York: Pantheon Books, a Division of Random House, Inc., 1972; London: Wildwood House Ltd, 1976), pp. 385–86.

[128]Martin Ralbovsky, *The Namath Effect* (Englewood Cliffs, N.J.: Prentice-Hall, Inc., 1976), pp. 30, 39.

[129]Kate Millett, *Sexual Politics* (New York: Avon Books, 1969); Germaine Greer, *The Female Eunuch* (New York: McGraw-Hill, 1971); Shulamith Firestone, *The Dialectics of Sex* (New York: Morrow, 1970); Jack Sawyer, "On Male Liberation," *Liberation* (August–October, 1970), 32.

[130]Warren Farrell, *The Liberated Man* (New York: Random House, 1974), pp. 4, 120, 126.

[131]Harvey Kaye, *Male Survival* (New York: Grosset and Dunlap, 1974), p. 199; Barry Farrell, "You've Come a Long Way, Buddy," *Life* (August 27, 1971), 52.

[132]"Dilemma of a Househusband," *Saturday Review of Literature* (January 2, 1965), 100; "Confessions of a Househusband," *Ms.* (November, 1972), 25–27; Warren Farrell, *The Liberated Man* (New York: Random House, 1974), p. 125.

[133]Steven Koch, "The Guilty Sex," *Esquire* (July, 1975), 54.

[134]Michael Korda, *Male Chauvinism* (New York: Random House, 1972), p. 50; Charles W. Morton, "Twilight of the He-Man," *Atlantic Monthly* (February, 1967), 111–12; "The Gent's Auxiliary," *Newsweek* (July 20, 1970), 75–76; Karen Durbin, "How to Spot a Liberated Man," *Mademoiselle* (April, 1973), 172–73.

[135]Quoted in "Now Men's Lib is the Trend," *U.S. News & World Report* (March 18, 1974), 49.

[136]Quoted in "And Now Men's Liberation," *Time* (May 10, 1971), 54.

[137]Warren Farrell, *The Liberated Man* (New York: Random House, 1974), p. 62.

[138]Mirra Komarovsky, *Dilemmas of Masculinity* (New York: W. W. Norton and Co., 1976), pp. 22, 154.

[139]Charles Winick, *The New People* (New York: Pegasus, 1968), pp. 350–51; Patricia Sexton, *The Feminized Male* (New York: Random House, 1969), p. 131.

[140]Stephen Goldberg, *The Inevitability of Patriarchy* (New York: Morrow, 1974).

[141]George Gilder, *Sexual Suicide* (New York: Quadrangle, 1973), pp. 7, 33, 96, 101, 109.

[142]Mirra Komarovsky, *Dilemmas of Masculinity* (New York: W. W. Norton and Co., 1976), pp. 26–27, 128–33, 138.

[143]"Now Men's Lib is the Trend," *U.S. News & World Report* (March 18, 1974), 49.

[144]Robert and Helen Lynd, *Middletown in Transition* (New York: Harcourt Brace Jovanovich, Inc., 1937), p. 177.

[145]Mirra Komarovsky, *Dilemmas of Masculinity* (New York: W. W. Norton and Co., 1976), pp. 222–24.

[146]Carol Tavris, "Masculinity," *Psychology Today*, X (January, 1977), 35 ff.

[147]Anthony Pietropinto and Jacqueline Simenauer, *Beyond the Male Myth* (New York: The New York Times Book Co., 1977), pp. 204–15; Shere Hite, *The Hite Report: A Nationwide Study on Female Sexuality* (New York: Macmillan, 1976).

[148]Anthony Pietropinto and Jacqueline Simenauer, *Beyond the Male Myth* (New York: The New York Times Book Co., 1977), pp. 128–43; Carol Tavris, "Masculinity," *Psychology Today*, X (January, 1977), 37.

[149]Carol Tavris, "Masculinity," *Psychology Today* (January, 1977), 36.

[150]Daniel Levinson, "Growing Up with the Dream," *Psychology Today*, XI (January 1978), 20–31 ff; Daniel Levinson, *The Seasons of a Man's Life* (New York: Alfred A. Knopf, Inc., 1978); Robert E. Gould, "Measuring Masculinity by the Size of the Paycheck," *Ms.* (June, 1973); Fernando Bartolome, "Executives as Human Beings," in Joe Pleck and Jack Sawyer, eds., *Men and Masculinity* (Englewood Cliffs, N.J.: Prentice-Hall, Inc., 1974), pp. 100–06.

[151]Peter Chew, *The Inner World of the Middle-Aged Man* (New York: Macmillan Co., 1976).

[152]Barry Farrell, "You've Come a Long Way, Buddy," *Life* (August 27, 1971), 52 ff; Karen Durbin, "How to Spot a Liberated Man," *Mademoiselle* (April, 1973), 172–73; "Special Issue on Men," *Ms.* (October, 1975); J. Harrison, "Changing Male Roles," *American Education* (July, 1977), 20–26; L. C. Pogrebin, "Househusbands," *Ladies' Home Journal* (November, 1977), 30 ff; David Gelman, "How Men Are Changing," *Newsweek* (January 16, 1978), 52–61; Carol Kleiman, "Secrets of the New Male Sexuality: Is it a Sign of Change, Backlash, or Just a Pop Fad?" *Ms.* (April, 1978), 45 ff; Caroline Bird, "Demasculinizing the Professions," in Roland Gross and Paul Osterman, eds., *The New Professionals* (New York: Simon and Schuster, 1972); Mike McGardy, *The Kitchen-Sink Papers* (New York: Doubleday Co., 1975).

EPILOGUE

Betty Friedan described in *The Feminine Mystique* a consciousness unique to modern women that was keeping them from growing up in the modern world. The vast majority of women were trapped, mesmerized by their grandmothers' tradition of serving men in a male-dominated culture. It has been my intention to suggest that men too have been trapped, that the identity and roles many men have assumed throughout American history have caused certain problems unique to male identity and fulfillment. There once *was* a frontier of open unsettled space, the very essence of which was that it beckoned to men to invest, expand, explore, grow, dominate, and progress, actions that occurred in both physical and psychological dimensions. Horace Greeley echoed a whole way of life when he exclaimed, "Go West, young man, go West." That way of life promoted a sense of Yankee invincibility and left behind a legacy of "how to get things done" and "how to be a man." Frontier culture exuded fresh hope and promise and spawned the belief that it was unmanly to let anything or anybody interfere with one's movements. Whether a cowboy or a robber baron, men in those days were puffed up with confidence and optimism; they scorned, even suppressed, doubt and cynicism. In all their relationships, such men seemed triumphant and fulfilled in their individualistic pursuit of happiness.

Or at least that has been the traditional vision of our past. What I have suggested is that the very terms of the dream—the vigor of the masculine paradigm embracing intense individualism, free enterprise, the self-made-man ideal, the moral athlete, in short, "the American way"—also contained within it certain doubts and frustrations bound to effect the way men behaved and related with one another and women. By the very nature of their successes, men often cut off from one another, from families, and even from culture and social change. In other words, American men caught up in the fever of the drive for success, power, and profit often found themselves severely limited in their attainment of what might have been significant growth and personal development. Thus, just as the feminine mystique obstructed the growth and development of women, the masculine mystique has exacted a price from men as the boundaries of physical space closed in on them.

As any student of history knows, myth and mystique attach themselves to people in strange ways. People often react to situations and events not according to what they know the facts to be but as to how individuals would like them to be, and there begins the inevitable distorting of reality as concept meets emotion. This common phenomenon elevates legend to truth and searches for heroes to idolize. The manifestation can be harmful when, for example it leads to claims of race and sex superiority and the subsequent denial of human and civil rights. While surveys suggest changes are taking place, he-man ideals and chauvinistic styles still abound, much to the encouragement of advertising, some admiring women, and many men caught up in the superheated dream life. The successful detective still gets his criminal with aggressive efficiency, and violence remains common TV and movie fare, as acceptable viewing for young adults. Meanwhile, sex education is suspect in many communities as a topic not fit for discussion in a classroom.

So, one might dare ask, what are the reasonable prospects for reforming male prejudice and stereotypes, given the heavy weight of the masculine mystique? At the ideological level there is the persuasion of human liberation (as outlined in Chapter 8), which might indeed make for a different kind of society in which, free from prejudice and peer-group pressure, a closer approximation of equality might succeed if human liberation were pursued to its logical conclusion. But history confirms that Americans are not predisposed to adopt new ideologies. And it is apparent that many Americans are especially squeamish about sex-role alterations. Conservatives register alarm about the prospect of such changes, basing their opposition on the assumption that the family structure would collapse if men failed to dominate and women were encouraged to seek careers. For this reason (along with others), many conservative men and women oppose the E.R.A., liberal divorce laws, open marriage, abortion, family planning, and, of course, gay liberation—the ultimate challenge to the masculine image. The argument posed is the just-as-Rome-fell syndrome. History verifies that these arguments are not new. They were raised in opposition to free spirits like John Humphrey Noyes and women like Charlotte Perkins Gilman and Mary Wollstonecraft, who seemed terribly radical in their day and dangerous to progress. More recently, critics have fallen on the counter culture, first noted in the 1960s, citing that it is all narrow, faddish, and in bad taste.

Of course, liberals have their difficulties, too. They cannot guarantee greater personal happiness through liberation or even creative fulfillment and satisfaction in the domestic and economic spheres. But change does seem to be taking place, which supports the contention that many people are reaching out for new concepts and that a paradigmatic shift is taking place, embracing significantly altered sex-identity behavior patterns. Man's physical conquest of his environment in space—the frontier ethos—has given way to a greater sensitivity to the quality of his inner life. Bookshelves are bending under the weight of titles covering a wide spectrum of personal feelings and problems. These are books on "self-actualization," dedicated to helping people cut through a lifetime of emotional red tape. There are books on transactional analysis, books on assertiveness, some on how to achieve meaningful intimacy by blasting away old inhibitions. Meanwhile, psychiatrists say they are seeing people in record numbers, especially men who are trying to work out a better perspective on their existence. With more introspection, the hope is that the grip of the feminine and masculine mystiques will lessen.

Whether or not ideological persuasion of liberation makes any headway, and beyond the consciousness-raising efforts and techniques of modern psychology, there remains another avenue to liberation. Betty Friedan made a major point by lamenting that education in America had too often stopped short of identity, leaving millions of young mothers without a strong core of human values whereby they might better understand themselves and in turn influence their children. The same can be said of boys—and men—from kindergarten to graduate or trade school. I have tried to demonstrate the excessive fervor with which we American men must do something *tangible* to be counted a success among our peers. Pressure is exerted on young boys to learn a skill or a trade, to make money, which helps "win a girl." Excellence in athletics is stressed because it assumes tenacity and forcefulness, which are assumed to attest to one's being able *to do something*. Specialization and technology, which have become such prominent features of modern America, aid and abet this mentality. Specialization and technology have made life easier, given us more time off—but time off to do what? A strong case can be made, however, judging from the reflections of middle-aged and older men who have been successful, that it is often the *intangible* things that give the greatest satisfactions in life. The satisfaction that comes to a man from reading, listening to or performing music, cooking, painting, or traveling is what can give diversity and spontaneity to an otherwise mundane life in which the preoccupation is always just the job, the job, the job—with the occasional let-up for golf.

In this regard, a liberal education, in which the goal is to provide a greater vision, appreciation of the arts, and an insight into anything from anthropology to zoology, as opposed to the acquisition of a specific skill, may be the most sensible educational choice. The objective of a liberal education is, after all, to liberate one from the biases, parochialism, and prejudices that restrict and limit human growth. The liberally educated man has a clearer understanding of himself because he understands his past, and his nation's past. He understands something about all the people living in his nation, its women, minorities, and their collective needs. He understands himself better by acquiring knowledge of people in other cultures. A man may be better able to confidently face the future if his education has succeeded in providing a solid base for a well-rounded identity. A great deal more research on masculine identity and fulfillment needs to be initiated to enlarge the historical, social, and psychological perspectives on the variety of issues and problems affecting masculine identity and fulfillment in American culture. Individuals as well as institutions, such as labor unions and corporations, need to be sensitized to these perspectives with an eye toward making adjustments where necessary.

Young men and women need training to do something in order to compete for jobs, but their education must not neglect that most of all they will want to *be someone*, someone of diverse substance and competence, not a prisoner of a myth or an image. If this goal can be achieved, we will have less reason to believe that Benjamin Disraeli's prophecy will prove that "youth is a blunder; manhood a struggle; and old age a regret."

ESSAY
ON SOURCES

The introduction to this book briefly summarizes the points of view of several key studies about masculinity and the male role. The notes throughout the text list specific sources I have used to document my observations about masculinity in America. In preparing this book, I have consulted many other sources for their useful perspectives. I hope that this essay can offer suggestions to others interested in related research.

Anyone approaching the history of gender relationships should see Peter G. Filene's *Him/Her Self* (New York: Harcourt Brace Jovanovich, Inc., 1974), in which Filene traces role changes from the end of the Victorian era to present. Any number of anthologies have appeared over the past several years that bring together a number of scholarly as well as popular articles on sexuality and sex roles. Joe Pleck and Jack Sawyer, editors of *Men and Masculinity* (Englewood Cliffs, N.J.: Prentice-Hall,

Inc., 1974), provide not only useful articles but a well-researched bibliography as well. Other helpful anthologies include *The Longest War: Sex Differences in Perspective* (New York: Harcourt Brace Jovanovich, Inc., 1977), edited by Carol Tavris and Carole Ottis; *The Forty-Nine Percent Majority* (Reading, Mass.: Addison-Wesley, 1976), edited by Deborah S. David and Robert Brannon; and *Masculine/Feminine: Readings in Sexual Mythology* (New York: Harper, 1969), edited by Betty and Theodore Roszak. Joe Pleck's essay "The Male Sex Role: Definitions and Problems, and Sources of Change," *Journal of Social Forces*, XXXII, No. 3 (Summer, 1976), 155–64, is an excellent starting point because it views the study of the male role in specific categories. "From Hero to Robot: Masculinity in America: Stereotype and Reality," *Psychoanalytic Review*, LIV (1967), 53–74, by Ralph Luce, examines ways in which certain types of men try to fulfill the traditional images. One should also see an essay, related to Luce's, by Roger Kahn, "Money, Muscles—and Myths," in *Mass Leisure*, Eric Larrabee and Rolf Meyerson, eds., (Glencoe, Ill.: The Free Press, 1958). The emphasis put on the traditional masculine activities tends to skew other values. The definitive work on homosexuality is Johathan Katz's *Gay Americn History* (New York: Thomas Y. Crowell, 1976), which has in it many articles from many men regarding the basic issues of identity, resistance, and love.

Myron Brenton's *The American Male* (Greenwich, Conn.: Fawcett Publications, 1966) contains a substantial amount of information about men and the masculinity trap. Another book that is often overlooked for what it has to say about masculinity-validating experiences is Charles Ferguson's *The Male Machine* (Boston: Little, Brown, 1966). Ferguson argues that the male psyche developed to a position of dominance in American history by using guns, machinery, and slavery. A more contemporary focus is offered by Herbert Goldberg in *The Hazards of Being Male* (New York: New American Library, 1976). To help enlarge the analytical framework, much can be learned by reading *The Lonely Crowd* (New Haven: Yale University Press, 1950), by David Reisman, Reuel Denny, and Nathan Glazer; and Margaret Mead's *Male and Female* (New York: Morrow, 1949). A general interpretation of American history that I found useful was Christopher Lasch's *The New Radicalism in America 1889–1963* (New York: Alfred A. Knopf, Inc., 1965), especially the chapter on the woman as alien. *Postscript to Yesterday* (New York: Harper, 1947), by Lloyd Morris, and *The Decline of Gentility* (New York: Columbia University Press, 1973), by Stow

Persons, focus on general aspects of American culture affecting sex-role concepts.

The literature on women and feminism in American history has a lot to say about masculine values. In the preface and epilogue I have already called attention to the significance of Betty Friedan's *The Feminine Mystique.* Kate Millett's *Sexual Politics* (New York: Doubleday, 1970) is a classic statement that incorporates the social and cultural male views of several leading authors, such as Norman Mailer and Henry Miller. Eva Figes's *Patriarchal Attitudes* (New York: Stein and Day, 1970) and Elizabeth Janeway's *Man's World and Women's Place In It* (New York: Morrow, 1971) are good interpretative analyses. Among the books on American women written by men, Eric Dingwall's *The American Woman* (New York: Rinehart, 1956) is dated but useful because he deals with sex identity in a broad social and cultural context. In the same way, Page Smith's book *Daughters of the Promised Land* (Boston: Little, Brown, 1970) is instructive in suggesting the tensions between industrialism and the family as an institution. *Everyone Was Brave* (Chicago: Quadrangle, 1969), by William O'Neill, concentrates on the feminist movement and its place in social reform. Vern Bullough's *The Subordinate Sex* (Urbana: University of Illinois Press, 1973) reveals how women have been treated through the centuries, but only the last chapter covers the American experience. The works of Morton Hunt are especially valuable because of his insights into social and psychological issues. *Her Infinite Variety* (New York: Harper, 1962) and *The Natural History of Love* (New York: Alfred A. Knopf, Inc., 1959) are highly worthwhile, as are Hunt's many essays, which have appeared over the years in various magazines and journals. To follow up a reading of women's history and liberation, there is also Gene Martin's *Male Guide to Women's Liberation* (New York: Holt, Rinehart and Winston, 1973).

Social historians are slowly getting around to the subject of sex and its influence in history. Paul Robinson's book *The Modernization of Sex* (New York: Harper, 1976) offers discussions and analyses of Havelock Ellis, Alfred Kinsey, and William Masters and Virginia Johnson. Modernism is defined by Robinson as a reaction against Victorianism. The thesis of *The New Sexuality* (New York: New Viewpoints, 1974), by Hendrick M. Ruitenbeck, is that what society terms "sexual perversions" really belongs to a wide variety of natural sexual experiences. Jessie Bernard, in *The Sex Game* (Englewood Cliffs, N.J.: Prentice-Hall, Inc., 1968), writes that each generation has to work out its own sexual identity. In addition to Lionel Tiger's *Men in Groups* (New York: Random House, 1970) and George Gilder's *Sexual Suicide* (New York: Quadrangle, 1973), one should also see *The Disappearing Sexes* (New York: Random House, 1965), by Robert P. Odenwald. Odenwald traces many contemporary ailments of society back to a lack of clear sex-role distinctions. In Midge Decter's *The Liberated Woman and Other Americans* (New York: Coward, McCann & Geohagan, 1971), the case is argued against women's liberation because the author maintains that women cannot manage the freedoms they already possess. From the disciplines of psychology and education, Anne Steinmann and David J. Fox contend in *The Male Dilemma* (New York: Jason Aronson, 1973) that the ambivalence resulting from role confusion is poisoning male–female relationships. Still another book that argues that sexual polarities are necessary (masculine rationality versus feminine intuitiveness) is Karl Stern's *The Flight From Women* (New York: Farrar, Strauss, and Giroux, 1965). *Beyond the Male Myth* (New York: The New York Times Book Co., 1977), by Anthony Pietropinto and Jacqueline Simenauer, is an excellent statistical survey on male sexual attitudes. Daniel Levinson's *The Seasons of a Man's Life* (New York: Alfred A. Knopf, Inc., 1978) examines the aging process and the expectations men have about their lives as they move from one stage of life to another.

Ronald Walters has gathered many good sources on nineteenth-century American sexuality and social history in *Primers for Prudery* (Englewood Cliffs, N.J.: Prentice-Hall, Inc., 1974). Walters draws heavily on the advice manuals, as does G. J. Barker-Benfield in *Horrors of the Half-Known Life* (New York: Harper, 1977). The latter is, in fact, one of the most thorough volumes to date on nineteenth-century male sexual values, mores, and fears. Charles and Carol Smith-Rosenberg have contributed a significant essay, "The Female Animal: Medical and Biological Views of Woman and Her Role in Nineteenth-Century America," *Journal of American History*, LX (September 1973), 332–56. Greater elaboration on medical theory, practice, and sexual advice can be found in *The Physician and Sexual Advice in Victorian America* (Urbana: University of Illinois Press, 1974), by John S. Haller, Jr., and Robin Haller. This volume runs the gamut from diet and posture advice to the evils of masturbation and prostitution. A very large number of advice manuals, self-help books, and guides for maturing young men and women existed during the nineteenth century; many libraries still have a small but representative collection. The Arno Press of New York, in a series titled *Sex, Marriage and Society*, has recently reprinted a selected few that demonstrate the intense concern about growing into proper manhood and womanhood. *Concepts of Insanity in the United States*, 1789–1865 (New Brunswick, N.J.: Rutgers University Press, 1964), by Norman Dain, points out that sexual excitement was a common explanation for mental illness. In *The Positive Thinkers* (Garden City, N.Y.: Doubleday, 1965), Donald Meyer analyzes the views of a few of America's most popular spokespersons, including Mary Baker Eddy and Norman Vincent Peale. One should not overlook *The Sex Radicals: Free Love in High Victorian America* (Lawrence, Kan.: The Regents Press, 1978), by Hal Sears. David Pivar's *Purity Crusade* (Westport, Conn.: Greenwood Press, 1973) explores the issues of vice control after the Civil War. To be read along with Pivar is *The Other Victorians: A Study of Sexuality and Pornography in Mid-Nineteenth Century England* (New York: Basic Books, 1960), by Stephen Marcus.

On the Civil War, books by Bell Wiley, *The Life of Billy Yank* and *The Life of Johny Reb* (Indianapolis: Bobbs-Merrill Press, 1952, 1943, respectively), reveal a lot about romantic and heroic soldiering and the morality of the troops. Set in a more intellectual framework is George Fredrickson's provocative *The Inner Civil War* (New York: Harper, 1965), which contains many insights on the literary New Englanders and a chapter devoted to the strenuous-life ideal. One of the very best discussions about children and how they were reared and socialized is Bernard Wishy's *The Child and the Republic* (Philadelphia: University of Pennsylvania Press, 1972). And despite its being full of biases and stereotypes of the time, G. Stanley Hall's monumental *Adolescence* (New York: D. Appleton and Co., 1904) is a landmark work on sex differences and the procedures recommended for bringing up young people "the right way." Although not everyone will agree with his conclusions, good use can be made of two books by Erik Erikson, *Youth, Identity and Crisis* (New York: W. W. Norton & Co., 1968) and *Childhood and Society* (New York: W. W. Norton & Co., 1950). Another perspective on youth and the maturity process is offered in Gerald H. J. Pearson's *Adolescence and the Conflict of Generations* (New York: W. W. Norton and Co., 1958), which discusses the problem of fathers' wanting to see their sons as extensions of themselves.

On the 1890s, *The Mauve Decade* (New York: Alfred A. Knopf, Inc., 1926), by Thomas Beer, has a chapter on the "titaness." Beer's work should be read along with Larzar Ziff's *The American 1890s* (New York: Viking Press, 1968), which explores the literature of the time, much of it having to do with sex and male and female roles. A better analysis of nineteenth-century literature, Robert Wasserstrom's *Heiress of All Ages* (Minneapolis: University of Minnesota Press, 1959) explores a number of the period's novels and short stories. Many of the works of Henry James, William Dean Howells, Frank Norris, Stephen Crane, Robert Herrick, Winston Churchill, and Jack London invite one to consider certain kinds of moods and attitudes that society was attempting to grapple with at the turn of the century.

Biographies, autobiographies, diaries, and letters offer many case studies that help to illuminate nineteenth-century social history. Some of the best are William Allen White's *Autobiography* (New York: Macmillan, 1946), Floyd Dell's *Homecoming* (Port Washington, N.Y.: Kennikat Press, 1933), Lincoln Steffens's *Autobiography* (New York: Harcourt Brace Jovanovich, Inc., 1931), Charles Francis Adams's *Autobiography* (Boston: Houghton Mifflin, 1916), John R. Commons's *Myself* (New York: Macmillan, 1934), Upton Sinclair's *Autobiography* (New York: Harcourt Brace Jovanovich Inc., 1962), Oswald Garrison Villard's *Fighting Years* (New York: Harcourt Brace Jovanovich, Inc., 1939), Theodore Roosevelt's *Autobiography* (New York: Charles Scribner's Sons, 1913), and Edward Bok's *The Americanization of Edward Bok* (Charles Scribner's Sons, 1913). Biographies of special value include Leon Edel's *Henry James: The Untried Years* (New York: Lippincott, 1953), F. O. Mathiessen's *The James Family* (New York: Alfred A. Knopf, Inc., 1948), Nancy Milford's *Zelda* (New York: Avon, 1971), and Mark Schorer's *Sinclair Lewis* (New York: McGraw-Hill 1961).

Several recent biographies—written from a psychoanalytic perspective—that are worth considering as models for studying other men and women with regard to sex roles and masculine values are Michael P. Rogin's *Fathers and Children* (New York: Alfred A. Knopf, Inc., 1975), which is about Andrew Jackson; Doris Kearn's *Lyndon Johnson and the American Dream* (New York: Harper, 1977); and Bruce Mazlish's *In Search of Nixon: A Psychohistorical Inquiry* (New York: Basic Books, 1972), which offers a controversial psychohistorical sketch of Nixon. *Eleanor and Franklin* (New York: W. W. Norton & Co., 1971), by Joseph Lash, provides a close look at one of America's most remarkable couples. The many works of Theodore Roosevelt, especially *The Strenuous Life* (New York: Century Co., 1900), written with a strong, *macho* undertone, are indispensable for learning about the ideals of national character that Roosevelt and many others championed around the turn of the century. A two-part essay by Glenn Davis, "The Early Years of Theodore Roosevelt: A Study in Character Formation," *History of Childhood Quarterly*, II (Spring 1975), uses psychonanalytic concepts to interpret Roosevelt's early years. James McGovern's "David Graham Phillips and the Virility Impulse of Progressives," *New England Quarterly*, XXXIX (September, 1966) is worth reading. My essay "Masculinity and Progressivism," *Psychoanalytic Review*, LXI (Fall, 1974) studies the Roosevelt–William Allen White relationship. Nathan Hale's *Freud and the Americans* (New York: Oxford University Press, 1971) offers a good synthesis of Freud's early writing and reviews some of the controversy surrounding his initial impact on America.

Although there are some new studies of the family, one of the old ones *The Social History of The American Family* (New York: Noble, 1917), by Arthur Calhoun, is still an important source—in spite of its age—for what it has to say about male and female roles. Sidney Ditzion's *Marriage, Morals and Sex in America: A History of Ideas* (New York: Bookman Associates, 1953) is a survey of many thinkers on a variety of issues closely related to family life. William O' Neill, in *Divorce in the Progressive Era* (New York: New Viewpoints, 1973), explores some of the reasons why the rate of divorce increased between 1880 and 1920. In earlier times, sex research and marital surveys were not frequently made, nor did researchers always ask the kinds of questions contemporary scholars wish they would have asked. But there are several that are still worth consulting (depending on the kinds of information desired), such as *Psychological Factors in Marital Happiness* (New York: McGraw-Hill, 1938), by Lewis Terman, and *A Research in Marriage* (New York: Boni, 1929), by G. V. Hamilton.

The impact or extent of the so-called sexual revolution is still a matter of debate among social historians. On this issue there is a good discussion by Daniel Scott Smith, "The Dating of the American Sexual Revolution: Evidence and Interpretation," *The American Family in Socio-Historical Perspective* (New York: St. Martin's Press, 1973).

One way of understanding the transition of values regarding American males is to study the subject from the point of view of the hero. In addition to the Ralph Luce article cited previously ("From Hero to Robot"), Dixon Wecter's *The Hero in America* (New York: Charles Scribner's Sons, 1941) is a good place to begin; Leo Gurko in *Heroes and Highbrows* (Indianapolis: Bobbs-Merrill, 1953) emphasizes that American heroes have been men of action, very often at the expense of intellectual and cultural standards. A better book on this particular aspect, however, is Richard Hofstadter's *Anti-intellectualism in America* (New York: Random

House, 1962). In *Heroes, Villains, and Fools* (Englewood Cliffs, N.J.: Prentice-Hall, Inc., 1962), Orrin Klapp describes certain social types and the roles they fulfill, his overall conclusion being that the quality of the national character is sinking.

Serious scholarship needs to be done on work and the attitudes about work and the impact these attitudes have had on sex roles and self-analysis. Some of the comments found in Studs Terkel's *Hard Times* (New York: Pantheon, 1970) and *Working* (New York: Pantheon, 1974) have aided in the preparation of this volume. In *The Unemployed Man and His Family* (New York: Institute of Social Research, 1940), Mirra Kamarovsky reports on the findings of a study of fifty-nine families during the Depression. Robert and Helen Lynd's *Middletown in Transition* (New York: Harcourt Brace Jovanovich, Inc., 1937) is a very substantial treatment of social and cultural values during the Depression years, and Maxine Davis's, *The Lost Generation* (New York: Macmillan, 1936) covers the effects of the Depression on youth. Frederick Herzberg's *Work in America* (Cambridge, Mass.: M.I.T. Press, 1973) helps in providing a perspective on work. Two books by Harry Levinson—a recognized authority on work and work-related problems—that should be carefully considered are *Emotional Health In the World of Work* and *Executive Stress* (New York: Harper, 1964 and 1970, respectively). *The Inner World of the Middle-Aged Man* (New York: MacMillan, 1976), by Peter Chew, analyzes the midlife-malaise syndrome many men face when they feel they are no longer as virile or vigorous as they once were. An earlier work, by Richard H. Huber, *The American Idea of Success* (New York: McGraw-Hill, 1971), suggests how cultural and social factors have a significant role in shaping attitudes about success and fulfillment.

It is hazardous to suggest significant titles that deal with the contemporary American social and sexual scene because the number from which to pick is so large. Perhaps one should begin with David Riesman's "Permissiveness and Sex Roles," *Marriage and Family Living* (August, 1959); *Premarital Sexual Standards in America* (Glencoe, Ill.: The Free Press, 1960), by Ira L. Reiss; Reiss's *The Social Context of Premarital Sexual Permissiveness* (New York: Holt, Rinehart and Winston, 1967); and Robert Bell's *Premarital Sex in a Changing Society* (Englewood Cliffs, N.J.: Prentice-Hall, Inc., 1966). Vance Packard, in *The Sexual Wilderness* (New York: David McKay, 1968), discusses sexual awareness and fulfillment in the context of changing values. Morton Hunt's *Sexual Behavior in the 1970's* (Chicago: Playboy Press, 1974) takes into account the youth revolt of the 1960s. Edward Shorter, in *The Making of the Modern Family* (New York: Basic Books, 1975), and Jessie Bernard, in *The Future of Marriage* (New York: Bantam, 1973), see marriage and the family as continuing institutions but subject to considerable pressures for change. Robert O. Blood, Jr., and Donald M. Wolfe's *Husbands and Wives: The Dynamics of Married Living* (Glencoe, Ill.: The Free Press, 1964) discusses role assignments around the house and indicates that traditional patriarchal values are collapsing but that specific sex roles are still very much in vogue. Advocates and opponents of change should consult Nena and George O'Neill's *Open Marriage* (New York: M. Evans and Co., 1972) and follow up on all the controversy it provoked. *The Affair: A Portrait of Extramarital Love in America* (New York: New American Library, 1969), by Morton Hunt, presents a study of adultery, what the author calls the hidden reality of American life.

Like the book shelves, magazine and periodical stalls have been bursting with any number of issues containing articles on various aspects of sexuality, sexual behavior, changing sex roles, family life, and so on. Worth mentioning here is *Playboy*, which since 1953 has offered many articles for and about men reflecting the "in" masculine image. The "Playboy philosophy" is a reasonably good representation of the values of a certain type of male. Since its inception, *Penthouse*, which calls itself "the international magazine for men," has competed against *Playboy* with a more sexually explicit format but fewer scholarly contributions. Many of the lesser pulp magazines for men available on the newsstands offer ample evidence that traditional masculinity still thrives. Publications such as *Brother, Liberation, Win, The Village Voice*, and *NOW* have contained numerous articles on consciousness raising to get men beyond the confines of the masculine mystique. *Psychology Today* and *Trans-action*, among others, have been good on analyzing current trends of the liberation movement. *Ms.* offers a perspective on men from the women's point of view. There have been lenghty discussions about men in issues of *Madamoiselle* as well as in some of the other women's magazines. Many of the books on men and men's issues contain specific references to articles and to special issues of other journals worth considering.

INDEX

317